PIMLICO
182

THE MYSTERY OF MALLORY AND IRVINE

Tom Holzel graduated in Economics at Dartmouth College, New Hampshire, and now works for a flat panel display company in California. In 1986 he organised and took part in an expedition to the north side of Mount Everest to search for new evidence of what became of Mallory and Irvine. He has invented and patented a new kind of oxygen 'rebreathing' apparatus for extended use at high altitude. He is the author of numerous articles for *Summit*, *Mountain* and the *American Alpine Journal*.

Audrey Salkeld has the most comprehensive private archive in Britain on mountaineering. She has translated from the German books by Reinhold Messner and Kurt Diemberger and has written the scripts for a number of television documentaries, including Leo Dickinson's *Eiger* and David Breashears' film *The Mystery of Mallory and Irvine*, for which she took part in Holzel's 1986 expedition and climbed to the North Col on Everest. She contributes regularly to mountaineering journals and is the author of a highly praised book on her Himalayan travels in Mustang and Tibet, *People in High Places*.

THE
MYSTERY OF
MALLORY
AND
IRVINE

TOM HOLZEL & AUDREY SALKELD

Revised edition, 1996

PIMLICO

PIMLICO

An imprint of Random House
20 Vauxhall Bridge Road, London SW1V 2SA

Random House Australia (Pty) Ltd
20 Alfred Street, Milsons Point, Sydney
New South Wales 2061, Australia

Random House New Zealand Ltd
18 Poland Road, Glenfield
Auckland 10, New Zealand

Random House South Africa (Pty) Ltd
PO Box 337, Bergvlei 2012, South Africa

Random House UK Ltd Reg. No. 954009

First published by Jonathan Cape Ltd 1986
Pimlico edition, with a new introduction, first and last chapter, 1996

1 3 5 7 9 10 8 6 4 2

Papers used by Random House UK Limited are natural,
recyclable products made from wood grown in sustainable
forests. The manufacturing processes conform to the
environmental regulations of the country of origin

Printed and bound in Great Britain by
Mackays of Chatham PLC, Chatham, Kent

ISBN 0-7126-7414-4

Contents

CONTENTS

For the witnesses:
Professor Noel Odell and Wang Hong Bao

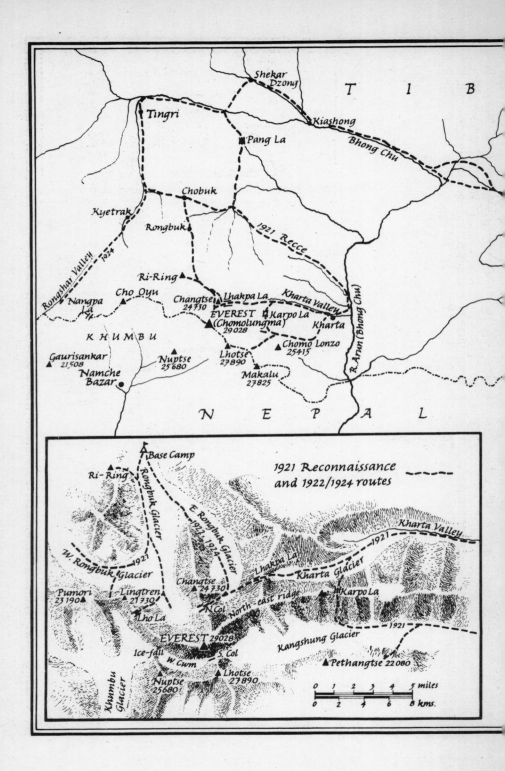

Shekar Dzong
T I B
Tingri
Kiashong
Pang La
Bhong Chu
Chobuk
Kyetrak
1921 Recce
Rongbuk
Ri-Ring
Rongshar Valley
1924
Cho Oyu
Changtse
24730
Lhakpa La
Kharta Valley
Nangpa
La
EVEREST
(Chomolungma)
29028
Karpo La
Kharta
K H U M B U
Chomo Lonzo
25415
R. Arun (Bhong Chu)
Gaurisankar
21508
Nuptse
25680
Lhotse
27890
Namche
Bazar
Makalu
27825
N E P A L

Base Camp
Ri-Ring
1921 Reconnaissance
and 1922/1924 routes
Rongbuk Glacier
E Rongbuk Glacier
1922, 1924
Kharta Valley
W. Rongbuk Glacier
1921
1921
Lhakpa La
Kharta Glacier
Pumori
23190
Lingtren
21730
Changtse
24730
North-east ridge
Karpo La
Lho La
N Col
1921
EVEREST 29028
Kangshung Glacier
Ice-fall
S. Col
W Cwm
Pethangtse 22080
Khumbu Glacier
Nuptse
25680
Lhotse
27890
0 1 2 3 4 5 miles
0 2 4 6 8 kms.

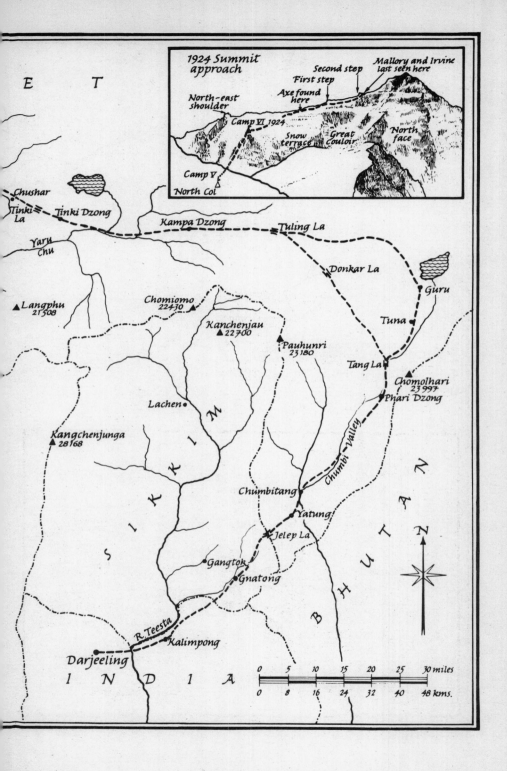

1924 Summit approach

North-east shoulder
First step
Second step
Mallory and Irvine last seen here
Axe found here
Camp VI 1924
Snow terrace
Great Couloir
North face
Camp V
North Col

E T

Chushar
Tinki La
Tinki Dzong
Yaru Chu
Kampa Dzong
Tuling La
Donkar La
Guru
Langphu 21 508
Chomiomo 22 430
Kanchenjau 22 700
Pauhunri 23 180
Tuna
Tang La
Chomolhari 23 997
Phari Dzong
Kangchenjunga 28 168
Lachen
S I K K I M
Chumbi Valley
Chumbitang
Yatung
Jelep La
Gangtok
B H U T A N
Gnatong
R. Teesta
Kalimpong
Darjeeling
I N D I A
N

0   5   10   15   20   25   30 miles
0   8   16   24   32   40   48 kms.

INTRODUCTION

The Mystery

by Tom Holzel, 1995

Trudging up to Camp III along 'the Corridor', a seemingly endless alleyway flanked by the wall of Everest's sister peak Changtse on the right and a flotilla of towering seracs on the left, I was acutely conscious that I was following the exact footsteps of George Mallory and Andrew Irvine who had perished high on Everest in unknown circumstances in 1924. Driving them on in the high, thin air was their ambition to become the first in the world to conquer its highest peak. What drove me on was the wish to discover whether or not they had succeeded.

The weather on that September day in 1986 was perfect, with brilliant sunshine and no wind. Even so, the gradual but unrelenting incline and the blazing sun caused me to sweat profusely. Mallory and his companions had climbed this same corridor in far worse conditions. Their expedition took place in the spring, which starts cold and warms up as the season progresses. Our expedition began at the end of August. We were to experience balmy weather early on and cruelly colder conditions as winter approached. A few hours below, Audrey Salkeld rested in Camp II, awaiting her turn to wend her way up to this 21,000-feet camp. A notch in the Changtse wall suddenly revealed the great massif of Mount Everest thrusting into the blue-black sky in monumental splendour. After all these years as an armchair historian in pursuit of 'the mystery of Mallory and Irvine', it called up a flood of emotions that overwhelmed me and I burst into tears.

My journey to discover the fate of these two pioneers of Everest had begun sixteen years earlier when I chanced upon a description in

1

the *New Yorker* magazine of the last sighting of Mallory and Irvine. Through a momentary break in the mists, the account read, they were spotted by a team member lower down on the mountain. Noel Odell claimed he saw the pair surmounting their final obstacle only three hours from the summit and 'going strong for the top.' After five minutes, mist intervened and the pair was lost to view forever. From my viewpoint in the Corridor, I could see this final obstacle clearly, a cliff encircling the summit. Where it blocks the Mallory route to the summit, this cliff is called the 'Second Step'.

For me, George Mallory and his tenacious will to succeed on Everest against almost impossible odds have become something of an ideal, as they have for generations of climbers, and I was surprised to find that no one had ever tried to discover whether his tenacity had gained him his hard-sought goal, even at the cost of his life and that of his young companion. Their story attracted me strongly, and so I began to spend my evenings and weekends researching the circumstances of their expedition at the New York Public Library close to where I worked. After six months, I came to the conclusion that a solution to this great mystery might still be discovered. It would not be found in libraries, nor in the scores of books that had been written on the subject. Rather, I believed, there were clues showing that the body of Andrew Irvine might yet lie on a snow terrace at 27,000 feet (8200m), almost 400 feet below the site of an ice axe discovered by climbers in 1933, and with it perhaps his camera. Eastman Kodak scientists, hearing of the possible existence of film frozen for so long, conducted extensive experiments and came to the conclusion that 'printable images' could still be recovered if the film had not been exposed to light or excessive cosmic rays.

Of course these were only speculations. It was not until the Japanese were rumoured to have obtained the first permit for forty years to climb Everest from the north (the last British expedition had been in 1938) that the real impetus came to mount a search. I wrote to the Japanese Alpine Club in 1979, telling them to be on the look-out for the bodies of Mallory or of Irvine and his camera, possibly lying on the '8200-metre snow terrace' on the North Face not far from the normal summit route. After hearing nothing from them for six months, I received an astonishing response.

Unknown to Western climbers, the Japanese had conducted a reconnaissance of the Tibetan side of Everest in the autumn of that year, when the Japanese climbing leader was approached by a Chinese high altitude porter with an incredible story. During the very large Chinese Everest expedition of 1975, Wang Hung-bao claimed to have discovered the body of an 'English dead', lying on the snow terrace at 26,600 feet (8100 m). The body had a hole in the cheek and was dressed in old-fashioned clothing that 'danced in the wind' when touched. The Japanese climber was amazed by this story – as I was – and it soon received world-wide publicity.

Wang's confirmation of my theory galvanised me into setting up an expedition to try to recover Irvine's camera. Lengthy correspondence with the Chinese eventually yielded that rarest of objects – a permit to climb Mount Everest from the north via 'Route No. 1' – the Mallory route. After years of hope, dreams were being replaced by action. Nine months later, on 25 August 1986, we found ourselves, 30 climbers-strong, at Mount Everest Base Camp.

The two lost climbers were last seen by Odell as he was climbing up in support of the pair. At about 26,000 feet, at 12.50 p.m., he chanced to look up as the mists parted to reveal the North-east Ridge running up to the summit. There, on that ridge 4,000 feet away, he was startled to see two tiny figures approach and then surmount the last fifteen feet of the rock cliff of the Second Step. He was startled because Mallory had written in a note carried down by porters that he hoped to be tackling this obstacle at 8 a.m. What could have caused their five-hour delay?

Up ahead, I saw a tiny knot of Advance Base Camp inhabitants gathered around the crevasse that had swallowed a yak a week earlier. They were busy bridging this ever-growing gap that cut menacingly across the Corridor. ABC – as we called this higher camp – was by now a small town of fifteen tents straddling a broad rock moraine, with Changtse flanking us on the right and the broad plateau of the head of the East Rongbuk Glacier (from which we chopped ice for water) on the left. Across the glacier rose the un-climbed North-east Ridge of Everest.

Our camp lay a mile from the base of the North Col. The col itself is the lowest part of Everest's North Ridge as it sweeps down to 23,000 feet and then up again to form the South Ridge of Changtse. The most dangerous part of our climb was the sixteen hundred foot ascent from the glacier to the col on which was placed Camp IV.[1] It is on this 45° slope that so many other Everesters have been killed. Mallory, leading a party up this slope in a last-ditch effort in 1922, was pulled down in an avalanche that killed seven porters.

Our Camp V was set up on the North Ridge at 25,400 feet. Soon, I hoped to climb up there and then to the 8100m-snow terrace. I had brought with me a chemical closed-circuit oxygen system to enable me to endure the altitude, and a metal detector specifically tuned to the Kodak VPK camera the climbers were known to have taken.

My controversial theory about the deaths of Mallory and Irvine, first published in *Mountain* magazine in September 1971, was that the two had split up shortly after Odell had seen them climbing the Second Step. It was at that point, at 1 p.m., that they would have had to face a critical decision.

They were laterally far from their highest camp and would need to assess whether they had enough resources to continue their climb. Could they reach the top and still make it back to camp before dark? Did they have enough energy, enough oxyen, and would the weather hold? I had theorised that the two climbers would have been ecstatic over their conquest of the Second Step and their successful use of the disreputable oxygen equipment. No other climber in the seven British expeditions to Everest before the Second World War believed that the Second Step 'would go' – except for Mallory. Once he and Irvine had conquered it, the summit would appear to be an obstacle-free three hours away.[2]

Still, it was a three hours that depended entirely on the climbers' continued use of oxygen. This late in the day, that essential element would be in short supply. From their known climb rates, I had calculated that each climber had one and a half hours of the precious gas remaining, clearly not enough for both to reach the top. There was also Irvine's safety to consider. At twenty-two years of age, he was the expedition's 'experiment'. Powerfully built, he had not previously climbed higher than 5,500 feet (!) The risk of his inexperience would have weighed heavily on Mallory, and would certainly slow them on the tricky, possibly night descent. Mallory, whose third, and clearly last expedition this would be, was obsessed with conquering Everest. He had toured Great Britain and the Eastern United States in speaking engagements to raise money for this trip, and had come very close to promising his audience that this time, he would not fail. Having just surmounted the final obstacle, at last success must have seemed as close as the summit standing out in bold relief just ahead. But it would require an evening descent to Camp VI.

Given this great dilemma – insufficient oxygen for two, the increased risk of going on, especially to Irvine, yet success within palpable reach – I came to believe that Mallory could have done only one thing. He would take Irvine's oxygen (its bulk would have been a severe handicap on the descent) and send him back to Camp VI along the safe route they had just climbed. Relieved of drawing Irvine into greater risk, and with the benefit of his additional oxygen, nothing seemed to stand in Mallory's way to the top.

If this theory is correct (and there is still deep, brooding opposition to it on ethical grounds among many older British climbers), Mallory and Irvine would have parted a little after 1 p.m., Mallory to climb the broad, steep 'final pyramid' of Everest's summit, Irvine to return to Camp VI in a long descending traverse across the 'yellow bands' of the mountain's North Face. I imagined Mallory lowering Irvine back down the rocky step on their rope. From there it would be a relatively easy traverse for the young man in clear snowless weather, the conditions at the time of their presumed parting. An hour later a bitter squall dusted the mountain with a coating of snow. And it was at the most exposed part of this traverse that climbers of the next expedition, that of 1933, discovered an ice axe which could have belonged only to one of the two climbers. It was lying loose on the route, as if wrenched from an exhausted climber's grip while he was attempting to arrest a fatal slip.

A glance at the map shows the terrain sixty-five feet below this supposed incident as levelling out into a broad terrace. Here, I calculated, at just around 8,200m (almost 27,000 feet), the tumble of a body down the steep slope might be checked. The theory stopped there, only to be galvanised ten years later by the Japanese report of Wang's discovery of the 'English dead'. Curiously, little serious interest was taken in the find by Western climbers.

The reaction of Zhiyi Song, our liaison officer, and a member of the Chinese Everest Expedition of 1975 on which Wang supposedly made his discovery, was disappointing. 'Sure, I've heard the Wang Story,' Song exclaimed animatedly through an interpreter at Base Camp. 'And none of it is true. Wang never reported finding an English mountaineer.'

Dampened, but not discouraged, I tried a different tack with Song. But now I was used to the reflexive denials of 'the Wang story' by Chinese officials, and by my worthy, if ageing, British opponents. I showed Song a copy of another article of mine, describing a much disputed Chinese climb of Mount Everest in 1960. Nearly all Western climbing experts at the time had discounted the Chinese claim because of a complete lack of summit photos, and a very vacuous description of the summit terrain. In my article I analysed those claims and was able to pierce the veil of propaganda to reveal information about the summit that could only have been obtained by eyewitnesses. Thus, they made it, I concluded, so becoming the first Western authority to support the Chinese claims with hard evidence.

Song was delighted with the article. Many of the climbers on that team were comrades of his, and he joyfully pointed out their faces in the accompanying photos.

'Mr Song,' I continued 'isn't it possible that Wang found the English body and didn't report it officially? Maybe he just told his friends.'

'If that is so,' Song replied carefully, 'I know who his climbing partners were, and you can meet them on the way back to Peking.'

With this important step set in place, I felt ready to make my move up to Camp IV and beyond. I had been at ABC for five days, and felt very fit. As I donned my climbing gear a commotion stirred outside my tent. I looked out to see the Sherpas milling around in a state of high agitation.

'Sherpa fall down North Col,' Dawang informed me tersely. 'Everyone go to help.' David Breashears, our climbing leader, was out in front, followed by other climbers and many Sherpas. Carrying an emergency inflatable toboggan, I fell in behind the group.

It was an unexpectedly tough climb. The route from ABC to the base of the col is very gradual, and everyone was walking as fast as they could. Nevertheless the mile-long journey was dotted with climbers standing still, puffing and blowing to get their wind back, and then starting up again. Despite several weeks acclimatising at this altitude, we could not move up at anything approaching sea-level speed. In fact, most of us had been at this altitude too long, waiting for the weather to clear, and it was all too evident insidious high altitude deterioration had already set in.

At the base of the col David found the body of Sherpa Dawa Nuru. His arm was sticking out of the snow. He had fallen several hundred feet and his neck was broken, perhaps by the oxygen bottle sticking out of his pack. The cause had been an avalanche triggered by a fellow climber above him as the two descended, widely separated, down the same fixed rope. For us, Dawa's death marked the beginning of the end.

Uncertainly we waited for better weather, each blustery day asking ourselves the same questions: had anything happened overnight to improve conditions up to the col? – had anything happened to make them worse? The answers were always the same: it had snowed more, and the weather had become colder still – loosening even more the delicate, underlying support of the stiff wind-slabbed snow on the surface.

Disheartened, we gave up at last and made our way back to Base Camp. As I climbed down alone, the weather turned brilliant again, as if the mountain was happy to see me leave. But I found myself moving woefully slowly. I, too, had spent too much time at altitude. The return to base took me nine hours, a journey that most fit climbers manage in five. When I reached Peking I discovered I had lost 35 pounds.

In the Tibetan capital, Lhasa, our liaison officer introduced me to Chen Tian Liang, Wang's Group Climbing Leader. He too denied that Wang had found a body at 8100m. And, Chen said, 'I should know. I was with Wang the entire time we were high on the mountain.'

I spent five hours interviewing Chen, frequently apologising for questioning him so intensely, but I could not reconcile the Japanese report, made in such great detail, with the bland denials I was getting from the Chinese. Chen felt certain that if Wang had found a body, it could only have been the same one that of the Chinese climber he had been sent up to look for. Wu Tsung Yueh slipped – perhaps he suffered a heart attack – and fell from almost at the same spot as I assumed had Irvine. But Wu's body was discovered a few days later by the team of nine climbers returning from the summit. Coming upon body parts on the descent, they had followed a trail of blood down to their fallen comrade. Of course Wang couldn't have found that body, we both agreed, because he would have recognised it instantly and rushed back with a report.

The interview dragged on. By 10 p.m. Chen was growing anxious to return home. Was there anything we hadn't covered, I asked dejectedly. 'Oh, yes,' he said suddenly. 'One thing. During a rest at our Camp VB[3], I received a radio call ordering me to climb up to a bivouac, Camp VII, to look for the missing climber.'

'Did you take Wang with you?' I asked.

'No. I went with a Tibetan porter.'

'So Wang was left at Camp VB all day, while you climbed up to Camp VII?'

'Yes.'

'Isn't it possible, Mr Chen,' I asked, 'that Wang might have discovered the English body during this time?'

Mr Chen gazed at me intently before answering. 'Yes,' he said, 'it is possible.'

7

'And who remained with him at Camp VB?'

'Zhang Yun Yan,' Chen answered. 'And he lives in Peking.'

Elated with that small victory, the next morning I worked again upon our liaison officer. Yes, he agreed, he would set up a meeting with Mr Zhang.

Getting to see Zhang in Peking met with unexpected delays. I sat around for nearly a week. On the afternoon of the day before I was due to leave for the States, I finally got a call from Mr Song. Zhang would meet me that evening in our hotel – a dismal place called the Bei-Wei. I was unexpectedly nervous while awaiting my guest. I had bet so much on the Japanese report, and had come away from this expedition with so little to prove, or disprove, my theory. What if Zhang gave me the same story that I had heard from everyone else? It would change a quixotic journey into a foolish one.

I had invited Zhang to dinner, and dispensing with the usual ten or fifteen minutes exchanging pleasantries, I plunged in with my question. Zhang was a tough-looking sort, and I could contain myself no longer. 'Mr Zhang,' I asked. 'What happened to you and Wang when Chen left to search for the missing climber?'

'I stayed in my sleeping bag,' Zhang answered, 'and Wang went out for a walk. He was gone for about twenty minutes.'

Good God, I thought to myself, how much ground can you cover on the North Face of Everest in twenty minutes? 'Did he say he found anything?' I asked with baited breath.

'Yes. He told me he had found the body of a foreign mountaineer. He didn't tell me this right away, but later, while we were descending. He told a few of the other climbers as well.'

I gaped in astonishment. So here it was – proof, or as much proof as anyone was going to get short of discovering the body of Mallory, or of Irvine, still lying on the snow terrace. I was struck momentarily speechless with elation at Mr Zhang's answer. As soon as I recovered, I could only splutter, 'Mr Zhang, do you drink champagne?'

T.H., May 1995

I

The Call of Everest

Brothers till death, and a wind-swept grave,
Joy of the journey's ending:
Ye who have climbed to the great white veil,
Heard ye the chant? Saw ye the Grail?

Geoffrey Winthrop Young, 1909.

In the spring of 1995 George Mallory II, grandson and namesake of the famous Everest pioneer, joined an American climbing party and was able to wrap up, as he said, a little outstanding family business. Following the same route up the Tibetan side of the mountain which his grandfather had advocated more than seventy years before, he carried the family name to the summit. Or, as many will maintain, 'once more to the summit'. After gaining the top, with others at 5.30 a.m. on 14 May, the younger Mallory jubilantly reported that 'the Second Step was easy, even in the dark.' He was convinced Mallory and Irvine could have climbed it in June 1924. His expedition, the professed aim of which had been to honour the pioneering spirit of the early British attempts, had proved – in his words – a 'whopping success', with thirteen people safely to the top and back again.

In fact it had been a whopping success of a season whichever way you looked at it, with no less than seventy-four people realising their ambition to stand on the world's roof, sixty-seven of them by this North/North-east Ridge route. Among them was the British woman Alison Hargreaves, who had climbed independently and without oxygen, topping out a day ahead of Mallory-the-Younger. Between them, these two can be said to have brought full-circle an epic chapter in the British Mt Everest story. What Alison, young George and all the others who were there that year remarked upon was how high winds had shot-blasted the upper slopes almost bare of snow, so providing conditions uncannily like those pertaining in

1924 when Mallory and Irvine made their final, fatal attempt.

Of course it is all but impossible to compare circumstances for climbers now with those far-off days. George, only two years younger than his grandfather was at the time he died, had the practical benefit of modern clothing and reliable oxygen equipment. He also had the more important psychological advantage of knowing that what he was attempting could be done. The route itself was well prepared with fixed ropes and, with no route-finding to worry about, he had only to clip in his jumar clamp and move swiftly. The dry conditions forced climbers up on to the ridge early, taking in First and Second Steps, although, that said, there was probably only one thirty-foot section on the exposed crest itself where the heart-stopping sweep of the East Face drops away beneath one's feet. The upper part of the Second Step still retains the ladder put there by Chinese climbers in 1975, and from the top of this an awkward but well-protected move delivers the climber to easier ground where the summit heaves once more into view, looking very close indeed.

Having set off from the team's high camp at 1 a.m., George reached the Second Step at 3.45 – his partner Jeff Hall and Sherpa Ongda Chhering in close step behind. In no more than thirteen minutes the formidable obstacle was behind him. While climbing, he noticed that the rock face to the right of the ladder was 'littered' with hand and foot holds, many of which he felt sure would have offered feasible passage to the first comers, 'given their adventurous attitude and GM's brilliant record on rock.' Especially, as he said, when one remembered that in those days they were used to climbing without modern protection and the leader simply 'never fell'.

Accepting the then and now as different enterprises, one nonetheless can gain encouragement on Mallory's and Irvine's behalf from the younger George' swift ascent. We are used to hearing the argument that Odell must have been mistaken in believing he saw the two men at the Second Step, because they could not possibly have surmounted it within the short space of his vision. Now we know. In exceptional circumstances, men (and women, too) can move with 'alacrity' over that sort of terrain at that altitude, with or without oxygen.

Alison, rejecting the fixed ropes, found the Second Step steep and 'quite awkward'. She had little option but to make use of the Chinese ladder – because it was there. And negotiating around the top of the step – that, too, was awkward, 'definitely the technical crux

10

of the climb',[1] yet even so she agrees it would have been physically possible for Mallory and Irvine in 1924.

Everest has claimed over a hundred lives since people began pitting themselves at its slopes, and throughout the Himalaya many have vanished in circumstances every bit as mysterious as those which swallowed up Mallory and Irvine. Why, of all such Himalayan disappearances, is theirs the most enduring, most compelling, best remembered of all? Of course it has to do with Everest-the-Unknown – as the mountain was at the time, if not also the-possibly-Unconquerable, as many believed for years to come. Yet in no small measure it also comes down to the man himself, the one to make that fatal misjudgement so long ago – George Leigh Mallory. We recognise a quality in him which speaks to us over the generations – a heroism, or altruism, call it what you will: some form of nobleness – and a questing spirit. He is seen as a spokesman for fair play, an inspirational figure, notwithstanding his ultimate failure to get back with life and story intact. He had, as he promised, given the mountain 'a good whack', and most people agreed with him that the game was worth the candle. He may have been approaching middle-age in mortal years, but in memory he is fixed forever as a flaming icon of youth, a James Dean, if you like, of mountaineering. And by association, his young companion shares his immortality. But always as an adjunct: always it is Mallory – and Irvine.

Mallory's instinctive sense of fairness is nowhere better illustrated than in the affair of Richard Brockbank Graham, a distinguished Cumberland climber who was selected to join the 1924 Everest team. A schoolmaster (like Mallory), this Graham was of Quaker stock and, as a pacifist, had been a conscientious objector during the Great War. The Everest invitation gave him tremendous pleasure; so to learn soon afterwards that some militarist members among the team nurtured conscientious objections of their own towards climbing with a 'non-fighter' was a bitter blow. The records no longer indicate who the principle troublemakers were, but the two to leap most spectacularly to Graham's defence were George Mallory and Howard Somervell. The minute he picked up rumours of the 'caddish treatment' afoot, Somervell cabled his resignation to the Alpine Club, declaring. 'I cannot conceive how the propriety of the Alpine Club could stomach such a low down trick after they had elected him in the full knowledge of his convictions . . . it is a dirty piece of work.'[2] And Mallory, no less vociferously protested his outrage to General Bruce in December 1923:

11

. . . the sooner members of the party who feel such things learn to control their feelings and make the best of the party as they find it the better it will be for all of us . . . I should have thought that a man who seemed to be good enough for yourself, Younghusband, Ronaldshay and Collie – as I suppose he must have done – may be good enough for any member of the party. And I further think that to ask a man to resign after he has been asked to join the expedition and the fact has been published in the press is simply a thing which is not done . . . I have the strongest objection to the action of any member of the party who is agitating to turn down Graham after the invitation has been sent; and I hereby agitate against *him* . . . precious few men are so valuable that I would want to keep them in if they are determined to kick out Graham at this stage; and I can't see why anyone outside the party should have a word to say on the matter.[1]

Mallory professes ignorance of the identity of the dissenters, while obliquely suggesting that squabbling among the organisers could be at the root of the trouble. However, the finger of suspicion did fall upon another member from Cumberland, a man to whom Mallory took an instant dislike, though later would learn to rub along with on the expedition; he was not one to bear grudges. Graham, finding his position untenable, withdrew and the invitation passed instead to John de Vars Hazard. Neither Somervell nor Mallory in the event were obliged to resign from the Alpine Club.

By today's standards, we would not consider Mallory's mountaineering qualifications in any way exceptional. Two visits to the Alps as a schoolboy and half a dozen summer holidays there when adult, with some short breaks snatched in North Wales and Cornwall, the occasional trip to the Lake District and five days on the Isle of Skye is a modest enough tally over a period of two decades. After university, Mallory lived and worked exclusively in the South of England, where sandstone climbing had yet to be developed along the Kent–Sussex border, and this was long, long before there were any artificial climbing walls. Between holidays and weekends away, the climber simply did not, could not keep up his activity. Nonetheless, it was a period of great change in alpinism and rock climbing, and Mallory with his natural athleticism and boldness very much epitomised the new breed of mountaineer, forsaking the security of cracks and gullies for airy ridges and tilted slabs. Even in his lifetime, his sense of balance and daring were legendary. Though he doubtless had friends in high places pulling strings for him, Mallory was a legitimate candidate for Everest.

True mountain experience cannot be measured in years and alpine seasons. Of course they are important, but the real mountaineer is defined from the moment he sets foot to his first hill. Physique and condition play a part – we hear often how Mallory had the 'ideal figure for a mountaineer' – as too do wind and stamina, but in the end, these have less to do with success than the state of mind and a constancy of purpose. Within a few days of grandson George's triumph on Everest in 1995, another mountaineer fulfilled his ambition to bag an 'eight-thousander' by making it to the top of nearby Cho Oyu, the world's sixth highest peak. This man's age, fifty-four, would in itself have rendered this a remarkable event not so many years ago, but when you consider also that Norman Croucher has lost both legs below the knee, you realise that condition and physical endowment played little or no part in his achievement. That was down almost solely to dogged perseverence and a steely resolution. Mallory and Irvine may have been played out physically after six weeks on the mountain and a month on the road from Darjeeling, but they lacked nothing in resolve. They were committed to climb this mountain, their mountain – a commitment they would not have relinquished lightly, and it is perfectly natural for us to speculate whether or not we think they succeeded in their mission.

II

The Young Recruits

To go climbing in the Alps in the early years of this century, it was usually considered necessary to employ the services of a guide familiar with the conditions of the area visited; and on extended routes, to take along also one or two porters to carry the required equipment and stores. The expense this entailed meant that from its beginning, mountain climbing had been a pastime reserved almost exclusively for the wealthy. But the old order was slowly changing. There was an increasing number of young climbers, many of whom had learned their skills on British hills, who now felt confident enough to tackle alpine routes without guides. It was a practice which outraged the traditionalists, but it brought alpinism within the reach of men and women of more modest means.

George Mallory was first introduced to mountains as a schoolboy in the summer of 1904 by Graham Irving, his housemaster at Winchester. Irving had been among the first to adopt guideless climbing. In fact, on lesser routes he drew particular pleasure from solitary mountaineering, which was considered to be even more irresponsible. He was ready enough, however, to acknowledge that a companion was advisable on glaciers, and indeed climbed regularly with a colleague on the staff at Winchester. When this friend died, Irving decided to search among the senior boys for likely candidates he could recruit to alpine mountaineering.

He did not have far to look. Living in rooms almost next to his were just the persons he needed. One was a lad called Harry Gibson, who he discovered developing photographs in forbidden hours, and who − conversation soon revealed − had already visited the Alps

14

and enjoyed mountain walking; the other was his friend George Mallory. Both were gymnasts, and both obtained permission from home to visit the Alps with Irving in the summer holidays.

Mallory was eighteen. Until then, he had climbed nothing higher than the Malvern Hills, and had shown no interest in mountains at all. There were a few books on mountain adventure in the school library, but Mallory had never discovered them.

After Mallory's death on Everest, Irving often wondered whether he had done right in introducing him to mountains. He wrote that it was tempting to say of a mountaineer as famous as Mallory and one 'so admirably built by Nature for mastering her own obstacles, and endowed with a knightly soul that was always striving towards a high ideal,'[1] that it was inevitable he should climb mountains. But there was, he believed, nothing inevitable about it. Mallory was a good all-round athlete with many other interests, and it was possible that mountains might never have meant anything in his life had he stayed at home that summer. It was pure chance, Irving maintained, that took him to the Alps instead.

The first mountain Irving attempted with his new recruits was Mont Vélan, less than 12,000 feet high and not technically difficult, but both boys suffered such severe headaches and sickness from the effect of altitude that they had to turn back. Soon afterwards, however, Irving and Mallory made two excursions by themselves, which Irving was to remember with pleasure all his life. One was an 'adventurous descent' of the Trient glacier in bad weather, an account of which, written by Mallory, is preserved in the records of the Winchester Ice Club (as it was decided to call their little climbing group); and the second, a traverse of Mont Blanc from the Dôme hut to the Grands Mulets, 'carried through after long imprisonment by storms on a few biscuits and scrapings of honey'.[2]

The following year Irving took Mallory to the Alps again, this time to Arolla. Gibson did not go, but two more recruits were found and added to the party. One of them, Guy Bullock, who was a year younger than Mallory, impressed everyone with his stamina and sound sense. 'A tough sort of fellow who never lost his head and would stand any amount of knocking about,'[3] Mallory was to recall years later when candidates were being sought for Everest.

Mallory went up to Cambridge at the end of that summer and it was several years before he was able to go to the Alps again. Irving, meanwhile, continued to introduce schoolboys to the Alps, and in December 1908 dared to deliver a talk to the Alpine Club entitled

15

Five Years with Recruits. By admitting to both solitary and guideless climbing in that hallowed atmosphere, he knew he was walking into a minefield. 'I dare say I was not qualified for the post of trainer,' he ventured in his opening remarks. 'To some of you it may seem sheer impudence to usurp the functions of the professional experts of Meiringen and Zermatt. It may even be that I shall be accused of corrupting the youth . . .'⁴ To many in the audience it did, and he was.

As Irving sat down a heated debate erupted, demonstrating just how high feelings ran on the subject. Later, when his paper was published in the club's journal, fourteen eminent members signed a Disclaimer repudiating responsibility 'for any encouragement which [its] publication . . . may give to expeditions undertaken after the manner therein described'.⁵ Some of those who put their signatures to the protest were predictable enough — Sidney Spencer, Douglas Freshfield, both well-rooted in a Victorian past — but the presence of others seems surprising: W.P. Haskett-Smith, a man often called the Father of British Rock Climbing because he was one of the first to realize the potential and to popularize guideless climbing throughout Britain; and T.G. Longstaff, who was usually sympathetic to young ideas. Most surprising of all, however, was the inclusion of Geoffrey Winthrop Young among the protesters. For more than half a century Young was an inspirational force in British mountaineering and personally encouraged a great many young people to take up climbing. In later years he worked vigorously to promote the ideals of the educationist, Kurt Hahn, believing that young people needed the stimulation of such physical challenge during their formative years, every bit as much as mental exercise. Captain Farrar, the Club's Vice President elect and assistant journal editor, refused to have anything to do with the Disclaimer and (according to the mountaineering historian T.S. Blakeney) 'wrote good humouredly but reprovingly to Geoffrey Young for signing the protest, when his own record made it so much a matter of Satan rebuking sin!'⁶

Irving's article appeared in the *Alpine Journal* of February 1909, the same month that George Mallory first met Geoffrey Winthrop Young. They were introduced by a mutual acquaintance, Charles Sayle. There would appear to have been no initial awkwardness as a result of Young's public disapproval of Irving's views, though he must surely have known that Mallory was one of the 'recruits', just as Mallory could scarcely have been unaware of Young's attitude.

Instead, the two became firm friends, sharing not only a spiritual, almost mystical approach to mountains, but also an appreciation of literature, of poetry and discourse, and a love of the manipulation of words. They would have been quick to discover, too, philosophical accord — a common idealism, the instinctive humanitarian view. But perhaps more even than these, they would have been aware of a bond of physicality. Both were men of action, athletes of near-perfect physique, both conscious of the beauty and rhythm of movement, men who expressed themselves to a large extent through movement, deriving a sensual, almost narcissistic, pleasure in their own fitness.

Young was ten years older than Mallory and at his peak as an alpinist. With the possible exception of Valentine Ryan (whose output of new routes was in any case less than Young's), there was no other British climber capable of producing alpine climbs of anything like the standard Young was regularly making, mostly in the company of Josef Knubel. It was a standard not bettered by British climbers until after the Second World War. Young's relation to climbing in those years running up to the First World War has been likened by Sir Arnold Lunn to that of Edward Whymper to the Golden Age, or A.F. Mummery to the Silver Age of Mountaineering. Claude Elliott (a past-headmaster of Eton, where Young, too, taught for five years) had trouble assigning Young to any particular period. He felt on the one hand that it was largely due to Young that there was such a 'fine flowering of the Victorian mountaineering tradition' during his active years; but he saw him also as having an Elizabethan flavour, in the way he combined a love of action with the mind of a poet. Young certainly had a deep love of mountaineering tradition; he was also a very modern man, interested in new ideas and developments. He was the second son of a baronet, but had a natural ease with people from all walks of life, and a special affinity with the young. His mountaineering reputation did not rest solely on his alpine climbing. In Britain, too, he was a pioneer, and as such, responsible for the emergence of a school of hard rock-climbing in Britain. But his real influence among British mountaineers lay not so much in his climbing successes as in his talent for sociability.

In those first decades of the century, it was possible, Young once said, to know the names of almost all the people who climbed. He certainly gave the impression that *he* did. He 'collected' around himself a highly talented group of mostly intellectual climbers — and 'collected' does not seem too odd a word to describe how, like an art connoisseur, he would seek out and win the fine or the unusual to

17

enhance his 'hill company'. His 'exhibitions' were the famous parties, or meets, he organized in North Wales, at first in the summer,
but later at Easter and even Christmas as well, and mostly at the
Pen-y-Pass hotel above Llanberis. To these, he invited widely and
with flair. Long days were spent on the cliffs, and evenings were
devoted to boisterous singing, wide-ranging discussions and im-
promptu theatricals. Always, at the hub of all activity, confident in
the affection of his protégés and friends, Geoffrey Young would
preside.

In contrast, Mallory would have seemed far less assured socially or
intellectually, immature even in many of his ideas. He was 22, with
the appearance of being even younger, and was in his last year at
university. But his circle, too, was wide and his interests varied. He
was reading History at Magdalene College, one of the smaller and
more intimate colleges in Cambridge with only about fifty students.
There he had the good fortune to be placed under the supervision of
Arthur Benson, who encouraged his talents for writing and debate
and took a pastoral interest in his developing personality. Together
they founded the Kingsley Club, a little essay group within the
College at which papers were read and discussed, and which pro-
vided Mallory with useful polemic training. Mallory's close friends
at Cambridge included the poet Rupert Brooke, David Pye, Hugh
Wilson, Geoffrey Keynes and James Strachey; he also met Lytton
Strachey, Duncan Grant and others of the Bloomsbury set. He was a
keen member of the Fabian Society and a founder-member of the
Marlowe Dramatic Society. In their first production, *Dr Faustus*,
Mallory made an undistinguished appearance as the Pope (Justin
Brooke was Faustus; Rupert Brooke, Mephistopheles; and Geoffrey
Keynes, the Evil Angel). David Pye remembers that it was at this
time Mallory took to 'dressing rather peculiarly in black flannel
shirts and coloured ties; and grew his hair long'. The house of
Charles Sayle (the under librarian in the University Library) provided a meeting place for a number of undergraduates and Mallory
became a prominent member of this rather literary clique. 'Sayle's
menagerie' it was called by J.W. Clarke; Cottie Sanders, writing
later, preferred 'the Cambridge School of Friendship'.

Even at their first meeting Mallory would have glimpsed in
Young something of the person he was aspiring to be. He could not
fail to have been dazzled by the diversity of Young's acquaintance,
quite apart from his impeccable standing as a mountaineer. For
Young, Mallory represented another 'collectable' find, a vivid and

youthful personality with which to enliven his circle. He immediately pressed him to join the 'hill company' at Pen-y-Pass the coming Easter.

Mallory was flattered by the invitation and responded eagerly. 'I am looking forward with unmixed delight to Easter,' he wrote, adding somewhat archly, 'though I don't expect to fulfil your sanguine expectations. If by chance we may prove that one of the more terrifying places is less difficult than it looks, I shall leap for joy.'[7]

He need not have worried. As Young had known he would, he fitted in perfectly. He climbed on Lliwedd, repeating Route I with Young, Marcus Heywood, Edward Evans and Page Dickinson one day, and inventing a route (through mistaken route-finding, and later called Wrong Chimney) with Evans on another day. Young has described in *Snowdon Biography* a typical image of those Pen-y-Pass meets, telling how, down from the hills, they would relax in sitz baths around a blazing stove, with shouts through the rain producing relays of hot water. 'Unforgettable are the endless discussions of details of climbs from bath tub to bath tub,' he said, '. . . and George Mallory or young George Trevelyan leaping to do slow circles over the roof-beam − until a blast of hail and protest let in the hot buckets and the boots together.'[8]

From now on mountains were to become the dominant interest in Mallory's life, rather than being just one of a number of activities he enjoyed. After the weekend, Young sent Mallory a form so that he could apply to join the Climbers' Club. He had obviously passed muster. Mallory wrote to tell Young he was perfectly serious in offering the traverse of the Malvern Hills as a qualification for membership. 'You will agree that an expedition of that sort is only undertaken by people who care about the mountains, the right people that is for any club of mountaineers.'[9]

Not long afterwards, Young pressed Mallory to join his party in the Alps that summer. 'I shall begin training on Ascension Day,' Mallory wrote, though it appeared that the training envisaged comprised only of going to bed at 11, 'or at least moderately early'. These were his last weeks at Cambridge and they were ones of feverish activity. At the same time he was desperately trying to finish an essay on Boswell for the Members' Prize Essay, which he felt he had high hopes of winning.[10]

In Switzerland, Young and Mallory spent a few days on training climbs together around Bel Alp before being joined by Donald

Robertson. These were marked, according to Young, by 'some of the hair-breadth happenings which are incidental to alpine inexperience'. His novice was evidently going to need a good deal more serious work 'as a corrective'. Accordingly they made the first ascent of a little peak they called Der Enkel. Then after further training climbs — Robertson having by now joined the party — they assayed in poor conditions a traverse of the Finsteraarhorn by its difficult southerly arête. It was a day packed with incident. Their first nasty moment came just below the summit. With Donald Robertson in the lead, they were picking their way delicately along the icy, corniced ridge when, without warning, Donald made a false move that sent him sliding down towards the Finsteraar glacier. Fortunately he was stopped short by the rope, and refusing to allow himself to be daunted by the incident, resumed the lead. They continued to the summit where, after a short stop, Mallory took over as first on the rope for the descent of the north side. He had not gone very far along the exposed ridge before Young noticed to his horror that between Mallory and Robertson the rope was hanging limply, and Mallory was perched none too securely on a tiny cut foothold on the glazed slabs with a vast sweep of emptiness below him. Young was terrified that if he shouted a warning, he might startle Mallory and precipitate an accident; instead, he whispered gently for him to stay exactly where he was, at the same time motioning Robertson to climb down and re-attach the rope that Mallory had forgotten to secure. In the event it was Robertson who from over-anxiety slipped, making such a clatter behind Mallory that it really did alarm him. He spun round on his tiny 'one-foot ice-nick'. Geoffrey Young hardly dared to look, for he felt sure that Mallory must tumble all the way to the glacier, 5,000 feet below. His panic was unnecessary. Mallory kept his balance. The reassurance of a rope never meant anything to him, commented Young afterwards. He was 'as sure-footed and as agile in recovery as the proverbial chamois.' It was, however, a subdued and shaken little party that continued the long descent.

Some days later Mallory did fall. It was getting late — past 6 p.m. on a long alpine day — and Mallory was seeking a way around the fourth and final vertical tower which blocked progress along the virgin south-east ridge of the Nesthorn. He had climbed fifteen or twenty feet above Young, and was attempting a gymnastic swing to surmount an overhang, when he fell off backwards. Young was aware only of a grey streak flashing past him and braced himself for the shock on the rope. Mallory fell clear for some forty feet before

Young, at the belay, checked his flight. It was miraculous that the rope did not snap with the shock, especially since they were using a woven rope which had, as Young later discovered, a very poor breaking strain. 'I suppose,' he reflected, 'that two rather abnormally resilient anatomies at either end of a rope may introduce a confusing element into the nicest theory of strains.'[11]

Mallory was unhurt and apparently unflustered. He had not even dropped his ice axe and was able to climb back up and rejoin Young on the ledge. All the while, Robertson — the third man on the rope, out of sight around a corner — was blissfully ignorant that anything untoward had occurred. They went on to complete the first ascent, returning to their hotel after midnight, having been out for 24 hours.

Forgetting to tie on was a clear demonstration of Mallory's chronic absent-mindedness, a fault he never managed to overcome. In an academic setting a certain fuzziness over material concerns might be considered endearing, might even be affected, but it is a dangerous commodity on a mountain. It would be unfair to say that Mallory was impractical, for he certainly displayed a mechanical aptitude as a gunner in the First World War, nor was he slipshod in the sense that he skimped effort, but he had always to strive consciously to remember simple precautionary procedures that other people might effect as a matter of routine.

During this first alpine season with Geoffrey Young, Mallory was still very much a novice. Experience could be expected to make him more circumspect and ensure he would not as readily over-estimate his abilities as he did on the Nesthorn overhang. He could have wished for no finer tutor than Young. Later in his life there were plenty of people ready to swear that Mallory was so in tune with rock it was impossible for him to fall, yet there also remained some who thought him reckless — or at very least impetuous.

One silly and avoidable accident which had long-reaching effects took place only a short while after his return from the Alps, and it so shook his confidence that it was several months before he could bring himself to relate it to Young. Having now come down from university, he was staying with Lytton Strachey's sister and her family in Roquebrune on the Riviera for several months to improve his French. From there he wrote to Young on 30 December:

I would have written you a letter long ago only it involved such a horrible confession. About three weeks after we came back from Switzerland I had a nasty fall while climbing on a little

21

sandstone cliff in Birkenhead and sprained an ankle which has caused much trouble, for the said ankle refused for a long time to get any better and I hobbled about shamefully. Indeed it is still in a poor state and though I can walk well enough for a short distance, it is no good for the mountains . . .

The whole affair is almost too disgusting to think of, the result chiefly of my obstinacy. I had been climbing about for some time with some friends when I suggested a possible new route. One of the other people who had never climbed before that day jeered greatly at the idea, so of course I was obliged to make the attempt at once. I like to think that I should have turned back if I hadn't been encouraged by a rope which was let down from above because my situation looked perilous, but at all events I went up on a hold I knew to be unsafe, persuading myself that if the worst were to happen, I could save myself with the rope. I deceived myself, of course, and when I slipped, I grabbed at the rope but couldn't grip it tight enough.[12]

The episode was a salutary warning, and Mallory acknowledged it as such. Even so, time and again, his courage appeared to outweigh reasonable caution. He seemed unable to guard against a certain impetuosity in his make-up.

The ankle obstinately refused to heal. Mallory remained in France until the Spring, by which time he was able to walk reasonable distances, but for many years afterwards, it continued to trouble him after serious exertion. In 1917, when he was serving on the Western Front, it became so bad that he was invalided home, and only then was it discovered that the original injury must have been a fracture, which through lack of treatment had mended badly. It required an operation to put right, and even then, went on giving him occasional twinges for the rest of his life.

Mallory as yet had come to no firm decision about a career. He felt drawn to teaching, but an interview with M.J. Rendall at his old school of Winchester had been far from encouraging. As he had nothing to teach, Rendall remarked, and anyway would probably teach it badly, there was not the least likelihood of his getting to Winchester — or for that matter, anywhere similar. He might try a private school for a year, then apprentice himself to a country parson. Mallory's father was Rector of Birkenhead, and during 1908 Mallory too had considered taking holy orders. He eventually dismissed the idea, unwilling to shackle his free-ranging religious explorations to the restrictions of church orthodoxy. In the long term, Mallory knew he wanted to write, but his father was quick to point out — as fathers are apt to do — that he could hardly expect to live solely on the hopes of some day selling whatever he chose to write. He would need to find a real job.

When he returned from the south of France, the opportunity arose for him to take a temporary teaching post at Dartmouth Naval College, an experience Mallory found he thoroughly enjoyed. Then in the summer another unusual and 'pleasant-sounding' possibility suggested itself — one, moreover, which would get him out to his beloved Alps again. It was to take a 15-year-old, John Bankes-Price, to Switzerland for August and teach him to climb. 'It isn't very clear to me', Mallory wrote to Geoffrey Young, 'that I am the ideal person for the situation, but I think I might behave with discretion if I was made responsible in this way. However, if you think I should endanger the boy's life, I won't attempt to go, but if, by chance, you think otherwise, then I should be very grateful if you would again employ your pen in my service.'[13]

Presumably, Young's pen did come to Mallory's aid, for the engagement was confirmed. 'Bear-leading' is how Mallory light-heartedly described it to his friends, but he was resolved all the same to do his best by the boy. Lytton Strachey thought it a ludicrous proposition. 'The imagination cannot create, it can only reconstruct and on this occasion mine has no materials except a snow mountain, laziness, energy, George, and a perfectly absurd companion aged 15 — and I can make nothing of them.' Not only was the whole prospect absurd, in Strachey's eyes it appeared also fraught with danger, and this at a time when, to him, Mallory seemed already set on an alarming downhill course. For Strachey fancied Mallory (at 24) to be growing fat and fast losing his good looks. 'His complexionless face [is] becoming rather washy and bulbous, its contours too lunar — like a cheese,' he bemoaned. To his brother James he wrote in characteristically dramatic fashion, 'And now I shall never see him again, or if I do, it'll be an unrecognizable middle-aged mediocrity, fluttering between wind and water, probably wearing glasses and a timber toe.'[14]

Lytton Strachey's fears about danger were unfounded. Unlike Mallory, young Master Bankes-Price found no spontaneous joy in mountains. Instead he promptly hurt his knee, thus preventing any real 'climbing' taking place at all. Mallory spent several disheartening weeks endeavouring to cajole the boy, who failed even to enjoy a

23

picnic, into some sort of activity. Such a 'jelly-fish mentality', as Mallory called it, always puzzled and irritated him; it was so alien to his own get-up-and-go instincts. His frustration was not eased by meeting several climbing friends in Zermatt, including Geoffrey Young, and hearing of the expeditions they were making. Towards the end of the month, some of Mallory's enthusiasm was beginning to rub off on the boy and they managed a couple of modest routes.

Meanwhile Mallory had secured a post as junior master at Charterhouse School in Godalming, despite Rendall's gloomy predictions. He started there soon after his return from the Alps in September 1910. Much has been made of the difficulty Mallory first experienced in keeping order and it is often called up as evidence that he was not a good teacher. If his natural diffidence was no great help to him when he started, neither was the impression he made on most people — however Lytton Strachey perceived him — of being little older than a sixth-former himself. He was also inexperienced. Apart from his few short weeks at Dartmouth, he had no 'teacher training' as one would understand it today. He was openly critical of many principles of school routine, which did not endear him to older, more traditional colleagues. He felt that the primary purpose of education was to be a civilizing influence; consequently he endeavoured to conduct his lessons in what he considered a civilized manner, encouraging a degree of familiarity with his students that was regarded with suspicion by other masters, and — it has to be said — by some of the boys as well. Yet, from the beginning, he had considerable success with individual students in whom he could detect a willingness to learn. Later, as his views matured, he began working towards educational reform.

There is no doubt that Mallory eventually became 'a schoolmaster by conviction' — which is how he was described by Geoffrey Young in an obituary notice for the *Nation*, and one who was 'notably successful in his history coaching and in stimulating young and older boys alike to an interest in literature, and a love of healthy nature'.

Robert Graves was one of the senior pupils at Charterhouse when Mallory arrived. Mallory recognized his poetic talent at once and encouraged it, introducing him to the work of writers who were not included in the school curriculum: Bernard Shaw, Rupert Brooke, Samuel Butler, John Masefield, James Elroy Flecker, H.G. Wells. For Graves it was literary exploration and very exciting. Later Mallory introduced him to Edward Marsh, founder and editor of *Georgian Poetry* and a patron of the arts for half a century, besides becoming private secretary to Prime Ministers Asquith and Churchill. But 'George Mallory did something better than lend me books,' wrote Graves in his autobiography *Goodbye to All That*, 'and that was to take me climbing on Snowdon in the school vacations.'[15]

Having derived so much pleasure and benefit from being one of Irving's schoolboy 'recruits' at Winchester, it was natural for Mallory, now that he was a schoolmaster himself, to attempt similar experiments with his own students. He did not take them to the Alps, but to North Wales and the Lake District. Robert Graves went with him on at least two occasions although dates are conflicting.

Graves describes one trip which he says took place 'in January' when it was snowy enough to enable them to do some ice-axe practice. Later they climbed Snowdon:

> We found the hotel there with its roof blown off in the blizzard the previous night. We sat by the cairn and ate Carlsbad plums and liver-sausage sandwiches. Geoffrey Keynes . . . and George, who used to go drunk with excitement at the end of his climbs, picked stones off the cairn and shied them at the chimney stack of the hotel until they had sent it where the roof was.[16]

Keynes recalled the incident in his own autobiography,[17] but had no personal recollection of Mallory being drunk with excitement after any of his climbs. *Goodbye to All That* he thought an 'entertaining but unreliable work'. Graves and Keynes were in agreement that they and Mallory were at Pen-y-Pass in the spring of 1914.[18] Graves:

> The practice at Pen-y-Pass was to have a leisurely breakfast and lie in the sun with a tankard of beer before starting for the precipice foot in the late morning. Snowdon was a perfect mountain for climbing. The rock was sound and not slippery. And once you came to the top of any of the precipices, some of which were a thousand feet high, but all just climbable one way or another, there was always an easy way to run down. In the evening when we got back to the hotel we lay and stewed in hot baths. I remember wondering at my body — the worn fingernails, the bruised knees, and the lump of climbing muscle that had begun to bunch above the arch of the foot, seeing it as beautiful in relation to this new purpose.[19]

25

Geoffrey Young always took an interest in Mallory's 'recruits' and made a point of encouraging the young Graves. He told him he had the most perfect sense of natural balance he had ever seen in a climber, a compliment which Graves admitted pleased him far more than if the Poet Laureate had told him he had the finest sense of rhythm ever met in a young poet.

Mallory 'never lost his almost foolhardy daring', according to Graves. 'Yet . . . one always felt absolutely safe with him on the rope.' Alan Goodfellow, another Charterhouse boy who went to Wasdale with Mallory in the summer of 1913, recalls how he and Mallory scrambled up without thinking to a small ledge and then found themselves faced with two almost equally precarious alternatives to get themselves safely down again: they must either climb back the way they had come, which is always difficult, or continue traversing without a rope:

> It must have been a very anxious moment for George with the responsibility of an inexperienced schoolboy climbing as his only companion; but he showed no trace of it and quietly suggested that we should eat all the bilberries before we went on. Then we effected the traverse unbelayed, with George leading the way and instructing me exactly where to put my hands and feet. He was quite the finest rock-climber I have ever seen, with a wonderful sense of balance.[20]

Geoffrey Keynes has acknowledged that Mallory was sometimes criticized for taking relatively unpractised climbers up difficult ascents, something he obviously did frequently. Even on the Everest Reconnaissance of 1921, Bullock felt Mallory took unwarranted risks with untrained and loaded porters on difficult ice. But Keynes asserts he never once felt himself to be in any danger when climbing with Mallory. He was a good leader, he said, capable of inspiring confidence in those on the rope behind him. 'Confidence breeds skill, which cannot be acquired without it. That was how George's pupils escaped injury.'

III

The Third Pole

When people began speculating on the possibility of climbing Everest towards the end of the last century, it seemed an idea more fanciful than probable, arousing hardly less public scepticism than did the anticipation of space travel in the early years of the present century. Yet the alpinist Edward Whymper, who made the first ascent of the Matterhorn, displayed a premature prescience when he remarked to a lecture audience in 1894 that there might be a boy present who would one day stand on a similar platform to recount his ascent of the world's highest mountain.

With a long tradition of exploration on land and sea, and with the expansion of the Empire into distant and often inhospitable corners of the world, the British laid claim to pioneering spirit as almost exclusively theirs. Victorian attitudes had overlaid a rambunctious past with a sense of duty that made a virtue of territorial gain. For a century before the First World War, the British had explored to spread the Gospel, they had explored for the Queen, for political treating and for hard commerce, they had explored in search of rare specimens, for sport and ultimately out of curiosity *to know*. The Royal Geographical Society was formed in the summer of 1830 with the express purpose of promoting exploration and collating the data of discovery. In its first hundred years most of the blank areas on the map of the world were sketched in, the dark continent of Africa crossed from coast to coast, the source of the Nile discovered, the desert interior of Australia explored. Such was the confidence of the Empire that Britons took it for granted that they led the world.

There had been failures too. The British suffered costly losses of ships and men in their abortive search for a northwest sea passage to link the Atlantic and Pacific Oceans, and, far more damaging to national pride in the early years of this century, they saw the conquest of both the Poles go to foreign explorers. Scott's failure to reach the South Pole ahead of Amundsen was a particularly bitter pill to swallow. Only the British were capable of making a heroic legend out of Scott's tragic defeat. His was the kind of sporting gallantry they understood. It was what made Britons great. Besides, the other fellow had not played fair: he had taken dogs all the way. This self-imposition of sporting 'rules' to enterprise is a curiously British phenomenon. Scott greatly diminished his chances of success by refusing to take dogs; one might draw a parallel with the later distaste felt for the use of bottled oxygen on Everest.

Once the South Pole had been reached, the only major geographical challenge left on this planet was Everest. Its lofty summit had taken over as the world's most coveted spot; it was even called the Third Pole. The British always assumed that with their strong influence over the Indian sub-continent, this last shining prize rightfully belonged to them, and that this time all likely competition could be firmly held at bay.

Yet nobody knew if men could safely venture into the diminished atmosphere that would be found at the top of Everest; for the highest anyone had ever climbed, anywhere, was to 24,600 feet on Bride Peak in the Karakoram in 1909. Everest was almost a mile higher. It could be approached only by travelling through the forbidden Himalayan kingdoms of Tibet or Nepal. At the time of the first British expedition, no European had been within 40 miles of the mountain, or indeed had seen more than its upmost slopes floating above intervening ridges.

Everest was first recognized as the highest mountain in the world in 1852, as a result of triangulations made from the North by the Survey of India. Before then, it had always been believed that the honour belonged to Kangchenjunga or Dhaulagiri. At that time, it was known merely by its surveying reference, 'Peak XV'. The height computed for Peak XV was 29,002 feet, later amended to 29,028 feet. No-one took great pains to find out what the Tibetans called it, or indeed if they had any name for it at all. Much later it was learned that to the villagers who lived nearby, the mountain had long rejoiced in the beautiful name of Chomolungma, or Goddess Mother of the World. Having convinced themselves that no local name existed, the officers of the Survey decided in 1865 that it should be called 'Everest', in honour of Sir George Everest, the Surveyor General in India.

Probably the first time anyone seriously suggested that an attempt should be made to climb Everest was in 1893, when a young Captain in the 5th Gurkha Rifles, Charles Granville Bruce, who had climbed with Conway in the Karakoram, put the proposition to Francis Younghusband, then Political Officer in Chitral. The idea caught Younghusband's imagination immediately, needing little of Bruce's boisterous enthusiasm to persuade him. He was a great romantic, and an adventurous traveller himself. Some years earlier, Younghusband had made an astonishing journey from Peking across the Gobi Desert and the Karakoram mountains to Rawalpindi, and on the way had stood atop a high pass and seen a peak of such appalling height that it had taken his breath away. That was K2. If Everest were higher than that, what a formidable objective it would be! Younghusband had yet to lead his controversial Mission to Lhasa, and Bruce, with his small band of hand-picked Frontier Scouts, was to go from one bloody skirmish to another on the troubled Northwest Frontier.

For the present, all talk of Everest remained academic, since the political problems of approaching the mountain appeared insuperable. Both Tibet and Nepal, from whose shared border the mountain rises, resisted all incursions from outside. It was not until after the Treaty with Tibet was signed in 1904, following Younghusband's Mission, that a glimmer of hope presented itself. Even then, by recognizing Chinese suzerainty over Tibet (which was something the Tibetans themselves preferred to ignore), it meant that permission to go to Everest would need to be sanctioned by both Peking and Lhasa.

Some years earlier, Cecil Rawling had seen Everest from a distance of 70 miles while on the Gartok Expedition of 1904, and was so captivated that he, too, conceived a secret ambition to climb it. Like Bruce, Rawling had been a soldier in the Frontier campaigns of 1897–8. Later he worked as a surveyor on the Tibetan borders, where in 1903 he mapped over 40,000 square miles of Himalayan territory and became familiar with the Tibetan language. In 1913, another Everest contender entered the arena, a young Lieutenant of the East Yorkshire Regiment, stationed in Calcutta, with the prophetic name of John Baptist Lucius Noel. Every summer, when his garrison retired from the heat of the plains into the hills for several months, Noel would take the opportunity to wander off with a small group of

29

native hillmen and explore the trails and passes leading into Tibet. He, too, had fallen under the spell of the highest peak in the world and his explorations were all directed towards the hope of one day reaching the mountain. Having identified a remote high pass to the north of Kangchenjunga that was not watched by border guards, he made an illicit sortie into Southern Tibet disguised as an Indian Mohammedan, hoping to discover a high-level route to the gorge of the Arun river and thence to the eastern glaciers of Everest.

From the Langbu La pass he obtained a splendid view of a chain of snow peaks ahead of him, which he knew to be too near and too low to include Everest. He gave the names Tarigban (meaning Long Knife) and Guma Raichu (Guma's Tooth) to the two most prominent in the group, and then, as the clouds shifted across this intriguing panorama, he glimpsed directly over the crest of the peak he had called Tarigban 'a glittering spire top of rock fluted with snow, which according to its magnetic bearing, could be none other than Everest itself'.[1] Some 1,000 to 1,500 feet of the summit was visible.

He estimated the mountain to be 60 miles distant, but impassably cut off from him by the mountain wall in between. He and his party tried skirting the barrier through the Tashirak Valley, but were forced back by hostile soldiers. 'Within forty miles, and nearer at that time than any white man had been! I leave you to imagine my chagrin and disappointment,' John Noel later wrote in his book *Through Tibet to Everest*.

The time had come for all those interested in climbing Everest to join forces. Accordingly, Cecil Rawling, with the support of the Royal Geographical Society, began laying plans for a two-stage expedition to take place in 1915 and 1916 with the object of first making a thorough scientific exploration of the Everest region, and following it the next year with an effort to reach the highest point attainable on the mountain itself. In his prospectus he wrote:

The experience of the Duke of Abruzzi [in the Karakoram], Colonel Bruce and others of recent years in the Himalaya has upset many of the old views as to the limits of attainable altitude. It may well be that Mount Everest is unclimbable on the north side by any mountaineer however skilled, or that even if the mountaineering difficulties were not insuperable, the altitude makes human advance impossible. These questions however have not yet been settled, and it is the aim of the expedition to do something towards their solution.[2]

Rawling's team was to include the young soldier-explorer John Noel and two other old Himalaya hands, Dr A.L. Kellas and Tom Longstaff. Kellas had made first ascents of Chomiumu, Kangchenjau, Powhunri and Langpo, each over 22,000 feet. Captain Morshead of the Survey of India and Dr A.F.R. Wollaston, a seasoned traveller who, like Rawling himself, had visited New Guinea, were also to join the group; and a close friend of Rawling's, the writer John Buchan, eagerly offered to help with the expedition planning.

Once more, however, political events intervened. 'The outbreak of war put a stop to these pleasant fancies,' John Buchan wrote in 1917 in *The Times*, when it was his sad duty to compile an obituary notice for his friend. Cecil Rawling had been killed at Passchendaele on 28 October, the victim of a casual shell.

The slaughter of the First World War, which so decimated a generation of young men, had a long-term effect on British mountaineering. Geoffrey Winthrop Young, Britain's finest alpine mountaineer, lost a leg, and several of his 'hill company' were dead, including Siegfried Herford, one of the most promising among a new breed of innovative and finely-tuned rock climbers. It meant that when attention again turned towards Everest, the pool of talent from which potentially good *young* high-altitude performers could be drawn was seriously depleted. Even those climbers like Mallory, who had survived the fighting, had earned their alpine experience before 1914, and were, by the time of the first expeditions, already well into their thirties. The older climbers, the experienced leader material, had not escaped either: Rawling was dead, Bruce had been severely wounded in the Gallipoli campaign, and Edward Strutt, a climber with exceptional snow and ice craft, had been wounded twice.

There was one significant change, however, which had a positive effect on aspirations to scale Mount Everest. The tense political situation within Tibet relaxed. Both the Russians and Chinese were occupied with revolutions at home and were in no position to take an active interest in Tibetan affairs. The Chinese garrison was withdrawn from Lhasa, and the India Office could no longer exercise restrictions over travel in Tibet under the pretext that it might damage Imperial policy.

In March 1919 the Royal Geographical Society invited Captain

31

John Noel to present an account of his 1913 Tibetan journey to its members in London. With hindsight, it is obvious that this was a carefully-orchestrated event to arouse public interest in an Everest project. When Sir Francis Younghusband took over from Sir Douglas Freshfield as President of the Royal Geographical Society the same year, he publicly avowed that while in office he would direct all his energies towards taking an expedition to Everest. On 26 April 1920 a joint meeting was held with representatives of the Alpine Club to determine precise objectives and strategy.

It was apparent from the start that the geographers were interested in producing accurate maps, while the mountaineers were anxious to get to grips with climbing the mountain. With self-righteous pomposity but a certain amount of reason, the geographers saw themselves as undertaking responsible scientific work and shouldering the brunt of the effort, while the alpine men were out to indulge their sport. With equal reason, the mountaineers knew that they were the ones required to step beyond existing knowledge, and that when it came to putting lives on the line, they would be taking all the chances.

The two organizations could never hope to be more than uneasy bedfellows. Nevertheless they agreed that the principal object of the expedition should be an ascent of Everest, and that all preliminary reconnaissance would be directed towards that end. The Royal Geographical Society would undertake all the organization up to base camp, and from there the responsibility would pass to the Alpine Club. Funds should already start being put aside for the enterprise, and no efforts spared in seeking official sanction.

Younghusband gave a stirring Presidential Address to the Royal Geographical Society, which was widely reported in the press over the following week. No gold would be found on Everest's summit, he predicted, and Mount Everest would not put a pound into anyone's pocket — indeed it would take a good many pounds out — but, he assured his audience:

> The accomplishment of such a feat will elevate the human spirit and will give man, especially us geographers, a feeling that we really are getting the upper hand on the earth, and that we are acquiring a true mastery of our surroundings. As long as we impotently creep about at the foot of these mighty mountains and gaze at their summits without attempting to ascend them, we entertain towards them a too excessive feeling of awe . . .

[but] if man stands on earth's highest summit, he will have an increased pride and confidence in himself in the struggle for ascendancy over matter. This is the incalculable good which the ascent of Mount Everest will confer.[3]

The *Daily News* was not swayed. 'It will be a proud moment for the man who first stands on the top of the earth,' its correspondent agreed, 'but he will have the painful thought that he has queered the pitch for posterity.' The *Daily Express* remarked on the fact that until recently the difficulty of ascending the highest Himalayas had been as much political as physical. 'Their would-be conqueror has either to evade avalanches or get round Lord Morley, and I don't know which is the more awkward obstacle.' Perhaps Morley's successor as Secretary of State for India would be less intransigent. Also Lord Curzon, who had been a strong supporter of the Everest project since his days as Viceroy, was now Secretary of State for Foreign Affairs, and a useful ally.

Invaluable help came also from an unexpected quarter. Lt-Col. Charles Kenneth Howard-Bury, a Himalayan traveller with an interest in politics, was planning a private visit to India and offered his services as mediator. He was a wealthy young man, a member of the family of Howard, Earls of Norfolk, and was prepared to pay his own expenses. For nearly six months he negotiated and carried messages between the Viceroy (Lord Chelmsford), the Governor of Bengal (Lord Ronaldshay), the Commander-in-Chief (Lord Rawlinson), and the Political Officer in Sikkim (Sir Charles Bell) and secured their support for the Everest plans. He met also the Surveyor General, various Indian government officials and the Tibetan authorities. He even visited the Flying Corps Headquarters in the hopes of persuading them to support an aerial reconnaissance of the mountain. As a result Bell was able to secure from the Dalai Lama of Tibet the long-awaited sanction to go ahead. It was a remarkable achievement.

Younghusband received the news in a letter from the India Office on 20 December 1920, and formal confirmation three weeks later. Immediately he set up an official Mount Everest Committee, which agreed that the expedition should be run in two stages: reconnaissance the first year, and a serious climbing attempt the next. The geographers were concerned lest the reconnaissance might be skimped once the mountaineers found their way on to the mountain; their chance was to come on the second stage of the expedition. So that there should be no misunderstanding a formal resolution was passed:

> The main object this year is reconnaissance. This does not debar the mountain party from climbing as high as possible on a favourable route, but attempts on a particular route must not be prolonged to hinder the completion of the reconnaissance.[4]

It had always been in Younghusband's mind that Bruce should lead the first expedition. His unique knowledge of the Himalaya, and especially his flair for getting along with Himalayan peoples, would make him an invaluable leader, and an ideal ambassador, which was almost as important. But Bruce, after waiting so long, had to pass up the possibility of going in 1921. He knew he could not get leave to go twice in successive years, and left it for the Committee to decide what he should do. It preferred to hold him back for the second phase and offered leadership of the first trip to Howard–Bury, who had been so instrumental in obtaining the permission to go.

Howard–Bury accepted without hesitation, adding generously, 'I hope Bruce will be given the leadership of the expedition in 1922. It is only right and his due that he should have it when the really serious attempt is made to climb Mount Everest.'[5] Once more, Howard–Bury offered to contribute towards his own expenses. Most of the rest of the expedition's funding was raised by private subscription from members of the Royal Geographical Society and the Alpine Club. The King and the Prince of Wales made generous donations, as did the Viceroy.

Howard–Bury had no easy task in front of him. To reach the mountain meant a long circuitous journey from Darjeeling and across the arid plains of Tibet that would take several weeks. Little or nothing was known of the northern approaches of the mountain, but to assist with the survey work, the Survey of India agreed to send two officers, Majors Morshead and Wheeler, and the Geological Survey of India one, Dr A.M. Heron. Their expenses would be met by their respective departments. Now, there was just the rest of the team to get together.

★

When it came to selecting personnel for each of three expeditions of the 1920s, the first two names to emerge naturally for consideration were those of Mallory and Finch. As early as March 1918, when the possibility of mounting a big expedition to Everest after the war was first rumoured, Captain Farrar (then President of the Alpine Club) wrote to his friend Henry F. Montagnier that he strongly favoured the inclusion of George Finch in the party — and also Maxwell Finch, his brother and regular climbing partner:

> They are at present gunners, but I believe we could easily get them seconded. I know them both very well and they are in my opinion two of the very best mountaineers we have ever seen and much more likely to carry out a job of this kind than any other men I know, whether a guide or a mountaineer of any nationality. They are both under 30 and the very men for the job.[6]

He repeated his view the following year, informing Montagnier that he had seen young George Finch, who was about to be demobilised and that he appeared to be quite willing to go: 'If he and his brother Max and young Kurz cannot do the job, then we have nobody who can.'[7]

George Finch was not at the time a member of the Alpine Club, though he had a fine alpine record. His climbing career had begun at the age of fifteen, when he and his brother Max scaled Beachy Head to the consternation of coastguards. Later the same summer, the adventurous pair evaded their tutor in Paris to attempt the walls of Notre Dame, but after that they settled down to more conventional routes. From 1907, George ranged freely throughout the Alps and Corsica, summer and winter, without guides and mostly with Max. Both were studying at the Polytechnic in Zürich, which Farrar has described as 'probably the finest mountaineering school in the world'. Students would organize themselves into graded parties and in this way, rapidly attain with reasonable safety an experience and proficiency that were remarkable for the time. Today it seems an obvious method of learning, but in those early years of the century it was still widely regarded necessary to build up alpine experience slowly over a number of summer seasons with accredited guides. Farrar wrote of George Finch, 'Save in the very few expeditions where he has been, by invitation or otherwise, a member of a guided party, Finch has been for some years past the recognised leader of his caravan.'

Not everyone held Finch in such high regard. He had not passed through the accepted social mill of British public school and university, and as a result of a somewhat nomadic adolescence, had acquired a cosmopolitan air of unconventionality that was considered decidedly rakish within the conservative enclave of the Alpine Club. In many ways he was ahead of his time; he was certainly out of step with the thinking of his contemporaries. A self-confident young man, forthright and uncompromising in his views, he recognized the limitations placed upon British mountaineering by its inflexible attitudes.

He was always holding forth about the enlightened climbing ethos that existed on the Continent, where a far more democratic system of clubs had developed, and the leaders of the sport were, for the most part, active young members. Though younger men were beginning to emerge in the provinces in Britain, what Finch wanted was a great national club which would open its doors to mountaineers from all walks of life. Such ideas smacked of heresy to the hidebound older generations.

The Alpine Club took pride in its exclusiveness; the very last thing it wanted was to open its portals to the hoi polloi; nor would it welcome the inevitable escalation in climbing standards such increased participation would engender. A long-serving club secretary once defined the Alpine Club as 'a club for gentlemen, who happen to climb'. Finch's publicly outspoken criticism in, of all things, a national periodical, only confirmed popular opinion that he was a brash, impudent upstart, and most certainly not a gentleman. He may have been the author of a number of fine new routes and traverses, but for many years afterwards he was treated by many of the club's elders with an aloofness verging on rudeness.

George Mallory, on the other hand, was the darling of the Establishment. He was socially ambitious and worked hard at burnishing the good contacts climbing afforded. He was elected to the Climbers' Club in 1909 and became a member of the Alpine Club two years later, at the age of twenty-five. He wrote frequently for the journals of both, elaborate articles in which he tried to convey the feelings and emotions of climbing rather than factual detail. Perhaps the most famous is his essay likening an alpine climb to a symphony.[8] In another he seeks to re-create a climb of five years earlier by summoning up his thoughts and sensations as he made it. 'What more after all are the events of life than moments in the stream of thought, which is experience?'[9] he asked. The spiritual thread he sought to trace in this article was coloured by a disordered stomach from too much sour wine the night before. The result was 'a wild performance', Mallory confided to Geoffrey Young. 'I fear the patient reader may be inclined to ask whether this disorder has yet been cured.' His writings, he knew, very often bewildered his audience. This one, he had submitted to George Yeld, Editor of the *Alpine Journal*, who — uncertain what to make of it — had forwarded it to Farrar. Farrar, Mallory related to Young with some amusement, declared he could not understand a word of it, and sent it on to H. V. Reade, 'who is now I suppose making up his mind what he shall say to me about it!'[10] Yet Mallory himself was treated with that sort of indulgence reserved for favoured children who attempt a sophistication beyond their years, only to be betrayed by unconscious naïvety.

It was primarily for his exploits on rock that Mallory was known. Finch, on the other hand, was a master on snow and ice. He climbed regularly in the Alps, while Mallory's visits were more spasmodic. It was not until after the war that two fine alpine seasons brought Mallory to a peak of fitness and confidence that led him to believe he had matured as an alpine climber. By this time his judgment had developed sufficiently for him to lead comfortably and competently, rather than 'to go over the top at the first rush', which, according to Geoffrey Young was his earlier notion of leadership.

At all events, the early explorations on Everest might be said to be the story of the two Georges — George Leigh Mallory and George Ingle Finch.

IV

The Two Georges

There can be no doubt that George Mallory was possessed of great personal charm, which for a long while was married to an improbably youthful appearance. He was regarded as the essence of idealistic youth, was dubbed 'Galahad' by Geoffrey Young, and affectionately lampooned by Geoffrey's brother Hilton in a Pen-y-Pass 'masque' as a seraphic pedagogue dreaming of Arcady.

In his early climbs, slips and miscalculations were not infrequent. After an ascent of the Girdle Traverse on Lliwedd with Mallory and H.V. Reade, Karl Blodig, an eminent Austrian mountaineer attending Winthrop Young's Easter party in 1911 remarked: 'That young man will not be alive for long!' This judgment dismayed Mallory who, according to a close friend, Cottie Sanders, used always to defend himself vigorously against any suggestion that he was not a perfectly prudent mountaineer:

> He *was* prudent, according to his own standards; but his standards were not those of the ordinary medium-good rock-climber. The fact was that difficult rocks had become to him a perfectly normal element; his prodigious reach, his great strength, and his admirable technique, joined to a sort of cat-like agility, made him feel completely secure on rocks so difficult as to fill less competent climbers with a sense of hazardous enterprise.[1]

Daring and coolness in face of sickening danger had been natural to Mallory since childhood. His sister Avie recalls that it was always fatal to tell George any tree was impossible to climb, for it was sure to act as a challenge to him. As a boy, he once told her that it would be quite easy to lie between the railway lines and let a train run over him. According to Avie, he used to climb up the downspouts of the house and clamber about on the roof with complete sure-footedness.

When George was born in 1886, his father was rector of Mobberley in Cheshire, which remained the family home until their move to the larger parish of St John the Evangelist in Birkenhead when George was eight. George, his younger brother Trafford, and their two sisters were left to their own devices while their parents struggled to minister to their flock in rather an abstracted fashion. Their father, who was said to have been a Cheshire squire, preferred to adhere to the conventions of his calling without enforcing any strict code of conduct on either his parishioners or his family. Only with reluctance would he engage in debate on the finer points of Christian teaching and usually confined himself to mild comments on the oddities of dress, and manners of others. George clearly had great affection for his father, who was, by all accounts, genial and kind-hearted. Curiously he seems rarely to have mentioned his mother. She gave the impression to many who encountered her of slipping easily from a devout Christian stance into vague eccentricity. Her ailments (never clearly specified) popped up and disappeared seemingly to suit purposes of her own. In later years, Mallory's wife found the gloomy Birkenhead vicarage an unlovely chaos, where servants were hard to come by and harder to keep. 'I don't see how anyone could have success in such an atmosphere.' She thought George's mother selective and muddled in her views on religion and human affairs and once remarked to George, 'I don't think your home can have taught you much.'

One year on holiday at St Bees, George determined to remain on a big rock on the beach while the tide came in; he wanted to know what it would be like to be cut off by water, but had taken no account that the rock itself would be submerged by the incoming tide. Quite unperturbed, he was rescued by a holidaymaker.

Mallory's impulsiveness did nothing to diminish his reputation as a climber of great style and dash. In his book, *The Epic of Everest* (written in 1926), Sir Francis Younghusband said that to Alpine Club members there was no question that 'he was the finest climber they had'. On the other hand, few shared Farrar's enthusiasm for Finch. Younghusband could have been referring to no one but Finch when he wrote:

A question had arisen about the inclusion of a certain other climber in the party. As a mountaineer this other was all that could be desired; but he had characteristics which several members of the Committee who knew him thought would cause friction and irritation in the party and destroy that cohesion which is so vitally necessary in an Everest Expedition. At high altitudes it is well known that men become irritable. And at the altitudes of Mount Everest they might find it wholly impossible to contain their irritation; and an uncongenial member might break up the party. It was an urgent matter; and to put it further to the test the Chairman consulted Mallory and asked him whether he would be prepared to sleep in the same bag with this man at 27,000 feet. Mallory, in that quick sudden way he used when he was intent on a thing, said that 'he didn't care who he slept with as long as they got to the top'.

According to Tom Longstaff, when Finch's name was discussed for the expedition of 1924, three others among the strongest contenders went to the Everest Committee and delivered the ultimatum: 'If Finch goes on this expedition, we don't!' Finch did not go. Farrar resigned from the Committee, disgusted at the shabby way in which Finch had been kept on a string about his possible participation until his technical expertise, so vital in getting equipment together, was no longer needed.

Longstaff did not include Mallory among those who had raised the objection. His version of the story has Mallory saying, 'I'm happy to share a tent with Finch — I'd share a tent with the Devil himself if it gave me a better chance of reaching the top of Everest!' The widow of Guy Bullock recalled it slightly differently. She understood that there had been serious differences of opinion between Mallory and Finch in 1922, largely over the use of oxygen. She believed that — 'according to Mallory's own statement to us' — he refused to join the third expedition if Finch were to be a member.

There were certainly arguments, if not on the mountain in 1922, after their return, and not only to do with oxygen but over lecture photographs. There is evidence that Mallory wanted to patch up these differences. Mallory's widow told Finch's family years later that her husband had wanted to see that Finch was accorded the honour due to him after the expedition of 1924. Of course, Mallory did not come back, but the description of his departure for that last expedition in the biography *George Mallory*, written by his son-in-law, David Robertson, substantiates the intention:

> On the 29th [February 1924] a strong wind hampered the tugboats and delayed the *California*. At last, having waved good-bye, Ruth returned to the children. George reminded Ruth that he hoped to see the Finches at Herschel House on his first weekend at home.[2]

There are few clues as to how the two Georges regarded each other in pre-Everest days. Certainly they were acquainted, for they were both present at Pen-y-Pass at Easter 1912. They also met up in Zermatt in 1920, when their hope of sharing some routes was thwarted by persistent bad weather. They sought to dodge the storms by keeping on the move.

> Finch and [Guy] Forster turned up on our slack day, and another day was wasted from our point of view. After this, the weather was hopeless. We spent two nights at the Bétemps hut, meditating an extensive scheme on the Monte Rosa; then crossed the Théodule and got to the Gamba once more . . . after a series of misadventures at nightfall next day.[3]

Who, then, was this man Finch, that he could stir up such violent reactions among fellow climbers? Why was there such a reluctance to climb with him? Did the antipathy felt towards him amount to a definite 'blackballing' of his name from the team in both 1921 and 1924?

George Ingle Finch was born in Australia in 1888. His father, Charles Finch, was Chairman of the Land Court of New South Wales and his mother, Laura, who was considerably younger than her husband, felt stifled and restless in Australian society. All the things that interested her seemed to be happening half a world away. Exciting new thoughts and movements were sweeping the European capitals, but they made little impact in New South Wales. In 1894 she heard Annie Besant lecture at the Sydney Opera House and immediately became fervently interested in Theosophy. For some years she was able to bury her frustration in the study of comparative religions and philosophy, until her husband, alarmed at her growing introspection and perhaps in a last-ditch attempt to rejuvenate their marriage, decided in 1902 to bring the whole family to Europe on a Grand Tour.

The Finches took their three children to England, cruised in the Mediterranean and stopped at fashionable hotels throughout Europe, finishing in Paris, which so beguiled Laura Finch that she immediately decided the children needed to be educated there if their horizons were to be widened. Tutors were engaged and young George, who demonstrated considerable scientific talent, began studying medicine. After a year abroad, George's father was obliged to return to his work in Australia, but he went alone. Laura and the children remained in the luxurious apartment they had rented overlooking the Jardin du Luxembourg and which was fast becoming a salon for Bohemian culture. The family never was reunited and only Dorothy, George's sister, saw their father again. Before another year had passed Laura had given birth to a third son, George's half-brother Antoine Konstant Finch (Konstant was the name of Laura's lover, a painter).

George, meanwhile, had decided that his interests lay not with medicine but with physical chemistry. He wondered if he should move to England, but was advised by one of his mother's friends that Zürich was the only place to study chemistry. At the age of nineteen he went to the Eidgenossische Technische Hochschule in Zürich, and later did well at Geneva University. The move to Switzerland gave him a unique opportunity to develop his mountaineering. Zürich at that time was the best known and most active centre in Switzerland. The Italian climber, Count Aldo Bonacossa, remembers meeting George Finch in Zürich one day in 1909:

> On that occasion I got acquainted with the elite of the mountaineers of Zürich . . . Among others I recall Heller, Keller, Marcel Kurz and Miescher . . . But the recognised number one mountaineer and the most outstanding personality among them by far was George Finch. He was tall and wore his hair long and untamed, quite unlike most men in Switzerland who used to wear their hair cut very short, and never took off their hat, as we can see in old photographs of mountaineers and guides; this gave him an exotic touch. Moreover he came from the Antipodes, and as a result was nicknamed 'the Australian'. He was also known for having introduced the anorak to replace the usual heavy jacket, which in hot weather became rather a nuisance.[4]

This was not the last time Finch employed his scientific inventiveness to improve climbing equipment and clothing. In 1921, in anticipation of being included in the Reconnaissance Expedition, he designed and made a two-layer eiderdown sleeping bag of the thinnest possible quilted balloon fabric, which he rendered air-tight and damp-proof with a coating of Duroprene. The total weight was just short of five pounds. He employed the same combination of balloon fabric and down in a suit, comprising lined coat, trousers, hat and gauntlets, which was made to his design by S.W. Silver & Co for Everest in 1922. Despite the sarcasm it provoked, the suit was a great success. (It was in effect the first duvet-clothing used on Everest and was years ahead of its time.)

Finch became President of Zürich's Akademischer Alpen Club in 1911. John Case, who climbed with him around this time, remembers him as an intellectual climber. He had a nose for route-finding and an eye for ground, but also studied the qualities of different kinds of rocks, the effect of weather on snow and ice, and the reaction of the body to cold and altitude. He had tremendous nervous energy.

On a mountain George gave the impression of being always master of his surroundings . . . On rock his strength was more apparent than grace of movement. He climbed very fast, going straight through from stance to stance, using holds far apart, without pause, rarely hesitating and almost never retracing a step. He seemed able to test each hold without loss of motion for I never saw a weighted one come away under hand or foot.

On ice he was superb, cutting steps far apart very fast with a minimum of powerful strokes. On steep ice he liked to cut straight up with his backer-up only a step behind and moving with him. His lead on the Marinelli route on Monte Rosa in the very dry year of 1911 with step cutting from the Imseng rocks to the ridge of the Grenzgipfel was a perfect example of this technique.[5]

George's brother, Max, was his most constant climbing partner. He lacked George's brilliance, but being steady and even-tempered, provided an ideal foil to his temperament, for already, according to Case, there were times when George could be an overbearing and difficult climbing companion.

Finch eventually became a research chemist and lived in England. During the First World War he fought with the Royal Field Artillery at Mons and then in Egypt, where he contracted a severe case of cerebral malaria, which gave him recurrent attacks for several years. He was assigned to bomb disposal work. There was one lucky escape when a bomb he was dismantling blew up in his face, but its only serious effect was a weakening in one of his eyes that in later life occasioned him to wear a monocle. It earned him mention in dispatches and an MBE.

After the war, Finch went back to Imperial College and devoted himself to teaching and research until, early in 1921, he was nominated for the Everest Reconnaissance Expedition and with his scientific background, was leant on heavily for advice on equipment and clothing.

Mallory, too, was a 'gunner' in the Great War. He was forced to wait nearly two years to get into uniform because schoolteaching was a reserved occupation and his headmaster stubbornly refused to release him. Many of his friends were pacifists and conscientious objectors. Though he, too, believed war to be 'inconceivable and monstrous', Mallory found increasingly that his fireside became 'an intolerable reproach'. Geoffrey Winthrop Young was in command of the Friends' Ambulance Unit in Ypres, and Mallory hoped he would be able to find a place for him also in the service. Later he considered applying for the Flying Corps, but eventually he crossed to France in May 1916 to serve with the 40th Siege Battery north of Armentières. After a year at the front he was invalided home with a recurrence of his old ankle injury. There was more irksome 'frittering away days and weeks in England as one only can do in the Army' before he returned to France at the end of September 1918 to spend the last weeks of the war with the 515th Siege Battery near Arras.

Throughout his time at the front, Mallory seems to have been able to distance himself from the horrors. He maintained a steady flow of letters to his young wife, Ruth, whom he married in 1914 after a whirlwind courtship, and to his friends, discussing philosophies and current affairs and the books he was reading; he even began work on a book of his own. 'The Book of Geoffrey' was conceived as a journal showing a young boy's intellectual and spiritual development, but more than anything it demonstrated Mallory's growing disenchantment with the public school system. He suffered agonies one day when he thought the precious pages lost:

My condition has been perfectly pitiable. For nearly an hour I have feared, or felt convinced, that the notes for the Book of Geoffrey were utterly lost. It was quite decided that my man

Symons, the model valet, who has the most detestable habit of shuffling papers away into holes and corners and other damned tidy places, should never touch my things again. Rather than see his fine fingers wandering over my possessions with infernal deftness, I was resolved to have no servant. And now I have just pulled the lovely sheet of paper, neatly folded, from an unsuspected pocket.[6]

In February 1921, Mallory was summoned to luncheon in Mayfair to meet a deputation from the Everest Committee. It comprised Captain Farrar, as President of the Alpine Club, Harold Raeburn, the Scottish mountaineer who — despite his age of 56 — had already been selected to look after the climbing side of the reconnaissance, and, as spokesman for the group, the quietly-persuasive President of the Royal Geographical Society. Sir Francis Younghusband had the trick of holding the attention of whomever he was addressing with an unblinking gaze from beneath a shock of white hair and rampant eyebrows. Mallory heard him out patiently although his mind had already been made up before he came to the meeting. He had been wrestling with indecision for two weeks beforehand, after receiving a letter from Farrar telling him that it looked as if Everest would really be tried that summer. 'Party would leave early April', Farrar had written, 'and get back in October. Any aspirations?'[7]

When, finally, Younghusband extended a formal invitation for him to join the expedition, Mallory gravely accepted. His demeanour came as a surprise to Younghusband, who was not prepared for such seeming diffidence in the face of so exciting a venture. Later he satisfied himself that within Mallory a fire did indeed burn, and if, as he said, Mallory was not 'of the conventional bulldog, heavy-jawed, determined type; and if he was not boisterously enthusiastic, he was evidently keen enough at bottom — keener than the most boisterous'. Neither exaggeratedly modest nor pushfully self-assertive, he impressed Younghusband as one who was 'conscious of his own powers and of the position he had won by his own exertions; and he had, in consequence, a not obtrusive but quite perceptible and quite justifiable pride in himself as a mountaineer'.[8]

To Mallory a more exciting invitation could hardly be imagined. It had come at a time when he was feeling he should be making changes to his life. He had been at Charterhouse — apart from his war service — since 1910, and had for a number of years been growing increasingly disaffected, both with prevailing teaching methods and the 'littleness of understanding' of young boys. Mountain climbing was his escape, his avocation.

He had already decided he might be happier teaching adults, but his real aspiration was to write. There was a tangle of ideas in his mind crying out to be set down. Were he to go to Everest it would provide him with a welcome break from his comfortable but unsatisfying existence, in which to contemplate his future, and it would only mean handing in notice to his headmaster a few months earlier than he planned. Against that, though, he was a married man with a wife and three young children, the youngest only a few months old. How could he be thinking of leaving them? How would they cope if he threw in his job, having no prospect of another, and disappeared to the Himalaya for six months?

Everest was not an opportunity that had come quite out of the blue. There had been wind of an expedition for some time. As long ago as Easter of the year before he had discussed the matter with his friend Geoffrey Winthrop Young. Young had lost a leg during the war and was now painfully relearning how to climb. While Mallory and Conor O'Brien were shepherding him up the Roof Route on Lliwedd in North Wales, he was endeavouring to persuade Mallory to lead the first attack on Everest. 'So undying is human hope', Young recalled afterwards, 'we were even discussing whether I might not still offer to accompany the expedition, at least as far as the foot.'[9] It was an impossible and short-lived dream, for the great Roof Slab, soon encountered, convinced Young that nature routinely designs holds on rockfaces for climbers possessed of four extremities, never three.

It was not just in climbing matters that Mallory sought Young's opinion. Young had directed Mallory into membership of the Climbers' Club and the Alpine Club; had written job references for him, had been best man at his wedding, had introduced him to influential friends and generally helped shape much of his thinking. Mallory scarcely ever made an important decision in his life without turning first to Geoffrey Young for advice, and the question of going to Everest was no exception.

Young visited Mallory and his wife Ruth in their house at Godalming to spell out how helpful he thought Everest celebrity could be to Mallory's career, whether this were to be as an educator or a writer. It must have been a convincing speech. In twenty minutes, Young had obtained both Ruth's and Mallory's acquiescence. Maybe Mallory needed little persuasion – the temptation to go must have been irresistible on so many counts — but to obtain Ruth's compliance and convince her that it was such a golden opportunity for them both, says a lot for her generosity as well as for Young's eloquence.

'I expect I shall have no cause to regret your persuasion in the cause of Mount Everest,' Mallory wrote to Young soon afterwards. 'At the present, I'm highly elated at the prospect, and so is Ruth — thank you for that.'[10]

It was less easy for Mallory to explain to his other relations that what he was about to embark upon was a responsible course of action for a family man with young children. 'I hope it won't appear to you a merely fantastic performance,' he wrote to his sister Avie. 'I was inclined to regard it as such when the idea was first mooted a few weeks ago, but it has come to appear now, with the help of Ruth's enthusiasm, rather as the opportunity of a lifetime.'[11] All the same, he was not able to purge all traces of guilt until he was actually in Tibet and the adventure took him over. From the ship on the outward journey he sent his friend and former student, the poet Robert Graves, a sombre assessment of his uncertain future:

> The Lord knows what I shall find to do hereafter or where it will be done. I can't think I have sufficient talent to make a life-work of writing, though plenty of themes suggest themselves as wanting to be written about. Perhaps I shall get a job at a provincial university. I decided before leaving Charterhouse that, if I were to teach, I would prefer to teach adults — unless indeed I were to be enthroned one day as a God Almighty Headmaster. Ruth is bravely content to be comparatively poor for a time, but I must make some money one of these days.[12]

V

Bald-headed into Battle

Organization of the Everest exploration had been put in the hands of a committee of eight, chaired by Sir Francis Younghusband. Members were drawn from both the Royal Geographical Society and the Alpine Club, each providing secretaries to the committee. J.E.C. Eaton represented the alpinists, but the bulk of the work fell to the energetic, opinionated Arthur Hinks of the RGS, whose expertise as a geographer did little to compensate for a total ignorance of the practical difficulties of field work and a boorish lack of diplomacy. Many Alpine Club members considered the communications he sent them offensive. His instinctive antipathy towards mountaineers got him off on the wrong foot with the star climbers of successive expeditions, including Finch and Mallory. From the start, Hinks disliked Farrar and it was inevitable that differences of opinion at those early committee meetings were generally worked out through heavy clashes of personality. Farrar was no whit less dogmatic than Hinks, and on alpine matters at least was not prepared to relinquish an inch of ground to him. Since most of the surviving correspondence is in Hinks's hand, it is hard to tell now how closely Hinks reflected the views of the Committee. He was usually careful to preface letters containing difficult proposals with 'I have been instructed by the Mt. Everest Committee to inform you' or 'The Chairman would like', but there is evidence that successive chairmen (for Hinks remained Joint Secretary to the MEC until the Second World War) found Hinks's manner and the more extreme of his views unpalatable. Yet, apart from a little calming-down behind the scenes when necessary, he was usually left to get on with the job.

One of Hinks's responsibilities was to mastermind the 'official record' of the exploration. He was at the time also the editor of the *Geographical Journal,* which meant that portrayal of the progress of the early expeditions, and the debate that surrounded them, was very often heavily weighted with his personal views and prejudices on the matter. Farrar was joint editor of the *Alpine Journal* − obviously another source of professional rivalry between the two men − and saw to it that his own views were likewise published. Between them, these two journals offer the best sources for coverage of the early Everest story and an insight into differences of opinion over such controversial matters as the use of oxygen.

Hinks catalogued the photographs sent home from Tibet, supervised the lecture programmes and negotiated with publishers for the production of books on the successive expeditions. He answered queries from the general public, reluctantly supplying bulletins and information where necessary. He had a deep aversion to 'publicity' and would have preferred no contact at all with the gentlemen of the press, if it could have been arranged that way.

Of course it could not; expeditions to Everest were news, and newspapers had a right to report them. Expeditions needed, moreover, the financial support that selling their story to the national press would provide. Through the agencies of John Buchan, a contract with *The Times* and the *Philadelphia Ledger* was negotiated for expedition despatches and with the *Graphic* for photographs. All but these were supposed to wait 24 hours before they could publish any news. This arrangement gave Hinks a lot of trouble. Some newspapers were unhappy at being excluded from news. In a leader the *Daily Telegraph* staunchly maintained that 'an enterprise too closely affecting India should not be made the subject of an exclusive scoop'. There were leaks when other papers took matters into their own hands and through resourcefulness gained access to expedition information. Matters came to a head when the Government of India asked the Survey of India for reports for the Indian papers. Hinks wrote in an injured tone to Colonel Ryder, the Surveyor General of India, on 20 June 1921:

This is the result of agitation which has been got up, nominally by certain Indian papers, but really I suspect by the representatives in India of certain London papers protesting against the arrangement made by the Mount Everest Committee with *The Times* . . .

All these questions of dealing with the newspapers and photographers are personally very distasteful to me, and I regret that the Expedition Committee thought it necessary to enter into them to some extent in order to provide the funds for the following year's work. As however they have done so, it is necessary for me to use every endeavour to see that the people with whom the Committee have made contracts get their full value, and are not let down by unexpected leakage . . . The correspondent of the *Morning Post* in Calcutta is the man whom I particularly suspect of enterprise not perhaps very strictly honourable. He got hold of the news of Kellas's death somehow, telegraphed it at urgent rates and got it into the *Morning Post* several days before we heard of it otherwise. Presumably he bought it from some telegraph operator on the line. That is an example of the kind of thing we have to fear . . .[1]

Newspapermen were all 'sharks and pirates' to Hinks. He drew up a draft agreement, which all members of all the expeditions were to be required to sign, binding them, among other things, 'not to hold any communication with the press or with any press agency or publisher, or to deliver any public lecture, or to allow any information or photograph to be published either before, during or after the expedition without the sanction of the Mt Everest Committee.'[2]

This agreement was to prove a constant source of discord between Hinks and expedition members. Mallory was one of the first to give voice to his reluctance to sign such an undertaking. He wrote to Hinks on 11 March 1921:

I feel I don't quite know where I am expected to be, nor where I shall be if I do as I am expected. No doubt we ought to have a clear business understanding; but I don't think the agreement which I am asked to sign (and which I have not yet signed) is altogether satisfactory. I expressed myself willing to sign an agreement limiting my freedom for a specified time after publication of the official account; but I am not sure that I am prepared to accept that. Naturally I should not wish to publish anything which the committee disapproves, nor interfere by any . . . action with what is being done for publicity on behalf of the expedition as a whole. But to obtain 'the sanction' of the Committee — what does this involve? It might mean submitting the lengthy manuscript to each member of a committee which had ceased to function for other purposes — an inconveniently cumbrous proceeding. Practically speaking, the agreement as it stands would place me unreservedly in the hands of the committee and while I have no doubt they are excellent hands, I think before I commit myself in this way, I should be taken fully into the committee's confidence as to what they are intending.[3]

Hinks was unsympathetic and curtly told Mallory to sign, 'as others have', and 'to rely on being treated with consideration'.

The mistake Hinks made was his failure to put any time limit on the commitment. Though members, however grudgingly, might expect to be constrained for a limited period, they most certainly were not prepared to do so in perpetuity.

On receipt of Hinks's letter in March 1921, however, Mallory decided against further fight and duly signed. There were more pressing worries concerning the expedition itself.

Lieutenant-Colonel Howard-Bury, as expedition leader, was anxious that his team should not be too large. As he said, they knew nothing of local conditions, or how much transport or supplies might be available there. 'Besides the eight Europeans, we shall have Assistant Surveyors, possibly an Assistant Surgeon and the corps of coolies to provide for.'

Raeburn, who had been appointed mountaineering leader, had a long record of fine guideless ascents in the Alps, Norway, the Caucasus and his native Scotland. The previous year he had been to 21,000 feet on Kangchenjunga, and seemed therefore to his Alpine Club proposers the perfect man for the job. He worked hard organizing supplies and equipment before departure, even when suffering badly from influenza, and little notice was paid to his increasing irritability. But the sad fact was that for years Raeburn had pushed himself harder than he was physically capable of going, and was already displaying signs of an ageing beyond his 56 years. His subsequent disappointment at being unable through ill-health to take any significant part in the reconnaissance, led to a complete mental collapse as soon as he returned home. He never recovered, growing increasingly weaker for four years until he died.

Dr A.M. Kellas, who had made seven journeys to the Himalaya, was another of the Alpine Club's nominees. He was only three years younger than Raeburn, and Farrar, for one, was not happy about his inclusion in the party. Some years before, when Kellas was being

51

considered as a possible Everest leader, Farrar had written to a friend, 'Now Kellas, besides being fifty, so far has never climbed a mountain, but has only walked about on steep snow with a lot of coolies, and the only time they got on a very steep place they all tumbled down and ought to have been killed!!'[4] Even so, Kellas had unrivalled knowledge of Himalayan travel and was moreover a leading expert in the new science of mountain physiology.

Nobody yet knew how high it was possible to climb as the air became more rarefied. There had been cases of collapse and even fatalities among balloonists who went to great heights, but the exact altitudes at which these took place were hard to determine. Balloonists were able to take aloft bottled oxygen to inhale. Whether it was feasible similarly to supply mountain climbers with sufficient oxygen needed to be investigated. From his own observations, Kellas was prepared to believe that if the difficulties of transportation up mountains proved too great, there was no reason why 'a man of excellent physique and mental constitution, in first rate training' could not climb Everest without resort to what he called 'adventitious aids'. Even if Everest were to prove difficult from a mountaineering point of view, Kellas felt that it should be possible to design an oxygen-supplying apparatus that would enable it to be climbed.

With some justification, Mallory and Finch expressed their misgivings on the make-up of the climbing party and on the equipment that was being collected for it. Mallory had already confided to Geoffrey Young in February that he thought the party inadequate in numbers. 'There is no margin,' he said then. 'Raeburn says he doesn't expect to get higher than about 24,000 to 25,000; Dr Kellas presumably will get no further; so the final part is left to Finch and me, and the outside chance that Wheeler and Morshead [the two surveyors coming from the Survey of India] will take to climbing and make a success of it. Perhaps, after all, I shall be the weakest of the lot; but at present I feel more doubtful of Finch's health.'[5]

Finch was still being troubled by the cerebral malaria he had picked up in Egypt during the war and underwent a drastic cure for it. Moreover, he was just getting over the break-up of his first marriage.

Mallory wrote to Young again on 9 March: 'We're having much trouble about equipment. Raeburn unfortunately was put in charge of the mountaineering "section" and is quite incompetent. Finch and I have had to put on pressure through Farrar, and I hope it will all come right; but such a vital matter as tents has not been properly thought out and no proper provision for cold at great heights came within Raeburn's scheme of things.' We might today think Raeburn displayed a little more modernity when it came to headgear, though this, too, displeased Mallory: 'He even advised us not to take pith helmets, an ommission [sic] which is pronounced to be mere madness by such men as Meade and Longstaff. So you see the difficulties are beginning early.' Mallory admits to moments of utter pessimism about their chances of getting up — or of getting back with toes on their feet. 'The temperatures at nights are bound to be low, minus 50 degrees or worse . . . and all the scientific lore goes to show that a rarefied atmosphere makes it much more felt and much more difficult ever to get warm again once one is cold.'[6]

In more cheerful vein (in the same letter), Mallory describes a reception which took place two nights previously, when proposed team members were guests of the Royal Geographical Society and had the chance of looking each other over:

> I very much like the look of Wollaston and Howard-Bury seems a nice gay person though I don't accept him without reserves. Finch and I have been getting on well enough and I'm pleased by the feeling that he is competent; his scientific knowledge will be useful and has already borne fruit in discussing equipment. I'm very glad Morshead is coming; I know two of his brothers; they are a nice family and from what I have heard I feel sure he must be a good chap . . . But Younghusband amuses and delights me more than anything — grim old apostle of beauty and adventure! The Everest expedition has become a sort of religious pilgrimage in his eyes. I expect I shall end by sitting at his feet, hearing tales of Lhasa and Chitral.

Geoffrey Young had warned Mallory that the expedition would be seen as a kind of romantic pilgrimage by the general public, too, once the press campaign got under way, and Mallory has to admit he has already been surprised and amused by letters received from respectable friends who have been easily wrought upon by the journalists.

As it turned out, the getting-acquainted party was somewhat premature. The team had still to undergo medical examinations. Finch and Mallory had no qualms when it came to submitting themselves to the two Harley Street consultants appointed for the purpose. They obviously regarded medical clearance as a rubber

53

stamp formality since their passages were already booked and they had each been given £100 towards a 'personal outfit' (with the solemn injunction from Hinks that they should consult Meade, submit vouchers, and confine expenditure to only what was really necessary). On 23 March Mallory joked in a letter to Hinks, 'Haven't heard from Wollaston as to whether I have the required number of red corpuscles.' In fact this would have been the same day as Hinks actually received the reports (*via* Wollaston, the expedition doctor), after a delay due to the marriage of one of the consultants.

Mallory, as expected, had passed with flying colours. His reflexes were normal, he had no cardiac murmurs or irregularities, no hernias, no haemorrhoids, no organic or functional diseases and all his joints were full and free. 'Height 5 feet 11 inches, weight 11 stone 5 pounds. This man is in every respect fit,' his report stated. The opinion on Finch was far less conclusive: he, too, had no cardiac murmurs or varicose veins, or hernias or haemorrhoids, and enjoyed free movements in all joints; moreover he was, the doctors said, a determined type and his 'cerebration' was 'active', but his general appearance they described as tired and sallow, adding that he was (at one and the same time, curiously) both 'spare' and 'flabby'. He was slightly anaemic, had been losing weight and his urine reduced Fehling. As if to add insult to injury, they further declared that 'his mouth is very deficient in teeth'. Such dental deficiencies could be cured by a plate and, they thought, his overall condition would probably improve considerably 'with training'.

Wollaston was in a quandary; should he or should he not reject Finch on the strength of this report? As doctor on the expedition, he would be responsible if Finch were to break down on the mountain. To him that risk was unacceptable and he recommended to Hinks that a replacement be found.

There is no record that the committee raised any objection to such a critical reversal in their plans. With no obvious replacement in view, Finch was advised nevertheless that he would not be required to accompany the party. To be rejected less than a month before he was due to sail was a devastating blow and Finch made no attempt to disguise how bitterly he felt about it. He knew he was not universally popular and could not erase from his mind the suspicion that this was a deliberate move on the part of his enemies to be rid of him. To have Hinks niggling for the return of his equipment allowance was the ultimate insult to his injury.

Finch's incredulous supporters were no less suspicious, and went so far as to suggest that the medical must have been fixed. Wollaston, on learning this, insisted 'the two medical people knew nothing more of these two young men than their names at the time of their examination'. All the same, he was seen by many as the villain of the piece. He complained to Hinks: 'It has got about that I was at the bottom of Mr. Finch's rejection. I expected this, but all the same it makes me exceedingly sick.'

Mallory, though disconcerted at the news, could not 'for a moment think the medical examination was unfairly done'. He had taken quite a shine to Wollaston and wrote to Geoffrey Young, 'I can't imagine him a party to that sort of thing, however much the idea of an examination may have been the hope of the party opposed to Finch. Wollaston told me that there could be no question of taking Finch after the doctor's report.'

It is in the '*no question*' of taking Finch after the doctor's report that the doubt lies. Was it really as cut and dried? A physical examination of Finch by the Department of Pathology at Oxford, to determine his fitness and his ability to tolerate oxygen deprivation, found him to possess 'an unusually vital capacity', and to be 'particularly resistant to altitude effects'. This report was dated 28 March 1921, only ten days after Finch had presented himself to the Harley Street doctors. Even their report had been equivocal, offering the opinion that all Finch needed was to get fit. The month at sea to India could reasonably have been expected to provide an opportunity for that. Besides, there was no obvious understudy waiting in the wings. Indeed, it had been a tussle getting the original team together, and the names the selection committee were now having to consider were infinitely less suitable than Finch. So why was the medical report not overridden? Applicants on this and later expeditions were accepted with far shakier medical credentials. It is difficult to escape the conclusion that the very strong faction which wanted Finch out of the show clutched with delight at this opportunity to be rid of him, even though, at such a deplorably late hour, it placed the success of the whole expedition in jeopardy.

The first substitute to be suggested was a friend of Raeburn, William Ling, president of the Scottish Mountaineering Club. From the outset Raeburn had been anxious to have him in the team, but despite his experience, Ling was 48 years old, which would leave Mallory (at 35) the only 'young' climber on the expedition. Mallory considered his situation carefully. In his view — and that of Geoffrey Young — all responsibility for success now rested solely with him;

there was nobody else of similar physical capacity. Mallory told Hinks of his misgivings on 27 March:

Since receiving your letter telling me that Finch is not coming with the expedition to Mount Everest, I have been thinking very seriously of my own position. The substitution of Ling for Finch, though it may make little difference in the earlier stages of climbing, will in all probability very materially weaken the advance party. It seems to me that our best chance of success lies in finding easy conditions in the final stage, for which we have considerable grounds for hope as the photos all show comparatively easy angles on the north side. If this hope is realised the question will be one purely of endurance and not at all of mountaineering judgement as to snow conditions, etc., or of technical skill in dealing with snow and ice. All that is likely to come in lower down, but for the final push we want men who can last and we ought to give ourselves the best possible chance of being such a party when the critical time arrives. I don't doubt the value of either Ling or Morshead but from the point of view of this final effort they have too much against them — Ling his age (it seems to me age must make it more difficult for the body to adjust itself to the conditions) and Morshead the fact that he will be engaged on his surveying work and consequently will not be able to train systematically for this mountaineering effort: and in any case we know very little about him as a mountaineer.

Looking at the matter in this way I consider we ought to have another man who should be chosen not so much for his expert skill but simply for his powers of endurance. I have all along regarded the party as barely strong enough for a venture of this kind, with the enormous demand it is certain to make on both nerves and physique. I told Raeburn what I thought about that and said I wanted to have Finch because we shouldn't be strong enough without him.

You will understand that I must look after myself in this matter. I'm a married man and I can't go into it bald-headed.[7]

Mallory clearly wanted Finch reinstated. Hinks was less than pleased. The letter had come to him via Farrar, and he felt sure he could detect the hand of Farrar in its sentiments. He loosed off to Mallory a peremptory reply:

I don't think that you need feel any anxiety about your own position, because you will be under the orders of very experienced mountaineers who will take care not to call upon you for jobs that can't be done. The fact that you have been in close touch with Farrar all along has no doubt made you imbibe his view which is hardly that of anybody else, that the first object of the expedition is to get to the top of Mount Everest this year. Raeburn has been given full liberty to get as high as possible consistent with the complete reconnaissance of the mountain, and it is left at that. As for Morshead, after all he has been more than half as high again as you have ever been, and he did this at rather short notice. I suspect you will find him a hard man to keep up with when he has been in the field for several months on his survey work, which is I should imagine the best possible training . . .

And I don't think that Farrar is the only authority. We have seen enough of him at the Committee to learn that he frequently talks at random, and when he differs on almost every point from Collie and Meade, who have both much Himalayan experience, I do not myself feel that Farrar is the best judge.

Mallory was quite naturally incensed. His first reaction was to reply equally insultingly to Hinks. But he hesitated. He had just had a brainwave of his own for a replacement for Finch, someone he liked better than Finch and with whom he would enjoy going on an expedition. Mallory had mentioned Guy Bullock's name before to Farrar, but now he learned that his old school friend was home on extended leave. It seemed an ideal solution to the predicament. He quickly laid the proposal before the Committee, and wrote in glowing praise of Bullock to Sir Francis Younghusband on 31 March:

I knew him at Winchester where he was a scholar and a very good runner, the best long-distance runner that anyone remembered in my time, good at all games and stolid, a tough sort of fellow who never lost his head and would stand any amount of knocking about.

He was a year junior to me and first came out to the Alps in 1905, my second season, with R.L.G. Irving, a Winchester master. He seemed to me then to have extraordinary stamina and looking back I can think of no one else about whom I have felt in the same way that he would probably last longer than

57

myself. As to his mountaineering qualifications I have asked Irving, with whom he climbed six years, to write to Collie. Since 1913 he has wandered about the world in the consular service, to New Orleans, Loanda, Fernando Po, Marseilles, Lima. He has kept himself fit, playing soccer as recently as six months ago. He will almost certainly be available now. I feel that he would be a valuable man in the party, level-headed and competent all round — a man in whom one would feel confidence in an emergency as one of the least likely of men to crack.[8]

Hinks meanwhile, perhaps realising that he had gone too far in his letter to Mallory, enlisted the help of Wollaston to calm down the situation. Wollaston obligingly got hold of Mallory alone and reported back (30 March): 'He was evidently hurt in his pride by your letter — which was perhaps just as well — and said that he was going to write to you, but I persuaded him not to do so, at all events in the way that he intended, and I don't think you or we will have any trouble with him.'

Mallory, for his part, wrote disarmingly to Hinks: 'I thought we had made good that evening of festival. I do not recognise the individual to whom your letter was written. Have a word with Wollaston — he'll put it straight.' He was not prepared, however, to back down over the composition of the party.

I stick to my point that in my judgement the party is too weak for the job (assuming Ling accepts), whether the job be reconnaissance on a big scale or a push for the top. I know nothing but what everyone may know about conditions, and I may be the first to 'konk out', but as a mountaineer I have my before-starting judgement about the party; it may be a judgement worth very little but it is one of the precious stars I have to steer by. In mountaineering the ultimate safety lies in reserve strength; no amount of experience or judgement can create that. And I repeat it looks to me as if this party as it stands is deficient in that quality.

For this reason I have asked Sir Francis Younghusband to consider taking a young climber who was at school with me who has great staying power; and I'm writing further about him to both presidents.

He signs off cheekily: 'Enough words. Epistolary warfare — lord save us from that!' Within three days it was all settled, and Mallory reported developments to Geoffrey Young, any real sympathy for Finch suppressed without a qualm.

When the Committee met they had Ling's answer refusing and Finch's name was not brought up again. I have not seen Farrar and I don't know why he suggested Wakefield. Anyway, Bullock's being on the spot and presumably available must have settled the matter, as they no doubt felt something had to be . . .

Finch always seemed to me rather a gamble; he didn't look fit and I felt no confidence in his stamina – we're not going to have very good opportunities of getting fit . . .

I feel sorry for Finch; the medical examination ought to have been arranged at a much earlier stage. But he forfeits sympathy by his behaviour. We shall be weaker on ice and in general mountaineering resources without him, but we shall probably be stronger in pure physique, much stronger in morale.[9]

Farrar was not at all happy with the way events had panned out. He could not share Mallory's optimism that playing soccer 'as recently as six months ago' in any way compensated for a lack of mountaineering experience. Announcing Bullock's inclusion in the team in the *Alpine Journal*, he first distanced himself from the decision, then added by way of apology, 'It should be understood that . . . inquiries were made of several well-known mountaineers as to joining the expedition. It is, however, possible to few men, at short notice, to arrange to be absent from England for seven or eight months.'[10] In committee, Farrar was more outspoken, and insisted on having his opinion minuted: 'Owing to the unavailability of Mr. Ling to join the expedition the remaining climbers Mr. Mallory and Mr. Bullock, whose mountaineering experience is limited and not of recent date, do not form a party sufficiently qualified to continue with safety the reconnaissance beyond the point at which Mr. Raeburn finds himself unable to lead.'[11]

Within five days Mallory was aboard the SS *Sardinia* with much of the expedition's equipment, bound for Calcutta. He was the only member of the expedition on board, most of the others having gone by another ship from Marseilles. It was a long, lonely voyage and he found himself a retreat in the bows where (as in the trenches) he could withdraw into himself, reading, writing letters, starting a journal and trying to finish his 'Book of Geoffrey'.

Finch worked out his resentment in the Alps, where his several fine ascents included a difficult route on Mont Blanc (almost identical to the one he had been going to attempt with Mallory the year before if the weather had allowed). Farrar could not resist informing Hinks with malicious glee: 'Our invalid Finch took part in the biggest climb done in the Alps this season.' In November the two doctors examined Finch again; this time there could be no doubt. Dr Larkins: 'He is now absolutely fit and has lost his glucosmia. In my first report on him I stated that I thought all he wanted was to get into training.'

It meant Finch was fit for the 1922 'show', but nothing could erase the ill-feeling that surrounded his rejection from the first expedition. Hinks in particular, Finch would never forgive.

VI

The Opening Round

Mallory's first exposure to Himalayan climbing could scarcely have been a more propitious adventure, though the expedition itself started badly with several members falling sick soon after crossing into Tibet.

To approach Everest from the north required a month-long march from Darjeeling, first through the jungles of Sikkim, and then across the arid plains of Tibet. Once there, four months were spent investigating and mapping the whole Everest region, exploring unvisited valleys and crossing many high passes, searching out the best approaches to the mountain. Though they were unable to cross into Nepal, by traversing around first west, then east, members were able to view the mountain from almost every aspect. It was four months of almost continuous physical activity, most of which fell to Mallory and Bullock, but it offered opportunities for discovery and acclimatization rarely enjoyed by climbers.

They were a raggle-taggle crew. The climbers had been given a small grant towards their outfit, but by and large the choice was left to them. To keep out the cold and the constant wind of Tibet, they brought their old tweeds and greatcoats, their woolly scarves and cardigans. They brought stockings knitted by their wives and their Alpine climbing boots. Their leader, Colonel Howard-Bury, as befitted the well-to-do squire of a country estate at Mullingar in Ireland, had set off rather more snappily dressed in dog-tooth check and breeches of the best Donegal tweed, and with his Kashmir puttees neatly wound, but several weeks on the road soon saw him as rumpled as the rest. When George Bernard Shaw saw pictures of one of the early Everest parties, he was amazed: it looked, he said, like a picnic in Connemara surprised by a snowstorm.

The journey to India had been a lonely one for Mallory. He travelled alone and missed Ruth a good deal. He worked on a series of exercises designed to tone up his muscles and strengthen the trunk, and wrote a good deal. 'I amuse myself sometimes by making gloomy remarks about this doomed ship,' he wrote, 'but it has ceased to be a good subject of jest. These last two days have laid low most of us, both passengers and crew — the Captain himself included — with some internal trouble. Luckily it seems readily curable with castor oil.'

It seemed to Mallory, anxious for action, that shipboard life was strangely artificial, giving the appearance of being civilized, yet all the while surrounded by the dark, evil presence of the sea. He even found it hard to shake off this sense of foreboding once he met the others in Darjeeling, where they all stayed as guests of the Governor of Bengal in Government House. It was here, as he confided to Ruth, that the manners and attitudes of the expedition's leader first began to grate on his nerves, and he already detected signs of friction developing between Howard-Bury and Raeburn.

Howard-Bury seems to be quite good at the organisation: but I don't find myself greatly liking him. He is too much the landlord with not only tory prejudices, but a very highly developed sense of hate and contempt for other sorts of people than his own; he makes himself very pleasant to H[is] E[xcellency] — too pleasant I sometimes think.[1]

These first impressions did not alter during the coming weeks. They marched as two parties, Mallory with Howard-Bury, Wollaston and Wheeler in the first group, Raeburn following on a day behind with Kellas, Bullock and Heron. There was nothing for it but to make the best of it, as he told Ruth on 24 May.

I felt I should never be at ease with him [Howard-Bury] — and in a sense I never shall be. He is not a tolerant person. He is well informed and opinionated and doesn't at all like anyone else to know things he doesn't know. For the sake of peace I am being very careful not to broach certain subjects of conversation; these are realms which are barred to our entrance together. However we are rubbing along quite well now. He knows a great deal about flowers and is very keen about them and is often pleasant and sometimes amusing at meals.

I saw, and still see, Raeburn as a great difficulty. He has some very tiresome qualities. He is very critical and unappreciative of other people in some ways — for instance about all our kit. Wheeler and Bullock have both commented on that. He is evidently touchy about his position as leader of the alpine party and wants to be treated with proper respect and he is dreadfully dictatorial about matters of fact and often wrong.

It was very evident in Darjeeling that he would not get on with Howard–Bury, to say nothing of the rest of us, and in these circumstances I rather view myself as a soothing syrup. Luckily I had a friendly little walk with Raeburn before we left Darjeeling and rather played up to his desire to give advice, so we got on very nicely. He has some very nice qualities and he has a good deal of fatherliness and kindliness; but his total lack of *calm* and of sense of humour at the same time is most unfortunate. I am rather sorry in a way that I am not with him now. I feel he is a weak man whom it might be my good fortune to help.

Dr Kellas had spent the month before the expedition exploring the mountains around Kangchenjunga and was far from fit when he joined the party in Darjeeling. He arrived dusty and dishevelled in the middle of a banquet given by the Governor of Bengal, having hiked several miles from a neighbouring village. Such obvious eccentricity delighted Mallory. 'Kellas I love already,' he told Ruth. 'He is beyond description Scotch and uncouth in his speech – altogether uncouth. His appearance would form an admirable model to the stage for a farcical representation of an alchemist. He is very slight in build, short, thin, stooping, and narrow-chested; his head . . . made grotesque by veritable gig-lamps of spectacles and a long pointed moustache. He is an absolutely devoted and disinterested person.'[2]

By profession, Kellas was a teacher of chemistry at the Middlesex Hospital Medical School in London, but his special interest lay in altitude physiology. He would spend many months of every year roaming the remoter valleys and passes of the Himalaya with a small band of trusted porters. The same men would go with him year after year, such was the loyalty he inspired, and it is Kellas who is credited with having discovered the supremacy of Bhotias and Sherpas for expedition work. He pushed himself hard on these trips, but just how hard no one really knew, for he rarely published more than the scantiest details of his journeys. Certainly, when he met up with the other members of the Everest party, no one had the slightest idea that he had so overtaxed himself in the few short weeks before that he had lost a stone in weight and was in a seriously exhausted and undernourished condition. When he contracted dysentery on the march-in, he simply had not strength enough to fight it.

Too feeble to walk beyond Phari, Kellas was carried on a makeshift litter by his own bearer and several Tibetans hired for the purpose. He travelled behind the main party and usually arrived in camp two hours or more after everyone else. He remained fairly bright, however, giving the impression he was on the mend, so that even Sandy Wollaston, the expedition doctor, did not fully appreciate the seriousness of his condition. When a porter came running into the camp at Kampa Dzong on 5 June with the news that Dr Kellas had died coming over the last pass (17,000 feet), the shock took everyone by surprise. Wollaston immediately hastened back to ascertain whether or not it was true.

'Can you imagine anything less like a mountaineering party?' wrote Mallory to David Pye, from Tinki Dzong, 30 miles farther along the road. 'It was an arrangement which made me very unhappy and which appals me now in the light of what has happened. He died without one of us anywhere near him.' And yet, as Mallory pointed out, it was hard to know what else they could have done. 'The old gentleman (such he seemed) was obliged to retire a number of times en route and could not bear to be seen in this distress, and so insisted that everyone should be in front of him.'[3]

On the first long stage from Phari, Mallory told Ruth, Bullock and he went out and met Kellas in the evening and walked in the last mile or more with him in the dark.

. . . generally speaking, one or other of us saw him on the way. Yesterday he was in a state of collapse on route and Heron and I got him down to a shelter while Bullock went off and got Wollaston who administered Bovril and brandy, but except for such incidents one scarcely saw him and he went to bed the moment he came in and never had a meal with us . . . His body is lying in a tent now and we shall bury him tomorrow or the next day . . .

My sadness at this event makes my thoughts fly to you . . . I know it is no use saying 'Don't be anxious', because anxiety is unreasoning and comes upon us unbidden, but it can be dispelled by reason. You mustn't let this event increase your anxiety in general . . . You must consider [Kellas's] case altogether exceptional — other people have suffered from diarrhoea and got over it perfectly well — everyone in fact has had it, but myself . . . It has been a distressing business.[4]

It was apparent to Mallory that people back home were very likely to criticize Wollaston for not having done more to save Kellas, and he enlisted Geoffrey Young's help to allay any such gossip. 'Wollaston is more my friend than anyone in the party', he explained, 'and has been greatly distressed.' He went on to describe Kellas's funeral:

It was an extraordinarily affecting little ceremony burying Kellas on a stony hillside — a place on the edge of a great plain and looking across it to the three great snow peaks of his conquest. I shan't easily forget the four boys, his own trained mountain men, children of nature, seated in wonder on a great stone near the grave while Bury read out the passage from the Corinthians.[5]

Kellas was not the only casualty in the party. Raeburn, having fallen twice from his horse, been kicked in the head and rolled upon, was now displaying symptoms alarmingly similar to those of Kellas; in particular he was suffering badly from diarrhoea. This time Wollaston was taking no chances. He accompanied him back down to Lachen in Sikkim where he could be placed in the care of some Swedish lady missionaries until sufficiently recovered to rejoin the expedition.

At a stroke and long before Everest had been reached, the expedition had lost its two 'senior' mountaineers and all its Himalayan experience (apart from that of the Survey of India men). Mallory realized that any mountaineering contemplated now would be up to him and he would have a fairly free hand in deciding what was done — certainly until Raeburn rejoined them, if indeed he ever did. By that time Mallory hoped he would have done enough useful reconnoitring work to be able to count on Howard-Bury to champion him should Raeburn prove tiresome. 'And Raeburn's capacity for being tiresome,' he confided in a letter to Geoffrey Young, 'it must be said, though I get on with him quite well, is unlimited.'

Mallory had high hopes of Bullock, 'my stable-companion, a very placid one, reserving energy and delighting a good deal in natural objects in his quiet way; I think he's going to turn out very useful, and before long, in a fortnight or so, he and I will be busy training coolies on easy expeditions useful for reconnoitring.' He had taken a shine to Morshead, too, one of the surveyors, 'who has been walking everywhere on the hills up to 18,000 all the way from Darjeeling and looks as fit and strong as possible — a very nice keen man.'

He was more guarded about the potential of Wheeler, the other surveyor, who had climbed a good deal in his native Canada, but was proving a 'lame duck' on this trip, being another smitten with a stomach disorder. He was not a man whom Mallory could instinctively like, as he confided to Ruth: 'You know my complex about Canadians; I shall have to swallow before I like him, I expect. God give me the saliva.'[6]

Heron, who had been seconded to the expedition by the Geological Survey of India, gave an initial impression of dullness, but on better acquaintance was proving cheerful and jolly. 'Solid treasure, and helps to keep an easy atmosphere,' Mallory wrote, 'but he won't be a mountaineer.' At the same time, he was not liking Howard-Bury any better. 'He is not a kind man,' Mallory wrote. 'His ultimate belief is in "strafing" inferiors. God help him,' but, Mallory rationalized, 'he's a keen mountaineer and a lover of flowers, so there must be some good in him,' adding, 'and he can't turn Everest into his connoisseur's possession.'[7] Whatever his faults, it was already clear that Howard-Bury was a strong walker and Mallory conceded he might make up the fourth in the climbing party, so all was not lost!

We're just about to walk off the map — the survey made for the Lhasa expedition. We've had one good distant view of Everest from above Kampa Dzong and I'm no believer in the easy North face. I hope we shall see him from 30–40 miles off from some slopes this (E) side of the Arun Valley in the next week or so. Geoffrey, it's beginning to be exciting.[8]

When they reached the Arun Valley the longed-for view of their objective was obscured by mist. In the hope that conditions might change, Mallory and Bullock left their ponies grazing on a patch of grass and scaled a small nearby hill. Their optimism was rewarded.

Suddenly our eyes caught a glint of snow through the clouds; and gradually, very gradually, in the course of two hours or so, visions of great mountainsides and glaciers and ridges, now here, now there, forms invisible for the most part to the naked eye or indistinguishable from the clouds themselves, appeared through the floating rifts and had meaning for us — one whole clear meaning pieced from these fragments, for we had seen a whole mountain range, little by little, the lesser to the greater until, incredibly higher in the sky than imagination had ventured to dream, the top of Everest itself appeared.[9]

As they arrived back in camp towards sunset that same night, the wind dropped and they were once more rewarded with a vision of Everest 'absolutely clear and glorious . . . The problem of its great ridges and glaciers began to take shape and to haunt the mind, presenting itself at odd moments and leading to definite plans. Where can one go for another view, to unveil a little more of the great mystery?'[10]

From then on the abiding presence of the mountain was to dominate their lives. They continued through Shekar Dzong, the White Glass Fort, where a cluster of gleaming monastic buildings clung like swallows' nests to the side of an abrupt hillside, that was crowned by a medieval fortress. Here they spent two nights camped on the valley floor in a little enclosure fringed with willows. Around midnight on the first night they were woken by yells and hammering as an intruder attacked their foodboxes. Bullock gave chase in the moonlight, brandishing his ice axe, 'and captured his gun rest'. The man was found to be a local lunatic and was returned safely to his parents the following morning.

Mallory and Bullock set off from Shekar ahead of the main party with a small group of porters, hoping to make a diversion that would afford them better views of Everest. They missed the bridge over the Bhong-chu and went several miles out of their way up a side stream before being forced to ford the river, getting thoroughly soaked in the process. 'Map is incorrect here,' Bullock remarked in his diary, and took delight in recording that Mallory had got wetter in the incident than he had. The next day they climbed their pass, both feeling very fit, and for a quarter of an hour before clouds rolled in, were granted a splendid view of Makalu (27,825 feet) and the whole Everest system.

The main caravan meanwhile established a first base on 19 June at Tingri, a small town of about 300 houses, on the side of a hill in the middle of a wide salt plain. It was a place of some strategic importance, lying on the ancient trade route into the Sola Khumbu valley of Nepal via the Nangpa La, a high ice-covered pass. Everest was still some 40 miles away to the south and clearly visible from the town. Here they were able to rent an old Chinese rest-house, which they noticed the Tibetans kept well clear of, believing it to be haunted. It boasted three courtyards: the outer one they gave over to the porters, the middle to the surveyors, retaining the inner one for the team members. A room was soon cleaned out for use as a dark-room.

It had taken a month of travelling from Darjeeling to reach Tingri, and they were the first Europeans to penetrate into this part of Tibet. The time had come to get down to the serious business of reconnaissance. Wheeler and Heron set off towards Kyetrak to begin their surveys, but Howard-Bury, who had hoped to join them the following day, was obliged to delay his departure while he recovered from the effects of inhaling toxic fumes in the dark-room. Wollaston arrived back after escorting Raeburn to the Lachen Mission only to find two of the porters dangerously sick with enteric fever. He was not at all impressed with the standard of hygiene in the Chinese rest-house, believing it 'the most filthy place for a camp imaginable, filled with dust of ages and the dirt of every day; the coolies are vile in their habits, and if it were not that many are going away I should insist on getting the whole lot under canvas.' It was obvious he must stay put to tend his charges,[11] but he despatched all available porters into the countryside around in search of natural history specimens. They would return each night with a selection of rats, birds, lizards, fish, beetles and other trophies for his collection.

Meanwhile, Mallory and Bullock, with sixteen porters, a sirdar and a cook, had headed straight for Everest. They planned a fortnight's exploration of the north and northwest side of the mountain. Two days later they pitched their first camp in the Rongbuk Valley under Everest and Mallory wrote to Ruth:

Shortly before we reached this spot we saw the great mountain standing up from its base at the end of [our valley], a more glorious sight than I can attempt to describe. Suffice it to say that it has the most steep ridges and appalling precipices that I have ever seen, and that all the talk of an easy snow slope is a myth . . .

My darling, this is a thrilling business altogether, I can't tell you how it possesses me, and what a prospect it is. And the beauty of it all![12]

The base of the North Face of Everest was found to be exceedingly steep. The mountaineering technique of the day was to avoid face climbs wherever possible in favour of obvious ridge lines, but at first sight none of these looked at all promising either. It became clear that the most likely course of attack would be to surmount a saddled ridge which they called the North Col, and which appeared to give the easiest access to the summit via the upper North-east Ridge. The problem was, how to gain this North Col.

Mallory and Bullock explored the Main Rongbuk Glacier and were rewarded with a fine view of the West Ridge and the North Col, but saw no easy way up to the latter. From this western side the slopes to the col are long, steep and windswept, shielded from the sun and prone to continual rock and snow slides. While not totally impossible, the climb presented such a dangerous proposition that they were quickly dismissed. There was no way they could ever encourage laden porters up such a place. Perhaps they could approach the col from its other side, if that were possible, in the hope of an easier climb.

First, though, they climbed a lesser peak, Ri-Ring, to get a better view of the country this side. From this vantage point they discovered the existence of the Western Cwm, hidden behind the bulk of the West Ridge. Some days later, from the top of the col separating the peaks Lingtren and Pumori, they saw into the hollow of this cwm — the Valley of Silence, as Swiss mountaineers later called it. They were looking right up the treacherous Khumbu Icefall towards the near-vertical ramparts of the Lhotsè Face, leading up to the South Col of Mount Everest. 'Another disappointment,' Mallory wrote, 'it is a big drop, about 1,500 feet down to the glacier, and a hopeless precipice. I was hoping to get away to the left and traverse into the cwm — that too, quite hopeless. However, we have seen this western glacier and are not sorry we have not to go up it. It is terribly steep and broken. In any case, work on this side could only be carried out from a base in Nepal, so we have done with the western side.'[13]

They then circled back around the mountain to view the great East (Kangshung) Face and, climbing the Kangshung Glacier were rewarded with a magnificent panorama of that triumvirate of mountain peaks — Everest, Lhotse and Makalu. 'I'm altogether beaten for words,' Mallory told Ruth on 9 August. 'The whole range of peaks from Makalu to Everest far exceeds any mountain scenery that ever I saw before.'[14] But it still did not yield, as they hoped, a suitable approach to the North Col, or any other feasible route up the mountain. It remained only to try the Kharta Valley approach.

During the expedition, members had been slowly compiling a map. It seemed obvious that a glacier must flow east from the North Col, and it had surprised Mallory and Bullock that neither the Kangshung nor Kharta had proved to be this glacier. What they had failed to appreciate in the early part of the reconnaissance was that a narrow stream entering the main Rongbuk Glacier from the east was in fact the outflow from the glacier they sought. They thereby managed to miss completely the presence of the East Rongbuk Glacier, which though it flowed east from the North Col, curved almost immediately northwards to run parallel to the main Rongbuk Glacier. Bullock began to get a suspicion of this when exploring the southern branch of the Kharta glacier some days earlier. Failing to find any way through to the North Col from the head of this valley, he had a hunch that the explanation for the elusive glacier had to be that it changed course somewhere along its length. At much the same time, Wheeler, painstakingly carrying out his photographic survey in the Rongbuk Valley, confirmed its existence and plotted the course of what then became known as the East Rongbuk Glacier.

The glacier in the Kharta Valley has two arms, a northern and southern branch. At the head of the southern branch is a relatively easy-angled snow col, the Lhakpa La (22,500 ft) which they hoped would finally lead them to the elusive North Col. Joined by Morshead, they set off at 3 a.m. on 18 August, planning to breast the Lhakpa La before the sun softened the snow. Appearances were deceptive. The long trudge up through soft new snow took them until 12.30 p.m. Mallory to Ruth:

> We were enveloped for the most part in thin mist which obscured the view and made one world of snow and sky — a scorching mist, if you can imagine such a thing, more burning than bright sunshine and indescribably breathless. One seemed literally at times to be walking in a white furnace. Morshead, who knows the hottest heat of the plains of India, said that he had never felt any heat so intolerable as this.[15]

When Mallory, Bullock and Morshead, with their porter Nyima, stood at last on top of the Lhakpa La, they saw through the clouds, across the basin in front of them, what they had for so long been seeking – the other side of the North Col.

Mallory saw immediately that, as a route, the North Col should 'go'. As they slowly retraced their steps back to camp, his mind was abuzz, formulating plans for one serious attempt to climb the mountain before they left for home. It was 2 a.m. when the weary group stumbled into their tents, Morshead almost totally played out, but Mallory borne along by his high spirits. He felt 'as fit and strong' as ever after a long day in the hills and ate a hearty meal in his dry, warm sleeping-sack, before settling down for an untroubled sleep. He could hardly wait to let Ruth know the good news:

> As we came down the long weary way, my thoughts were full of this prospect and this success [of having found a way to the North Col]. I don't know when I have allowed myself so much enjoyment from a personal achievement. I fairly puffed out my chest with pride and the consciousness of something well done; of a supreme effort made and happily rewarded . . . For this success brings our reconnaissance to an end, we have found out the way and we're now planning the attack.[16]

This was to be the last voice raised in pleasure. While Mallory would continue to improve his acclimatization, it would be at the expense of waning physical strength, which was slowly deteriorating due to his extended period at high altitude. He would continue to feel fit at these heights, but would have even greater difficulty in climbing up to them. This is the true state of human acclimatization. A few can acclimatize permanently to 17,000 feet – that is, they can live healthy lives at that height. There are no permanently inhabited villages higher, and no-one can live higher indefinitely. Many people can reach greater heights on a short-term basis. But that temporary extension is purchased at the cost of rapid muscle deterioration.

Upon rejoining the main party in the Shangri-La of the Kharta Valley, where the expedition had set up a new Base Camp, Mallory received the surprising news of Wheeler's discovery of the entrance to the East Rongbuk Glacier that would lead directly to the north-eastern side of the North Col. It was obviously the key for which they had so long been seeking. Here was a direct route, relatively sheltered, which ascended gradually right to the foot of the col. However the discovery came too late to be tried out in 1921. The main party, which by this time had very little left in the way of reserve strength, could not again make the long 3-day haul round to Rongbuk. Would it not be quicker to reclimb the Lhakpa La and gain the North Col by that arduous but proven route, as Mallory had already planned? They agreed to give it a try.

Almost immediately, two weeks of bad weather set in, preventing the attempt. Though annoying, it offered a much-needed break in which to recuperate from the strenuous climbs of past weeks, and it also gave Mallory and Bullock (who had been exploring together for two months) time to iron out their mounting antagonisms. 'I have established somehow, I hope, a fresh relation with Bullock,' wrote Mallory to Ruth:

> We weren't getting on quite happily. We had rather drifted into that common superficial attitude between two people who live alone together — competitive and slightly quarrelsome, each looking out to see that he doesn't get done down in some small way by the other. I have been thinking B[ullock] too lazy about many small things that have to be done (indeed he certainly was, at one time), as a result of which I have sometimes tried to arrange that he shall be left to do them; and he has developed the idea that I habitually try and shift the dirty work onto him; and so we have both been forgetting Christian decency and even eyeing the food to see that the other doesn't take too much — horrible confession! But a passage has happened between us to put it all right, or so I hope; and we've been talking together today, much more friendly and cheerful than usual.[17]

There are two lessons buried in this letter. The first is that living in close proximity for long spells inevitably produces friction — the more so, the fewer of you there are — and such friction is exacerbated by high altitude; no matter how well acclimatized, tempers will flare between otherwise equable friends. This was generally known among mountaineers, but perhaps not anticipated by Mallory and Bullock. The second lesson — a more subtle one — is that this irritation can paradoxically be further exacerbated by a democratic relationship, where each partner is expected to do an equal share and have an equal say. So much time and energy is expended in sifting and weighing to make sure one is not getting gypped.

Mallory's spirits, always mercurial, were subject to the same wild exaltations and deep troughs on Everest as elsewhere. One day he could write with enormous gusto about the thrill of walking off the map, and the next be gloomily sceptical about the whole enterprise, as when he confided to a friend on 12 July:

I sometimes think of this expedition as a fraud from beginning to end, invented by the wild enthusiasm of one man, Younghusband; puffed up by the would-be wisdom of certain pundits in the A.C.; and imposed upon the youthful ardour of your humble servant. Certainly the reality must be strangely different from their dream. The long imagined snow slopes of this Northern face of Everest with their gentle and inviting angle turn out to be the most appalling precipice, nearly 10,000 feet high . . . The prospect of ascent in any direction is about nil and our present job is to rub our noses against the impossible in such a way as to persuade mankind that some noble heroism has failed once again.[18]

Had Bullock been subject to similar changes of mood, the two could have expected to spend far more time bickering than they actually did. Bullock managed to maintain a remarkable cheerfulness throughout; he was steady, stoical, loyal, and apparently blessed with the gift of being able to sleep anywhere — a most useful attribute in the field. In other words he was probably the perfect companion for Mallory on a venture such as this.

After the first month of exploration Mallory made the bitter discovery that practically all the photographs he had taken were useless, because he had put the plates into the camera the wrong way round. 'I know nothing about plates and followed instructions given me by Heron,' he complained to Ruth. 'I have taken enormous trouble over these photos: many of them were taken at sunrise from places where neither I nor anyone else may go again — for instance, those on our ascent of Mount Kellas. However, I'm determined to replace them as far as possible . . . It will mean two days spent in the most tiresome fashion, when I thought all our work in those parts was done.'

This confusion of simple tasks is another effect of high altitude — an unnoticed diminution of intellectual ability. Bullock also ruined a day's photographs by incorrectly installing the plates in one instance, and by tearing the film in another.

While Mallory went to Lingtrennup to photograph the west side of Everest, Bullock toiled up the Lho La and secured pictures of the Khumbu Icefall and the North Col. Their leader, however, showed scant appreciation of their efforts and the incident only served to confirm their uselessness in his eyes. He complained to Hinks that neither of them had ever shown the slightest willingness to help, to which — in a later batch of mail from home — he received a sympathetic acknowledgment. 'The failure of Bullock and Mallory to photograph anything is deplorable — they must be singularly unintelligent people not to be able to learn the elements of the thing in a day or two,' Hinks commiserated on 6 September.[19]

The sad fact was that Howard-Bury and Mallory did not understand one another. Mallory hinted at the awkwardness to Geoffrey Young. '[Bury] is a queer customer as I'll tell you one day.' Perhaps it was just as well they did not have a lot to do with each other. Of necessity, Mallory and Bullock operated very much as a self-contained unit with little recourse to the main group. But when persistently too few supplies arrived for his party, Mallory's sense of grievance mounted and was only compounded by a difficulty in passing intelligible messages back to the others because of the distances involved and language problems with the porters.

Mallory had expected interpretation to be laid on as part of the organization — and indeed had Kellas survived to travel with the exploring party, there would have been no problem, since he spoke several native dialects. As it was, Mallory was endeavouring to communicate with his sirdar by means of 150 words of basic Tibetan scribbled in his notebook. And the sirdar left much to be desired, being 'a whey-faced treacherous knave, whose sly and calculated villainy too often, before it was discovered, deprived our coolies of their food.' It turned out that the man, Gyalzen, was selling porter rations for huge profits on the side, and the men were too frightened to say anything about it. Mallory and Bullock had been puzzled that the porters were always so hungry, and shared with them the chocolate and nuts they received in food parcels from home. Even after the matter had come to light, the question of stores for Mallory's party remained a source of friction between him and Howard-Bury. On 1 September Mallory wrote to Ruth:

Frankly, I was quite glad Bury was away. I can't get over my dislike of him and have a sense of gêne when he is present, which he too feels, even though we talk quite cheerfully. And now I've had trouble with him about stores — a most miserable petty business, so miserable I really can't bring myself to explain it. But his attitude amounted to an accusation of greed on my part in taking more than I ought up here for the use of the higher camps; and meanwhile B[ullock] and I are providing meat and tea for the coolies out of our own money, because we know they must be fed and encouraged in this way if we are to get them up the mountain; and Bury will allow nothing outside their base rations. He has economy on the brain and I can't bear his meanness.[20]

On 1 September, to everyone's amazement, Raeburn suddenly reappeared in Base Camp. He had experienced considerable difficulty crossing Tibet on his own, and serious flooding in many parts of the country had not helped matters. Rivers were unfordable and bridges had been washed away, frequently causing him to detour miles out of his way. His appearance was quite shocking; he seemed to have aged enormously since his illness. The other members greeted him warmly enough, though their greetings concealed mixed feelings. Howard-Bury reported to Hinks, 'Raeburn turned up yesterday after a three month absence. He passed five bags of our mails at Chushar near Tinki and he made no attempt to bring them on! Can you imagine anyone being such a fool.'[21] Mallory wrote to Geoffrey Young to say how extraordinarily old and grizzled Raeburn had become. Not just in his looks, but behaviour too. 'When he is not being a bore I feel moved to pity, but that is not often,' Mallory admitted. To Ruth he was even more frank. Raeburn was, he told her, a broken figure. At least he was unlikely now to reassume the climbing leadership. That was some consolation to Mallory, though Howard-Bury felt they were entitled to an explanation from Raeburn of his 'curious want of cooperation'.

Letters to family and friends at home were collected and sent out to Phari for despatch with a couple of mail-runners once a fortnight, but receiving mail from England was a far more erratic affair. They were so much on the move, it took a long time to catch up with them. The privations of nomadic life left everyone desperate for news of the world outside Tibet, which was why Raeburn's inexplicable failure to bring on the sacks he had seen in Chushar so angered Howard-Bury and the others. When the missing post finally found its way to Kharta not long afterwards, having been held up by the floods, it proved a mixed blessing for it brought waves of homesickness along with its gossip and good wishes. To H. V. Reade, Mallory wrote:

. . . not only seven weeks' letters from home but seven weeks' news of the civilised world as selected by the *Statesman and Friend of India* and we have wet days to read it all. And in the *Statesman* one may read of strange things at home — how the drought came to an end at last and holiday-makers had wet seats in charabancs, how Lloyd George with the King for his second blacked Lord Northcliffe's eye — and finally what de Valera has said; that's the last despairing news, that Daíl Eirean has rejected the P.M.'s offer. What does it mean and what is one to think?[22]

and, more intimately, to Ruth,

My dearest . . . It's always a wonderful moment when the mail comes and love flies in among us and nestles in every tent; but when we have waited for six weeks and more and suddenly there in our hands is six weeks' love in envelopes, which we bear away for long silent reading to our tents, it's as though some great floodgates have been opened and the quiet waters were bearing us gently away on their smooth delightful bosom.[23]

A letter from Geoffrey Young, recognizing the extent to which the adventure was taking Mallory over, brought a plea for caution: 'don't lose sight of the "rightness of the attempt",' he urged Mallory, 'and let no desire for result spoil the effort by overstretching the safe limits within which it must move.'[24] It might not be possible for the summit to be reached this time, he said, but the important thing was to maintain 'the resolution to return, even against ambition!' How Mallory wished he had Geoffrey Young with him now, with whom to talk things over — any of the climbing friends he felt comfortable with would do at a pinch, but Geoffrey, especially. He could do with some of his sound philosopher's wisdom. It had been exciting, and that last push up the Lhakpa La was the biggest effort he had ever been called upon to make on a mountain, but, he complained,

The whole thing is on my shoulders — I can say this to you. Bullock follows well and is safe; but you know what it means on a long, exhausting effort to lead all the time . . . Geoffrey, at what point am I going to stop? It's going to be a fearfully difficult decision; there's an incalculable element about other men's physical condition, and all the more so under these strange conditions. I almost hope I shall be the first to give out![25]

The thrill of exploring new terrain never quite returned to Mallory after his discovery that an approach to the North Col did exist from the Lhakpa La. It is almost unavoidable after moments of high elation for a reactionary sense of flatness to set in, particularly when these moments occur as the culmination of intense mental and physical effort. Inactivity and general weariness can only compound the condition. As September progressed with little improvement in snow conditions, Mallory found it very hard to wait idly for the weather to improve, and to shake off his feeling of depression. Already it was almost too late for a successful outcome to any attempt. He wrote to a friend, 'the later the season the colder will be the nights, the more uncomfortable the coolies and the less likely to carry on our burdens to the highest camps'. To Ruth he conceded that his 'chance of a lifetime' would have so sadly dwindled by the time the weather did decide to improve, that he no longer rated the odds on success higher than one in a thousand.[26]

Then on the morning of 16 September, 'Wonder of wonders! . . . We just woke and found it different.' Mallory's optimism had returned! He and Bullock began at once to organize their expedition back across the Lhakpa La, or Windy Gap as they called it, in order to reach the North Col. On 20 September the full climbing complement – Howard-Bury, Raeburn, Wollaston, Mallory, Morshead, Bullock and Wheeler – was gathered with the porters in an upper camp, from which Mallory and Morshead led fourteen laden porters and two without loads off towards Windy Gap. They succeeded in getting eleven loads on to the col, and two days later tents were pitched and occupied in a hollow at the top. On their way up, they saw for the first time tracks in the snow, which the sherpas claimed were those of the Yeti, or abominable snowman. These human-sized footprints were probably animal tracks grossly enlarged by the action of the sun on high altitude snow.

After a cold night, Wollaston, Howard-Bury and Morshead went back down to join Raeburn in the lower camp, leaving Mallory, Bullock, Wheeler and ten of the porters to cross over the pass and descend into the basin of the East Rongbuk Glacier. At last, after four months of circling it, they were within striking distance of setting foot on the mountain itself.

A further camp was made on the glacier at around 22,000 feet and from there, after a miserably cold night, a reduced party set off to climb up the icy cliffs of the North Col. Even Mallory had now to admit that the party was entirely without hope of climbing Everest, but that the reconnaissance must be pressed as high as possible.

> It was evident by this time that on north slopes at all events we should find no good snow this year . . . Moreover the North Col was itself a more formidable obstacle than we . . . had expected. We were not unprepared for a steep snow wall, but the height of the wall we saw above the glacier surprised us; we estimated it at 1000 feet. It was doubtful whether we should be able to get up . . .
>
> I had the good fortune on these last two days to feel effects of elevation less than the others and it seemed to me about the rest of the party that they hadn't a kick left of any real strength. However, three volunteers were forthcoming . . . when we asked for some coolies to come on with us to the North Col; and they proved stout-hearted enough. Two of them between them did most of the plugging in deep soft snow, and very exhausting work it was. We had no serious difficulties.[27]

The ridge itself was stepped, forming a kind of double shelf. The lower shelf was relatively sheltered and would become the camp-site of later years. It was only when they breasted the crest of the col proper that they caught the full force of the wind. Mallory had eyes for one thing only — the route to the summit. He looked up at the blunt north ridge rising at a not very steep angle to join the north-east ridge, and was encouraged. 'No obstacle appeared, or none so formidable that a competent party would not easily surmount it or go around it. If one harboured a doubt about this way before, it was impossible to keep it any longer.'[28]

The technical difficulties then were not great, and yet it was impossible, as Mallory said, to look at the route ahead without a shudder, for from top to bottom the ridge was exposed to the full fury of a gale from the north-west. It was as much as they could do to stand their ground without being plucked from their feet:

> And higher was a more fearful sight. The powdery fresh snow on the great face of Everest was being swept along in unbroken spindrift and the very ridge where our route lay was marked out to receive its unmitigated fury. We could see the blown snow

deflected upwards for a moment where the wind met the ridge, only to rush violently down in a frightful blizzard on the leeward side.[29]

For a few moments they hesitated, leaning into the wind. They took a few desultory steps forward into the teeth of the gale, then hesitated again. Wheeler had been against the attempt from the beginning; he was not prepared to go any further and turned his black-bearded face around to face the way they had come. But Bullock knew how much this attempt meant to Mallory:

I was prepared to follow M[allory] if he wished to try and make some height, but was glad when he decided not to. It was lucky he didn't as my strength proved to be nearly at an end.[30]

Nothing more was said. It would have been folly to press the assault further. They retreated out of the biting wind and started back down the snow slope once more.

During the descent from the North Col two noteworthy incidents occurred. Mallory and Bullock both noticed that their ascending track had cut loose a small avalanche, which Mallory described later in the expedition book:

[An] occasion when we had to face and determine the possibility of an avalanche was in traversing the slopes of the North Col. Here our feet undoubtedly found a solid bed to tread upon, the substance above it was dubiously loose. It was my conviction at the time that with axes well driven in above we were perfectly safe here. But on the way down we observed a space of 5 yards or so where the surface snow had slid away below our tracks. The disquieting thoughts that necessarily followed this discovery left and still leave me in some doubt as to how great a risk, if any, we were taking. But it is natural to suppose that at a higher elevation or in a cooler season, because the snow adheres less rapidly to the slopes on which it lies, an avalanche of new snow is more likely to occur.[31]

It is a sadly prophetic observation and shows that Mallory was not unaware of potential avalanche danger on the slopes of the North Col. Yet, within nine months, when he was back, attempting these same slopes under a covering of fresh monsoon snow, he failed utterly to recall how dangerous they had become.

The other disquieting incident occurred at the bottom of the North Col slopes, when Bullock was left behind 'at his own request' to rest, intending to follow twenty minutes or so behind Mallory, Wheeler and the porters. Mallory later reported to Younghusband that 'it was nearly two hours after we came in when Bullock appeared saying that he felt very weak and had had difficulty in reaching the camp'.[32]

Mallory cited this incident as an indication that their decision not to continue above the North Col was well founded. They had pushed themselves as far as they could reasonably go. But the subject of leaving climbers behind, for whatever reason, or sending porters down from high camps unescorted, was a volatile one. And while it occurred quite frequently on Everest in the 1920s and 1930s, it was a practice that never met with approbation. Depending on who left whom behind, and what the outcome of the decision was, the reaction of the Alpine Club members varied from ignoring the incident altogether (in the case of Norton leaving Somervell) to vehement condemnation (when Finch sent a porter down alone). Mallory wisely omitted the Bullock incident from the official expedition report.

Bullock's weakness apart, it was as well they retreated when they did, for Wheeler was already showing the first stages of frostbite. It took several hours of rubbing on Mallory's part to restore any feeling to Wheeler's feet. On reflection, Mallory realized it was not a question 'as to what might have happened higher, but what would have happened with unfailing certainty,' had they given in to the temptation to press on. Thank God, they had not. As he acknowledged to Geoffrey Young, 'it was a pitiful party at the last, not fit to be on a mountainside anywhere.'[33]

As the bedraggled climbers reassembled for the journey home, Mallory wrote to Ruth of the anti-climax he felt:

This is a mere line at the earliest moment, in the midst of packing and arrangements, to tell you that all is well; that is to say, that I am well in spite of all efforts and disappointment. It is a disappointment, there's no getting over it, that the end should seem so much tamer than I hoped . . . As it is, we have established the way to the summit for anyone who cares to try the highest adventure; and I don't much regret having failed to beat a record, as we could have done easily had fortune favoured us.[34]

Brave words, but the disappointment festered throughout the long journey home by sea. Mallory wrote to his friend David Pye from Marseilles:

> Never mind Everest and its unfriendly glories. I'm tired of travelling and travellers, far countries and uncouth people, trains and ships and shimmering mausoleums, foreign ports, dark-skinned faces, and a garish sun. What I want to see is faces I know, and my own sweet home; afterwards the solemn façades in Pall Mall, and perhaps Bloomsbury in a fog; and then an English river, cattle grazing in western meadows . . .[35]

And to Geoffrey Young:

> I think it was disappointment more than anything else that prevented me from writing before: the terrible difference between my visions of myself with a few determined spirits setting forth from our perched camp on that high pass, crawling up at least to a much higher point where the summit itself would seem almost within reach, and coming down tired but not dispirited, satisfied rather, just with the effort; all that, and on the other hand the reality as we found it — the blown snow endlessly swept over grey slopes, just the grim prospect, no respite, and no hope.[36]

VII

The Damnable Heresy

Mallory's post-expedition tristesse is understandable. He had wanted to accomplish so much, to put on a good show, perhaps even to reach the summit — at least to get some substantial distance up the slopes of Everest's great North Face. Yet the mountain reconnaissance had been eminently successful. The country around Everest was now mapped, and a feasible route had been discovered through the mountain's close defences, which looked as if it should lead right to the summit. Moreover, the work of the reconnaissance, which was to have been directed by its older experienced men, had ended up in the hands of its youngest members — the lieutenants who were to have learned their trade from their betters. The rightness of this Mallory had never doubted, but he would like to have proved it in everyone's eyes with more glorious achievement.

Before they had set out Mallory had complained to Hinks about the advanced age of the team, and been rebuffed with a harsh insult. Now Hinks had been shown that Mallory was right. But the matter of age was a sore point with Mallory too — not the least because at 35 he felt himself past the first flush of youth. We know now that Himalayan climbers very often reach their peak in their mid-thirties, but Mallory was fearful his powers could only diminish, and it was a fear that would haunt him increasingly as time went on.

At the same time he could see the irony in the gulf that existed between the debate that went into planning and what actually happened in the field, when faced with the need for snap decisions from a collection of individuals suffering privations and exhibiting all the human frailties. To David Pye, he wrote:

> When I think of that wonderful Everest Committee and all the solemn divergences of opinion that must have passed between nodding their heads, the scrutiny of photographs and the discussion of letters, with grave doubts coughed up in phlegmy throats as to whether the party are really 'on the right track', and all the Glaxo-loving public — lord, when I think of it, something bubbles up inside me. The effervescence is sternly repressed, of course. I settle down to pondered judgments; and then — a bubble outs and bursts.[1]

Yet part of Mallory's disappointment may have been less a reflection of his past adventure than a yearning for another one. For George Mallory, Mount Everest had begun to spin its fascinating web. Such adventure was more fulfilling to him by far than being a school teacher. At last he had found a challenge to which he was ideally suited, both physically and emotionally.

The highest altitude reached by Mallory in the Reconnaissance Expedition was 23,000 feet, higher by more than a mile than the highest mountain in the Alps. Even though he became superbly acclimatized during the five months of the expedition, he realized clearly how much climbing effort was limited by the difficulty of breathing in the thin air. In the Alps, the difficulty disappears after a few weeks of acclimatization. At much higher elevations, no amount of acclimatization eliminates completely the often desperate wheezing and gasping for air that takes place during strenuous exertion. As climbers age and become less strong, they maintain their climbing level by skilfully drawing on their accumulation of experience. In the Himalaya, breathing is the primary limiting factor in climbing performance.

Mallory became interested in devising any breathing techniques that might help him climb more easily, and he experimented with different methods. During his five months away he developed what he later called his 'secret' breathing technique, or at least, so he later told Noel, promising to reveal it after their return from Everest in 1924. Mallory did not return, and so it was believed the secret was lost. Mallory had already described one special technique in the Expedition report of 1921, and this in all probability is the 'secret' to which he referred:

The importance of breathing hard and deeply had impressed itself upon us again and again. I had come to think of my own practice as a very definite and conscious performance adopted to suit the occasion. The principles were always the same — to time the breathing regularly to fit the step, and to use not merely the upper part of the lungs, but the full capacity of the breathing apparatus, expanding and contracting not the chest only, but also the diaphragm, and this not occasionally but with every breath whenever the body was required to work at high pressure . . .

I came to employ two distinct methods of working the legs with the lungs. As soon as conscious breathing was necessary it was my custom deliberately to inhale on one step and exhale on the next. Later, at a higher elevation, or when the expedition of muscular energy became more exhausting, I would both inhale and exhale for each step, in either case timing the first move-ment of lifting the leg to synchronize with the beginning, so to speak, of the breathing-stroke.[2]

Success in using his special technique may have caused Mallory to believe he would be able to do without oxygen breathing equipment when that question arose later. The trick certainly seemed to work well for him while scaling the intermediate Everest heights in 1921. But as he was to climb higher and higher on the mountain in future expeditions, his breathing capability was ever more severely tested. As a last resort on both the expeditions of 1922 and 1924, he would abandon his technique in favour of all-out attempts using oxygen, although not without moral struggle, and not without first making unsuccessful bids breathing naturally.

From Mallory's descriptions of his desperate huffing and puffing during climbs around the base of Everest, arose conjecture as to whether anyone could survive, much less climb, above the North Col. The British military had run into similar problems with high-flying aeroplanes during the First World War. Professor G. Dreyer, who during the war had been a consultant to the Air Board on the use of oxygen at high altitude, had expressed strong views about the need to use oxygen to climb Everest before the reconnaissance party set out. 'I do not think you will get up without it,' he had said, 'but if you do succeed you may not get down again.'[3]

Professor Dreyer made a convincing case for the use of oxygen, and easily persuaded Captain Farrar of its necessity. George Finch submitted himself to tests in Dreyer's vacuum chamber to simulate climbing at altitude. There had been no time to get together a satisfactory oxygen kit for 1921 although Dr Kellas had intended carrying out oxygen experiments in Tibet. His death prevented anything being done, since no one else was competent (or sufficiently interested) to take over the work.

On the expedition's return Dr Wollaston urged that the matter be taken up again and proposed Dr Longstaff as a suitable Oxygen Officer. Longstaff had climbed above 23,000 feet without undue distress, and, like most climbers, had an instinctive resistance to the use of oxygen. At the same time he doubted if the summit could be reached without it. Scientifically he was curious to see if there was any ceiling for unassisted climbers. Farrar was shrewd enough to see that if Longstaff was only a half-hearted believer, and moreover lived a great distance from London, little progress was likely to be made if the question were left to him to resolve. Here was an opportunity to bring Finch back into the arena after the unpleasantness of his rejection from the reconnaissance. Accordingly, he wrote to Younghusband:

> We have in Finch a man qualified to take entire charge of the oxygen apparatus. He is Chief Assistant to Professor Bone FRS, the Head of the Fuel Research Department, and Finch was, so Strutt tells me, Special Gas expert at Salonika. Hence our risks are reasonably minimised. We must not hide from ourselves for a moment that the ascent of Everest is essentially a very dangerous proposition, not perhaps so much from a mountaineering point of view as from the effect of altitude and the incidence of cold, about which, as Professor Leonard Hill constantly reiterates, no one possesses any definite experience.[4]

An Oxygen Committee was formed comprising Captain Farrar, P.J.H. Unna, Howard Somervell and George Finch and they put themselves under the advice of Professors Dreyer and Hill at the Air Board. Finch and Somervell both performed further low-pressure experiments in vacuum chambers at Oxford, during the course of which Somervell exercised himself to unconsciousness. When oxygen was administered, he vigorously denied feeling any ill effects, thus confirming the scientists in their belief that the main symptoms of oxygen lack were mental confusion and a tendency towards truculence.

When the results of these tests were reported to the Everest Committee, a sum of £400 was voted to obtain 10 open-circuit oxygen sets and a supply of cylinders for the expedition.

Low pressure chamber tests on unacclimatized subjects greatly exaggerate the performance differences oxygen would make on the mountain. The effect on acclimatized people of breathing oxygen is less beneficial than the effect on those who are not acclimatized. Given the antipathy towards the use of oxygen, had these physiological factors been better understood, it is perhaps possible that it would never have been used at all.

Most of the climbers were suspicious of the gains promised by the use of oxygen, and for good reason. An increase in performance was difficult to substantiate outside the low-pressure chamber, but the weight and awkward bulk of the complex apparatus was all too apparent, as was the greatly increased porterage required to place the oxygen cylinders in position on the mountain. This would consume porters who would otherwise be available to allow additional, non-oxygen-aided attempts. Besides, the equipment was pathetically unreliable — a fact that has never yet been satisfactorily explained — and climbers were loth to throw in their lot with such an untrustworthy aid.

The cylinders sent out with the 1922 expedition arrived, as Finch reported, in good condition: 'but the apparatus — through no fault of the makers, who had, indeed, done their work admirably — leaked very badly, and to get them into satisfactory working order, four days of hard toil with soldering-iron, hacksaw, pliers, and all the other paraphernalia of a fitter's shop were necessary . . . The masks from which the oxygen was to be breathed proved useless.'

However justified their prejudices were, a split soon developed between those who believed in the theoretical benefits promised by oxygen use and those who saw only its many practical disadvantages. Once this division had taken place, neither side could see any merit in the other's claims or complaints. The issue became so emotional that facts could no longer change men's minds, and the argument ran on for nearly a quarter of a century. The real debate was about the ethics of its use, for 'fair play' was of paramount importance to the generations preceding the Second World War. Thus 'science' had little chance of settling the argument and successive physiologists were mystified why none of the factual evidence they produced ever swayed opinion. The debate continued into the late 1940s (and indeed has re-emerged in recent years since the ascent of Everest has now been proved possible without using oxygen).

Because of his idealistic view of mountain climbing, and his great faith in his breathing technique, Mallory was initially strongly against the use of oxygen equipment, favouring acclimatization over oxygenation. When, on 31 January 1922, Sir Walter Raleigh discussed with Mallory the physiologists' opinion that oxygen would be needed, Mallory claims to have retorted, 'I told Sir Walter that the physiologists might explode themselves in their diabolical chamber, but we would do what we could to explode their damnable heresy.' In 1922, on the ocean voyage to India, Mallory wrote to his friend David Pye:

> I thought it a rather grim business to be bound for Everest again with so small a chance of getting up and with so many things in life one might do that would seem more worth doing. And when I think of mountaineering with four cylinders of oxygen on one's back and a mask over one's face — well, it loses its charm.[5]

Yet in short order, Mallory's favouring of acclimatization over using oxygen began to waver. There were several causes for the slow metamorphosis which overtook his thinking on the subject, but perhaps the strongest was the influence of George Ingle Finch.

VIII

Preparing the Attack

Mallory received his invitation to take part in the second expedition while still on his way home from the first. He had two main recommendations for the Everest Committee after his experience of the Reconnaissance. To begin with, he was sure they had gone in the wrong season. It would be far better to tackle the mountain in May and June, before the monsoon snows. He also argued that the climbing team needed to number at least eight men. While public interest was high and relations with Tibet were good, the Committee was anxious that no time be lost in sending out the next party, but if it was to be in position in Tibet by the spring, they only had a few months in which to get everything organized. Mallory could not see how enough suitable people could possibly be assembled in so short a time, and therefore did not feel prepared to commit himself immediately. He advised Hinks he would give him a decision when he reached home after spending a little time with his wife in the South of France.

In a letter to his sister Avie he remarked, 'I shall tell them they can get the other seven first. How they'll pore over the A.C. list and write round for opinions about the various candidates! I wouldn't go again next year, as the saying is, for all the gold in Arabia.'[1]

Hinks did not like ends left so untidily; surely Mallory realized there was a lot to be organized. Why could he not give a straight answer? Besides, in his last letter, the man had touched a raw spot by criticizing the sketch map that he (Hinks) had prepared for *The Times* to accompany the expedition's despatches. Sourly, Hinks wrote to Mallory: 'It is really very important that we should see you as soon as possible because though you may not be coming out next year other people are.' He had to have the last word, too. 'I am prepared to bet you a £1 treasury note', he wrote, 'that the sketch map of Mt. Everest which I made . . . is more accurate than that which you sent me in your letter.'[2]

Mallory, as it proved, had underestimated the Committee. Though it did not manage to produce the eight climbers he sought, a reasonable-looking team of six was quickly put together and Mallory agreed to join it — without the lure of Arabian gold! Right from the start when a two-stage assault was first planned — reconnaissance one year, serious attempt the next — several contenders had 'pencilled in their names' for what they saw as the more interesting second stage. Three of those who had been most persistent in trying to go to Everest were included in the party: Bruce, Longstaff and Noel.

General Charlie Bruce was to be the overall leader. He had waited nearly thirty years for this opportunity and it had come almost too late. In 1919, following three years' strenuous work in the Bannu district, one of the hottest spots on the frontier, he had been invalided out of the Army after three medical boards concluded he was suffering 'cardiac debility with great enlargement'. They told him to go home and live quietly for the rest of his life. He was in his late fifties. For a congenitally active man it was a bitter pill to swallow. Joking about it afterwards, Bruce would say that scarcely any organ in his body remained unaffected. 'Even my liver was found to be so large that it required two men and a boy to carry it.'[3]

Bruce came home to his native Wales, railing against the injunction to lead a quiet life. He quickly took up a post with the Glamorgan Territorial Association, which improved his spirits no end, but he still longed to get back into the mountains. Accordingly, he placed himself under the care of a climbing physician, Claude Wilson. In 1920 Wilson allowed him to do some mild climbing and it improved his condition wonderfully. In 1921 he was allowed to climb as much as he liked in the Alps and he came back very fit indeed. Now here he was, in 1922, to lead an expedition to Everest! Admittedly he was not expected to go higher than Base Camp, but there were many who were not sanguine that he would make it that far. It was known that Howard-Bury would have liked to lead the second expedition. Indeed, having more than fulfilled expectations during the period of initial negotiations, and then so successfully carried through the reconnaissance, to many it seemed only right that he should be given the chance to finish the job.

He was clearly encouraged into thinking this might yet happen by Hinks, who was no great admirer of Bruce. Hinks's letters to him while he was in Tibet, carried frequent reference to Bruce's uncertain health, and after the death of Kellas, Hinks had written: 'I wonder if Wollaston examined Kellas medically at Darjeeling. It would have been a very hazardous enterprise because he was a very obstinate little man. The experience so far seems to point out the great necessity of medical control and I cannot think what sort of figure Bruce will cut if he is overhauled in the autumn preparatory to being considered for next year.'[4]

Later, he was even more forthright, telling Howard-Bury, 'My own opinion is that Bruce certainly ought not to go, and that no physician would pass him, but our experience of this year shows what funny views committees take.' Hinks was well aware he was speaking out of turn, for he added, 'the President is a bit sticky on the subject of Bruce, and I have told him I am writing to you'. Sticky the President certainly was. It was a point of honour with Younghusband, that because he had been present at the birth of the idea all those years ago, Bruce should be involved with it now, when, as was fondly assumed, it was coming to fruition.

Given that he was not going high, Bruce managed to convince the expedition doctors of his fitness — his various scars and bullet wounds were dismissed as being of no consequence and his slight arteriosclerosis seemed to them outweighed by his general health and physique. It was a great relief to both Bruce and Younghusband. Bruce: 'I am mightily rejoiced . . . so if the Council will have me, I'm your man. Don't think I am possibly giving this job up.'[5]

Bruce's appointment was announced to the press before the reconnaissance party reached home. Howard-Bury took umbrage at the way the news was handled. It seemed to him that by making it public with such alacrity, the impression was being put about that his effort had been a failure. Bitterly he complained that the expedition was becoming purely a climbing venture, and no interest was being shown in anything beyond the climbing results 'where unfortunately we were unable to achieve any records for you'.[6]

Bruce's Climbing Leader, who would take over from him above Base Camp, was to be Lt-Col. Edward Lisle Strutt, a very experienced alpinist, then aged 48. He was a distinguished soldier-diplomat and a man of enormous courage, who in 1919 had rescued the Emperor and Empress of Austria from the teeth of revolution and conducted them safely into Switzerland. He was on intimate terms with many of the noblest families in Europe and for a short time held the post of High Commissioner in Danzig, before leaving abruptly after an undiplomatic clash with the Foreign Secretary, Lord Curzon. Clashes of personality were not infrequent where Strutt was concerned; indeed he is most often remembered now as trenchantly opinionated and prone to ludicrous outbursts, and for his inspired snobbery. He resisted all progress in mountaineering style and standards, and during the ten years it came under his editorship, the *Alpine Journal* became known for too readily adopting 'the role of a shocked and censorious maiden aunt'.[7]

The active climbing team was to comprise George Mallory, George Finch, Howard Somervell, A.W. Wakefield, and Major E.F. Norton: all considered capable of reaching the summit. Somervell and Wakefield both originated from Kendal, in the Lake District, and were medical men — Somervell a surgeon, Wakefield a general practitioner who had been working in Canada for a number of years. Somervell was extraordinarily tough, thirty-two, with a fine alpine reputation, although his best season, when he climbed no fewer than 32 peaks, was still a year ahead of him. At Cambridge he had gained a double first in Natural Sciences, and he was also gifted musically and artistically. On the way to Everest he made a collection of Tibetan folk tunes that he later transcribed for Western instruments; and at every stop of the long journey, he would perch awkwardly on piled packing cases to produce vigorous pastel sketches of the changing scene. Wakefield was known mainly for the rock exploits of his Cumbrian youth; he was so keen to join the expedition that he sold his practice in Canada.

Major E.F. (Teddy) Norton was the great find of the expedition. He was a grandson of the alpine pioneer Sir Alfred Wills who had made the first ascent of the Wetterhorn. As a boy he had spent his holidays at the family chalet near Sixt in the Haute Savoie. There, he and his brother became adept at scrambling over steep, loose ground in search of chamois, taking on slopes where even local hunters would not go. Tall and limber, Norton was a fearless horseman; he had served as a Horse Gunner and enjoyed polo and pig-sticking. With his modesty and cultured interests he proved an ideal expedition man, offering the bonus that he could speak several Hindustani dialects. On a later expedition, there was good cause to be thankful, too, for his quiet authority and organizational skills when, at short notice, he was obliged to take over leadership in the middle of Tibet.

The official doctor to the expedition was Tom Longstaff, and like Wollaston the year before, he doubled as naturalist and collector. He had more Himalayan mountaineering experience than anyone in the team, but at forty-seven was already past his prime. When he submitted himself for his pre-expedition medical, the doctors unkindly commented, 'this man is not a very good specimen'. John Noel, on the other hand, was told that his balancing powers were good and his altitude test extremely good. He, too, now finally had the opportunity of realizing his Everest dream. He would be the expedition's photographer and film-maker, and began his preparations immediately. His clockwork camera would require special modifications against the cold, and as he intended to process all his film at Base Camp, he needed to find a light-proof, dust-free darkroom tent.

As Transport Officers, General Bruce nominated his nephew Captain Geoffrey Bruce and Captain John Morris (both serving with the Gurkhas), to be assisted by Colin Crawford of the Indian Civil Service. Once he arrived in India, Bruce approached the Survey of India for the release of Morshead. He wanted him as a climber this time, rather than a surveyor — and this was agreed. With Morshead and Crawford, then, who was also a noteworthy climber — and indeed also Geoffrey Bruce, who though he was not a climber, took to it readily — the General had shrewdly strengthened his team, with no reference back to the Committee. It was to prove, by and large, a very happy and cohesive party.

Bruce travelled to India ahead of the main party in order to make all the necessary transport arrangements. He estimated he would need at least 500 mules to get all the equipment to Base Camp, and was determined to procure a better selection of animals than they had the year before. A great deal of the scientific apparatus was too delicate to be entrusted to muleback and would need carrying in by porters. Captain Noel, he ragged Hinks, would be arriving at Darjeeling with a box 40 feet long, and he was currently 'scouring the country for an adequate mule'. To ease their passage through Tibet, Bruce had also taken care to procure suitable gifts for the Dzongpens and other officials they would meet. 'I am taking brocade for the Rongbuk Lama,' he reported, 'and twenty-four Homberg hats — the nearest way to the heart of all subordinate officials.'

On 23 March he was able to report to Hinks that they were actually on the move. 'The outfit is rather tremendous.' There were 40 climbing porters, 8 photographic porters, 10 oxygen porters, a sirdar or head-man, an interpreter, a cobbler, a tent-mender and several first class cooks.

Hinks felt things were getting out of hand. Bruce was spending money like water. An unofficial estimate had put the costs of carrying the oxygen outfit alone, from Calcutta to the North Col, at £600. He had always felt the whole business of taking oxygen added an element of farce to the project. After witnessing the first gas drill, he had written to Bruce telling him that 'a most wonderful apparatus' had been contrived that was certain to make him die laughing. And he had scornfully questioned in print many of the recommendations of the oxygen sub-committee, as well as the recommended lay-out of oxygen bottles on the mountain. Farrar was furious. 'I will say quite frankly that I do not like the somewhat satirical tone of your article,' he told him. 'You will be seen as a doubter.'[8]

The offending piece was a progress report Hinks had prepared for the *Geographical Journal*. It was unsigned and since, in it, Hinks lapsed frequently into the royal 'we', it did not so much portray *him* as the doubter, but the whole geographical establishment. What in particular so incensed Farrar was the way Hinks managed to convey that the Everest Committee was prey to the whims of boffins and atypical mountaineers:

The party was equipped this year with oxygen at the strong desire of a section of the climbers who had convinced themselves, or had been convinced, that they would never reach the summit without it. The Committee, feeling bound to supply whatever in reason might be demanded, cheerfully faced the large expenditure required . . .

It is more than likely that some of the climbers will find it impossible to tolerate the restraint of all this apparatus, and will develop new and interesting varieties of the 'claustrophobia' that afflicts men shut up in pressure chamber or the diving dress. And this will be a good thing, because it seems to us quite as important to discover how high a man can climb without oxygen as to get to a specified point, even the highest summit of the world, in conditions so artificial that they can never become 'legitimate' mountaineering.[9]

For Hinks to comment thus was an outrageous transgression beyond his remit, but he was unrepentant. He told Farrar, 'I should be especially sorry if the oxygen outfit prevents them going as high as possible without it. The instructions laid down by Dreyer say clearly that oxygen should be used continuously above 23,000 feet. That I am convinced is all nonsense. Wollaston agrees. If some of the party do not go to 25,000–26,000 feet without oxygen, they will be rotters.'[10]

Farrar retorted:

Strictly speaking, I do not think that oxygen is any more of an artificial aid than food. The human frame is attuned to a certain supply of oxygen. All we have endeavoured to do is to make up the supply to the normal quantity. I certainly (with very considerable experience of mountaineering – equal at least to anyone of the present party) do not agree that 'if some of the party don't go to 25–26,000 feet without oxygen they will be rotters'. I start with the strong conviction that, whatever they do, no party in *similar conditions* could do more.[11]

A copy of Hinks's article was later to reach Finch at Base Camp at the start of the expedition. He was convinced he could detect in it a sinister attempt to subvert the expedition's whole purpose. What was even more distressing, he believed that in this, it had in some measure succeeded:

Instead of the aim being to climb Mount Everest with every resource at our disposal, the opponents of oxygen . . . had so successfully worked upon the minds of the members of the expedition as to induce them to entertain a fresh objective, namely to see how far they could climb without the aid of oxygen. It were pleasant to think that the writer who could thus acclaim possible failure and, in advocating a new objective, destroy the singleness of purpose of the expedition, was not a mountaineer.[12]

The main group of climbers travelling out from England sailed together aboard the liner *Caledonia*. Finch was anxious to put the time to good use and instigated drills with the oxygen apparatus, which no one took at all seriously. He complained in his diary that 'most of the others think it is all so simple that it does not need concentrated practice', but added with some satisfaction that 'today some made rather fools of themselves, getting muddled over the question of valves: so shall probably do better next time.'[13] It was not the valves that bothered Mallory, they were 'simple enough', it was the suffocating intimacy of the rubber face-masks, and most particularly the emergency procedure if the standard mask failed to work. This involved holding a rubber tube in the mouth. 'I sicken with the thought of the saliva dribbling down. I hope it won't be necessary to use it,' he told Ruth.[14]

The journey passed peacefully enough, as Mallory wrote, 'sunshine day after day and the members of the expedition are a happy smiling company with plenty of easy conversation.' Wakefield and Somervell indulged in deck tennis to keep fit, they all played some deck cricket, and Finch (who Mallory said was 'behaving very well so far') rigged up a punchball.

A good deal of scientific discussion takes place ranging often round the subject of breathing oxygen. Wakefield is somewhat distrustful of the whole affair and is usually found on the opposite side to Finch who is dogmatic in his statements. I think Wakefield is sometimes irritated by him. I must say in this company I am amused by Finch and rather enjoy him. I'm much intrigued by the shape of his head, which seems to go out at the sides where it ought to go up. He's a fanatical character and doesn't laugh easily. He is greatly enjoying his oxygen class and talks of what he has got to do about it somewhat egoistically. However, the drill is being abandoned, so perhaps we shan't hear quite so much on this subject, which nevertheless is extremely interesting and Finch has been very competent about it.

How different people are from one's first thoughts. I had imagined Strutt from one brief meeting at the Alpine Club a dry stiff soldier, but he turns out to be anything but that . . . and is rather a chatterbox and quite entertaining, though never profound . . . Over one affair, he tells me, Curzon tried to get him court-martialled as a traitor to his country, so I conclude he must be a good man.

I've never in my life been so idle, really because we have a lot of talk. I particularly like Noel. We had a long yarn a few nights ago and he told me the Everest film, which is to be a complete story in itself apart from a lecture, should be worth £15,000 for foreign rights alone and goodness knows how much in England, which gives me some hope that there will be generous terms to the lecturers.[15]

On board ship Finch met the Calcutta Manager of Lightfoot's Oxygen Company, who offered to inspect the expedition's oxygen cylinders when they arrived in India. The bulk of the oxygen apparatus was in fact travelling on a separate ship, the *Chicka*, which they had overtaken on the voyage, so that Finch was obliged to kick his heels impatiently, awaiting its arrival, while the others went on to Darjeeling to meet General Bruce and all those who had come direct from other parts of India.

They found Norton in hospital in Calcutta with a bad attack of piles after a pig-sticking event, but it proved unnecessary to operate and he was able to continue with the rest of the party.

Bruce greeted them with a boisterous show of cheer on the road outside Darjeeling, and very soon had the factions welded together. 'I'm very happy, dearest one,' Mallory told Ruth. 'It seems a congenial party — to think of the difference between Bruce and Bury!' It was a comparison he could not fail to draw since one task of the journey-in was to correct the proofs for the book of the previous expedition. Bury's chapters seemed worse than he expected, 'quite dreadfully bad' as he told Ruth, spun-out and lamentably childish, which was all the more a pity because he had collected quite a lot of interesting information:

> There is not a word of appreciation of anyone's work or qualities — nothing even that gives the feeling that the author liked any one of the party in the whole of the 180 pages, whereas on the other hand there are quite a number of remarks quite gratuitously pointing to their weaknesses, as for instance when he says that Wheeler had some chances of shooting duck but missed, that Morshead and I felt the height on the occasion when I took Bury up a mountain, and that Bullock and I went the wrong way from Shekar Dzong without mentioning the ultimate success of our expedition. These small things don't worry me in the least and I must say that about the larger issues of the reconnaissance he has not been unfair to me, but I don't like sharing a book with this sort of man.[16]

Finch, when he arrived, remained the odd man out. His unpopularity with other members of the team was a continuing problem. He might have been passed over, as he was in 1921, had not Strutt spoken up in his defence. He told Younghusband, '[Finch] is the one man I would back to reach the summit and we should always remember that.'[17] If the General and he were well aware of the difficulties, Strutt said, surely they could be relied upon, between them, to prevent any serious outbreak of friction? Yet despite these fine words, Strutt himself was not above exhibiting flashes of appalling prejudice, as John Morris recalls:

> Strutt's objections were based upon George Finch's unusual background. He had been educated in Switzerland and acquired a considerable reputation for the enterprise and skill of his numerous guideless ascents. Besides, he was by profession a research chemist and therefore doubly suspect, since in Strutt's old-fashioned view the sciences were not a respectable occupation for anyone who regarded himself as a gentleman. One of the photographs which particularly irritated him depicted Finch repairing his own boots. It confirmed Strutt's belief that a scientist was a sort of a mechanic. I can still see his rigid expression as he looked at the picture. 'I always knew the fellow was a shit,' he said, and the sneer remained on his face while the rest of us sat in frozen silence.[18]

Morris had yet to meet Finch and wondered what to expect. Later he was pleasantly surprised to find him a man of 'equable temperament' and very 'professional' in his attitude, though he did notice, when Finch caught up with the party for a few days in Darjeeling, that he seemed ill at ease. Morris put this down to Finch's knowing full well that neither he nor his oxygen equipment was particularly welcome. Throughout the expedition, Finch remained the butt of much sarcastic comment and practical jokes.

For his part, Finch confided to his diary the impressions he gained of the rest of the team. He tried to assess how far his companions might get on Everest, and was interested to see the extent to which his views would be confirmed or otherwise by future events. By their own admission, General Bruce, Longstaff and Noel were non-starters who never expected to get high on the mountain, for they had other responsibilities, though Noel had hopes of reaching considerable altitudes if not on Everest itself. Finch based his opinion of the others on their physical appearance, their attitudes and their mountaineering experience. Geoffrey Bruce, for example, was too narrow-chested to promise much in the way of stamina, and Morris wore glasses and was clumsy, his body disproportionately long on its short legs. Neither he thought of as climbers. Despite good stamina,

Norton was also no mountaineer, and Wakefield, his age more against him than it ought to be, might squander his energy in a nervousness that amounted to hysteria. To an extent Finch gauged right here, for Wakefield failed to acclimatize. Strutt could go higher, Finch felt, but his lack of confidence and gloomy view of himself told against him. The heavy Somervell might, like Strutt, and perhaps Norton, get to 24,000 feet, though he could become muscle-bound. In the pressure tank at Oxford 23,000 feet had finished him. Only Mallory, whom Finch was 'inclined to look on as the strongest of all',[19] had much chance of approaching 25,000 feet. For himself, Finch hoped he could 'hold his own with Mallory', but he did not want to be called upon to make the attempt without oxygen. So unpopular was the bottled gas, he doubted if anyone else placed reliance upon the use of it. Indeed, both General Bruce and Longstaff had let it be known to him that oxygen was not going to be used at all in the first attempt.

Far from being convinced that Everest was possible without oxygen, Finch did not believe that an individual who has pushed himself 'to his extreme limit' in attempting to break the existing height record (24,600 feet), or to climb Everest, without oxygen, would be equal to another attempt the same year, even with oxygen. It had been decided not to use oxygen below 23,000 feet and that, he considered, might already be far too high for any man who has worn himself out on a previous attempt without oxygen. At this stage, of course, all was speculation. They would see what they would see. In Darjeeling Bruce had engaged forty Nepalese porters, including thirteen from the previous year's climbing party. It was not as many as they would have liked, but they hoped to be able to engage a few Tibetans later on. Immense quantities of stores were already well on their long way to Tibet. On 27 March Mallory wrote to Ruth from Kalimpong:

Today we came up the Teesta Valley to railhead, a three hour journey . . . but a very lovely one, Bruce with his head out of the window most of the time, brimming over with joy and waving his handkerchief to passers by and Noel on the roof of the train working his cinema apparatus.[20]

It was very hot at the railhead and most, like Mallory, were content to ride from Teesta Bridge on ponies. Not the General. He was 'making heroic exertions to get rid of his tummy', and chose instead to walk the 4,000 feet uphill. 'You may imagine how he watered the paths, but what energy!' commented Mallory.

The oxygen cylinders had still not arrived when the first two groups were ready to leave and Finch again had to wait behind. Crawford remained with him. This was a serious blow as it seemed to Finch that in all probability he would not now catch up with the main party before Base Camp on or around 20 May, which meant none of the oxygen drills he had planned for the journey could take place. He began to doubt if the team would be sufficiently proficient – or interested – to use the apparatus on the mountain. He had pointed out as much to General Bruce before he left, but, 'without however insistence as I do not wish to appear to be an unruly nuisance'. He thought that only he and perhaps Somervell were at that moment capable of using oxygen, and since the monsoon could be expected to break in early June, there would be little time for any thorough training with it before Everest would need to be attempted. An added frustration was that his tools had gone on ahead with the vanguard, so that he was prevented from testing or overhauling the equipment on the journey. It did not seem to Finch that oxygen was being given a proper chance, but things were not quite so bleak as he feared. The cylinders caught up a week later and, by dint of forced marching, Finch and Crawford were able to rejoin the main party at Kampa Dzong on 13 April, whereupon the General ordered a two-day rest period to allow them to recuperate so that everyone could continue together. Here, at least, was a chance for Finch to reinstate his oxygen drills.

'A usual and by now welcome sound in each new place is Strutt's voice cursing Tibet, this march for being more dreary and repulsive than the one before, and this village for being more filthy than any other. Not that Strutt is precisely a grouser, but he likes to ease his feelings with maledictions and I hope feels better for it,'[21] Mallory told Ruth. For his own part, although he had difficulty remaining aesthetically stimulated when treading known ground, Mallory was finding that the naked forms of the country began to grow upon his consciousness. It had been very wintry since they passed on to the Tibetan plateau and several of them caught colds. Bruce ordered another additional rest-day in Tinki Dzong to allow Longstaff to recover from a chill. Mallory, remembering Kellas and Raeburn, felt anxiety at how alarmingly frail the little doctor suddenly looked. To Ruth, he wrote, 'He hasn't the physique for this job and carries it all through on his tremendous spirit – no one is more splendidly full of humour, so gay and talkative.'[22] He and Longstaff had been putting their heads together to work out a plan of campaign for the General, who wanted to launch an attack on the mountain without delay. 'L[ongstaff] of course from his past experience knows far more about this sort of thing than anyone else and I was very glad to find that we were in agreement about all the knotty points.'[23]

The knottiest of all was, of course, the oxygen apparatus. Everyone was getting fed up with the time and energy it was consuming, and Mallory no longer found the endless scientific talk as amusing as he did on board ship. 'It is becoming a little difficult not to acquire a Finch-complex,' he told Ruth. 'I hope we shall manage to get on.' Quite apart from the two weeks' training Finch vigorously declared was necessary before anyone could safely use the apparatus ('fantastic nonsense' in Mallory's view, 'two days would be ample'), the whole outfit — sets and cylinders — weighed between eight and nine hundred pounds. That was a daunting amount to convey on to the mountain. According to Mallory, Longstaff dogmatically asserted that they never would be carried to the North Col because there was simply not the power to get them there. Other qualms were felt, too. 'After tea, Finch gave an oxygen demonstration, largely for the benefit of the novices, an interesting entertainment as it showed up several weaknesses which had developed in the apparatus which we had used to practise on board. Nothing that is incapable of adjustment, but showing only too well how many chances are against its working properly.'[24]

In *The Making of a Mountaineer*, Finch exhibited a flash of sarcasm when he remarked that his oxygen drills 'were deservedly popular, being held, as a rule, each evening at the end of a long day's march, when everybody was feeling particularly fit and vigorous'. Longstaff, he knew, thought it a great mistake to have brought the stuff at all, and everyone else seemed to treat it more or less like a younger sister on a lovers' picnic, grudgingly taken along because Mother said so. Certainly none of the high climbers (bar himself) saw oxygen as the key to success on Everest, and who could tell if anyone would bother with it even after the proposed oxygenless first attempt?

The General was certainly wary of the apparatus, although immediately after Mallory and Somervell returned from a scouting trip to the North Col, he did begin having it ferried up to Camp III at the head of the East Rongbuk Glacier. (The expedition this time took the shorter approach via the full length of the East Rongbuk Glacier.)

The oxygen was thus in a position where it could conceivably have been made ready and used for the first attempt had Mallory so desired. Bruce wrote home to Hinks:

Finch is working very hard at oxygen arrangements and getting people trained in the proper use of primus stoves etc, but I myself am rather terrified at the oxygen apparatus. It seems to me to be so very easily put out of order and also so liable to be damaged by hitting against rocks, or by catching its indiarubber tubing on rocks; also the change of bottles on steep slopes when the apparatus has to be taken off and readjusted by very weary and hungry men seems a danger. The pressure I am told at the start and during the climb will be kept at a height of 15,000 ft [equivalent] and the weight of the apparatus is 33 lbs. This seems to me to require a tremendous effort to go all day carrying this weight without food or drink as the apparatus once put on cannot be removed from the mouth. However, Finch seems very confident. I am very glad to say however that they are going to make a good trial at an elevation where if the apparatus is taken off no harm can occur.[25]

Besides ten open-circuit sets, the expedition had also been pro- vided with 'oxylithe' bags, designed by Professor Leonard Hill, which were intended to produce oxygen by the chemical action of water (or urine) on a cake of sodium peroxide. Their performance did nothing to allay Bruce's reservations about all these new-fangled contraptions. He reported to Hinks:

The Leonard Hill oxylithe apparatus is a sham and a delusion high up. Apparently at diminished atmospheric pressure, a great quantity of caustic soda is given off with the oxygen and the results have been anything but satisfactory . . .

This was something of an understatement. A few days earlier Captain Noel, complaining that the air in his well-sealed dark-room tent rapidly became de-oxygenated, had begged Finch for some oxylithe to remedy matters. He was given a tin on to which, once inside the tent, he poured the requisite amount of water. About ten minutes later he was startled by a small explosion and a biggish flash of flame and the whole tent filled with a mist of caustic soda solution. Remarked Finch, 'It strikes me that oxygen from oxylithe will want

101

some watching. Tomorrow I am going to give our Leonard Hill's bags a try-out, but I am not going to take any chances!'[26]

It had been arranged that the first assault would be made by Mallory and Somervell without oxygen, following which Finch and Norton were to carry out a second attempt using oxygen. On 14 May, Finch looked out of his tent and was devastated to see Norton and Morshead leaving with the first party. Existing plans had clearly been abandoned in favour of an onslaught in force. Finch had been left out in the cold. There was no way, as he saw it, that any of them could possibly be fit for a further attempt without lengthy recuperation: 'Hitherto, I had been sanguine in the extreme about getting to the top, but when I saw the last mountaineers of the expedition leave the Base Camp, my hopes fell low. Any attempt I could now make upon Mount Everest would have to be carried out with untrained climbers.'[27]

While the first assault party was away up the mountain, Finch and Geoffrey Bruce began sorting and testing the main oxygen equipment. They experimented with the apparatus up the steep slopes to the North Col and were delighted how quickly they pulled away from their porters who were not using it, and who were carrying loads no heavier — and in some cases less heavy — than themselves. 'Our oxygen experiment was an unqualified success,' Finch noted. 'The going was hard owing to the new snow — we had much step-cutting. Time up about 3 hours only, down back to Camp III only 50 minutes going easy. Returned fit and fresh to Camp III. Oxygen consumption exactly 3 bottles each. We beat the coolies who were carrying as much (or less) as ourselves hollow.'[28]

At the foot of the North Col, on 22 May they had met the first party coming down in a sorry condition. 'They were obviously in the last stages of exhaustion, as indeed men should be who had done their best on a mountain like Everest,' remarked Finch. Morshead, who had been the liveliest when they set out, had suffered so badly from the effects of cold and altitude, he had had to be left in Camp V while the others made their high bid, reaching as they thought 26,985 feet.[29] Instead of benefiting from the rest, Morshead was in even worse shape when they returned to escort him down, and could barely find the strength to descend the easy slopes, leaning heavily on the arms of his companions. But shortly after meeting Finch's party on their way up, Morshead came to a spot where a little trickle of water had been melted by the midday sun. Lying prone, he lapped from the puddle until he had consumed about a quarter of its content.

'Instantaneously', he afterwards claimed, 'my strength returned and I realised that my whole trouble had been simply due to the impossibility of obtaining sufficient liquid at the high altitudes.'[30]

Climbers require up to six litres of liquids per day to counter the effects of altitude dehydration. Laboured breathing results in a great deal of the body's precious moisture being lost in exhalation, but there was no repository of such experience and basic truths in 1922. Although the climbers were all aware of their chronic dehydration, they made little serious effort to combat it in any of the pre-war expeditions.

All four were close to collapse and suffering various degrees of frostbite. Finch was right: there seemed little chance that any of them could recover sufficiently for another attempt. In retrospect, it seems foolish to have spent four of the best men on a single forlorn attempt. Finch, as he had suspected, was left with no other companions for his assault than the non-climber Geoffrey Bruce and the Gurkha Tejbir Bura. It was as well he had given them both a crash course in snow and ice craft.

IX

A Bitter Defeat

The experience of the first assault team cannot have failed to make Mallory examine his own attitude towards oxygen. Despite his aversion to it, he must have been curious to know how much it might have improved his own performance. Finch's pro-oxygen logic had begun to sway his opinion on the boat coming over, and he had expressed then 'good hopes that it will serve us well enough and without physiological dangers from a camp at 25,000 feet'. Now they had climbed to almost 27,000 feet without it, but even clambering up to the North Col (23,000 ft) on 17 May with Climbing Leader Strutt and their party of ten porters, the first effects of the thin air were already discernible.

> My recollections of going up to the North Col are all of a performance rather wearisome and dazed, of a mind incapable of acute perceptions faintly stirring the drowsy senses to take notice within a circle of limited radius. The heat and glare of the morning sun as it blazed on the windless long slopes emphasized the monotony.[1]

The thin air was not their only concern. It was not known whether or not they might suffer damage from the ultra-violet rays. Better to be safe than sorry. Mallory wore two felt hats, Strutt and Somervell their solar topees. The others took no such precautions — and seemed none the worse for it. They plodded slowly and silently upwards and as Strutt struggled up the final slope, he gasped, 'I wish that bloody cinema were here. If I look anything like I feel, I ought to be

104

immortalized for the British public.' Mallory, relating the incident afterwards, said, 'We looked at his grease-smeared, yellow-ashen face, and the reply was: "Well, what in Heaven's name *do* we look like? And what do we do it for, anyway?" '[2]

After fitting out the North Col Camp on its lower ledge, where they could be sheltered from the wind by the bluff of ice cliffs, they had gone to bed on the 19th in confident mood. Mallory:

Now, as darkness deepened, it was a fine night. The flaps of our two tents were still reefed back so as to admit a free supply of air, poor and thin in quality but still recognizable as fresh air; Norton and I and, I believe, Morshead and Somervell also lay with our heads towards the door, and, peering out from the mouths of our eiderdown bags, could see the crest above us sharply defined. The signs were favourable. We had the best omen a mountaineer can look for, the palpitating fire, to use Mr. Santayana's words, of many stars in a black sky. I wonder what the others were thinking of between the intervals of light slumber. I daresay none of us troubled to inform himself that this was the vigil of our great adventure, but I remember how my mind kept wandering over the various details of our preparations without anxiety, rather like God after the Creation seeing that it was good. It was good. And the best of it was what we expected to be doing these next two days.[3]

This is an eloquent moment, as Mallory lay there gazing up at the starlit crest of Everest, and it may have been then that the germ of an idea formed in his mind, not fully considered until the last attempt of the next expedition, to make a night ascent.

The next day started clear and fine, as predicted, and they set off at 7 a.m., rather later than they had hoped, with Morshead again pushing out in front. 'Illusory hope of early sun begot!' quoted Mallory. 'We presently became aware that it was not a perfect day: the sun had no real warmth, and a cold breeze sprang up from the west.' Mallory put on an extra shirt and jumper, but Morshead delayed too long before wrapping himself up properly. The porters were all feeling the cold very badly. To crown it all, in a clumsy moment, Mallory, gathering up the rope after a rest-stop, managed to jerk Norton's rucksack from his lap; Norton lunged for it and missed, and the rucksack with its cargo of rations and warm clothing bounced irretrievably from ledge to ledge down the mountain. It says a lot for Norton's good nature and remarkable phlegm that he did not rage at Mallory for his carelessness. Instead, he watched as the precious bundle vanished into the abyss, then broke the shocked silence with a gentlemanly, 'My rucksack gone down the *kudh*!'

Two small tents were pitched 50 yards apart in the lee of some rocks around 25,000 feet with a double-sleeping bag spread out in each. The sherpas were sent back down. Somervell melted snow and with a lot of labour produced a 'perfunctory meal' before all four turned in for a cold and uncomfortable night, higher than anyone had camped before. None of them appreciated they were already exhibiting the preliminary signs of frostbite: Mallory had three frostnipped fingers, Norton's ear was swollen to three times its normal size, and it was obvious that Morshead was far from well.

'None of us, I suppose,' wrote Mallory, 'after a long, headachy night, felt at his best. For my part, I hoped that the mere effort of deep breathing in the first few steps of the ascent would string me up to the required efforts, and that we should all be better once we started.'

Another rucksack was accidentally knocked down the mountain, but came to rest, fortuitously, on a ledge 100 feet below from where Morshead gamely retrieved it. That proved sufficient effort for him and, at his own request, he was left behind in the small camp as the others pushed on up the slabby slopes.

Mallory wrote, 'Ultimately, the power of pushing up depended upon lung capacity. Lungs governed our speed making the pace a miserable crawl . . . But our lungs were remarkably alike and went well together.' But in the way Mallory so often demonstrates in his writing when, having made one point, he quickly goes into reverse to contradict himself, he continues, 'Personally, I contrived a looseness of the muscles by making an easy, deep-drawn breath, and by exercising deep breathing I found myself able to proceed.' Our lungs were remarkably alike, in other words, but mine were different!

With the occasional help of the hands we were able to keep going for spells of twenty or thirty minutes before halting for three or four or five minutes to gather potential energy for pushing on again. Our whole power seemed to depend on the lungs. The air, such as it was, was inhaled through the mouth and expired again to some sort of tune in the unconscious mind, and the lungs beat time, as it were, for the feet. An effort of the will was required not so much to induce any movement of the limbs as to set the lungs to work and keep them working. So long as they were working evenly and well the limbs would do their duty automatically, it seemed, as though actuated by a hidden spring.[4]

They were hoping to reach the North-east Shoulder where the North (Col) Ridge joins the North-east Ridge, but they knew they should turn back not much later than 2 p.m. By 2.15, after crossing the head of a conspicuous couloir on the North-east Face, and still some 500 feet below the shoulder, they agreed that 'the only wisdom was in retreat'. They were not, in Mallory's view, at the end of their powers, but there was Morshead to consider back at Camp V; it was important to get him down to the North Col that night. They had a clear view of the summit and reluctantly turned their backs upon it.

By 4 p.m. they regained Camp V where Morshead was waiting, still weak and now suffering from frostbite, and with him proceeded on downwards. New snow had obliterated all their earlier tracks and so altered appearances that they could not be certain, as they traversed back towards the ridge, that they were following exactly the same line as before.

Fresh snow had to be cleared away alike from protruding rocks where we wished to put our feet and from the old snow where we must cut steps. It was not a difficult place and yet not easy, as the slope below us was dangerous and yet not very steep, not steep enough to be really alarming or specially to warn the climber that a slip may be fatal. It was an occasion when the need for care and attention was greater than obviously appeared, just the sort to catch a tired party off their guard.[5]

It must have been very like the conditions that would have faced a returning climber on the last fatal descent in 1924. As it was, a nasty slip did occur which resulted in three of the party being pulled from their footing. Tragedy was only averted by Mallory having the presence of mind to thrust in his axe and make a quick rope belay around it, which, with luck, was strong enough to hold their combined weight.

It was dark when they reached the heavily crevassed section above the North Col, but luckily the wind had dropped and they were able to light their candle lantern and pick their way gingerly back to the camp, arriving after 11 p.m. It had taken 7½ hours to descend 2,000 feet. Even then, their difficulties were not over. In their enthusiasm the porters had cleared the camp of all cooking equipment. They were forced to make do on an improvised 'ice cream' mixture made from a combination of strawberry jam, condensed milk and snow.

Exhaustion and oxygen deprivation were taking their toll. Mallory afterwards dimly remembered congratulating Morshead on safely overcoming the ordeal, but persistently calling him 'Longstaff':

> I had already transposed the names several times, and he now protested; but it made no difference, as I could remember no other. 'Longstaff' became an *idée fixe* though the entity of Morshead remained unconfused − I did not, for instance, give him Longstaff's beard − he was fixedly Longstaff until the following morning.[6]

(Such irrationality is a typical symptom of oxygen deprivation; Smythe in 1933 chatted happily to a friendly companion, even at one point offering him a sandwich, when all the while the 'companion', if not the sandwich, was an altitude-induced hallucination. It was Smythe, too, who observed − in days before flying saucers − curious round dark objects hovering above the ridge of Everest, objects which became known to his unsympathetic companions as 'Frank's pulsating teapots'.)

At the highest point reached by this first party Mallory's aneroid registered 26,800 feet; it was later 'measured' by theodolite at 26,985 feet, and it is this second figure that has entered the history books. But on the next Everest expedition, that of 1924, Norton sent home a sketch of the mountain with various locations noted on it. On it, he shows the 1924 Camp VI as higher (and slightly more to the east) than the highest point reached by Mallory, Somervell and himself in 1922, yet believes it to be under 27,000 feet and comments: 'so I guess we took the wrong point with the theodolite last year.' They were still more than a mile from the summit horizontally, and a little over 2,000 feet below it in vertical height.

In the expedition report Mallory answers the unspoken question of why they turned back when they did. This is always a sensitive issue with climbers because of the implicit suggestion of having given up too soon. But Mallory's is a sensible answer, and he is forthright in bringing the subject up. He will not be so forthright the next time he makes an unsuccessful attempt without oxygen.

Instead, keeping his own counsel, he will spin on his heel and shoot back down the mountain in his rush to regroup with the controversial gas.

And if we were not to reach the summit, what remained for us to do? None of us, I believe, cared much about any lower objective. We were not greatly interested then in the exact number of feet by which we should beat a record. It must be remembered that the mind is not easily interested under such conditions. The intelligence is gradually numbed as the supply of oxygen diminishes and the body comes nearer to exhaustion.

Looking back on my own mental processes as we approached twenty-seven thousand feet, I can find no traces of insanity, nothing completely illogical; within a small compass I was able to reason, no doubt very slowly. But my reasoning was concerned with only one idea; beyond its range I can recall no thought. The view, for instance – and as a rule I'm keen enough about the view – did not interest me; I was not 'taking notice'. Wonderful as such an experience would be, I had not even the desire to look over the North-east Ridge; I would have gladly got to the North-east Shoulder as being the sort of place one ought to reach, but I had no strong desire to get there, and none at all for the wonder of being there. I dare say the others were more mentally alive than I; but when it came to deciding what we should do, we had no lively discussion. It seemed to me that we should get back to Morshead in time to take him down this same day to Camp IV. There was some sense in this idea, and many mountaineers may think we were right to make it a first consideration. But the alternative of sleeping a second night at our highest camp and returning the next day to Camp III was never mentioned. It may have been that we shrank unconsciously from another night in such discomfort; whether the thought was avoided in this way, or simply was not born, our minds were not behaving as we would wish them to behave. The idea of reaching Camp IV with Morshead before dark, once it had been accepted, controlled us altogether.[7]

The descent off the North Col the next morning took far longer than expected. Partly because of the effort of cutting steps under a hot sun, but also because all four were now suffering severely from dehydration, it took four hours instead of one. At the bottom of the

109

slopes they met relief in the form of Finch, Geoffrey Bruce and Wakefield coming towards them with oxygen cylinders on their backs and proffering two thermos flasks of tea, which they thankfully gulped down.

Leaving Wakefield to escort the tired men safely down to Camp III, Finch and Bruce continued upwards, testing their performance with oxygen. Mallory was surprised to see Finch so full of vigour. When he had last heard of him before they had set off for their attempt, Finch was 'in bed with dysentery at Base Camp'.

Finch was soon ready to make his oxygen attempt on the summit. With Geoffrey Bruce and the Gurkha, Tejbir, he left the North Col camp on 25 May at 9.30 a.m., an hour and a half after their ten porters who were not using oxygen. They caught them up at 11 a.m. at an altitude of 24,500 feet when, after three hours of climbing, the tired porters had stopped to rest. Finch:

> A moment's calculation will show that we had been climbing at the rate of 1,000 feet per hour. Leaving the porters to follow, we eventually gained an altitude of 25,500 feet, where, owing to bad weather, we were constrained to camp. It was not until two o'clock in the afternoon that the porters rejoined us, despite the fact that our progress had been hindered by the necessity for much step-cutting.[8]

Dumping their loads, the porters were happy to scurry down to the relative safety of the North Col, leaving the three climbers huddled in their little tent on the crest of the ridge (500 feet higher than the Camp V of the previous party). Before long a fierce storm began to blow outside and a fine dusting of snow penetrated the pores of the tent fabric, covering everything.

There was to be no sleep for them that night. As the storm rose to a hurricane, they were obliged to remain on constant guard to hold down the ground sheet and prevent the wind getting underneath. 'We knew', said Finch, 'that once the wind got a hold upon it, the tent would belly out like a sail, and nothing would save it from stripping away from its moorings and being blown, with us inside, over the precipices on to the East Rongbuk glacier.' They took it in turns to go outside in any lulls in the storm to try and patch up the damage to the tent. Three of the guylines snapped 'with pistol-like reports' and later a slab of rock struck the tent and ripped a huge hole in its windward side.

The storm kept them pinned down for most of the next day. The tent was becoming decidedly tattered and it was no longer possible to fasten the door. When the wind finally blew itself out in the afternoon, they decided against retreating to the Col but to stay put a further night and make an early start up the mountain the following morning. Their main concern now was that they were running short of food. They had been told by 'a certain fashionable gentleman'[9] that it would be impossible to eat much at altitude, and consequently brought with them the skimpiest of rations. The altitude had not had the slightest effect on their appetites; they were ravenous. 'It was a pity one of the scientists could not have been up there with us,' Finch used to say afterwards, 'and the fatter the better, because we would have eaten him!'

Late in the afternoon they were surprised to hear voices outside and found to their delight that six porters had climbed up from the North Col to bring them thermos flasks of warm tea. It was a rescue mission, for the men had hoped to escort the three climbers back that night and took a lot of persuading to return without them.

Despite their contrived good humour throughout their stay in their high camp, spirits flagged disastrously as the cold began to seep into their limbs during the second night. They were very tired by this time and weak through lack of food. Suddenly Finch remembered the oxygen. He hauled one of the sets into the tent, fiddled with its control valves and quickly had a flow going. They passed the mouthpiece around, taking doses in turns and treating the matter very much as a joke. 'Tejbir took his medicine without much interest,' Finch wrote, 'but his face soon brightened up. The drawn, anxious look on Bruce's face gave place to his usual one. In my own case, I felt the painful, pricking, tingling sensation due to the fact that my blood was beginning to circulate again, restoring warmth to my half-frozen limbs.'[10] Finch connected up the apparatus in a way that they could all breathe a small quantity during the night and he was convinced it was this that saved their lives.

At six o'clock the next morning, the three men, suffering acutely from hunger, set off from their high camp along the ridge towards the shoulder. Finch and Bruce were each carrying loads of more than 40 lbs, Tejbir nearer 50 lbs. The plan was for Tejbir to stay with them as far as the shoulder where they would relieve him of his load and send him back, but he had not gone more than 500 feet before he collapsed and they had some difficulty in reviving him. Obviously he could go no further, so they left him with sufficient oxygen to see him back to camp, and continued without him. It was a dismissal for which Finch was later roundly criticized. At a height of 26,500 feet they were forced to leave the ridge on account of the violent and penetratingly cold wind:

> The thousand feet from our camp up to this point had occupied one and a half hours, some twenty minutes of which had been employed in re-arranging the loads when Tejbir's broke down. Our rate of progress, therefore, had been 900 feet per hour.[11]

Forced on to the face, they gained little in altitude, but steadily made horizontal distance across the difficult, slabby ground, upon which lay considerable quantities of fresh snow. When about half-way across the face, they struck upwards once more in an endeavour to regain the summit ridge, but had not gone far when Geoffrey Bruce caught his oxygen apparatus against a rock and broke one of the pieces of glass tubing. One of the direst warnings of the scientists had been that if the supply were suddenly cut off from a climber employing oxygen at high altitude, death would be the fairly instantaneous result:

> I had just reached a ledge at the top of a steep slab . . . when I heard Geoffrey Bruce give a startled cry: 'I'm getting no oxygen!' Turning round immediately, I saw him struggling ineffectually to climb up towards me. Quickly descending the few intervening feet, I was just in time to grasp his right shoulder with my left hand as he was on the point of falling backwards over the precipice. I dragged him face forwards against the rock, and, after a supreme effort on the part of both, we gained the ledge where I swung him round into a sitting position against the slope above.[12]

Finch passed his oxygen tube to Bruce and endeavoured to locate the fault. When he, too, began to feel the effects of oxygen deprivation, he contrived a T-piece connection which enabled them both to breathe oxygen simultaneously from his apparatus, and was thus able to find the broken glass connecting-piece in Bruce's set and replace it. Resupplied with their own systems the two men continued after a short rest, with Finch keeping a watchful eye on Bruce's condition:

Now I saw that Geoffrey Bruce, like Tejbir, had driven his body almost to the uttermost. A little more would spell break-down. The realisation came like a blow. My emotions are eternally my own, and I will not put on paper a cold-blooded, psychological analysis of the cataclysmic change they under-went, but will merely indicate the initial and final mental positions. Reasoned determination, confidence, faith in the possibility of achievement, hope − all had acquired cumulative force as we made our way higher and higher; the two nights' struggle at our high camp had not dimmed our enthusiasm, nor had the collapse of Tejbir, rude shock and source of grave anxiety though it undoubtedly was. Never for a moment did I think we would fail; progress was steady, the summit was there before us; a little longer, and we should be on the top. And then − suddenly, unexpectedly, the vision was gone.[13]

Finch realised they had only one hope left, to turn back and lose height rapidly. At Camp V they spotted porters on their way up and committed Tejbir into their care, while they continued down, reaching the North Col Camp at 4 p.m. Exhausted, they would have preferred to stop there, but since Crawford and Wakefield were in occupation for one night, they were compelled after a quick snack to keep going downwards to Camp III. Captain Noel, who had been in support on the col for the four days of their attempt, came with them now, shepherding them safely down the steep snow and ice slopes. They arrived, in Finch's words, 'dead, dead beat':

Since midday, from our highest point we had descended over six thousand feet, but we were quite finished. The brightest memory that remains with me of that night is dinner. Four quails truffled in *pâté de foie gras*, followed by nine sausages, only left me asking for more. With the remains of a tin of toffee tucked away in the crook of my elbow, I fell asleep in the depths of my warm sleeping bag.[14]

They had reached a vertical height some 500 feet above that achieved by the first party, but not without cost. Bruce's feet, particularly the left one, were badly frostbitten. All the same, Finch was satisfied that the advantages they had derived from the oxygen apparatus far outweighed any disadvantage in its weight. He felt certain that on any further attempt on Everest, oxygen would form a most important part of the climber's equipment. The benefit was no longer merely theoretical. He had demonstrably proved its value with his climb, and General Bruce, who had been fearful initially, was now sufficiently impressed to endorse the use of the controversial gas. The General was further convinced that if Finch and Geoffrey Bruce had not been forced to traverse out across the face of the mountain, but had been able to continue directly up the ridge:

> . . . they would undoubtedly have reached the point on the main Everest crest which is marked at 27,390 and have progressed along it to a greater altitude. There is no doubt in my mind whatever of this: not only would their route have been far more direct, but the actual ground over which they would have to climb would have been easier. It is quite certain that with the same exertions on the same day they could have reached a higher point than they did. That does not, however, in the least detract from their performance. [15]

Finch slept for fourteen hours after his ordeal and, when he awoke, was 'still too done in to walk at first'. Geoffrey Bruce was in an even worse state, and the pair of them were dragged on a sledge by four porters down the glacier. They spent that night at Camp I, still catching up on their eating and sleeping, and from there the next morning Finch managed to stagger on under his own steam ('tottering along like a centenarian'), although Bruce still needed to be carried. They arrived in Base Camp in time for lunch and there spent the next four days recuperating.

*

Base Camp was a dismal place, with everyone very fractious. The older climbers, considering the effort over, were happy to be winding up affairs, but there were bitter regrets among some of the younger ones about having to return with no positive success. Their despondency was only exacerbated by the fact that weather prospects appeared good. It was then that Mallory began to nurture the idea of going up for one last try. He slipped away from camp to write to Ruth, knowing she would be unhappy for him to put himself at risk once safely out of it, but desperately needing her accord. 'You will feel chiefly as I do,' he asserts hopefully, 'that it would have been unbearable for me to be left out.' In higher camps, he assured her, he would be thinking of her whenever important decisions needed taking. 'Dear love, believe that I will never forget the beautiful way you have behaved about this adventure.'[16]

But much as he tries to bring comfort to Ruth by glossing over possible dangers, he is not himself under any illusions, and to David Pye confides: 'It's an infernal mountain, cold and treacherous. Frankly the game is not good enough: the risks of getting caught are too great; the margin of strength when men are at great heights is too small. Perhaps it's mere folly to go up again. But how can I be out of the hunt?'[17]

It was while he was resting in his tent on 2 June that Finch first got wind of what was afoot. 'Heard a pretty little plot concocted in tent next to mine,' he noted in his diary. It was proposed that Dr Wakefield would examine Mallory, Somervell and Finch and pronounce them all fit for another attempt, using oxygen, and with Finch in command. Finch knew he was still far from recovered – indeed he seemed to be declining in strength, if anything. The others at least had the advantage of 10 days' rest since they descended – but he, too, could not shake off a sense of failure at his earlier defeat, and needed little persuading to subscribe to this third attempt.

On 3 June the three climbers set off once more up the glacier, supported by Wakefield and Crawford, but by the time they reached Camp I, Finch could see he was deluding himself. He had not the strength to go on. A heavy snowfall in the night signalled the arrival of the monsoon, and that clinched it for him. He gave Somervell a last-minute briefing on the oxygen and retreated to Base, where he was able to join the departing party of Longstaff, Morshead and Strutt.

For Finch, that was the end of his struggle with Everest. The others continued – to disaster. The party was caught in an avalanche on the slopes of the North Col and seven of their porters were killed. Somervell, Mallory and Crawford were leading 14 porters on four ropes up through new snow when they were all swept away. The last two ropes, nine men in all, were swept over ice cliffs of some 40 to 60 ft high, and of these, only two survived. Those on the other ropes were carried down some 200 feet but were able to free themselves without difficulty once the snow-slide came to a halt. Captain Noel, who had been following up behind with his bulky cameras, had turned back some time before finding the soft snow heavy going. At the time of the accident, he was having a meal in Camp III with Wakefield. Every five minutes or so the two men would glance up to watch the climbers making their slow progress up the slopes. Suddenly, there were no longer any black figures on the snow cliff. It took a few seconds to register what had happened. Then, horror-stricken, the two men rounded up all available porters and set off at a run across the glacier with blankets and warm drinks, not knowing what they would find.

When they arrived among the tumbled debris at the foot of the col they could see no one. Then they caught sight of some huddled figures up on the cliffside, squatting at the edge of a sheer drop, too frightened to move. Climbing higher, they heard voices, and found Mallory, Somervell and Crawford digging frantically with their ice axes into the loose snow that choked an enormous crevasse. Several men had been killed by the force of the fall. Bodies were lying on the ground, and a climbing rope disappeared ominously into the snow within the crevasse. Noel and Wakefield immediately lent a hand. One man, Narbu, had already been pulled out dead, four oxygen cylinders still tied to his back. When they reached the second, Angtarkay, he was unconscious but miraculously still breathing. Another man, buried deeper in the snow, was extricated but he too was dead, and the rope from his waist led still deeper into the packed snow. At its end yet another must lie buried, they knew, but despite all efforts it proved impossible to reach him. At the request of the surviving Sherpas, all seven dead – their friends and brothers – were left in the snow where they had died.

It was a dejected party that trailed back down the mountain, the expedition at an abrupt end. Somervell later confessed that the single thought gnawing at his brain as he made his sad way back was, 'Only Sherpas and Bhotias killed – why, oh why could not one of us Britishers have shared their fate?'[18] He felt he would gladly have been lying dead in the snow to demonstrate that the sahibs shared in their loss.

Yet the burden of responsibility lay with Mallory – as he well knew. He went over and over the sequence of events to see if there were any clues he had missed that could have foretold the tragedy. On 9 June he wrote a long letter to Ruth ('I will answer what I imagine to have been your first thought: it was a wonderful escape for me, and we may indeed be thankful for that together. Dear love, when I think what your grief would have been I humbly thank God I'm alive'.[19]) Two days later he prepared an official report for Sir Francis Younghusband. He also wrote, climber-to-climber, to Strutt, hoping he might be able to forestall any accusation that it was the result of recklessness. More intimately and at length he described the accident to Geoffrey Young; and not for the first time longed for Geoffrey's consoling presence:

I'm quite knocked out by this accident. Seven of these brave men killed, and they were ignorant of mountain dangers, like children in our care. And I'm to blame, so you wouldn't expect much sense. But I want to tell you something about it.

I suppose the whole plan of making another attempt once the first burst of the monsoon had brought heavy snow is open to criticism. Actually we left this camp [Base] on the 3rd with the clouds still threatening. The snow came on the following night and day and during the long day we spent at Camp I I thought out my position. Of course if we had come back saying that the snow made Everest impracticable and that now the monsoon had come it was time to go home — no one would have said a word against our decision. But it seemed to me not unreasonable to expect a break of fine weather, as there was last year, before the monsoon set in continuously and that in some balance between the old fierce west wind and the monsoon current we should have a calm day and our chance at last; at all events the proper ending would be to be turned back by some definite danger or difficulty on the mountain, or, to be beaten by height as before — I have little doubt besides that using oxygen and given the opportunity, Somervell and I would have reached the top — for whatever that performance might be worth.

On the 5th we went up in clouds and intermittent snow to Camp III, and the 6th all rested there in glorious warmth and sunshine. As you may remember a steep slope has to be crossed below the shelf on which our North Col Camp is established: but the snow solidifies with wonderful rapidity and I reckoned that with fine weather it would probably be safe to cross it on the 8th. Meanwhile we could establish tracks so far and get the hard work done. The first part of the ascent had previously been a steep ice-slope; when we started up on the 7th it provided a test of the snow — and the snow was binding so well that we made new tracks up it without cutting steps (about 10.30 a.m., so that the slope had had 5 hours sun). Above, the slopes are comparatively gentle and except in one place where a dozen steps had to be cut we had previously found good snow. The

117

new snow was up to our knees, but binding well, not a powdery substance. No one of us three had an inkling of danger or the thought of an avalanche on such easy slopes. The avalanche started from under some ice cliffs not far above us on the left, it was not of the sort that peels a whole slope; looking at the debris afterwards I conjectured that the snow under the cliffs had had less sun and remained powdery; at all events it was lying at a steeper angle and had sufficient weight to push down the lower snow; but the whole slide was only about 200 feet on the average — a very small affair to have such fatal consequences; the trouble was the ice cliff below and the fall of from 40 feet to 60 feet must have killed most of the men at once.

Thinking it all out with the wisdom after the event I come back simply to my ignorance, generalisations on too little observation and the lifetime it requires to know all about it. But I also remember Donald Robertson and the great sleeping ones that have but to stir in their slumber. And perhaps you'll remember that for me. At all events you won't believe we were pushing recklessly on; and the story I think does not accuse us of being careless of coolies' lives; we three were in front to take turn in making the track.

The bitterness is partly in the irony of fate. Somervell and I had had experience enough of Mount Everest to feel that one must take no chances with that mountain. I was never so resolved to be careful and half our talk had been how to ensure the safety of the coolies — perhaps you don't realise that in Finch's show they had been going up and down unconducted and unroped — a party of them actually arriving among the crevasses of the North Col in that state at 11 p.m., and perhaps we were a little consciously virtuous in condemning this example and resolving to arrange otherwise.

Do you know that sickening feeling that one can't go back and have it undone and that nothing will make good?

I don't much care what the world says, but I care very much what you and a few others think . . . I shall be home before the end of August. I shan't feel much like showing my face but I would like to see yours before too long.[20]

General Bruce was also desolated by the loss of so many fine porters. He had the unenviable task of arranging compensation for their families before leaving for home. He kept out of the public debate but admitted privately that the accident ought never to have happened and if Finch had been a fit man, it would not have done. 'There wasn't the least necessity to risk men's lives, let alone their own, to recover a few tents from the North Col . . . above the col was in a complete smother of snow.'[21] To Bruce, it was not only a tragic ending to the expedition, it was an especially humiliating one, for he considered what had led to its outcome 'to have been entirely unnecessary'.

X

Casting Asparagus

Leaving the expedition ahead of the main party, Finch, Strutt and Longstaff knew nothing about the fate of the third attempt and the loss of the seven porters until they reached Dover some six weeks later and read about it in the Sunday newspapers.

The news hit them hard. Longstaff, in particular, felt the blow keenly. In many ways the expedition had been a disappointing time for him, for he had not stood the altitude at all well, which was perhaps surprising for a man who even then held the record for the highest peak ever climbed. Twice he had been laid low by a 'flu-like condition, which left him so weak at one stage that he had to be carried down to Base Camp on the back of one of the porters. ('Oh the disgrace of it!' he had mourned.) As expedition doctor, Longstaff became extremely anxious whenever he felt climbers were taking unreasonable risks, and he was shocked at the level of risk the younger men seemed prepared to take. On 28 May, after Finch and Geoffrey Bruce had returned from their attempt, frostbitten but otherwise safe, he had noted in his diary, 'Must put my foot down: there is too little margin of safety. Strutt agrees.'[1]

He began putting his resolution into effect the following day when he examined Norton and Mallory and issued General Bruce with a written report to say they were both unfit for further attempts. Finch he looked at on 2 June. His heart was enlarged from effort, its apex beat very indistinct, and in Longstaff's opinion, it was going to need at least a fortnight to recover. Longstaff told his patient, by way of consolation, that Mallory's condition was even worse. His heart was exhibiting a worrying 'thrill' and his fingers were all frostbitten.

120

Somervell alone appeared unaffected. With some amazement, Longstaff remarked that he seemed 'physically incapable of exhibiting the symptoms appropriate to his physiological environment'. Apart from a few superficial frost-bites on his fingers, he bore no trace of exhaustion.

Longstaff handed Bruce a second statement declaring that neither Finch nor Geoffrey Bruce were fit for further action. It seemed important to Longstaff that these diagnoses were preserved in writing for he did not want anyone afterwards, unaware of the true position, accusing his companions of faint-heartedness. He received little thanks for his pains, however, since the climbers themselves were not yet prepared to admit defeat. 'Luckily, neither Morshead, Norton, nor Geoffrey Bruce could walk, so they were in my power,' he remarked ruefully. 'But Mallory and Finch persisted in joining Somervell in the last attempt.'[2]

When the 'pretty little plot' was hatched for Wakefield to re-examine Mallory and Finch and find them fit enough to launch a final bid, Longstaff had justifiable reason to be concerned for their health and safety. More than that, he could not restrain a feeling of bitterness that his authority was being so openly challenged. There was obvious friction in the camp. Mallory wrote home to his wife, 'Longstaff . . . is in one of his moods of bustling activity, when he becomes tiresome, interfering and self-important.'[3]

In happier days, when the team had first come together at the start of the expedition, Longstaff had jocularly announced to the company: 'I want to make one thing clear. I am the expedition's official medical officer. And I am, as a matter of fact, a qualified doctor, but I feel it my duty now to remind you that I have never practised in my life. I beg you in no circumstances to seek my professional advice, since it would almost certainly turn out to be wrong. I am however willing if necessary to sign a certificate of death.'[4] Little had he expected his words to be taken so literally, but here were Wakefield and Somervell colluding to override his diagnoses. It was obvious there were too many doctors on this expedition. Longstaff gave up all hope of dissuading the climbers from their purpose. Instead, he concentrated all his energies on Morshead, whose frostbite injuries were giving serious cause for alarm. Both his hands and feet were so badly affected that it was plain he must lose several digits. He was in constant pain and no opiates brought any relief. Although he strove bravely to put on a cheerful face, Somervell, for one, noticed how, whenever he could, Morshead would slip away by himself and cry

121

like a child. The longer he waited for proper medical treatment, the worse the permanent damage would be. It was clear that some surgery would soon be required; nobody relished the idea this should be undertaken at Base Camp or on the journey home. Bruce readily agreed that Longstaff should escort Morshead back to India by the shortest route.

They left on 5 June, and in the prevailing atmosphere of disagreement and suspicion it would have been with considerable relief that Longstaff shook the dust of Base Camp from his boots. Strutt and Finch took the opportunity to come away at the same time. Strutt had spent nearly a fortnight at or above 21,000 feet and was showing marked deterioration, with loss of weight and increased tetchiness. Finch, as Longstaff had predicted, really had been quite unfit for that final move up the mountain. He was now totally played out.

When he looked back at Everest the following day and saw it covered from head to foot in fresh snow, Longstaff noted in his diary: 'Everest a snow peak. Will take 3–5 days' sun to clear. Impossible now.'[5] That, he hoped, would put an end to any thought of further attempts — whatever the ambitions of some of the climbers. It was a lighthearted party that trotted back through Tibet and Sikkim in record time, savouring the reappearance of vegetation and creature comforts, all lingering anxiety evaporated away. Morshead was placed in safe hands, and Strutt cabled Hinks from Darjeeling:

22.6.22 SITUATION UP TO JUNE 6 AS FOLLOWS. MAY 21 PARTY WITHOUT OXYGEN ATTAINED APPROXIMATELY 26,800 FT. MAY 27 DIFFERENT PARTY WITH OXYGEN REACHED ABOUT 27,300. WEATHER BAD BOTH ATTEMPTS. BOTH PARTIES MORE OR LESS FROSTBITTEN, DOING WELL. ANOTHER ATTEMPT [WAS] TO BE MADE BETWEEN JUNE 6 AND 14. MONSOON BROKE JUNE 3. LONGSTAFF, FINCH AND SELF RETURNING ENGLAND IMMEDIATELY. REST OF PARTY PROCEEDING KHARTA VALLEY JUNE 14 TO RECUPERATE BEFORE HOMEWARD JOURNEY. LONGSTAFF CONSIDERS WHOLE PARTY PLAYED OUT. STRUTT.[6]

What a shock then to arrive back in England on 16 July, on the very day that the news of the avalanche disaster reached there. Longstaff's first reaction was one of anger, and though he still blamed Mallory and Somervell for contriving to make the third attempt possible, the real force of his wrath he now vented on Hinks, who from the isolation and security of his office in the Royal Geographical Society had continually pressed the General for better results.[7]

When Hinks received Strutt's cable he wrote immediately to Bruce: 'If Mallory and Somervell could climb Makalu, that would give the news a welcome fillip.' That we must assume was Hinks's little joke; he was certainly not at all amused by the early return of the three climbers. To him it smacked of desertion, particularly in the case of Strutt. As Bruce's Second in Command and Climbing Leader, Strutt, he considered, should have stayed at his post until all climbing was over.

Longstaff firmly believed that it was Hinks's unreasonable expectations that had forced the General into the ignominious position in which he now found himself. The fact that his leadership and organization had in all other respects been superlative and his arrangements worked like clockwork, that through the sheer force of his personality, relations with local *dzongpens* were now excellent, and that the party itself had been basically a cohesive and happy one — all these aspects, Longstaff felt, had been undermined and called into disrepute by the tragic folly of the third attempt.

Hinks called a Special Meeting of the Everest Committee on 17 July to hear the reports of the three who had returned. (No time was lost — they had landed in England only the day before.) It was a frosty session. Younghusband, as Chairman, welcomed them home and congratulated Finch on his record climb, but all three climbers had the feeling of being on trial. Longstaff afterwards wrote to his friend, Wollaston (who was a member of the Committee), to explain that the reason the meeting was so edgy was because they all three felt that the Committee ('which probably means HINKS') had consistently treated Bruce meanly. By not appreciating his difficulties, and by 'quite unnecessarily and most ungenerously' urging him to repeated attacks on the peak, they had been landed with an accident that made them all feel horribly humiliated.

According to Longstaff, Hinks had written 'a somewhat ungenerous and extremely rude letter to Strutt in which he cast asparagus at both of us for returning', and that while on the expedition, either Bruce or himself had received an unpleasant letter from Hinks or Younghusband by pretty well every post:

We had only just heard of the accident the day before and were furious. They groused about Bruce not writing enough tosh for

123

the papers – he can't do that well I admit – and yet almost *every* statement they themselves gave to the Press contained the most absurd lies. All three of us 'had it in' for Hinks and Y-H. We have no grouse against anybody else.

Bruce was a splendid leader. His organisation was perfect. He worked hard. We were a mixed party of 13 and thanks to Bruce there was never a hot word amongst us the whole time. When things looked like heading towards peevishness Charlie always turned it into a laugh by some ready silly wheeze. He really carried out his instructions to the utmost, even when such were against his own far better judgement. You know more or less what stores were sent out; we required 350 transport animals. He delivered every single scrap at the Base Camp on May 1st. You and I expected most of it to remain at Darjeeling or Phari. Of course Geoffrey Bruce and John Morris did the driving work, but it was Charlie Bruce's organisation.

In the same letter, Longstaff gave his impressions of the rest of the team and his own assessment of the causes of the avalanche tragedy:

Mallory is a very good stout hearted baby, but quite unfit to be placed in charge of anything, including himself. Somervell is the most urbanely conceited youth I have ever struck – and quite the toughest. He was very politely scornful of our refusing to countenance the German–alpine, forlorn–hope, success-at-any-cost, death–don't–matter, stunt. He was honestly prepared to chuck his life away on the most remote chance of success. Wakefield could not face the altitude at all – rather worse than I was, and is ignorant of the arts of mountaineering.

Norton was a huge success in every direction. Fine eye for country. Sound climber. Bird man. Plants. Always on for *any* job and always did the job well. He got down Morshead alive. Latter most plucky: suffered abominably: 2 grains of opium would not make him sleep at night from pain. But you will realise that the cause of frostbite is carelessness or ignorance or both. We so dreaded Finch that we were relieved to find his manners very passable: his temper agreeable: his mountain knowledge not overrated. He had *very* bad luck on his climb. With any reasonable conditions he would have stood on the final ridge. With luck he would have got to the top. But he is very Australian: he must have made a great effort to be nice to us!!

As to the accident that is due (1) to Charlie not prohibiting a third attempt, as Strutt and I urged him, and as he wished to do, because of the continuous urgings of Hinks and Y-H. (2) to the absence of knowledge of snowcraft on the part of Mallory and Somervell. I should not be surprised to find that old Crawford tried to dissuade 'em. Mallory cannot even observe the conditions in front of him. To attempt such a passage in the Himalaya after new snow is idiotic. What the hell did they think they could do *on Everest* in such conditions even if they did get up to the North Col. Route above is slabby with strata the wrong way, and most dangerous after new snow. Bruce had warned 'em rather to sacrifice equipment at Camps IV and V than to risk men's lives bringing it down. By their ignorance and unwillingness to take advice Mallory and Somervell have brought discredit on old Bruce — and that's why we were so savage the other day.[8]

Longstaff went on to say that he was proposing Finch for membership of the Alpine Club. 'If they pill him I shan't rage: nor will Strutt. But I shall try and get him in, tho' I think it would be unwise for me to canvass widely.' Strutt, on their long shared journey home, had obviously lost all trace of the reservations he had held about Finch at the start of the expedition. Bruce still needed some convincing, but he too eventually added his weight to Longstaff's proposal. Farrar, of course, had long been a champion of Finch, so all told, the proposal came with the strongest of recommendations. There *was* an attempt to 'pill' Finch by a faction who disliked his connections with the Anglo-Swiss Club, but this was thwarted when he got wind of it by Sir Douglas Freshfield. Finch was duly elected a member of the Alpine Club. But it was not long before there were some bitter regrets — certainly on the part of Bruce.

★

The end of any failed expedition is always a time for general recrimination, the more especially when there is loss of life. As the climbers straggled home, it became apparent that Longstaff was not alone in blaming Mallory and Somervell for the avalanche accident. Hinks wrote to Norman Collie (Alpine Club President) on 19 July:

The returning people at present are disposed to say nasty things

— about Howard-Bury last year and Mallory this year. Wakefield was a complete failure. I think they are all cross and jumpy like the people who came back last year and want handling carefully.[9]

Again on 21 July:

All who have come back think *Mallory's* judgement in purely alpine matters was bad and inferior to Norton of whom everyone speaks very highly. They evidently had sharp disagreements about the appropriate way to ascend the North Col, Finch going a different way from Mallory.[10]

Collie had no quarrel with this; he already had a very high opinion of Finch's mountaincraft, and to him Mallory's choice of route on the fateful day was totally wrong. 'To *traverse* snow slopes is always dangerous,' he said, 'and the best way is always to go *straight up*. It looks as if they zigzagged up. Evidently Mt. Everest is not a mountain to be monkeyed with, and it will need a very experienced mountaineer to guide a very hardy young climber to finally get to the top.'[11] (This idea of partnering an older, wiser man with a youthful vigorous one is especially interesting, and was to recur ever more frequently in debate.)

Strutt, on receiving Mallory's letter about the accident, had told him,

I am awfully sorry for you, and I know well how much you are feeling this disaster . . . I will not criticise from a distance. When Longstaff, Finch, and I read Charlie's account in the paper, going up to London from Dover, I remarked, 'We never saw an avalanche on the mountain, and Mallory therefore concluded that the snow evaporated instead of sliding' . . . I will add, if you will allow me, that after the great fall of fresh snow, seventeen persons on the North Col was fifteen too many, even after *two* days' perfect weather. Don't think that these are criticisms; the man on the spot must be the sole judge, and he gets the reward or pays the penalty.[12]

Geoffrey Young told Mallory to put it *entirely* from his mind 'that anyone has ever thought of placing any responsibility for the accident on you or the mountaineers.'

In this case, I have no doubt. You made all the allowance for the safety of your party that your experience suggested . . . The immense percentage of 'chance', or we may call it of the 'unknown', present still in this hitherto unattempted region of mountaineering, turned for once against you. Well? What then? You took your full share, a leading share, in the risk. In the war we had to do worse: we had to *order* men into danger at times when we could not share it. And surely we learned then that to take on ourselves afterwards the responsibility for their deaths, to debate with ourselves the 'might-have-beens', was the road to madness.[13]

Younghusband, too, told Mallory, 'However much you may blame yourself, I certainly am not one to blame you, for I have done precisely the same thing myself in the Himalaya, and only the purest luck can have saved me and my party from disaster.'[14]

Bruce had never been happy about the third attempt. 'By way of prophecy,' he had written on 1 June, 'I do not expect it to do better than the previous two. The flower of the men's condition must have gone, also the weather has distinctly got rougher, and when it's rough on Everest, it really is rough, and one full exposure to it is enough to sap anyone's strength for a very long time.'[15] Now, of course, he deeply regretted having given it his reluctant blessing, but he, too, was not one of those to blame Mallory (and Somervell) for what happened. On the contrary, in the confidential report he wrote to Hinks on his team (4 July) they both come out fairly well, although he could not resist making play with Somervell's big-headedness and Mallory's scatterbrain:

SOMERVELL — Stands by himself from the point of view of the Himalaya in his capacity as an absolute glutton for hard work, not so much that he is better on any particular day as for his extraordinary capacity for going day after day. He is a wonderful goer and climber. He takes a size 22 hat, that is his only drawback.

MALLORY — Second to Somervell in going capacity. Genuinely anxious to look after all his men. Everything else you know all about him. He is a great dear but forgets his boots on all occasions.

NORTON — The great success of the expedition. Is a first rate all round mountaineer, and full of every sort of interest. Is recovering now but was very overdone.

MORSHEAD — A first rate goer, absolutely unselfish. Just the man for this sort of expedition, irrespective of his professional qualifications.

FINCH — Probably the best snow and ice man on the expedition, but has a curious constitution. On his day can probably last as well as any man, but apparently very soon shoots his bolt. I should say not a very robust man for a long strain and has a delicate inside. Is extraordinarily handy in all kinds of ways outside his scientific accomplishments. A convincing raconteur of quite impossible experiences. Cleans his teeth on February 1st and has a bath the same day if the water is very hot, otherwise puts it off until next year. Six months' course as a lama novice in a monastery would enable one to occupy a Whymper tent with him.

CRAWFORD — Very good technical climber. Came as a transport officer at which he was entirely useless. Very cheerful. Does not stand very great height well. I freely acknowledge this is my blob.

WAKEFIELD — A noble and worthy old gentleman. Assistant doctor. Came as a climber. Does not stand great heights well. A complete passenger. Please note that this is the Committee's blob. Dear old thing for all that though I'll never forgive him for breaking the drums of both my ears.

NOEL — Stupor mundi. St. Noel of the Cameras. He is an R.C. Please approach the mountaineering Pope for his beatification during lifetime.

G. BRUCE/MORRIS — Shan't say anything about these two till I get back and have your private ear. As both the damn things would blush.

Good old T.L[ongstaff] and Strutt were naturally first class at their jobs. Strutt is a first class mountaineer in judgement and I wish to goodness he had had command of the last party which went up. I hope you will get both of them and have a good talk.[16]

In an earlier bulletin, Bruce had reported to Hinks that Strutt was 'fed up to the world' and 'it may possibly be that we are a little too young for him — still his mountaineering judgement is excellent and he has been of great use in moderating the views of the extreme pushers and the highbrows.'[17]

As can be seen, Bruce's boisterous sense of humour is never far below the surface. He is every bit as convincing a raconteur of tall stories as he claims of Finch. Reading his letters and reports now is a joy, but they proved a trial for Hinks who preferred the more businesslike accounts of Howard-Bury or, later, Norton. On 10 April 1922, Hinks had commented to Mrs Bruce, 'I have a most cheerful letter from your husband . . . it ends up with the statement that he is going to sleep in a palanquin for the first week, but does not say whether the palanquin is going to be carried over the Jela Pass with him in it. I fear that he sometimes allows his good spirits to mystify us.'[18]

It will be seen that jokes at Finch's expense were still, in Bruce's book, fair game despite his finding him 'an extraordinarily handy and accomplished person'. An interesting thing about Bruce's scurrilous remark regarding Finch's personal hygiene is its similarity to an anecdote Finch himself would regularly retail in his lectures, which makes one suppose they were both embroidering for their own use a joke heard somewhere else. Finch would warn his audiences that if they ever wanted to speak to a Tibetan, they should be careful to stand on the windward side of him. A very noble Tibetan had told him once that he had two baths, one at his birth and one on his wedding day. 'Having neglected to stand on his windward side,' Finch would continue gravely, 'I had great difficulty in believing him. Of course, in the case of priests, you should be careful there is a very strong wind — you see priests or lamas don't marry.'[19]

*

With the return of the main party, the business of evaluating all its experience began. Bruce was most anxious that momentum should not be lost, especially since the Tibetans were so friendly. You never knew with the delicate politics of High Asia how long such a state of affairs would last. It was generally felt, however, that there was too little time remaining to put together a new attempt for 1923. All energies should be directed instead towards a major enterprise in the spring of 1924.

129

There were four aspects in particular that were going to need careful preparation, and all of which provoked furious contention. First, there was the question of making sure that sufficient funds were available for an unstinted attack. Experience had proved that at least £1,000 was needed per head per European. While abroad this year, the expedition had run up an overdraft of £3,000 (£2,000 of which was guaranteed by the RGS, but it needed a sharp letter from Hinks to the Alpine Club to make sure it guaranteed the rest: 'If you Alpine Club people cannot somehow publicly or privately guarantee a thousand pounds of the overdraft, I fear some of your eminent members will be left in India to work their passage home').[20]

The make-up of the party would also need careful consideration in order to avoid, if at all possible, the inclusion yet again of those who could not acclimatize and became mere 'passengers'. It was thought that there should be, ideally, eight climbers capable of reaching the summit and that their average age should be considerably less than on the two previous attempts. Longstaff and Strutt had both been impressed that the porters who performed best were all about twenty-two, and concluded that twenty-five to thirty was probably the optimum age for Europeans, though this, they granted, would be subject to considerable individual variation.

Then, there were tactics to discuss — and these were infinitely arguable. Finch, Longstaff and Freshfield all wrote papers for the *Alpine Journal*. As the general public became more familiar with the intricacies involved, it too took an interest in the problem, seeing it in some measure as one of national importance. Considerable press comment and advice was generated. One area where there was enormous division of opinion was in defining the limits of acceptable risk. Traditional mountaineers wanted to be assured that Everest was being tackled in a sufficiently sporting and circumspect manner. They did not approve the new aggressive attitudes of a rising group of continental climbers, who with their newfangled ironmongery and inventive methods of assisted-rope techniques, were responsible for a tide of new routes on alpine faces that had previously been considered inviolate. To them, this unhealthy development threatened not only to pervert the nature of the sport, but failed also to accord a proper dignity to the mountains thus challenged.

Finch's remark in the 1922 expedition book, when it came out, that on Everest the margin of safety must be narrowed down — if necessary, to vanishing point — seemed to echo this alarming trend. Old Guard mountaineers deplored the apparent nihilism of his conclusion that the climber must drive his body on and on, no matter how intense the pains of exhaustion, 'even to destruction if need be'. He was firmly convinced that the key to success was an unswerving faith in the possibility of success. He believed that the body's warning mechanism of pain provided a wide margin of safety which someone committed to success would need to be prepared to override.

Finally, there was the very vexed question of oxygen — should it or should it not be used, and could it be improved? Finch and Farrar continued to be amazed by the fervour with which it was still resisted, and quite unreasonably resisted in their opinion. But subtle shifts in the debate were becoming discernible.

Freshfield, for one, could not see what all the fuss was about. 'So long as the summit of Mount Everest is gained, who cares whether it is with or without the use of oxygen?' he demanded. 'One might as well claim merit for going up the Matterhorn without a rope or an ice axe, in dress-shoes or shirt-sleeves.' In his view a lesson could be learned from the 'more tragic parallel' of the unfortunate prejudice against the use of sledge dogs by British parties in the Antarctic.[21]

It was an argument Finch expanded more fully in his lectures and writings. Loosely to apply the term 'artificial' to bottled oxygen (and thereby imply its consumption to be unsporting) was in his view a slipshod use of the term. In this enlightened twentieth century, he averred, most people had learnt to respect progress and appreciate adaptability. No one demurred at warm clothing — it was commonsense to wear it — or at hot tea from thermos flasks.

> Nonchalantly, without fear of adverse criticism [the climber] doctors up his insides with special heat and energy giving foods and stimulants! From the sun's ultra-violet rays and the wind's bitter cold, he boldly dares to protect his eyes with Crookes' anti-glare glasses; further, he wears boots that to the average layman look ridiculous! The use of caffeine to supply just a little more buck to an almost worn-out human frame is not cavilled at despite its being a synthetic drug, the manufacture of which involves the employment of complicated plant and methods.[22]

If science could prepare oxygen in tabloid form, or supply it in thermos flasks to be imbibed like tea, Finch believed all stigma of 'artificiality' would be effectively removed. It was because it needed to be carried in special containers that the whole essence of mountaineering was held to be altered by using it. When all was said and done — and this is Finch the scientist and logician speaking — the inhalation of a little life-giving gas did not smooth away rough rocks or quieten the storm, nor did it waft the climber magically upwards. 'Oxygen renders available more of his store of energy and so hastens his steps, but it does not, alas! fit the wings of Mercury on his feet. The logic of the anti-oxygenist is surely faulty.'

Farrar echoed similar sentiments when he reminded *Alpine Journal* readers that Dr Collie ('whose authority no one will gainsay') had stated the case once for all when he remarked, 'What is oxygen but air?' It was fairly certain that a climber could get up with its help, but by no means so without it! 'Do we want to be *fairly certain*,' demanded Farrar, 'or should we spend further thousands of pounds on an off-chance?'[23]

XI

Epistolary Warfare

In order to boost funds for the next attempt, a series of lectures on this year's expedition was proposed. There was also the cinematograph film that Captain Noel had shot — now in the process of being edited. Longstaff was confident that, handled properly, the film alone could easily pay for another expedition. Always the entrepreneur, Captain Noel outlined plans for exploitation of the film, which, he said, should be placed in the hands of himself and Hinks. To these the Committee agreed, provided they were kept informed. Privately, Noel felt confident that from foreign rights alone, they should earn £15,000. It was to be the first-ever film of its kind, and there was some justification for such high hopes. The sad reality was that his optimism was unfounded, and in that first season the film was a flop. Through their innocence in such matters, Hinks and Noel managed to grant the German rights twice over, resulting in costly legal fees.

To set up the lecture programme, Hinks got in touch with Gerald Christy, whose agency handled arrangements for speakers after the reconnaissance expedition. Hinks's idea was that as many speakers as possible from the expedition should be allowed to deliver talks, but Christy advised otherwise (17 July 1922):

> I think it would be wisest if one, or perhaps two, of the actual climbing party were deputed by the committee to be, so to speak, the 'star' lecturers for the big centres, rather than have four or five members lecturing on more or less equal footing [which] would tend to cheapen the whole scheme. It may seem

133

invidious to make distinctions, but from my own feelings in the matter and from what I gather from conversation with people generally, Mr. Mallory and Captain Finch are the two who stand out most prominently in the minds of the public and would seem to me to be the two who should be 'starred'.

We all know Mr. Mallory can speak well and I happen to know that Captain Finch is most effective on the lecture platform and can tell a story admirably.[1]

In his own handwriting, Christy added 'Mr. Mallory would do big things in America. Our representative over there is very anxious to have him go as soon after Xmas as convenient.'

Leaving that tempting proposal in the air, arrangements went ahead for a British tour much on the lines Christy had suggested. Shackleton's Lecture Tour circuit of 1909–10 was used as a guide (a number of famous explorers were on Christy's list). Cities and institutions were allowed to choose which of the two main speakers they wanted — Finch or Mallory — and as bookings came in, Hinks was reluctantly obliged to agree that Christy had been right — the two men appeared equally sought after. ('It is now pretty clear that there will not be much to choose between.')

When putting together his lecture, Mallory approached Finch for permission to use some of his photographs. This was a sore point with Finch. He had already had a contretemps with Hinks about copyright of his pictures, and Hinks's high-handed reply still rankled. Finch was a very fine stills photographer – at least as good as Captain Noel, the expedition's official cameraman – and he had brought back some of the best pictures taken on the mountain that year, particularly what one would call 'human-interest' pictures, unposed shots of members about their day-to-day affairs. He was not prepared for Mallory to claim any credit for them in his lectures. He wrote back:

My style of lecturing is, as you perhaps know, essentially different from yours and is, among other things, chosen to set off my slides to their best advantage. Any other than my own lecturing methods would not only fail to let them be seen to proper advantage but would plagiarise them in the eyes of the public; that I cannot permit as I wish to use these slides later when free to lecture on my own behalf.[2]

Mallory could pick from the full range of the Everest Committee's photographs, he said, of which he only expected to use four or fewer.

Like everyone else, Finch had been obliged to sign one of Hinks's agreement forms, placing all results obtained under the control of the Committee, and agreeing to have no dealings with the press. Like Mallory he had balked at this — to no avail. Indeed, in Finch's case, Hinks made a special point of stressing that 'nothing should be allowed to appear which looks like an individual advertisement'.

'You won't mind my saying,' Hinks had written, 'that certain pictures appeared last year in the illustrated papers when it was hoped that you would be a member of the party, [that] gave an unfavourable impression,' and he followed this, rather oddly, by adding that of course their appearance 'had nothing whatever to do with the fact that you could not be accepted last year owing to the medical report'.[3] (The only reason for Hinks to volunteer this last bit of information would seem to be to quell some general suspicion or belief that it had.)

'I am quite ready to believe,' Hinks had continued, 'that what happened last year was due to the injudicious action of a friend, who was perhaps making money for himself out of pictures of you, but I am sure that this year you will do your utmost to put a stop to anything of the kind.'

Though it must surely have riled Finch to receive such a letter, he was in a delicate position. So soon before the expedition's departure in 1922, he dared not jeopardize his place again. He duly signed, commenting only, 'I take it that I am not to be the official photographer of the expedition and that any snapshots I take, or sketches and paintings I make, remain my property subject to the control of the Committee as before.'[4]

Hinks was forced to concede that the *ultimate* ownership of any photographs taken privately doubtless did remain with the taker, but reiterated (at great length) that so long as the Committee wished to retain control, pictures could not be used independently by individuals. Finch had no intention of handing any negatives over to the Committee if he could help it, but thought it best for the moment to let matters ride.

Now, here was Mallory also seeking to take advantage of his pictures. It was too much. Back from the expedition, it no longer seemed so important to keep his lip buttoned. He wrote the following day to Hinks advising him that since he had spent over £200 of his own money on photography and, by taking part in the expedition, had lost half a year's salary and some consultancy work, and since now, on account of the Everest lectures, he was having to curtail his own normal lecturing programme, it was surely not unreasonable to expect some better return for his pains. He thought a third of the net proceeds from Everest lectures — plus travel and subsistence expenses — would be reasonable, with a guaranteed minimum of £25 per lecture.

The Committee did not meet to consider Finch's request. Instead Hinks replied abruptly that 'Sir Francis thought' 30 per cent adequate and that no minimum fee could be guaranteed. There seemed nothing more to be done and the lecture tours went ahead as planned.

From the middle of October, and throughout November and December, Finch and Mallory gave more than fifty lectures in town halls, assembly rooms, schools and concert halls up and down the country, starting with the joint meeting of the Alpine Club and the Royal Geographical Society on 16 October, at which they both spoke. Mallory was anxious that for this lecture at least Norton, too, should be included in the programme. 'He'll do it well — he does everything well,' he assured Hinks, brushing aside the little matter of Norton's aversion to public speaking:

> We're all yours to command I suggest for this occasion. I can't imagine anyone of normal modesty wanting to give tongue on such an occasion. The instinctive reaction of a lion to a lion show is to sulk in a corner and refuse to roar. However, for the nonce we've got to roar, so there's an end to it.[5]

Hinks was anxious to know the content of the proposed lectures. At the bottom of his letter (above) Mallory scribbled in pencil a line to say that his manuscript was with Farrar. It apparently contained 'some unmistakably adverse comments' about oxygen, which he must have known were likely to upset Finch — as indeed they did — and Farrar, on reading them, urged Mallory to modify them. Forwarding the manuscript to Hinks, however, Farrar could not resist a good-natured dig:

> I did not know that one of your duties was to control papers that are read [before the Society]. Good job I am not reading one, as you would not control me! . . .
>
> Sorry to see from your letter you do not get on with Finch.

Maybe he requires a little handling, but when you get to my age you may possibly have learnt how to do it! Still hope for you![6]

In view of the heavy programme he was about to undertake, Mallory enquired (22 October) whether it would be possible to travel First Class before a lecture in order to be able to arrive fresh and prepared. Hinks replied that it was for him to decide, but, predictably, urged 'reasonable economy'. By this time, it should be noted that Hinks and Mallory enjoyed a cordial relationship despite their scratchy start during the preparations for the 1921 reconnaissance. We don't know what Mallory felt about Hinks personally, but he now had his measure and appreciated the way a working relationship with him needed to be played. He employed his characteristic charm to disarm Hinks, and it obviously worked. Finch, on the other hand, did not go in for such games. He made no efforts to conceal his irritation at the slights and insults he felt directed at him by the Committee, and by Hinks in particular. There is no doubt that he *was* baited by Hinks, who had quite obviously disliked him from the beginning and enjoyed fanning discord between Finch and Mallory.

Years after Mallory's death, Finch was publicly to regret the rivalry and animosity that he considered had been manufactured between them over Everest. We were young and foolish, he said, and should never have allowed ourselves to be used in this way.

The little flare-up over oxygen continued for a couple of weeks at least. On 31 October, reporting to Hinks that the lectures were going fairly well, although afternoon audiences were depressingly small, Mallory said: 'There are things that pass man's understanding and this certainly passes mine. I can't tell Finch's story in minute detail because I wasn't of his party, but I tell it in such a way that all my audiences have very heartily applauded his performance.' He would like to see verbatim reports of Finch's lectures, if Hinks had them, but added in a more conciliatory tone, 'It may in any case be said about it, that the results depend not only upon what one says but how one says it.'[7]

Hinks was not inclined to be so charitable and replied, somewhat spitefully, 'I certainly have not got Finch's verbatim reports. I would not touch them. He is now sad because Howard-Bury referred to you as the greatest climber on the expedition and did it twice. He asked me how I justified such action on the Colonel's part.'[8]

Mallory did not want to get caught up in the petty mud-slinging which Hinks so obviously enjoyed, and tried to wind down the exchange by replying (2 November), 'La question Finch m'ennuie. It may interest you to hear that a cheque of his drawn to me for a sum under £2 was returned from my bank with the ominous letters R.D. However he has since made good . . . But this explains some parts of his conduct.' Indeed, if Finch really was suffering financial hardship as a result of taking part in the Everest expedition, no wonder he needed a fairer deal from his lecturing. On the oxygen question, Mallory continued:

> In Oxford on Saturday I made the *amende honorable* to Dreyer, saying, however, at the same time that I saw no reason to suppose that acclimatisation necessarily ceases short of the summit — which pleased Haldane whom I saw afterwards and who has his knife into Dreyer. Haldane was very interested, and I remember Somervell saying that he knows more than anyone about the whole physiological effects, etc.[9]

Meanwhile plans for Mallory's American lecture tour were taking shape. Christy wrote to Hinks recommending Lee Keedick of Fifth Avenue, New York, as manager for the tour. On 23 September Christy pressed Hinks again to use Keedick since he was, he said, 'the only man in America who would run the lectures in the tactful and dignified way which the Mount Everest Committee would desire. Mr. Keedick is a man of taste and refinement and in quite a good social position.' An introductory letter from Keedick was enclosed, outlining his terms:

> I agree to manage the American lectures of Mr. G.L. Mallory, or any other speaker or speakers that you may desire to send to America to speak on the Mount Everest Expedition, for the consideration of 45% of net profits derived from the lectures. Net profits shall be determined by subtracting out-of-pocket, or actual, expenses of the lectures from the gross receipts received by me for the lectures. The steamship fares from England and return, the hotel and railroad expenses of the speaker shall be included in the expense of the tours.
> It is my understanding that Mr. Mallory will arrive in New York by February 1st to begin his tour.[10]

The Everest Committee thought the agent's fee too high and hesitated. For the British lectures, Christy's were taking one third and the Everest Committee two-thirds. The lecturer was paid from the Committee's percentage, and the balance put towards the next expedition. Christy wrote to Hinks again on 13 October, effusive in praise of Keedick:

> I am quite certain that there is nobody else in the United States who can compare with Mr Lee Keedick in knowledge, ability and experience as manager of lectures. He is a man of highest integrity; and, as perhaps you may know, he has given complete satisfaction to all the famous people whom he has engaged to deliver lectures in his part of the world. He is a gentleman, is well received everywhere, and knows exactly what to do and when to do it. I never hesitate about him, as I have known him for a long while and in all my dealings with him, everything has shown how hard he works and how anxious he is to obtain the best possible results.[11]

He assured Hinks that the terms Keedick offered were the same as, if not even a little more favourable, than those accepted by other well-known men and women whom he had sent to him. The organization of lectures in the United States, Christy maintained, was a very expensive enterprise for the manager and involved considerable risk. He concluded, 'I am confident that Keedick is making as good an offer as he possibly can.'

Still the Committee demurred. Transatlantic cables began arriving, urging that delay would harm the advertising of the tour. Hinks could see the wisdom of this and recommended to Younghusband that they accept Keedick's terms promptly. 'I do not think we can get better terms from anybody else in America,' he said.

So the plans went ahead. If they wanted him to be in New York at the beginning of February, Mallory could book a passage on the elegant White Star liner, the *Olympic*, which would cost £57.10, or he could sail on a smaller Cunarder for only £31. Mallory left it to Hinks to decide, bearing in mind it had to come out of expenses, but said that Christy recommended the *Olympic*, 'as it would be a sort of advertisement,' adding, perhaps a little wistfully, 'there may just be something in that'.

Once again they bowed to Christy's opinion. It was on the *Olympic* that Mallory sailed for his three-month tour. Hinks rather hoped he might be persuaded to stay on in the United States and Canada afterwards to promote Captain Noel's film.

It was a bitterly cold day when Mallory stepped ashore in New York on 17 January 1923, to be met by the illustrious Mr Keedick. It came as something of a shock to discover that, despite his unrivalled knowledge of the American lecture scene, Keedick had so far not been able to secure very many definite engagements for his client, and the first lecture, in Washington, was not for another ten days. Meanwhile Mallory was ensconced at the luxurious Waldorf Astoria − presumably this too by way of advertisement − where he spent the days working on his lecture notes and chapters for the expedition book, and talking to a number of newspaper reporters.

Living on the 12th floor of a 13-storey hotel was something of a novelty − it was in the days before skyscrapers had made an appearance in Britain − and Mallory joked to the reporters that he got his Everest training by rejecting elevators and walking up to his room 'without oxygen tanks'. Before leaving, he hoped even to scale the summit of Mount Woolworth, he said.

*

Early in 1923 discussions began in earnest about who should be included in the following year's expedition. Bruce wanted to see Somervell, Mallory and Norton go again, but there was some doubt that the latter two could be available. And much as the idea lacked appeal for him, he could see no alternative but to invite Finch again. As he told Sidney Spencer, Secretary of the Alpine Club, 'It is those scientific requirements', and, of course, his expertise on snow. With Finch and Norton, Bruce considered they would have two *first class* snow men, but they needed more. In fact, what they really needed were some young climbers around twenty-five years of age. 'Is there no one who started young?' lamented Bruce.[12]

Longstaff, too, had strong ideas about who should be included, but his primary concern was that the selection should not be made behind closed doors. On the two previous occasions the matter had been left in the hands of the Everest Committee, and there was a suspicion that patronage had a hand in the final choice. By the time names were announced, it was a *fait accompli*, too late for the views and experience of rank-and-file Alpine Club members to be considered.

What Longstaff was suggesting was a formal sub-committee to

handle the selection, proposed or at least approved by the Club, which would take account of recommendations made to it. Spencer was dubious of the wisdom of this. 'I do not much like the idea of the club being let loose on the job,' he protested. 'You run the risk of having quite unsuitable men chosen.'[13] It offended his sense of rectitude to grant democracy to the possibly uninterested. Those who did not give any encouragement by subscribing to the expedition fund, he contended, could hardly expect to be consulted.

A few days later, however, Spencer was persuaded to Longstaff's view. 'If you propose it, and you see you have a seconder ready, there it is, fixed up,' he told him. And so it proved. At the club meeting on 10 April the selection committee was adopted. It comprised G. Solly (the Club's Vice President), Mallory, Noel Odell, G. Sang, Strutt, Longstaff, R.P. Bicknell and W.M. Roberts, as well as those AC members already serving on the Everest Committee, namely: Bruce, Collie, Farrar and Spencer.

Its first task was to decide on a Climbing Leader. There was no question but that everyone wanted General Bruce to be overall leader again, so what had to be found was a man capable of being his second-in-command. There was a suggestion this might be Finch, but it was quickly quashed. Longstaff felt it should be Strutt again, or someone who was 'almost the reflection of him'. The two alternatives that the committee finally recommended were Norton (Major E.F. Norton of the previous expedition) or his brother, Major J.H. Norton. In the event it was the tried-and-proven Norton, 'the great success' of 1922, who was invited and was able to go.

Much has been made of the significance of Norton's appointment. Was it, as some have said, a deliberate snub to Mallory? Mallory was after all the only person to have been twice to Everest and — in the eyes of the public at least — his was the name most closely associated with the mountain. He was the leading climber in the sense that it was generally felt he had the greatest chance of reaching the summit — not because of his superior climbing skill, which was probably matched by that of Finch and Somervell, but more especially because of his intense drive to succeed. His unquenchable ambition was plain for all to see, and that, rather than mere skill, is the hallmark of most successful Himalayan climbers. All the same, it was precisely this driving ambition of Mallory's that could be held responsible for mounting the disastrous third attempt in 1922. Longstaff among others felt that at very least the North Col accident called Mallory's snowcraft into question.

141

To be a leading climber is not the prime requirement for a Climbing Leader. Because he has the tactical responsibility for all activity on the mountain at the high camps, he needs, more than anything, organizational, or managerial, skills. Even Mallory's staunchest supporters could not claim organization as one of his strengths. His impracticality and absentmindedness were well known and were in themselves sufficient to render him eminently less suited to the role of Climbing Leader than Norton, without taking into account his impulsiveness and impatience for action. To be employed to positive advantage, these really needed outside direction.

There was one very important consideration that no one liked to discuss, though it must have been perfectly apparent to all the selectors. The continued good health of the General could not blithely be taken for granted. His heart condition was again giving cause for anxiety. There was a fair chance that whoever was chosen as second-in-command, at some stage during the expedition, might have to assume supreme control. And this would mean not just directing climbing operations, but supervising the whole baggage train to and from the mountain. In such an eventuality, Norton's military training would prove invaluable whereas Mallory's abstractedness could be positively disastrous.

What gives the final lie to the idea that the choice of Norton was a snub to Mallory is, however, the fact that Mallory was a member — and an influential member — of the committee that chose Norton, and that, at the time the decision was taken, Mallory was far from certain he would go to Everest a third time.

As it happened, the General did fall ill on the next expedition, and Norton was obliged to take over command. As anticipated, he did it admirably, and his first job as Leader was to cast Mallory (to Mallory's delight, it must be said) in the role of Climbing Leader.

There was a close bond of respect between these two men. They were in fact loosely related by marriage, Mallory's wife Ruth being the niece of Mrs Rosamund Wills, who was also aunt to Norton. It would be hard not to get along well with Norton — the only man on those early Everest expeditions for whom nobody had a bad word. He was a splendid, natural leader, secure in his abilities. He sought out advice from his men and took it when it made sense. When he gave orders, he gave credit freely to those whose ideas he was adopting, and when he wished to chart a course that was unpopular, he did so for reasons all could see as at least being logical. He was the best sort of military man. Respect for his judgment was such that none questioned his authority.

★

While Mallory was enjoying critical acclaim in America – if not financial success – back at home the British lecture programme was tailing off. Noel's film was enjoying a moderate success in London, but had received a disappointing response in the provinces.

For Finch, who had maintained his youthful contacts with Swiss mountaineers, there was the prospect of giving a few lectures in Switzerland during his summer holidays. He saw no reason why this should involve the Everest Committee, and was by now in any case anxious to extricate himself from the stranglehold of the Agreement. Just how binding was it, he wondered. He consulted counsel and was told that legally it was not binding at all, being 'neither reasonable as between parties, nor consistent with the interests of the public'. Feeling, thus, fairly sure of his ground, he wrote on 26 June 1923 to Hinks to tell him that from the middle of the following month he would consider himself free from all moral and legal restrictions and able once more to lecture on his own account.

Hinks was away when the letter arrived at the RGS offices, but it caused a great flurry none the less. It was forwarded to Sydney Spencer at the Alpine Club, as Joint Secretary, and Spencer rang General Bruce, who had taken over from Younghusband as Chairman of the Everest Committee. Together they decided that an emergency meeting should be called. Only four members were able to attend and failed to agree what should best be done. J.J. Withers, a prominent member of the Alpine Club and a lawyer, thought it very doubtful an injunction could be obtained to prevent Finch from doing as he wished. The implication that the matter might get into courts horrified Bruce, as it did some others, although they were all agreed that Finch's action was ungentlemanly and ill-timed with regard to the forthcoming expedition. Bruce wrote to Spencer on 30 June:

> Well at any rate he's torn it now. There are compensations for everything and I think this action on his part definitely rules him out of the next expedition . . . What an absolute swine the man is. I now regret insisting on putting him up for the AC.[14]

Maybe Finch could see the writing on the wall and adopted his stance after realising it was unlikely he would be asked to go to Everest again. If the Everest Committee had already decided against Finch, that might explain Farrar's resignation from the Committee at the end of May. It would certainly explain why Finch was prepared to make himself further unpopular by challenging his 'Agreement' and risking legal action. At all events, Farrar took it on himself to have a word with Finch about his ultimatum early in July, and then wrote to Spencer on the 5th:

> I sent for Finch as it is a pity that a very able man who has done good service to the Everest expedition should put himself in a false position. I questioned him very narrowly. There has been as I anticipated constant friction with Hinks who is a man of great ability and strong personality, but not of equal tact in handling men of independent spirit.
>
> I expressed to Finch very clearly that his letter was not a proper one. He has accordingly agreed to withdraw it and to submit his case in a more moderate manner — I have seen the proposed letter to which if I were a member of the Everest Committee, I should give every consideration.[15]

He added that 'the only use of the older man is to curb the impetuousness of the younger one!'

Taking Farrar's advice, Finch offered to postpone his proposed action until the autumn, and in his own defence, reminded the Committee that he had given 80 lectures on its behalf, written three chapters of the expedition book, and supplied prints of photographs taken on his own apparatus, as well as lending negatives. He received little sympathy, and Farrar once more tried to modify the Committee's hard line on the affair. He wrote (10 July):

> I agree that if a man signs an agreement, however arbitrary and possibly not binding in law, he is *morally* bound to observe it. But on the other hand, I think the other party is equally morally bound not to demand the full pound of flesh . . . Of course it was a great thing to go on the Everest expedition but we must not assume that there are plenty of men available or forget that he rendered splendid service and brought his party safely out of a most perilous adventure. With a less competent and resourceful leader than Finch is, we might have had to record the loss of

other than porters — I put his name forward in a full knowledge of his thorough competence in alpine matters so that nothing should occur to prejudice the name of the Club. *That is always my main concern*. The result, last year, bears me out.

It had little or no effect. Hinks replied to Finch on 26 July, saying the Committee was unable to accept his suggestion since it was 'necessary for the protection of interests of the expedition of both those of 1921, 1922 and of any future expedition that all questions of publication and public lecturing should be treated as part of a whole.' He was to consider himself still bound *in honour* by the undertaking he signed.

There is some doubt that this letter reached Finch before he left for the Alps that summer, and a curious postscript hovers over the episode, for within a week and a half, Hinks was writing to Spencer (who was also holidaying in the Alps): 'I am interested to hear that you, the General and Finch are all hobnobbing together at the Hotel Monte Rosa!'

Hobnobbing or not, it could not have been a very amicable party. Spencer reported that he had attended a lecture Finch had given there, adding with some glee that it was not very well attended. Meanwhile Hinks complained to Christy and reported to Spencer: 'I don't suppose he will book any more lectures from Finch.' Finch himself — feeling strapped financially — wrote to Hinks at the beginning of September declaring himself 'perfectly willing to continue to lecture under the auspices of the Committee during the coming winter.' He would accept a reduced fee of £10 plus £2. 10s. expenses. It proved too much for the Committee, who asked him to furnish an account of his Swiss lectures, and resolved to follow this up three weeks later with a solicitor's letter.

XII

George and Ruth

'Dear girl, it is much more difficult to go without you in this country than ever it was in India,' wrote Mallory to Ruth in some dejection during his American tour in February 1923. 'I don't know why, but I don't feel I can really be happy at all without you. I have most of the time a dreary mechanical feeling about life as though it just had to be got through until we can be together again.'[1]

It was not that they were unused to being apart; long separations had been the pattern of their life together. They had married in the week that war broke out, a time when it seemed impossible and inappropriate to settle down comfortably to domestic bliss. Friends were going away to fight, many of them to die, and it was not long before Mallory, too, began fretting to get into uniform. Eventually he joined the Army late in 1915, just after the birth of their first daughter Clare. At the end of the war, he and Ruth had two more or less settled years, and then began the Everest adventure. In almost ten years of marriage, George and Ruth Mallory spent less than half that time together.

That he should miss Ruth quite so acutely while in America was perhaps surprising. Of course there were always moments of great homesickness whenever he was away, during which time he would long desperately for her calm and her overriding sanity, but for the most part he was able to draw comfort from the certainty of her existence. The absence of all the petty intrusions of everyday life guaranteed that his idealized image of her remained pure and intact. Ruth was his guiding inspiration, the anchor for his dreams. He had written from France in 1918, 'As regards your appearances to

146

me, I don't greatly worry about their corporeal form. You appear more as an atmosphere with which I have a tender relation, and a beautiful presence.' And from Everest in 1922: 'I am conscious of you at the other end, and very often, dearest one, I summon up your image and have your presence in some way near me.'

Why, then, should their separation affect him so much more acutely when there was no shortage of things to do and see in New York? Mallory was rarely obliged, as he said, to feed in solitude, for when he was not the special guest at some luncheon party or other, there were usually invitations from friends, or friends of friends. With trips to the opera and theatre, concerts, and visits to the Morgan Library to read its collection of Boswell letters, he was left with little enough time for all the writing he planned to do while he was away, let alone to brood.

In all likelihood, Mallory's loneliness away from Ruth was not attributable to any single cause. He had been on tour now almost continuously for three months, and though he enjoyed the limelight, it was none the less an interruption to his life. He had managed to spend only six weeks at home since returning from Everest and, sooner or later, would need to decide whether to go back to teaching or to try to make out as a writer. His dejection also owed something to a sense of alienation in a strange land, for despite all the bustle and activity − or perhaps because of it − he found he could not like New York. The city was stimulating, certainly, but superficial social intercourse had never interested him. He wanted to talk about matters of moment − France's policy in the Ruhr, the worrying situation in Turkey − but could find few New Yorkers sufficiently versed to discourse on such matters. Some were prepared to admit that there was no continuity in American foreign policy, and that it was all at sixes and sevens, but Mallory concluded to Ruth, 'they are so lighthearted about the faults of their own politics that one despairs of them ever getting things better.'

He was both fascinated and appalled by the blatant display of wealth by society women at the opera. It called to mind the court of Louis Quatorze and seemed to him vulgar. 'The whole social atmosphere is sprightly and superficial,' he complained, 'at least wherever women are present.' To Mallory, American women were very ill-educated and only appeared intelligent on first meeting through employing 'the knack of putting all the attractive goods in the shop window . . . they are utterly unable to follow a subject. They just break in at any moment with any floating and often irrelevant idea.' This jaundiced view returned afresh each time he came back to New York. He felt far more comfortable when travelling around to other cities.

His first engagements in Washington and Philadelphia were on the whole encouraging. Mallory had been concerned that he might not be able to hold American audiences with his unfamiliar manner of speech. He had even practised an American accent on the Atlantic crossing, though he maintained that this was to enable him to communicate with railway porters and the like. He did not intend to employ it on stage.

Just before midnight on 26 January, his suitcases packed for an early start next morning, he wrote to Ruth from Washington to let her know how the first two engagements had gone.

> This afternoon they were the most unresponsive crowd I ever talked to – never a clap when I meant them to applaud and almost never a laugh. They weren't comfortable with me. I don't know why. But they *were* held, just. And afterwards much handshaking and kind words, as though it had been a *grand succès*. I believe they were just like the Torquay audience, only kinder.
>
> And this evening it came right off, from the first word to the last. I did what I liked with them; they took all my points; it was technically better than any lecture I've ever given, either year, and had any amount of spontaneity, too. There! if it doesn't 'take' now – well, I can do no more, and I'll come home.[2]

In Philadelphia the next day, it was an even better story. More than a thousand people turned out to hear him in the Witherspoon Hall, and the evening papers carried a full-page feature on his visit. He spent the night as guest of the Geographical Society's president, a local businessman and big game hunter who lived ten miles outside the city, and the following day – after lunch and tea parties – addressed another large and enthusiastic audience, this time of more than 2,000 people. Well satisfied, he returned to New York, where he was to spend a week before his big debut there at the Broadhurst Theatre on 4 February. A good reception and good press coverage in New York would ensure further bookings, which Mallory was disturbed to learn were still very slow coming in.

Mallory's initial dealings with Lee Keedick, his American impresario, seemed favourable enough and he was prepared to accept

Keedick's assurances that things would soon improve. It was something at least that he set such great store by advertising. When, two days after his arrival in America, Keedick had taken Mallory to see a show at the Broadhurst Theatre, Mallory had been impressed to notice that on every seat there was a folded leaflet advertising his own lecture. More handbills adorned the smoking room. Keedick also employed a press agent to ensure that a string of reporters called to interview Mallory in his hotel — but not before he had been well rehearsed in what to say to them! 'I don't know that that made much difference,' Mallory reported wryly to Ruth.

The Waldorf Astoria, too, had its own press agent, whose job it was to write about the hotel's celebrated guests. He called for a long talk with Mallory, explaining that what he was after was 'a contrast of value', as that always stimulated interest. Mallory wrote to Ruth,

> The young man wanted me to say that the great mountaineers of the expedition were all men of scientific training, or that mental training had more to do with the matter than physique. Can you imagine anything more childish? But I expect that is just what Americans are — boyish.[3]

There was one important engagement before the big lecture, and that was to attend a dinner as guest of the American Alpine Club, a gathering of about forty people. He sat between the president, a genial Presbyterian parson, and a lady he judged to be of partly foreign extraction, who told him she had 'climbed a peak in Alaska and endured a temperature of minus 60 degrees!!' She obviously made no better impression on Mallory than other New York socialites he had met, for, as he remarked afterwards, her intelligence appeared to have remained frozen ever since. The president introduced Mallory by reading extracts from the 1921 Everest book.

> Three others spoke after him, rather well, then I rose; everyone else rose too as is the custom here, clapped for a little — sat down again; I had several things to answer from other speeches and then gave a serious discussion of the problem of climbing Mount Everest. There was not much fun or fizz over it, but it went well enough. After that we sat on round the table and I was bombarded with questions. Altogether a very pleasant, homely party.[4]

The occasion lasted over four hours, and by the end Mallory was feeling 'very dry'. With prohibition still in force, nothing more stimulating to drink was provided throughout the evening than water. It was with some surprise and delight, therefore, that Mallory found himself whisked off afterwards to one of the 'swellest' of New York Clubs. 'We went down to the old wine cellar, which is now lined with lockers; one of these was unlocked, a bottle of gin was produced and handed over to a barman, who then mixed three long drinks known as Tom Collins.' It was not a drink Mallory had met before, though he thoroughly enjoyed it, and, thus fortified, sat pleasantly talking and drinking with his new friends into the small hours of the morning. 'Quelle vie!' Mallory wrote that night.

On the day of his New York lecture, Mallory was furious to find that preparations were very slap-happy. The operator had not bothered to turn up early enough to get things ready and had only just discovered that 'his wire was not long enough to fix up an electric signal'. Mallory was not surprised to find that he also made a hash of showing the slides.

> The Broadhurst Theatre, which only holds about 1,100 people, was only half-full, and that too was depressing. However, I had friends in the audience, amongst them *all* the members of the American Alpine Club who had been present at the dinner they gave me, so I didn't worry. I got them all right at the start; and they proved quite a pleasant, appreciative audience − they really went away *fizzing*, and I had reports of nice things said as they were going out, so that was all right.[5]

The most encouraging praise of all came from an old Cambridge friend, Reginald Poel, whom Mallory had encountered unexpectedly in New York. Poel, like himself, had been one of the founder-members of the Marlowe Dramatic Society, and had now landed a small part as the ghost in a Broadway production of *Hamlet*. Mallory went to see it and found it 'mostly bad', but he respected what he called Poel's critical knowledge of the stage, and was therefore delighted when Poel told him that Mallory's performance could hardly be bettered.

The following morning over breakfast, Mallory eagerly scanned the newspapers for reviews and was bitterly disappointed to find they contained very little. *The New York Times* managed to twist its third of a column story into 'anti-prohibition propaganda' with a

Above: Family group at the silver wedding of George Mallory's parents. George (centre back) is flanked by sisters Mary (left) and Avie. His brother Trafford (later Air Chief Marshal) sits left, with dog.
Below: At Pen-y-Pass, Easter 1919, George Mallory (driving), Winthrop Young (front seat), with Cecil Slingsby and Eleanor Winthrop Young behind. Ruth Mallory stands extreme left.

Above left: John Percy Farrar of the Alpine Club.
Above right: A.R. Hinks of the Royal Geographical Society.
Below left: Dr A.M. Kellas who died outside Kampa Dzong, 1921.
Below right: Geoffrey Winthrop Young as Special War Correspondent in 1914.

Above: The North Face of Everest from site of 1920s Base Camp.

Below: George Ingle Finch (right foreground) supervises one of his 'popular' oxygen drills at the end of a long day's march.

Above left: Captain Noel and his 'bloody cinema'.
Above right: The Second Summit Assault team, 1922,
Geoffrey Bruce (left) and George Ingle Finch.

Below: Time for Tiffin, Camp III, 1922–
left to right: Strutt, Wakefield, Morshead, Norton, Somervell, Mallory.

Frostbitten and exhausted, Geoffrey Bruce is assisted down to Camp II, 1922.

Above: George and Ruth.

(Inset) Andrew 'Sandy' Irvine.

Howard Somervell. Noel Odell. Teddy Norton.

Above: Mallory and Irvine leave Camp IV for their final summit attempt, 6 June.
Below: The shocked survivors return to Darjeeling—Hingston, Hazard, Norton,
Beetham, Geoffrey Bruce, Somervell, and General Bruce who met the party.

Left: The Second Step at 28,500 ft showing the ladder left by Chinese climbers in 1975. The cracks below and left of the ladder are frequently choked with snow.

Below: Jon Tinker's photograph, looking down the northeast ridge from about 28,700 ft. His Camp 3 (indicated) lies on the '8100m-terrace' where the English dead is believed to lie.

ABC

② ③

Yellow Band

Second Step

headline which ran 'SAYS BRANDY AIDED MT. EVEREST PARTY — A Swig 27,000 Feet Up "Cheered Us All Up Wonderfully," Mallory Tells Audience.' When the *Tribune* ('a very important, more or less liberal paper') came out later in the day, it painted a far more sympathetic picture, praising Mallory's 'unaffected manner of speech, which made him immediately a friend of the audience'. This was more like it! 'At all events', Mallory reported to Ruth, 'the second-in-command in Keedick's office bought a hundred copies to send about, so I have hopes there may be some engagements fixed up as a result.'

Far from any immediate improvement, however, there was yet further disappointment. Two days later Mallory arrived in Canada to fulfil two engagements, only to be told that his Toronto lecture had fallen through. 'An incredible muddle,' he told Ruth, the result of 'some idiocy' on the part of the local agent. He was beginning to have doubts about the efficiency of Keedick's organization. In Montreal, there were more technical hitches with projector — something Mallory was coming to expect — although the lecture itself went down well. There were no further firm bookings after that until Detroit on the 17th.

Mallory had hoped the tour would enable him to see far more of the United States than it did. His great dream was to travel across to California, but there seemed little chance of that. The sparsity of bookings was doubly frustrating now that he had discovered how much he enjoyed lecturing, considering it not the least of the opportunities Everest opened up. Mallory was clearly a performer at heart and no longer had any fears that he would not 'get hold' of his audiences. His speaking voice was good, and he had a pleasant, relaxed stage manner. American critics commented on the modest way he kept his personal part of the story in the background.

David Pye was impressed by how quickly Mallory learned this new skill. His lectures of the year before were vigorous enough, but patchy with a tendency towards the metaphysical and poetical. There had been a straining after pictorial effect, he said, which he did not 'get across'. Mallory himself had written:

I am much intrigued by the whole art of casting a spell upon an audience; it's rather amusing to practise one's guile on two or three thousand expectant persons, but I wonder if the experience will ever be related to anything more useful in the future.[6]

Everest had given him, Pye said, 'a far more eminent platform than

151

the one in his classroom'. For all his grand ideas on the way forward for education, there is no indication that Mallory had any hankering at all to return to ordinary schoolmastering. It was two years since he had given up work, but any decision on what to do next could safely be postponed for as long as lecture bookings kept coming in.

When Mallory returned to New York after an enjoyable weekend learning to ski in the Laurentian Hills with the 16-year-old son of his Canadian host, there was no improvement in the situation. Keedick could only promise three more firm engagements, with one or two other vague prospects. The tour had not 'taken', as he hoped. It is hard to know how much this was due to lack of public interest and how much to the fact that Keedick refused to lower his hire fee to enable more clubs and organizations to stage the lectures. He said it would only get him into trouble with those who had already paid the higher prices. He was not prepared, either, to run the risk of hiring public halls himself. The New York lecture had lost money and the one in Montreal made only 48 dollars.

'What a washout!' Mallory told Ruth in exasperation. 'Don't be terribly disappointed. We shall be poorer than I hoped for a bit.'

At home, Ruth was indeed finding things rather tight financially. They had recently acquired a car and were now having a garage built to accommodate it, which was proving more expensive than they thought. At the same time the car was acting up and Ruth already regretted having bought it at all. Mallory was sympathetic, but begged her, 'Please don't sell it before I come home!'

In the circumstances, the expense of the 'advertisement' of living in the Waldorf Astoria seemed no longer justified. Mallory decided to join his friend, Reginald Poel, at the Flanders Hotel on West 47th Street, where he could stay for 2 dollars a night, instead of 8. For that price, though, he had to choose between a room with a view or one with a bath. He did not much like his new quarters, and still went round to the Waldorf for tea if he was meeting anyone important. Meanwhile, he had been granted temporary membership at two clubs, where he was able to write or read or take meals, so that he was not obliged to spend much time in his hotel room.

In Boston, Mallory was the guest of Mr and Mrs Alston Burr, whom he found exceptionally charming and cultured. Altogether he found it a very agreeable city, and the people 'much more like the English than the New Yorkers'; there was even quite a lot of 'goodish talk'. His first lecture there was at Harvard, where 80 per cent of the audience were undergraduates. The student newspaper, the *Harvard Crimson*, ran a full report under the heading 'MALLORY THRILLS UNION AUDIENCE.'

> Before an audience that filled the Living Room of the Union, Mr. George Leigh Mallory described the attempt to ascend Mount Everest which took place last May . . . Mr. Mallory introduced his speech by asking 'What is the purpose of climbing Mount Everest?' He answered his question by saying in jest that it was of no use other than to fulfil the desire of the geologists for a stone from the summit and to show the physiologists at just what altitude human life becomes impossible.[7]

What is remarkable about the Harvard lecture is that Mallory sought to convince the students that 'the oxygen tanks which weighed 32 pounds proved unsuccessful because of their weight', although conceding that the attempt made with their aid reached 'the record height of 27,235 ft' — significantly higher than his own climb without it! Mallory gave no hint that he planned to use oxygen himself on the proposed third attempt. His attitude towards oxygen on this occasion is the more strange because in his lecture in New York City and elsewhere he had told his audience.

> Taking in the oxygen apparently forced the body processes to proceed so much faster than the normal rate that it burned up their tissue very badly. However, it seems to be an advantage and we will probably all use the tanks on the next trip.[8]

In his biography of Mallory, David Robertson comments that adverse remarks about oxygen which Mallory intended to include in his first public lecture after the 1922 expedition occasioned a flare up with Finch. When remonstrated with by Farrar, Mallory had merely remarked that 'indiscretions would bubble out', to which Farrar urged restraint. Mallory had therefore restricted himself to a plea for acclimatization and some injudicious digs at the oxygen boffins:

> I always, as a matter of course, take off my hat to scientists, as latter-day Olympians breathing a different if not purer air than common mortals. But the air of Mt. Olympus (a base little lump after all) is not that of Mt. Everest, and experiments made there with a pumped-out tank, interesting as they may be, are of

no value in determining where precisely on that other hill of
unrivalled altitude persevering man will be brought to a standstill; for it must be supposed of the persevering man that he has
been acclimatised to rarefied air, while the Olympian and other
victims of those experiments are only acclimatised to the
atmosphere of Mt. Olympus, which, I am given to understand,
is particularly dense.[9]

Robertson does not indicate the nature of those 'indiscretions' that
Mallory presumably excised from his first performance, but this
Cambridge lecture gives the clue. It was no wonder Finch thought it
'very naughty of George' if Mallory was dismissing his oxygen tanks
as unsuccessful, when, with their use, Finch had attained a record
height!

Mallory reported to Ruth that the Harvard audience was as good
as any he remembered. 'They received me very well and were
evidently thrilled and amused. There is no doubt that people over
here are really impressed by the story and I shall feel that the lectures
have been worthwhile even though the number remains small for the
time spent in the country.'[10]

After another performance in Boston to the Appalachian Mountaineering Club ('a combination of the Rucksack Club and the
Pinnacle Club'), Mallory departed for a second visit to Philadelphia,
and then for Toledo, before detouring on his own account to secure a
sight of Niagara Falls.

> The day I was there was the worst sort imaginable, a black East
> wind, followed by a blizzard. Even so, the tossing rush of
> waters, swooping down one slant after another for miles above
> the fall, then the clean apple-green swirl as they turn over is
> wonderfully impressive.[11]

Then it was on to Chicago, and then to Iowa City, the farthest west
he journeyed. ('It's a long way from my dream of seeing the Pacific
Coast.') The country was still in the grip of ice and snow, as it had
been ever since he arrived. The lecture in Chicago was another that
did not materialize, the Geographic Society offering 200 dollars to
hear him, which Keedick refused. The one redeeming feature of the
whole business was that Mallory felt free enough to make a pro-
visional booking to return home.

'Oh, my dearest one,' he consoled Ruth, 'you won't have long to wait after receiving this. How lovely it will be and what a nice long 'spring we'll have together. I shall be angry if it's too early.'

In the remaining fortnight he visited his uncle in Toronto, and returned to give another, and final, lecture in Boston. He sailed home on the *Saxonia*, which left New York on 31 March.

★

Mallory's anxiety to be back in time to share the spring with Ruth was two-fold. All his life he had a passionate love of nature and spring was always for him a season of restless excitement. It was a feeling that had only intensified since he had known Ruth. They had fallen in love in springtime. Now, each year, as the air warmed and the first scented blossoms appeared, it seemed to George like a reaffirmation of their love and he needed her with him to relive some of the magic of their early romance.

It was in 1914 that they had discovered each other when Mallory had been invited to spend the week before Easter in Venice as guest of the Turner family. Thackeray Turner lived with his three unmarried daughters — Marjorie, Ruth and Mildred — in a large house on a hill just outside Godalming, and had met Mallory when he was playing in a local dramatic production. It was not long before Mallory became a frequent visitor at Westbrook, enjoying a game of billiards with Thackeray Turner. Just before leaving for Italy, and surprised at how eagerly he was looking forward to the visit, Mallory told Geoffrey Young, 'I should be sorry to induce a friend to run such risks as I am to run now.'[12] If risks there were, he capitulated without a struggle. Ruth, the shy and wise middle daughter, so bewitched him one idyllic day among the mountain flowers above Asolo, and he her, that within a few weeks they decided to be married.

'What bliss! And what a revolution!' Mallory wrote to his mother on May Day to tell her of the engagement. '*Ruth Turner* — she lives just over the river from here in a lovely house and with lovely people, and she's as good as gold, and brave and true and sweet. What more can I say!'[13]

There had been young women in Mallory's life before he met Ruth. During his student days he had considered himself madly in love with a doctor's daughter who lived near his home in Birkenhead; she was only sixteen, but they would marry one day, he promised her. The girl's mother laughed at his youthful ardour. Then, over a number of years he enjoyed a close and comfortable friendship with Cottie Sanders (the novelist Ann Bridge), one of

Geoffrey Young's 'hill company'. With her he exchanged affectionate and newsy letters, and when she married a diplomat the year
before Mallory met Ruth, they remained the best of friends. But
George Mallory had never fallen headlong in love as he did now with
Ruth. Her father wanted to know if Mallory had given any thought
as to how they would live. Was the young schoolmaster expecting to
rely on his wife's income? Mallory was outraged.

'Oh, I couldn't possibly marry a girl if she had her own income!'

'You couldn't possibly marry her if she *hadn't*,' observed his future
father-in-law dryly.

All three daughters were promptly whisked off for a fishing
holiday in Donegal. It would do no harm for the young lovers to
spend some time apart, to make certain of their feelings for one
another.

The three weeks seemed an eternity. George and Ruth wrote to
each other almost every day, dreaming of how it would be when
they were together. It was a pity that all the endearments Mallory
wanted to shower upon her had been used so many times before.

'Sometimes I fear that the words that come out of my mind are
only a literary echo,' he lamented. 'I want a new vocabulary of love
words. Can't we make them one?'

When she read his letters, she was to remember that 'the loops
are all kisses and the tall strokes and the tails are all arms to embrace
you.' It would be their secret code. 'Shall I go through my letter and
make them all longer?' he asked.

Ruth carried the precious bundle of letters around in her pocket
wherever she went so that she could re-read them whenever there
was a quiet moment. 'I shan't be able to keep them in there much
longer, there will be too many.' She told him, 'Life with you is going
to be very perfect.'

Alarmed at the responsibility, Mallory warned her she must be
prepared for a few downs with the ups, she must always remember
to be critical of his faults. 'I can see, my dearest Ruth, that you have a
dangerously unselfish disposition, but you shan't spend your life
doing little jobs for me; I hope that I shan't be horribly selfish — and
that you sometimes will be.' Though he may affect her growth and
she his, he told her, they must be separate individual growths all the
same.

On 16 May Mallory wrote:

I suppose the real model lover would have written to you

yesterday, but then the model lover is entirely idle and it's easy to achieve fidelity on paper. I didn't write because I went to a tennis party and a dinner party — anything but idle! Tennis at the headmaster's — the Friday levée, where a dozen or so pedagogues contend. Mrs. F[letcher, the headmaster's wife] meant to be very nice and said she thought you very *pretty*; this gave me a horrid shock and I didn't know what to say . . . so I let it pass with a vague approval and have felt very angry ever since and much want to go back and explain to Mrs. F, who means to be so nice . . . the horrid irrelevance of that silly word *pretty* — when applied to *you*.[14]

Ruth's beauty transcended mere prettiness. Mallory had just been preparing a series of art lectures for the older boys at school and Botticelli had emerged as one of his favourite painters. *Botticellian* was how he would have described her. Curiously it was a comparison frequently applied to him, too, not only by Lytton Strachey and Geoffrey Keynes, but by his old housemaster Graham Irving.

'Have you received any wedding presents yet?' he asked her two days later, having himself just been sent a cheque for £100. 'Bah! . . . I believe it really is a serious annoyance to me that you, my dearest, are rich and I am poor. Never mind — you'll have to keep what you've got. That'll be your job, and mine shall be not to make more than we want.'

Ruth replied gravely that she thought he had more sense than to bother about money and whose it was, adding, 'I'm glad it's there: it will make you freer, and also enable you to think about it less.'

He assured her that money was 'wholly irrelevant' to him. He supposed that one day they might have to think a bit more about it, but never enough, he hoped, to cramp their existence. 'The idea of possessions doesn't interest me unless I have some part in producing a beautiful whole with them according to a preconceived idea.'

David Pye has said that until he met Ruth, Mallory lived a good deal in the clouds, where the things that mattered were literary or intellectual considerations. 'Practical concerns he treated either with a casualness which bordered on the sublime or, if they seemed of sufficient importance, with a good deal of rather elaborate discussion.' As a married man, he would have to take an interest in a few material things and some social niceties. It was lucky for him that Ruth was inclined to be practical. Her father was an architect (much under the influence of William Morris) and her mother had been a gifted needlewoman; for as long as Ruth could remember, great store had always been placed on good design, craftsmanship and practicality. She enjoyed making things and had a special flair for painting china. With her sisters, Ruth had attended Prior's Field, the avant-garde school for girls, founded by Julia Huxley, where self-expression was encouraged and Mrs Huxley's own love of literature and the arts was passed on in an atmosphere of kindliness and calm. Less attention was paid to such mundane subjects as arithmetic and spelling, and Ruth's spelling remained imaginative all her life. It delighted Mallory, who regularly teased her about it in his letters. 'Spelling', she told him, 'I'm afraid you must take that as one of the worses in the better or worse of the marriage service.' But she was anxious to learn from him in other directions, and wrote,

> Do you know dear I'm afraid I am rather only half grown-up. I haven't thought nearly enough. I have come to the conclusion that that is the biggest wickedness in my life. I have only realised it lately . . . Of course, I know that really we go on growing all our lives, still I think I ought to have got further at my age. But I am glad there is a lot of growing to do with you. I would rather grow with you than anyone in the world. I think you have made me grow a good lot already. [15]

Ruth's aunt, Rosamund Wills, wrote to Mary Ann O'Malley (Cottie Sanders), apparently unaware that Mallory was a friend of hers,

> My niece, Ruth Turner, is engaged to be married. She is one of the 'twice-born': a soul of the most crystal wisdom, simplicity, and goodness — pure gold all through. She is going to marry a young Charterhouse master, George Mallory — I hope he is good enough for her, but it is hardly possible. [16]

Amused, Mary Ann replied that Rosamund's niece would be marrying one of the rarest spirits of his generation, and it sounded, on the whole, as though *she* might be nearly good enough for *him*!

At first the young couple would need to live in rented accommodation, although they planned to move into a house of their own before too long. The headmaster's wife, idly curious, asked Mallory about his 'arrangements for the future':

> . . . too many questions, I thought, but I suppose women can't

help being like that however nice they are — e.g. what colours our rooms were to be, black or purple or anything of that sort? A reference, I suppose, to my Posty [Post Impressionist] tastes, and quite typical of the world's way of classifying such things. Mrs. Fletcher, like almost everybody, has divided them into proper and outré; and mine are outré, and therefore probably I like black rooms. I don't know in point of fact that I've ever thought about a black room and I dare say it might be rather fine, but I hate people's minds working squintwise . . . Let's be really high-toned and have an emerald room and a sapphire room and an amethyst room! Or really Romantic and have a room like Monte Cristo's cave and a room like the bottom of the deep green sea, with mermaids sitting on the mantelpiece, an octopus in the corner, and seats of sponge and coral! Or shall I take orders, and we'll go in for mid-Victorian culture and get me made a headmaster in no time and then a bishop? If life is meant for fun, then a bishop I would be — if only for a week or two. [17]

Ruth replied that an Alpine room would seem more suitable than a deep sea one. 'And the chairs could simply be boulders, which would be cheap. Then we will ask Mrs. Fletcher to dinner.' She had been reading Whymper's *Scrambles Amongst the Alps*, the better to understand Mallory's passion for mountains, and had induced her sisters to make an ascent of the mountain across the lough from where they were staying. It was a ten-hour expedition and Mallory was impressed. 'Ten hours in this climate is equal to about fifteen or more in the Alps for most people,' he told her, 'so I expect you would make nothing of an ordinary expedition there, and in time — who knows?'

He began to think of spending part of their honeymoon climbing in the Alps. Geoffrey Young was horrified. The deaths of H.O. Jones and his young wife in the mountains two years before were still fresh in his mind, and he wrote sternly to Mallory.

Both of them were steeped in the double romance of themselves and the mountains. And the accident came of his over-care for her, his distraction from the single eye of the mountaineer, that he *must* have, and that he *cannot* retain if he is throwing himself into someone else's being, outlook, and performance.

Now — forgive my going on, but I feel this sincerely — your weakness, if any, is that you *do* let yourself get carried away on occasions in the mountains . . . I think that it is your failing, the consequence of your combination of extraordinary physical brilliance in climbing and of power of mental absorption in it, that you do not, or at least have not, held back from allowing yourself to sweep weaker brethren, carried away by their belief in you, to take risks or exertions that they were not fit for, and which, had the crisis come, neither you nor any man in climbing could have the margin to cover for both . . .[18]

Mallory was crestfallen. It was not the fear of leading her into danger that bothered him, but a solicitude over how she would cope with strenuous exercise. He began rather earnestly to collect what information he could about the physical state of young women immediately after marriage. 'My mother, who is most particular in such matters, said that it was a period when women ought to take more exercise than usual and quite approved of the Alps.'

The outbreak of war immediately after their wedding at the end of July put paid to all ideas of going abroad. The young couple went walking instead in Somerset and Hampshire, sleeping out under the stars. In the jittery political climate, they were arrested on suspicion of being German spies when discovered one night on a beach near the New Forest.

Ruth had written during the three-week separation of their courtship that she could not think how couples coped with being apart for long periods. 'It must be awfully dreary and worrying, the exchanging of ideas, the answers to questions, everything in writing is so slow.' It was something she was to face frequently in the coming years, and not just the loneliness, but her fears for George's safety. The actual moment of parting was always painful, although even in that she gradually learned to mask her distress, telling him after he returned to France in September 1918, 'The gloom and sadness was a little relieved by seeing York Minster, as you no doubt thought it would be. I did part with you cheerfully, in true British fashion, didn't I. I'm getting stronger at those times than I used to be. I suppose the adversity of war hardens one's fibre.'

Whenever they were apart, they corresponded assiduously, sharing the detail of their days, the books they were reading, as well as their deepest reflections. Mallory hoped that his letters to her were not too 'literary', to which Ruth replied that she was probably not the best judge, but 'I do know that they are very nice and say much that I want to know. If they are . . . they will perhaps counteract mine a little in some world balance.' As time went on, they appeared to communicate more freely by letter than in discussion. 'What can be more lovely than you reading this letter diligently probing and testing my words to find out all that has been in my mind because you love me, and holding it all up for truth's sake to your own true mirror of experience, and that I should be trusting you to behave so?' Mallory wrote to her from France.[19]

Like all soldiers, Mallory wondered how he would react under fire. 'Curious how I have found myself going back for reassurance to old football days at Winchester.' He promised he would always tell her the degree of danger he was in, but found himself for several months unable to confess that the first night he went up to the Observation Post, a bullet passed between him and the man walking a yard in front of him. 'I've never had a narrower escape . . . but we settled long ago that there's no reckoning with Death. Everyone out here who goes anywhere near the fighting line has narrow escapes and you may have a million or a dozen.' It was no use worrying about 'imaginary evils', he told her. They must both put their trust in God.

'There is an awful feeling of futility sometimes when I pray for you and that you may not be killed,' Ruth told him. 'Every one out there has someone passionately praying that they may not get killed and yet one knows some must and certainly will. I think you would say that praying for a definite thing like that is bound to put you in that sort of position, so you don't do it. But I must. It's all I can do, and I must.'[20]

In an endeavour to reassure her, he wrote in July 1916:

The saying I quoted you about the complete safety of the actual front trench was amply borne out, I was fortunate too in finding a very safe way of getting there and back — rather a gruesome way, however, as one meets a stark sentry. Altogether the gruesome enters in a good deal. Happily my nerves are quite unaffected by the horrible — not so my nose: but oh! the pity of it! I very often exclaim when I see the dead lying out; and anger I feel too sometimes when I see corpses quite inexcusably not buried.[21]

Two days later, two of his party were killed on this safe way back from the trenches. They had been walking a little way behind Mallory carrying between them a reel of wire on a stick, when they heard a shell coming. He supposed the burden slowed them down in their dive to take cover. Afterwards, when they did not respond to a whistle to come on, he went back and found them lying face down in the mud.

Physical discomfort never concerned Mallory. As a small boy, he used to sleep in winter under a single blanket to inure himself against cold. He could never bear houses — or tents — to be hermetically sealed against fresh air. Living in a dugout caused in him no special distress.

'I'm quite well protected in my little hole and it is the greatest comfort of life that I have such a little sanctum.'

On periods of duty at the Observation Post, his bed was nothing but crumpled chicken wire in a damp clay hole, but it was not a bad life, and he told Ruth he felt very fit.

'Darling,' she replied, 'I am very glad you find the present life youth-giving and that you look well and happy, even if you aren't always. When I told the others that your life was youth-giving, Father said if you were going to get any younger he did not know what would happen and Marjorie that I should be dandling you on the other arm with Clare. They are sillies.'

Ruth could also be disarmingly candid. She wrote to him about life in his father's vicarage in Birkenhead. 'Your mother is a queer person. Isn't it funny the way she shuts her eyes when she is speaking of religious things.' She even remarked that his mother certainly wasn't 'radiating love for her fellow beings and passionate sympathy for them in their troubles.' Mallory once acknowledged that, instead of cowering like 'a peasant slave' before some VIP, he wished, like Ruth, he had the courage to loose off a 'direct hit'.

When winter came, the dugouts had their drawbacks. Heavy rain flushed the men out of their holes during November 1916 and threatened collapse of the whole warren. They were faced with frantic remedial digging. The scene reminded him of a Millet peasant painting, only 'more *there*'. Mallory procured a stove for his refurbished retreat and wrote home for his climbing boots and warm clothes.

'I have not been very content with myself just lately,' he complained. 'One falls into the way of making so many arrangements for avoiding discomfort, that one gets into the habit of thinking too much about comforts altogether and living in a spiritually lazy fashion.'

After his first leave that Christmas, they were both delighted to learn that Ruth was pregnant once more. It was very cold when he got back to France and found he had been moved out of the battery mud to a new dugout in a chalk gully, which, though he was obliged to share it, was far more comfortable. 'How wonderfully lucky I've been . . . I have almost forgotten that mud existed and I can hardly remember what it was like to spend a cold day in a wet trench.'

He began keeping 'a literary notebook' for jotting down random ideas as they came to him, and in an effort to resolve his philosophical thinking. 'Since coming to France I have regarded inefficiency in my own person as the unforgivable sin. I have actually on one or two occasions experienced a sense of sin, almost new to me, in its intensity,' was an early entry. He was deeply affected by his reading of Thomas Hardy's *Tess of the D'Urbervilles*:

I feel bruised and broken and pierced in a way that leaves me no thought beyond the tragedy I have just witnessed. No one can ever have possessed such power as Thomas Hardy to harrow the human heart. If he weren't a supreme artist, it would be impossible to read such a story as *Tess*, but he has that quality that one reads on because one can't help it, as one reads *King Lear*, seeming to experience life itself from the depth of human truth in the story. It's not a useless sorrow this, like that of some sordid Zola or Balzac or Flaubert, it is a great spiritual experience, however disagreeable, to feel such great pity. I think perhaps more good may come to the spirit by the deepening of that sense than in any other conceivable way. What do I feel towards you now, dearest, just that it would break my heart to cause you the least pain, and a tremulous longing gently to kiss you so as to assure myself that all is well between us.[22]

Mallory was allocated a servant, but it was hard to know how to employ him. In February they went together to man the observation post in freezing conditions, and Mallory wrote home, 'There is almost nothing for him to do except wash up my plate and frying pan. I don't wash or shave up here and I sleep in my clothes, but I'm very glad to have him here and he will learn to observe. He seems a very nice man, a barber by trade.' This was a useful accomplishment, at least. Normally he shaved Mallory in bed every other morning, which, as he remarked to Ruth, was a luxury 'almost worth a war'.[23]

Billeted with a man called Dunbar, a rather 'unhappy little bird, full of trifles and little grouses' and without much idea of amusing himself, Mallory decided to cheer him up by reading him poetry as they huddled over the fire. 'He seemed to like Shelley but didn't care much about Keats,' he reported back to Ruth, 'but I'm pleased to observe that he's picked up the book now and is reading it.' As spring approached, Mallory kept a little bowl that Ruth had painted, full of flowers, on his makeshift table.

A recurrent theme in Mallory's letters is a desire to lie among flowers. He loved his garden at The Holt, their house in Godalming, with its formal beds above the virgin copse overlooking the Wey Valley. Sometimes the only clue to be gleaned from his correspondence that Mallory was missing home when he was away, was when he went in for long-distance gardening. Ruth would be sent pages of instructions on seeds to plant, special watering requirements that must not be forgotten, and other important tasks. In one of his early letters from France, he had requested Ruth to send him some seedlings for the overgrown cottage garden where they were billeted. With her usual resourcefulness, Ruth promptly despatched a selection by post, but Mallory was moved on very soon afterwards and never knew whether they grew or not.

Improbable parcels followed him around France. Ruth sent him cakes, cheeses, sausages, and, later in the war, 3½ lbs of flour every week. In July 1916 he wondered how fresh butter might travel, 'a sudden nausea has come upon all of us at the sight of the tinned stuff we get. Will you send out a pound as an experiment? I believe that if wrapped well in paper and packed in a tin or wooden box it might arrive quite fresh.' Ruth had been making butter during the food shortages at home, and accordingly parcelled up some, as requested. She continued to send it regularly until the weather got so hot she felt it would never arrive in a state fit to eat.

'Our other great need is vegetables,' George told her, 'especially potatoes — they are exceedingly difficult to procure out here and poor when we do get them. I think it would be quite worthwhile to get a large quantity sent out by rail — 5 stones of new potatoes would make us happy for a month or more, and I could charge the cost to the mess account. Please try and do this, my dear . . . the railway people will tell you the best way.'

Ruth sent the potatoes.

'It so often happens,' he told her, 'that for some days I see nothing but the *Daily Mail* and the Harmsworth popular press disgusts me in its present stage of rampant jingoism over the great push.'

Ruth saw to it that he received bundles of *The Times* each week, together with the *Literary Supplement*. When rat poison was required, that too Ruth sent. His cleaning and mending came home for her to do.

'You'll see what's happened to the drawers. My stupid owl of a servant confesses that he was looking out of the window as he was drying them at the fire. I don't know whether they can be patched?'

Towards the end of the war, when they were no longer engaged with the enemy and relatively settled, it was velvet curtains for the officers' mess that Ruth provided.

In April 1917, just before Mallory was sent home to have his ankle operation, he told Ruth that he had lost a secret code book, warning her he would probably be shot at dawn. She wished he would not say such things, even in jest, and tell her really what would be done about it, but he continued to tease. 'Sentence alas has not yet been passed, but practically remains to be decided at what hour. I'm inclined to think dusk and not dawn.'

Invalided home for the summer, and then stationed at Winchester, only thirty miles from Godalming, Mallory was able to spend time with Ruth before their second daughter, Beridge, was born on 16 September. It was a whole year before he finally got back to France for the last few months of the war. With the Armistice daily expected, there was little action, and plenty of time to reflect. If he had any regrets, it was that his share of the fighting had been too small. 'I should have liked to return home, if not a hero, at least a man of arms more tried than I have been.'[24]

He was aware from Ruth's letters that she, too, was wondering if life could be made better on a more personal level. If it was to be 'springtime in heaven', as he had promised, why did a certain petty friction remain?

'Do I appear as a domestic tyrant, irritable and unkind?' he asked her. 'From what you say, I think that must be the case — not always, I hope.'

'You do criticise me quite a bit, and I don't mind, except that I'm sorry not to come up to scratch,' she told him.

Mallory wondered 'how to avoid those little moments of opposition which rub the bloom off married life.' He frankly confessed he never expected to be a good person to live with, and that the fault when she had been 'not quite sweet-tempered' lay in some untender way of his that had irritated her.

'I suppose it's impossible that anyone can always be open — even you sometimes have shut periods, usually when you are busy,' Ruth had said to him.

Mallory sought to reassure her. 'The only possible jar to our happiness after the war will be my personal ambitions, so you must help me to keep them in order. You must be patient with me, please, my dearest one, and always remember that I love you very tenderly.'

Ruth: 'I do want us dearest always to be close together in mind, and able to share thoughts and to grow closer and closer together. I do want to be able to help you by showing you you are making a barrier, if you are, but you seem to do so singularly little, and I think it is because you have always valued friendship so much that you have trained your mind to open itself instead of shutting itself up.'

Teasingly, Mallory wrote to her shortly before the news of Armistice came through late on 10 November: 'I decided that it would be necessary for me to leave all the practical part of our life together to you, so that I should be better able to intensify my spiritual life. Isn't that beautifully unselfish of me?'

As the weeks passed, he grew impatient to be home. 'I look forward to a life with you and the children, at The Holt, or wherever it may be, as a wonderful bliss.' He rented a room, hoping to be able to get down to some writing away from the distractions of the mess, but found it hard to settle to serious work when daily he expected to be ordered home. In the spring of 1919 he and Ruth were finally reunited and able to move back into The Holt with the children. They were happy to be together again, keeping open house for their friends, yet Mallory was not content that life should drift on as before. The war had profoundly changed his thinking, particularly his views on education. He hoped that Geoffrey Young and David Pye might be persuaded to join him in opening a new sort of school. When he received the invitation to accompany the Everest Reconnaissance of 1921, he resigned his teaching position at Charterhouse with very little regret. It was lucky, as Ruth had said when they first met, that there was sufficient money to allow him a measure of freedom; and lucky, too, that when he was not there she had learned to manage the day-to-day domestic affairs and the children (of whom by now there were three, his son John having been born in August 1920). They were to have a very interrupted home life from now on.

*

166

Sailing back across the Atlantic after his American tour, Mallory was besieged by feelings of anti-climax and failure. His lecture tour had been a flop. His writing had been limited to chapters for the expedition books — hardly what he had in mind when he dreamed of being a writer, and certainly not profitable either. Financial difficulties were eating into his relationship with Ruth. In his contribution for the 1922 expedition book, he was forced once more to face the terrible consequences of his unfortunate decision to make his last-ditch attempt. Taken all round, there seemed little enough in his life at present to occasion much pride. He had failed on all fronts, and he had no idea what he should find to do when he got back home.

What he could not know was that one day when Hinks was travelling on a train to Cambridge, he had bumped into an old acquaintance. D.H.S. Cranage was now Secretary of the Board of Extra Mural Studies at the University and was, he told Hinks, on the lookout for an assistant secretary and lecturer. University extension courses, designed largely for the working class, were expected to play an important role in postwar Britain. Hinks immediately suggested the name of George Mallory as a possible candidate. To Mallory's surprise, therefore, when he arrived home, he found himself under consideration for a position that seemed tailor-made for him. There were other candidates, but he rallied as much support as he could from his friends. Arthur Benson, Frank Fletcher, F.E. Hutchinson, all put in a word for him, and on 18 May, Mallory was able to report to Hinks,

> There was a rather fierce battle in the end between me and another man with very strong academic qualifications and I rather thought I was going to be turned down. The fact that you had mentioned my name to Cranage before I applied was just one of the things that turned the scales in my favour. I'm very glad you put me on to the job.[25]

He added that there was no question now of him doing any more lecturing on behalf of the Everest Committee, as he was required to start work 'more or less at once'. He went on:

> An even more serious matter is my poor diminished chance of going with the next expedition. I didn't at any point dare to bring up that question for fear of jeopardising my chances; and

it will be difficult to bring it forward now. However, I'll have a talk with Jim Butler and see what can be done.

Nothing much does appear to have been done, however, for another five months. Mallory put Everest far from his mind as he threw himself enthusiastically into his new life. He moved at once to Cambridge, living in rented accommodation while he looked for somewhere more permanent. Ruth and the children remained at The Holt until he could send for them. Mallory was delighted to be back among his many academic friends. It has been suggested that this new job was rather less than someone of his aspirations might have hoped for. To be in Cambridge, but not 'of the University', could be considered being nowhere. This seems harsh. It is probably true that Mallory would have liked one day to be offered a fellowship, but it was not beyond the bounds of possibility that this could yet have happened, given influential friends in the right places. No, he was teaching adults at last, which was what he wanted, and the fact that it was giving educational opportunities to young working class men and women well satisfied his Fabian instincts. It was not a position he was going to threaten by premature discussion of Everest.

When the selection committee met to finalize names on 16 October, Mallory could do no more than put question marks after his name. He was informed that Bruce and Norton especially wanted him to come again, and that Hinks would be writing to Cranage, on behalf of the Everest Committee, to see if he might be released. Mallory wrote to Ruth two days later, advising her that in the circumstances, he had brought the matter up with Cranage himself, even though Hinks's letter had not yet arrived. 'He [Cranage] has not turned it down definitely, but I don't think they will hear of me going. It will be a big sacrifice for me either way. It is wretched not to be able to talk to you about this darling. You must tell me if you can't bear the idea of me going again, and that will settle it anyway.'[26]

He wanted the decision taken out of his hands. To Hinks on the same day he wrote, 'I'm having a horrible time on the tightrope. I suppose it is certain that Bruce feels as strongly as you put it? It might make a difference if he didn't.' Hinks rushed to offer reassurance. 'If it's any use to you I think I can say that not only Bruce but all the members of the Committee are anxious that you should come. I have not heard any expression except of fear that the University might not be able to spare you.'[27]

When Cranage eventually received Hinks's letter, he felt he could not very well refuse his request, given that Hinks had been so instrumental in finding Mallory in the first place — and Mallory had proved exactly the man for the job. Reluctantly, therefore, he acquiesced, agreeing to put Mallory on half-salary during his absence. The moment had passed for Mallory to say 'no'. Once more, he had let others make an important decision for him. Yet once made, he put his reservations behind him. He wrote to Geoffrey Young,

> A line to let you know I am going out once more. Not the slightest opposition from the syndicate here. But a big tug for me with the ends of this new job gathering in my hands; and Ruth will feel it more this time too.[28]

He explained to his father that though it was a wrench to be going off again instead of settling down to make a new life in Cambridge with Ruth,

> We have both thought that it would look rather grim to see others, without me, engaged in conquering the summit; and now that the prospect revives, I want to have a part in the finish . . . Ruth comes in, of course. She has written that she is willing I should go, and we shall discuss it this weekend. Taking that for granted, my present feeling is that I have to look at it from the point of view of loyalty to the expedition and of carrying through a task begun.[29]

Geoffrey Winthrop Young, the man who persuaded Mallory to go on the first expedition, and was delighted when Everest celebrity ticketed him socially, has told how he pressed Mallory *not* to go this third time. 'He said he *must*, unless the syndicate objected. And I clearly understood and hoped they *would*,' Young recalled. His wife, Eleanor, remembers how Mallory expressed an interest before he left to talk to Captain Scott's widow, Kathleen, who was now married to Hilton Young, Geoffrey's brother. 'In the taxi coming back,' she said, 'Mallory confessed to us that he did not want to return to Everest again.'[30] Geoffrey Keynes remembered a similar conversation.

> He said to me that what he would have to face would be more like war than adventure, and that he did not believe he would

return alive. He knew that no one would criticize him if he refused to go, but he felt it a compulsion. The situation has its literary counterpart in Melville's Captain Ahab and his pursuit of the White Whale, Moby Dick.[31]

It will be seen that these expressions of foreboding attributed to Mallory stem from comments made by friends *after* his death, and it is impossible now to say whether they were merely fleeting moments of guilt at leaving Ruth and his responsibilities, or something more substantial.

Meanwhile, in the few months left to them, Ruth and the children joined Mallory in Cambridge. They had acquired a fine, large house in Herschel Road and were enthusiastically planning its redecoration. 'They will have to spend a lot of money,' remarked Benson when he was shown over it. 'The place was full of interesting and mouldering lumber — birdcages, ladies' dress stands . . . They speak of having paying guests.'[32] Later he wrote peevishly after a dinner party with the Mallorys, 'They have made the house rather grand, but with rather too calculated a simplicity.' Benson was delighted to have Mallory back in Cambridge, but he had lived a bachelor existence too long to accept Ruth readily or her startling frankness. 'She is beautiful, self-conscious, brusque and extremely inattentive,' he noted in his diary. 'She believes herself to be a suggestive and humorous talker, but she is a thin and truculent performer.' (As a measure of his general acidity, he remarked that the other dinner guest was 'a stout pale fish in electric blue'.) Luckily for Ruth, Mallory's other friends welcomed her more warmly, and were very supportive when Mallory went away, 'really, I think, more friendly than they were at Godalming', she wrote just after he sailed.

Mallory urged her to enjoy herself while he was away and not to let domestic matters become a burden.

I much hope you will find some time for painting china this summer, dear one; it is so good for you and makes you so nice. Don't think you must spend hours of time knitting knickers for John, etc. If that must be thought of from a money point of view, you could probably sell the china for the money you would pay for getting a large part of such work done for you, or buying things readymade . . . put the spiritual sort of thing first.[33]

Fine words, but not so easy for Ruth to achieve! She had The Holt to sell, and she might as well let Herschel House for the summer once she had seen the building work finished and the garden laid out. She fell down a ladder trying to stow all Mallory's climbing things into the loft; the bank manager told her they were overdrawn; and a blizzard soon after Mallory sailed caused her to use a ton of coke to keep the place warm.

All the same she apologized for recent friction between them. 'I know I have rather often been cross and not nice, and I'm very sorry, but the bottom reason has nearly always been because I was unhappy at getting so little of you. I know it's pretty stupid to spoil the times I do have you for those when I don't . . . I do miss you a lot.'[34]

XIII

Out of the Blue

In the summer of 1923, Andrew Comyn (Sandy) Irvine, a second-year engineering student at Merton College, Oxford, took part in a university expedition to Eastern Spitsbergen. He was one of a four-man sledging party, led by geologist Noel Odell, with R.A. Frazer as surveyor. They left the expedition's support ship at Cape Dyum on the north-east coast of Central Island and traversed the unknown and mountainous mainland. After a month spent exploring, they rejoined the ship on the opposite side of the island. Both Odell and Frazer had taken part in the university's first expedition in 1921, but neither Irvine nor the fourth member of the team, his close friend Geoffrey Milling, had any previous Arctic or expedition experience. They had been recruited solely for their strength and fitness, which they owed to being oarsmen. Both rowed in the Oxford boat. Several members of the Alpine Club had given financial support to the Spitsbergen venture, and the club was well represented on the team, for besides Odell and Frazer, Tom Longstaff came as naturalist with the shipboard party.

Odell had been obliged to turn down the offer of a place on the 1921 Everest Reconnaissance having already agreed to go to Spitsbergen that year. This time the dates did not conflict, and before he sailed north, he already knew that he would be going to Everest in 1924. Both he and Longstaff were, of course, on the screening committee and would naturally have been on the look-out all the while for likely Himalayan candidates among the university men. Everest must have been a popular topic of conversation, on board ship and while camping in the interior.

One day during the sledging trip, Frazer and Milling having gone off to climb Mount Newton, the highest mountain in the Spitsbergen archipelago, Odell and Irvine skied away to the west, across the Lomme Bay Glacier, towards a group of mountains they could see thirteen or fourteen miles away. These proved to be high rock-peaks 'of such truly alpine aspect,' Odell wrote, 'that their existence came as a surprise in a region where great snow-domes and broad ridges are predominant.'[1] The two men followed the south-east ridge up an elegant peak which Odell afterwards named Mount Irvine. It offered 3,000 feet of magnificent climbing on hard metamorphic rock, to Odell's mind, not unlike to the Tower Ridge of Ben Nevis but on a much larger scale.

It was one of those perfect, God-given days of which lasting memories are made, and it confirmed Odell in his opinion (if indeed he needed further conviction) that here was the ideal companion for such a rigorous undertaking. Besides his physical strength, the quality young Irvine most exhibited – and one which would serve him well on any future expedition – was perpetual good humour. Of his resourcefulness, Odell had long been in no doubt. Several years before while honeymooning in North Wales, Odell and his new bride were just approaching the summit of Foel Grach, having just tramped over Carnedd Llewellyn, when they were astonished to see a young man on a motor-cycle combination riding towards them. He pulled up and politely enquired, 'Is this right for Llanfairfechan?' Odell was intrigued, but it was four years before he learned the identity of the 'freak motorist', as he called him. It was none other than the schoolboy Irvine. They met again on the tideway in Putney, when Irvine was training with the Oxford crew for the 1923 boat race and Odell was considering the make-up of his sledging party. Seeing Irvine again, so full of energy and keen to win, convinced Odell that he typified exactly the spirit he wanted for the expedition.

'Adventurer by nature that he was, he jumped at the idea,' Odell recorded later, 'though I must admit I abundantly emphasised the labour and hardships of sledging and spoke little of the delights of skiing over virgin glaciers, and exploring unknown peaks.'[2] Irvine plunged enthusiastically into preparing himself for the venture. That Easter he went with Odell to North Wales, leading on sight up the Great Gully of Craig yr Ysfa, an impressive first lead for any novice. Once in Spitsbergen, he was so thoroughly taken with expedition life that he could hardly wait for further adventure. In his diary he noted some simple practical hints which would make life more

173

comfortable on future trips. They included: 'socks that don't shrink' and 'a sleeping bag that doesn't moult'. 'Pockets in sledging suit' was another recommendation which he took to heart. In the group photographs taken on Everest in 1924, we see Irvine is the only one with useful zipped pockets in the front of his Shackleton smock.

They arrived home from the Arctic during the first week of September, a month before the selection committee was to meet and finalize names for the 1924 party. Already the point had been stressed in committee that what was needed were young, strong applicants. With the exclusion of Finch from the party, someone with an aptitude for mechanical gadgetry would also be vital to take charge of the day-to-day running of the scientific apparatus. Odell had been placed nominally in charge of oxygen, but he was totally out of sympathy with it, and the old Everest hands — Mallory, Norton, Somervell — were all singularly unhandy in such matters. Irvine was known to be both practical and inventive. His name came before the committee at just the critical moment. Offering youthful vigour and mechanical skills, he must have seemed the answer to all its prayers. Not that his acceptance went through totally un-challenged: the fact that his ice experience was limited to just one Spitsbergen trip counted against him, as did his age — he was at the time only 21, which was rather younger than the committee had been advocating.

Irvine himself was very keen to go, and looked around to see who might speak up for him. He approached George Abraham, the Lakeland photographer and rock climbing pioneer, who duly wrote (10 October) — not to the selection committee of which he was probably unaware, but to Charles Meade on the main Everest Committee — to say how in his opinion Irvine would be 'an ideal chap for the job' and adding that Odell, too, wanted him along. 'He is up again at Oxford now, where on the athletic side he is excep-tionally good, a good tempered youngster of wonderful physique.'[3] Meade passed the recommendation on to Hinks (21 October) com-menting only that Abraham's 'opinion carries weight with me as far as it goes', but (covering himself), 'as you know it does not go as far as India'.[4]

The Alpine Club's selection committee had already met on 16 October, when they had placed Irvine as their second preference on a shortlist of five names being considered for the last two available places (or three, should Mallory find himself unable to go). By 24 October the matter was decided and a formal letter was sent to Irvine advising him he had been chosen. The necessary medical tests gave him no problems, and his college was prepared to grant him two terms' leave. Mallory informed Geoffrey Young, 'Irvine represents our attempt to get one superman, though lack of experience is against him.'[5]

Irvine was anxious to do what he could to remedy that situation in the short time before the expedition sailed. He decided on a period of glacier-skiing around the Aletsch Glacier and sought advice from Arnold Lunn, who was an early promoter of winter sports and the 'inventor' of downhill skiing. Christmas 1923 found Irvine in Mürren as guest of the Lunns, learning a few basic skiing turns, sufficient to enable him to go off and explore the higher snowfields. Arnold Lunn remembers him as a beginner of extraordinary promise:

> After a few days he went in for the elementary test . . . designed to show that the candidate could negotiate the descent of a steep slope by a series of linked turns. The course was started just above the half-way station of the Allmendhubel. When it came to his turn, Sandy pointed his ski straight down the slope, and let go. By a miracle he stood up for most of the way then, at top speed, he came an almighty purler and vanished into a cloud of snow. To the astonishment of the spectators (who all thought he must be badly hurt) he was up in a moment, shook himself, and finished the course . . . in 40 seconds. On that day the next best time was five minutes.[6]

At the end of three weeks Irvine entered and won, against strong opposition, the Strang-Watkins Challenge Cup for Slalom-running and a few days later passed his Second Class Test. Thus prepared, he set off to cross the Oberland glaciers. Poignantly, in the light of what happened on Everest so soon afterwards, he wrote to Arnold Lunn, 'When I am old, I will look back on Christmas, 1923, as the day when to all intents and purposes I was born. I don't think anybody has ever lived until they have been on ski.'[7]

Irvine's family used often to wonder, had he returned from Everest, what he would have made of his life. His brother Hugh, in particular, found it hard to envisage him settling down in any conventional job. Herbert Carr, the editor of *The Irvine Diaries*, believes that, at the time of Everest, Irvine might already have been considering a career in the Canadian Arctic, as were two of his Spitsbergen colleagues, Geoffrey Milling and George Binney, who both went on to work for the Hudson Bay Company.

Irvine was given the role of Equipment Officer on the Everest team, and immediately began familiarizing himself with all the stores they would be taking. He managed to procure one of the 1922 oxygen sets to strip down and study in his workshop at home. Some of its design features struck him even then as unsatisfactory, and he sent a list of suggested improvements to the manufacturers, Siebe Gorman. These were not acted upon, and it is unclear now whether this was through lack of time, or because of an unwillingness (on Siebe Gorman's part) to take advice from a college student. When Odell and Irvine finally had a chance to check the gas equipment that was sent out − which was not until they were well on the road in Tibet − they received an unpleasant shock. Irvine wrote home to Geoffrey Milling:

> The ox. ap. has already been boggled. They haven't taken my design, but what they have sent is hopeless, breaks if you touch it, leaks, is ridiculously clumsy and heavy. Out of 90 cylinders, 15 were empty and 24 leaked badly by the time they got to Calcutta. Ye Gods! I broke one today taking it out of its packing case.[8]

Before leaving home, Irvine had drawn up a list of tools he thought should be taken to guarantee all equipment could be maintained while they were away, and throughout the expedition his tent had the atmosphere of an engineering workshop. Not only did the oxygen sets and stoves require almost constant adjustment, but he would carry out running repairs on all manner of personal items that gave trouble en route: Beetham's camera, Odell's tripod, Geoffrey Bruce's table, a camp stool, the expedition torches, Noel's cinema-motor, Mallory's bed, saddle, axe and crampons; he also fashioned tin shades to replace the cardboard ones supplied with their folding lanterns, which were continually catching fire, and fabricated a 60-foot rope ladder for use on the way to the North Col. His ingenuity and industry seemed limitless. Even on those days when his diary records that he felt quite 'seedy', he would stoically work away, often well into the night, after all the other climbers were tucked up in their warm bags or discussing poetry and philosophy in their tents.

From the very start, the names of Mallory and Irvine were linked by the press. The *Liverpool Post*, releasing the names of the team on

11 January 1924, ran as its headline: MOUNT EVEREST EXPEDITION —
TWO BIRKENHEAD MEN IN THE PARTY. Mallory wrote to his mother:
'Irvine is the star of the new members. He is a very fine fellow, has
been doing excellently up to date, and should prove a splendid
companion on the mountain. I should think the *Birkenhead News* — is
it? — ought to have something to say if he and I reach the top
together.'⁹

No one can say precisely when it was that Mallory first met Irvine.
Mallory is known to have lectured to the Oxford University Mountaineering Club, but this may well have been before Irvine's climbing days; certainly, such an occasion is unlikely to have provided
much of an opportunity to get properly acquainted. When it was
decided that they would both be sailing to India aboard the SS
California, along with J. de V. Hazard and Bentley Beetham, Mallory
wrote to Hinks suggesting that as he and Irvine would be starting
together from Birkenhead, it might be convenient for them to share a
cabin. Hinks had more than enough to organize and replied brusque-
ly that it was up to Mallory to arrange this himself with the ship's
purser. Nothing further was done. Mallory shared his cabin with
Hazard, but took meals with Irvine in the dining saloon. He wrote
home that he found Irvine sensible and not at all highly strung. He
looked just the sort of person to depend upon for anything — except
perhaps conversation.

The four climbers sailed from Liverpool on 29 February, having
been entertained to a farewell dinner the evening before by the
Wayfarers Club, at which the fathers of Mallory and Irvine were also
present as guests of honour.

General Bruce and Norton were already in India by this time; they
had sailed on a mail steamer arriving in Bombay on 16 February. All
members were to meet at the Mount Everest Hotel in Darjeeling
by the third week in March. Odell was making his way from the
Persian oilfields, and Somervell from Travancore where he had
recently begun work as a mission doctor. Geoffrey Bruce would
again be Transport Officer, having obtained dispensation from his
regiment on the North-west Frontier. He was to be assisted this time
by E.C. Shebbeare of the Bengal Forest Department, another
accomplished linguist. The doctor/naturalist was Major R.W.G.
Hingston, an Irishman, who had been on the Indo-Russian Survey
Expedition of 1913 and was now an RAF surgeon in Mesopotamia.

Captain John Noel was to be the photographer and film-maker
once more, but in a rather different capacity than before. Early in

June 1923 he had put the astonishing proposal to the Everest Committee that he pay them £8,000 for full photographic rights to the expedition; or, alternatively, for the film rights alone, he was prepared to pay £6,000. This money he would pay in advance of departure. It did not take the committee long to agree to the larger of the two offers. It could scarcely have concluded otherwise: not only would its financial worries be instantly resolved, but, at the same time, its administrative problems would also be reduced. By removing from the budget all expenditure allocated to photography, the Committee had effectively secured a further saving of £2,000.

Noel was to be responsible for providing all his own equipment and filmstock, transporting it to Tibet, paying any photographic assistants he required, and for his processing costs. To raise this money, he set up a company, Explorer Films Limited, and elicited donations from the public against the promise of a share in anticipated profits. Sir Francis Younghusband was persuaded to become the new company's chairman. The Aga Khan also bought shares.

Clearly Captain Noel was gambling on the hope that this time the mountain would be climbed, and that if it were, a film of the event would be of sufficient public interest to break into the main cinema circuits. This was where its chief hope of income lay, for there was no reason to feel particularly encouraged by traditional methods of exploitation. Sale of photographs from previous expeditions had not been remarkable, and the management of the earlier film – handled by Hinks and Noel – had been disastrous. It was quite a risk Noel was taking, but he obviously considered the stakes to be sufficiently high. He was never one to be short of ideas for catching public attention. Among other ruses, he designed his own Everest 'postage stamps' and franking device for expedition postcards.

On the expedition in 1922 he had processed all his own negative film at Base Camp in a special dark-room tent heated by a yak-dung stove. It meant breaking and melting ice to get water for mixing his developer, and, despite the stove, there were repeated instances when the film froze hard in the intense cold. A special muslin inner tent did little to remove the copious amounts of dust which the fierce winds blew up off the moraine. This time he arranged to have a laboratory custom-built in Darjeeling. All exposed film would be sent back by relays of horsemen in sealed air- and water-tight containers. There, for seven days a week, over a period of four months, Noel's photographic assistant, Arthur Pereira, and another young assistant, worked at developing film and lantern slides, and fulfilling the expedition's obligations to supply pictures to *The Times* and other papers.

★

From the mailboat on his way to India, Bruce wrote in his usual good spirits, 'Here we are all a-blowing and a-growing. I am just specially dropping a line being anxious for two things, to wit: (1) The Book of Stores, (2) The typewriter. Without them I am nothing worth.'[10]

He was quickly reassured that they were on their way. Doubtless the Book of Stores had great practical merit, but the typewriter was in a class by itself, worth its weight in gold! Bruce had never been good at writing. He loathed it. It was far too solitary an occupation for a storyteller who thrived on a rapport with his audience. Hand-written letters from Bruce were always sorry, scrappy, barely legible affairs — but, give him a typewriter and the ear of a sympathetic typewriter-operator (in the form of one of his Transport Officers) — then that was an altogether different matter. Bruce would lyrically expand, would discourse and gossip, and with unerring eye, would describe the ridiculous and quirky elements inherent in most human situations. It is easy to imagine how the business of sending home regular expedition reports, far from being a chore, became a source of welcome entertainment, with the two men guffawing away as they sought just the right phrase to shock or baffle poor Hinks. 'Please note that I am doing my best for this expedition,' Bruce had urged in 1922 when they were running short of funds. 'I have interviewed the Viceroy, I have preached to Boy Scouts, and I have emptied the poes in a Dak Bungalow. This is the meaning of the term General. They are cheap at home, they are more expensive out here. Hurry up with that thousand [£] please!'[11] And in 1924: 'You will be amused to hear that all silver coinage has been called in by the Tibetans and that we are now provided with five complete mule-loads of copper coins.'[12] Earlier, he had written, 'It was lucky the oxygen equipment was sent to Lightfoot's for overhauling as 11 bottles were empty and another 11 half-full. As the G.O.C. Rawalpindi Division remarked when the mule kicked him in the stomach: '"This must not occur again."'[13]

When it came to recruiting native personnel in 1922, one of the first to present himself was Gyalzen, Mallory's 'whey-faced, treacherous knave' who had sold off the porters' rations the year before. Instead of rejecting him, Bruce employed him as sirdar, telling Hinks, 'Although he is not an angel, after I had passed a sufficient number of remarks, calculated to wound him in the tenderest places, he has turned out a very valuable and useful man. Possibly the fact that I am acquainted with the little slips of his life, including the poisoning of a lama in the Upper Kosi Valley, may have something to do with his present angelic behaviour.'14 On the subject of porters, 'This year we have had no trouble at all from drink, certainly not among the cooks. There were one or two little drops taken at Phari, but there wasn't a man who couldn't lie comfortably on the ground without holding on.'15

Bruce would tell how once a Tibetan woman had sent for him and told him that ever since she had seen his face, she had been unwell. What did he propose to do about it?

What it appeared was necessary, was that I should wash her face, which I should add was not only scored by wind and dust, but bearded, and to be perfectly frank, rather dirty. Soap and water having been duly provided, I prepared to set about my unusual task. But alas, it was not to achieve cleanliness that the good lady was so anxious to have her face washed, for no sooner was that rite performed, than she poured the soapy water into a jug and drank it, assuring me that after that she felt much better, indeed completely recovered.16

Younghusband said of Bruce that he remained a boy all his life. 'Bubbling over with all the jollity of a child, he was unique . . . his joviality was infectious. Any circle he entered became instantly alive. His jokes were of the simplest, but he himself laughed so immoderately at them, that no one could help laughing with him.' As a young soldier he had been appointed to the 5th Gurkha Rifles, and remained with the regiment for most of his military service. Gurkhali he spoke fluently, and a good many other dialects besides, though paying scant regard to grammatical niceties. He had a natural empathy with most Asian peoples and his ready fund of bawdy stories made him extremely popular wherever he went. It was said that his wheezy laugh was a tonic the length and breadth of the Himalaya.

On arrival in Darjeeling at the beginning of March, Bruce was greeted by an army of Sherpa porters, many of whom had been with the two earlier expeditions and who, despite the avalanche accident, were anxious to join again. Out of some 300 men, 70 were chosen. Selection was supposed to be subject to the medical approval of Hingston, but Noel remembers that as often as not, when an old favourite presented himself before the General and saluted, Bruce would slap him on the back and steer him quickly past the doctor. 'Why, here is old Chemshar again,' he would say. 'Fine! Of course he must come.' One who was there waiting was Sherpa Angtarkay, one of the two men rescued in the 1922 disaster. There could be no question of leaving him behind. 'I don't think poor Angtarkay . . . ever really recovered from that terrific experience,' wrote Bruce afterwards, 'for he was dug out unconscious, firmly fixed in the snow, standing on his head, having fallen some 60 feet. We felt bound to take him on again, but he soon broke down, and returned with me.'[17]

Karma Paul, a young educated Tibetan, who had been interpreter for the 1922 expedition, when he impressed everyone with his polite efficiency, was again enlisted, with Gyalzen, the erstwhile wicked sirdar, as his assistant. At last, the bandobast (plan of operations) was complete and the huge baggage train started its long journey towards Everest. Bruce was convinced it was going to be third time lucky, for this year's team – if not larger – was considerably stronger than before. His main concern was that he should bring it 'burly and fit' to the foot of the mountain. 'It is almost like dealing with the crew of a university boat,' he said. 'They must be brought up to scratch without having suffered in any way from the arduous 300-mile journey across Tibet, or from degeneration in any form from the effects of a somewhat elevated route at a very early season of the year.'[18]

It was Bruce's own health, in the event, which collapsed under the rigours of the Tibetan spring, when the blizzards that sweep across the Phari Plains can knock the stuffing out of the strongest party. It had not been without trepidation that Bruce's doctor, Wilson, had agreed to let him take part in the 1922 expedition. He had told him then:

I hope you will keep fit, but I take it there will be some second in command. In my view no *one* should be essential. What would have come of this last show if Mallory had not been good enough to step in the leadership when Raeburn failed? . . . Of course, with all care, you might knock up like Raeburn did – though I don't think you'll die, like poor Kellas. You are not

181

quite fit, and if I have any special medical doubts about you, it is as to how you will stand prolonged camping, especially if it is cold and damp — the proposition is different from the Alpine climb, with a good hotel to come back to. So you must be jolly careful.[19]

Bruce was. In 1922 he did not risk climbing above Base Camp, and remained rudely healthy throughout. He seemed impervious to cold, wearing his shorts most of the time. To Bruce goes the uncertain honour of introducing shorts into the British Army: when training his select band of Frontier Scouts to work and fight on steep hillsides, Bruce discovered that by lopping their trousers off at the knee, they were able to range over rough territory with far greater freedom. After initial opposition from Army top brass, the fashion caught on throughout the service.

Wilson was sufficiently encouraged by Bruce's performance in 1922 to write up the case in the *British Medical Journal*. His patient, he said, while in Tibet was 'never sick nor sorry for a day, and now looks ten years younger than he did in 1920'.[20]

Unfortunately, the improvement was not maintained. When the two Harley Street doctors examined Bruce in 1924, they expressed serious reservations about his condition. Dr Larkins reported: 'Bruce's blood pressure has definitely risen since last examined, the heart has definitely dilated on the left side and the mitral murmur markedly increased. He has definite albuminurea.' Dr Anderson found that the altitude test occasioned Bruce some distress, and pronounced him fit to go only to 15,000 feet, not a lot of good when Base Camp is at 16,500 feet. Larkins wrote to Wilson, 'I passed him for the expedition [in 1922] because in spite of his defects I felt he was fit for the job, but this time I honestly do not feel comfortable about passing him.' Wilson was forced to concede that if Bruce were to have an electro-cardiogram, it would probably 'not be ideal'. He did not want Bruce to see a modern heart specialist, who would almost certainly turn him down — if not for his heart, then for his blood pressure. 'I don't want him frightened and I don't want him turned down,' Wilson declared loyally, 'and though I know there is a risk, I am willing to take full responsibility for letting him go, assuming that he keeps feeling as fit as he is now.'[21]

If Wilson was fool enough to take that responsibility, that was his concern, but Larkins had no intention of allowing himself to be pressured into going along with it. He told Wilson, 'I . . . cannot possibly let the Committee take him on without expressing a pretty strong warning.' Even so, Larkins knew full well the committee members would agree to take Bruce on Wilson's say-so, simply because he was considered so indispensable. Let them. 'If he gets apoplexy out there, they have only themselves to kick,'[22] he said, washing his hands of the whole affair.

For his part, Wilson confided in Spencer that though he would not recommend Bruce to an Insurance Office as a first class life, he was sure he had sufficient physiological reserves to carry him through another year of moderate effort. Thus, it was agreed that Bruce could go — with the sole proviso that he allow himself to be examined again before proceeding beyond Darjeeling.

From Yatung, in Tibet, Bruce reported that he had duly submitted himself to the tender mercies of Hingston, the expedition doctor. 'Innumerable instruments were applied to every square inch of my body,' he told Hinks with some relish. '[Hingston] came to the conclusion that Larkins had treated me with extraordinary ferocity and that I might be allowed to proceed. All is well.'[23]

This was written on 3 April, the same day that Andrew Irvine recorded in his expedition diary, 'Had a day off today while most of the first party went on with Norton while the General, who has been a little bit seedy, stayed behind.' The next night Irvine noted that 'the General must be better as he had some good stories for dinner,' but Somervell voiced concern, 'General Bruce not feeling up to the mark; fever, and he doesn't look fit.'[24]

On 7 April Bruce celebrated his fifty-eighth birthday in Phari with a bottle of 'the old family rum', specially sent by his brother from England. Feeling fragile the next morning, he elected to travel not with the rest of the party, but with Hingston and John MacDonald (son of the Trade Officer) by a longer but lower route around the Dochen Lake. Mallory explained the detour to Ruth.

The General's trouble has been an irregular pulse and he and Hingston are both nervous about the effects of these altitudes on his heart — consequently he is not coming with us to Kampa Dzong . . . but (in six days instead of four) by another way which will allow him to camp lower. It is difficult to know how much to make of his trouble (don't mention it); I think it is 10 to 1 he will be all right.[25]

When Bruce's party set off, they were in sufficiently high spirits to attempt to round up a herd of wild donkeys, but later in the day, at Tuna, Bruce collapsed with a severe attack of malaria. From the remarks made by other members, he would seem to have been suffering from a chill for some days, brought on no doubt by sudden exposure to the icy winds of the plain after the warm climate of India. Word was sent to the main party that 'the General was seedy and Hingston had broken all his thermometers'. Hazard rode off to investigate, and returned after dark with the news that the General had a bad chill and MacDonald was ill with mountain sickness.

The following day Bruce had a second malarial bout, which left him so ill he had to be brought back the 50 miles to Yatung on a litter. Although both attacks yielded promptly to treatment, Hingston had been sufficiently alarmed to take no more chances. He knew that full recuperation would be difficult, if not impossible, unless he could get him lower. It was no longer a question of keeping fingers crossed and hoping for the best. Bruce must not be allowed to go on. Hingston insisted on escorting him back to India as soon as he was well enough to travel. To the Everest Committee he reported that Bruce had suffered 'solely the recrudescence of old malarial infection, which must have been dormant in his system for many years and has been rendered active by the cold and wind of Tibet.'[26] It could not possibly have been foreseen, he told them.

No mention was made of the irregular pulse. Hingston went so far as to say that 'General Bruce has suffered in no way from the effects of altitude and his heart had remained sound throughout.' He had lost about two stones in weight and his spleen was dangerously enlarged. Yet within a week of his attack, Bruce was fretting to get back to the expedition, and Hingston was having a hard time restraining him. In desperation, he cabled the Committee, 'Bruce anxious rejoin expedition. I insist relinquishment. Await report. Hingston, Yatung.' In London an emergency meeting was held: what was to be done if Bruce was obdurate and refused to give up?

Spencer declared that if Bruce did not accept the position, it would be necessary to take steps forcibly to stop him rejoining the expedition. Collie's view was that 'Bruce was quite old enough to look after himself. If every explorer who had fever were to turn back, a great deal of exploration would never be done.' Hinks merely complained, 'It is a great nuisance that people cannot be explicit in cablegrams. What does Hingston mean "await report"?' All the same, he was enjoying the drama and wrote to Mrs Bruce, 'I am very much hoping that the General will have taken the doctor by the neck and insist that if he feels well enough, he shall go forward, because, like you, I don't believe very much in doctors, who always play for safety (to themselves). It seems to me the General must be the best judge whether he is fit to travel again.'[27]

The General gave in without further fight. On 19 April the interpreter, Karma Paul, rejoined the main party in Chiblung with the news of Bruce's return to India. Norton then assumed leadership of the expedition and appointed Mallory his second-in-command and leader of the climbing party.

Writing to Younghusband that evening to assure him Bruce's life was no longer in danger, Mallory remarked, 'We shall miss him a good deal in the mess as you may imagine and we shall miss his moral force behind the porters later on and the absence of his genial chaff.'[28] Indeed, it was difficult to size up exactly what practical difference the General's absence would make. His instructions when appointed leader had been to 'father' the whole expedition rather than to take part in any climbing, and that is precisely what the expedition had lost — its caring father figure.

XIV

Vanishing Hopes

Mallory was thrilled at his promotion to Climbing Leader. In a letter to Sir Francis Younghusband, he demonstrated his euphoria by praising Norton to the skies:

> I must tell you, what Norton can't say in a dispatch, that we have a splendid leader in him. He knows the whole bandobast from A to Z, and his eyes are everywhere; is personally acceptable to everyone and makes us all feel happy, is always full of interest, easy and yet dignified, or rather never losing dignity, and a tremendous adventurer — he's dead keen to have a dash with the non-oxygen party. He tells me (and I tell you confidentially, as I'm sure he wouldn't have it broadcast) that when the time comes he must leave it to me in consultation with Somervell to decide whether he'll be the right man for the job. Isn't that the right spirit to bring to Mount Everest?[1]

To Ruth, Mallory could be a little more candid: 'He will do it much better than I could have done in his place, if only because he can talk the lingo freely.'[2]

Mallory was not the only one to express his pleasure at the change in leadership. Hinks, who had always found General Bruce's juvenile sense of humour and irrepressible high spirits a source of irritation, conveyed his satisfaction to Norton, once more factually informative despatches began arriving from the Expedition.

Your cable from Kyiashong was published in *The Times* on the

12th May. We all thought it extremely interesting. I do not know whether the inspiring air of Tibet has made you break out into poetry or whether Mallory was partly responsible, but anyhow the two cablegrams that have come since you have been in command have been in my opinion far better than those written by the General, though I cannot go so far as to say that the Day Editor of *The Times*, who has in my opinion a rather vulgar taste, prefers your style of humour to that of Bruce's.[3]

The bandobast was the subject of long, drawn-out debate. It was an amicable argument, but it had already been going on for months. Norton first put his ideas on paper — his cockshy, as he called it — as long ago as the previous Christmas, and had sent a copy to Mallory, but Mallory had his own view of how things should be tackled. The four days spent in Kampa Dzong, waiting for news of General Bruce, gave them a chance to discuss it further but still they failed to see eye to eye. Norton:

We had so far reached something of an impasse . . . At Darjee-ling, and again at Phari, we had held lengthy discussions — Mallory, Somervell, Geoffrey Bruce, and myself — and, failing to agree altogether, had decided to continue our arguments across the endless plains of Tibet. At Kampa we hoped for a final decision and a cut-and-dried plan of which the details could be worked out on the fortnight's trek still ahead of us . . . But we were to leave Kampa with our plan still in the air.[4]

On 17 April Mallory wrote in haste to Ruth from Tinki Dzong, 'I've had a brain-wave — no other word will describe the process by which I arrived at another plan for climbing the mountain.' It involved concurrent attempts being launched on the summit by parties with and without oxygen, the pair with oxygen starting from Camp VI and the gasless pair from Camp VII. If things went according to plan both parties would meet on the summit. If not, their camps would be in position and they could hope to have sufficient reserve power for another attempt. Mallory boasted to Ruth:

This plan has such great advantages over all others that Norton has taken it up at once and this evening we had another pow-wow and every one has cordially approved.

187

I'm much pleased about this, as you may imagine — if only for this it seems worth while to have come, for Norton's plan was fundamentally unsound I'm sure and might have had very bad results . . . in this one there is much greater safety.

It is impossible yet to say who the parties will be. Norton and I have talked about it; he thinks Somervell and I should lead each of these two parties; he puts himself in my hands as to whether he should be one of them — isn't that generous? We shall have to judge as best we can of people's fitness when we reach the Base Camp. Odell has not been showing up well, but either he or Irvine must be of the gas party.[5]

Some form of announcement was required before Base Camp, however, and by the time they reached Shekar Dzong on 24 April, the issue was decided. Mallory again reported to Ruth:

The difficult work of allotting tasks to men has now been done — Norton and I consulted and he made a general announcement after dinner two days ago. The question as to which of the first two parties should be led by Somervell and which by me was decided on two grounds:
(1) On the assumption that the oxygen party would be less exhausted and be in the position of helping the other, it seemed best that I should use oxygen and be responsible for the descent.
(2) It seemed more likely on his last year's performance that Somervell would recover after a gasless attempt to be useful again later.[6]

The plan of assault was to be for Geoffrey Bruce and Noel Odell to establish Camp V, but not to make a summit attempt. Then, Somervell and Norton would make the unaided attempt, while Mallory and Irvine set off with oxygen.

How the experienced Odell felt about being expended on a non-summit attempt, while the star climber planned to use Odell's inexperienced protégé is not recorded, but Irvine at least was delighted at the prospect. He wrote in his diary, 'I'm awfully glad that I'm with Mallory in the first lot, but I wish ever so much that it was a non-oxygen attempt.' Mallory explained to Ruth (24 April) why he chose Irvine instead of Odell.

It was obvious that either Irvine or Odell should come with me in the first gas party. Odell is in charge of the gas, but Irvine has done the principal engineering work on the apparatus — what was provided was full of leaks and faults and he has practically invented a new instrument, using up only a few of the old parts and cutting out much that was useless and likely to cause trouble; so Irvine will come with me. He will be an extraordinarily stout companion, very capable with the gas and with the cooking apparatus. The only doubt is to what extent his lack of mountaineering experience will be a handicap. I hope the ground will be sufficiently easy.[7]

The idea of climbing with Irvine had begun to germinate in Mallory's mind on the boat coming from England, when he had watched fascinated as Irvine overhauled the equipment. He was already determined that his attempt at least would be made with oxygen, and it struck him what an irresistible combination for the purpose was offered by Irvine's quiet efficiency and his youthful vigour and strength. On 17 March Mallory had written to his sister Mary:

Irvine is a great dab at things mechanical and has some criticisms to make; and there are certainly a good many chances that it [the oxygen] will go wrong or break if we use it. We broke one of the high-pressure tubes that are supposed to stand any amount of bending, putting it away into its box today. However, I rather expect we shall use it, as we can carry 50 per cent more oxygen than last year with the same weight. Norton was keen to go up without oxygen from 26,000, but we've got to camp higher than that to have a chance. Anyway, we've got to get up this time; and if we wait for it and make full preparations, instead of dashing up at the first moment, some of us will reach the summit, I believe . . . I wish Irvine had had a season in the Alps.[8]

No matter how casually stated, the intimation is implicit: Mallory at that time was expecting to climb with Irvine. It is extraordinary that he should have come to such a conclusion so quickly. He had only just met Irvine, he had never climbed with him before, yet here he was favouring him above any of his more experienced, but older, companions. His complete conversion to the use of oxygen is emphasized in a letter to Longstaff the following day:

It's going to be a good party. What we shall do first God knows, and everything will depend on that. I'm dead against trying without oxygen from 26,000 — we should simply knock out three or four of the best and be jolly lucky if they had the sense to turn back in time . . . I'm dead against making ill-prepared dashes; it's got to be all or nothing this time; we don't want to break any more records for height until we reach the summit; and the only way is to start as high as possible . . .

At present, I'm inclined to think that the first job will be a strong reconnaissance with oxygen from [Camp] IV to choose the best camp site and build . . .[9]

Mallory had become convinced that undertaking assaults lightly provisioned, so as to permit a rapid ascent and retreat, would not work on Everest. Being lightly laden — climbing without all the oxygen paraphernalia — does not, as one might expect, enable climbers to ascend faster. Finch had proved the contrary to be true. Only when carrying the heavy load of oxygen could climbers move rapidly. The use of oxygen, however, made it necessary to be placed and stocked in advance, and this would have to be done by climbers capable of getting near the summit but not permitted to climb it. To turn back when forward progress is still possible goes very much against the grain. Everyone harbours the urge to reach the top. Mallory recognized that 'some poor blighters' had to be regarded in effect as high altitude porters and might well be expended getting the job done. It was a tough but inescapable fact of life — not his life, of course, for he would be in a summit party:

The whole difficulty of fitting people in so that they take a part in the assault according to their desire or ambition is so great that I can't feel distressed about the part that falls to me. The gasless party has the better adventure, and as it has always been my pet plan to climb the mountain gasless with two camps above the Chang La [North Col] it is naturally a bit disappointing that I shall be with the other party. Still, the conquest of the mountain is the great thing, and the whole plan is mine and my part will be a sufficiently interesting one and will give me, perhaps, the best chance of all of getting to the top. It is almost unthinkable with this plan that *I* shan't get to the top; I can't see myself coming down defeated. And I have very good hopes that the gasless party will get up. I want all four of us to get

190

there, and I believe it can be done. We shall be starting by moonlight if the morning is calm and should have the mountain climbed if we're lucky before the wind is dangerous.[10]

This style of climbing — constructing a pyramid of camps and supplies, with no summit attempt until the whole train is in place — is known as siege- or Himalayan-style climbing. These days the term is often used pejoratively, the tendency being towards smaller parties and lightweight Alpine-style tactics, but it is, nevertheless, a logical means of ascent on a very big mountain, particularly when large numbers of climbers and porters are involved and manpower is no great problem. It offers surer safeguards against unexpected delays and weather changes, but has the disadvantage, because it takes longer, of exposing more climbers to greater periods of high risk.

Mallory had been giving considerable thought to how much oxygen they would require, and in his letter to Longstaff, remarked,

By the way — it occurred to me only yesterday, though I must have thought of it before when these things were fresh in the mind — by your calculations what was Finch's height per hour on his last day up. I understood that they started at 6.30 and made 1800 feet by noon (from 25,500 to 27,235), not more, therefore reckoning four and a half hours going rate equals 400 feet, a maximum. But Norton reckons 600. It is a vital point, as my reckoning would mean laying out bottles for a party starting from 26,000. I hope I shall find a copy of the book at Darjeeling to look that up.[11]

The question of climbing speeds with and without oxygen had become completely muddled. Had it not, there could have been little objection to oxygen use if the real goal was to climb Everest in any way possible. Yet here was Mallory reckoning Finch's ascent speed to be 400 feet per hour, Norton 600; whereas Finch, the man who actually did the climbing states clearly that his climb rates were 1,000 feet an hour from Camp IV to Camp V, and 900 feet an hour above Camp V! This pathological confusion extends to the present.

As they crossed Tibet, Irvine worked hard trying to salvage the best he could from the oxygen apparatus. Odell wrote a full report home from Shekar Dzong certifying that all eleven sets had been found to leak, and 38 of the oxygen cylinders had also leaked more or less badly, despite having been checked and recharged where

191

necessary in Calcutta. Nine of the carrying frames were defective. After great effort, Irvine had made five of the sets safe enough to use, but of these, only on four could emergency tubes be fitted. Everyone was impressed at his ingenuity. By inverting the oxygen bottles and doing away with some of the fragile valves and pipework, Irvine had managed to save 4 or 5 lbs in weight 'besides making a much more certain as well as more convenient instrument', as Mallory informed Ruth on 24 April. That evening four of the team spent an hour and a half testing Irvine's 'Mark V' apparatus by climbing the loose rock up to the Dzong. Mallory:

> I was glad to find I could easily carry it up the hill even without using the gas, and better, of course, with it. On steep ground where one has to climb more or less the load is a great handicap, and at this elevation a man is better without it. The weight is about 30 lbs, or rather less. There is nothing in front of one's body to hinder climbing, and the general impression I have is that it is a perfectly manageable load.[12]

The expedition entered the Rongbuk Valley on 27 April, passed the Monastery the following day, and arrived at Base Camp on the day after that.

'April 29. Bloody morning, light driving snow, very cold and felt rather rotten.'[13] So starts Andrew Irvine's diary on the first morning at Base Camp. The arrival of the ten sahibs and their army of over 200 porters and Sherpas marked the change-over from moving supplies by beasts of burden to the carrying of them by porters. For the third British Everest Expedition, arrival at Base Camp marked the beginning of a long siege, high hopes and ultimately a tragedy that would reverberate through generations of climbers.

The Rongbuk Valley is a barren channel carved out over aeons by the flow of the Rongbuk Glacier, which itself is fed by the snows of Everest's vast North Face. The great Rongbuk Monastery lies about half way up the valley, some 16 miles from Everest, at 16,500 feet. Until the Red Guard destroyed it in the Cultural Revolution, it was home to some 20 lamas and several hundred Buddhist monks. The British climbers set their Base Camp a few miles up-valley from the monastery, in full view of Everest's great North Face. In the sharp, clear air, the mountain looked close enough to touch, but they were still 12 miles from its foot.

Norton began at once to organize the assault. Before any climbing could start, several tons of food and equipment needed ferrying up the long, gradual incline of the Rongbuk and East Rongbuk Glaciers, which came to be known as *via dolorosa*, to Camp III at 21,000 feet, beneath the steep slopes of the North Col. Usually sheltered from the continuous blast of westerly winds, Camp III is the jumping-off point for the real climb of the mountain. This far it is a long uphill plod, but ahead is the treacherous ascent up the steep cliffs of the Col to Camp IV. Exactly how this considerable mass of stores and gear was to be delivered to the base of the mountain in time to allow the climbers to make their summit attempts, and still beat the arrival of the summer monsoon storms, was a subject that had much exercised their minds on the march in. Taking his lead from the onset of the monsoon in 1922, which had hit the mountain on 1 June, Norton was determined to stock Camp III in time to reach the summit by 17 May.

In charge of leading the first carry of equipment to Camp III, Mallory saw to it that oxygen equipment rather than extra food or material went up first. Perhaps he was concerned that if it did not go up on the carry he was leading, it might not find a place on anyone else's. The stocking of Camp III soon turned into a minor disaster. Mallory, with the first group of porters, reached the camp safely on 5 May, but the second group, which was scheduled to arrive the following day, carrying essential food and additional bedding for both groups, ran into a blizzard shortly after leaving Camp II. Mallory came half-way down from Camp III to guide the porters the rest of their way, but to no avail. The porters could not continue in the fierce storm, and Mallory was forced to have them dump their loads short of the higher camp. That night was unusually cold. There was little food and inadequate bedding at Camp III for the porters, most of whom were already suffering from mountain sickness.

By morning the porters were in very bad shape indeed, far too sick to carry loads, and most of them vomiting. Mallory was faced with no alternative but to send them all back down to Camp II. He escorted them part of the way and then turned round to guide up a further small group of laden men. These porters, too, were in an exhausted condition. Mallory and Irvine bundled them into tents, distributed among them some of the high altitude sleeping bags and got a primus going. The temperature remained around zero and there was no let up in the strong wind.

It would be easy to criticize Mallory for the foul-up at Camps II and III, were it not for the fact that it was Norton's plan to have such large numbers of porters carry up in close convoy. Just as with the decision to send two summit parties up simultaneously — Mallory's 'Brainwave' — this stocking plan allowed no margin for error or the effects of bad weather. Unjustified as it may be, it is difficult to avoid reading into Geoffrey Bruce's expedition report a gruff reproach to Mallory for the effects of the storm:

> We [Bruce and the reserve porters] arrived at Camp II on May 8th, and found the tents pitched in the same spot as they were two years ago beside the frozen lake, with the high wall of glittering ice cliffs closing it in on the lower side. Instead of finding the camp empty except for a cook and an odd porter or two, we found it fully occupied. There had been a severe breakdown, which would undoubtedly have developed into a complete collapse of the porters had Norton not been present at the critical moment to keep them on their feet and restore their ebbing courage and spirits. He explained to me what had happened on the two previous days.
> He and Somervell reached Camp II on May 7th without incident, but on arrival discovered that No 2 party based there had encountered such appalling weather that Mallory had decided to form a dump on the glacier, a mile short of camp, and send them back. That evening between four and six o'clock they observed some porters staggering wearily down the glacier from the direction of Camp III. These men belonged to the first party, and had made one journey to the camp with full loads two days before. They had since then been confined to their tents in Camp III, with only one blanket apiece, and a little uncooked barley to eat, and were now driven out unable to bear it longer, utterly exhausted.[14]

The blizzard continued unabated. Climbers and porters huddled in their tents, the insides of which became covered with fine spindrift that penetrated everywhere. It was too much to bear. Norton called the dispirited climbers down from the mountain, and retreated with them the full 12 miles to Base Camp above the Rongbuk Monastery. Recuperation was essential if the expedition was to entertain any hope of carrying out the assault on the mountain. Irvine reports the reassembly of the party at Base on 11 May, and champagne has added sparkle to his usual matter-of-fact style:

George [Mallory] and I and Noel came to the base camp to find Hingston just arrived and very cheery, having left the General quite fit again. We had a very amusing dinner with a couple of bottles of champagne. A very dirty and bedraggled company. Hingston clean shaven and proper sitting opposite Shebbeare with a face like a villain and a balaclava inside out on the back of his head. Hazard in a flying helmet with a bristly chin sticking out further than ever. Beetham sat silent most of the time, round and black like a mixture of Judas Iscariot and an apple dumpling. George sitting on a very low chair could hardly be seen above the table except for a cloth hat pinned up on one side with a huge safety pin and covered with candle grease. Noel as usual leaning back with his chin down and cloth hat over his eyes, grinning to himself. Everyone was very happy to be back in a Christian mess hut eating decent food.[15]

With the enforced rest each climber had time to drain himself of the tension of constant reaction to the mountain's seemingly malevolent efforts to thwart access to her flanks. He could gather his thoughts, write letters and, in general, loaf about waiting for strength slowly to return. It also allowed time to feel the inexorable pressure of opportunity slipping by.

Irvine, as usual, spent most of this unexpected period of inaction repairing other people's belongings, making gadgets for Noel's camera, tinkering with the oxygen and giving porters lessons in lighting primuses. Mallory fretted, unable to sit still. He went bouldering with Somervell and Odell, but his sights were fixed on climbing far higher than the walls of the Rongbuk Valley. Possessed by a will to reach the summit, he spent much of his time working out a new deployment of the porters and climbing team up the mountain.

His plan was to shift the original time-table so as to result in a summit attempt from Camps VI and VII on Ascension Day, 29 May. 'He seemed to be ill at ease, always scheming and planning,' wrote John Noel, who had invited Mallory to share his tent at Base Camp.[16] As the week slipped away, and still they could not get to grips with the mountain, Mallory felt what he considered a sheer waste of time even more keenly. In fact, it is now recognized that to follow an initial exposure to high altitude with rest at a lower level, is the *ideal* method of building acclimatization. Norton's retreat, with hindsight, therefore, was a fortuitous event that allowed the climbers to achieve a level of performance on the mountain that was not significantly bettered until 1978 when Reinhold Messner and Peter Habeler eventually became the first to climb Everest without using oxygen. Yet, at the time, the climbers were unsure even if man could survive at altitudes never before attained. With the monsoon storms threatening to blanket the mountain with impassable snow, they were growing increasingly pessimistic, and were almost beaten before they had really started.

The porters were still demoralized by the cold, wretched week spent on the glacier. Several had developed pneumonia, one had a broken leg, another his feet frostbitten to the ankles and one of the Gurkha NCOs a suspected clot on the brain. The latter two could only have been saved in a hospital, and in a few days, both died. Hot baths and champagne dinners notwithstanding, it was a gloomy and worried Base Camp crowd during the week of 12 May.

The climbers believed themselves to be weaker this year than on the previous expedition. Somervell attributed this to the enervating week spent holed up in Camp III. Mallory was convinced that both Somervell and Norton were below their form of 1922, and felt himself to be 'the strongest of the lot, the most likely to get to the top, with or without gas'.[17] It was an appraisal that must have been shared by Norton, who was never more than one day away from Mallory. Beetham had not been well since leaving India. First he had persistent dysentery and now was incapacitated with sciatica. It looked doubtful whether he would be able to make much contribution at all, although he had been one of the highest hopes at the start. Hazard kept himself very much to himself. Mallory described him to Ruth as 'the only difficulty' adding, 'he and Beetham don't love each other'.[18] The sad fact was that none of them had much love for Hazard — only Odell was able to get on with him at all. According to Somervell, Hazard had 'built a psychological wall round himself, inside which he lives. Occasionally he bursts out of this with a "By Gad, this is fine!" — for he enjoys (inside the wall) every minute of the Tibetan travel, and even hardship. Then the shell closes, to let nothing in.'[19] Geoffrey Bruce, though his role was to supervise the porters, would obviously play a climbing role again this year, if his form was anything to go by. He was the most forceful personality in the camp, and in Somervell's view, the most essential member of the whole expedition:

Some people know naturally what is the right thing to do,

others have the ability to make others do what they think ought to be done. Geoffrey is one of the few people I know who combines these two qualities. He knows exactly how to get the best out of the porters, and does it with strength combined with kindness.[20]

Bruce was very close to Norton, and had considerable influence when it came to decision-making. With his efficiency and his military sense of order, it is no wonder he often felt Mallory to be disorganized. He took no pains to conceal his disdain for shambolic organization, as his report of the fiasco of the first attempts to stock Camp III demonstrates. The surprise of the expedition was young Irvine, the blue-eyed boy (Somervell again), 'neither bumptious by virtue of his "blue", nor squashed by the age of the rest of us. Mild but strong, full of common sense . . . He's thoroughly a man (or boy) of the world, yet with high ideals, and very decent with the porters.' Mallory felt he showed more of a winning spirit than the other newcomers, but worried that 'hard things seem to hit him a bit harder'. Would he learn to pace himself, he wondered, and conserve his energy on easier ground?

What was going through Mallory's mind during that week of enforced idleness as he sat in Base Camp each evening, Everest brooding impassively in the distance? On his shoulders, as he well knew, rested the best chance of reaching the summit, and he was supremely conscious of the burden of responsibility he bore for such hopes. He felt entrusted to reach the summit. At almost thirty-eight years old, he did not expect another opportunity. The possibility of defeat could hardly be entertained, for it would mean not only that he had missed the one chance, as he now saw it, to make something significant of his life, but that he had failed to live up to other people's expectations of him. He had lectured boldly about his third attempt on Everest, assuring Harvard students that 'Mount Everest is asking for trouble' and that soon there would be a different story to tell.[21]

'May 17th', Andrew Irvine's diary reads. 'The day we were scheduled to reach the summit. Not a cloud on the mountain up till 11.00 a.m. Perfect day, no wind early. What a pity!'[22] It marked instead the day they started moving up the glacier again for a fresh attempt. By the evening of 19 May they were once more in occupation of Camp III.

The North Col can be reached by traversing upward across a series of gentle terraces, and this easy route still lures the unwary — with regularly disastrous results. When Mallory descended from the North Col in 1921, he spotted an avalanche that had started five yards below their ascending tracks. He analysed this ominous event at great length in the expedition report, correctly assessing the deceptively innocent nature of snow conditions on the Col's east slope.[23] Yet the warning was not enough: in 1922, it was while diagonally crossing a steep scoop here that the avalanche occurred which wrenched Mallory and his party down the slope, killing seven porters. Adopting a direct line up the steep slope is safer by far than the easier zig-zag line. It is unrelenting, hard work, but avoids cutting a horizontal track that can release an avalanche.

Mallory and Norton decided on a line to the right, or north, of that used in 1922 and began working their way up, Odell and one of the Sherpas, Lhakpa Tsering, following in their tracks. The route involved negotiating a narrow ice chimney, which Mallory led, as Norton said, 'carefully, neatly, and in that beautiful style that was all his own'. Higher up, however, they were left with no option but to tack across steep slopes to attain the sheltered shelf, where Camp IV was again to be situated. In the expedition book Norton described this section:

We both had unpleasant recollections of this traverse, which had changed little since we last crossed it on our descent in deep fresh snow two years before, when at every step it looked as if the whole surface snow was bound to peel and carry us with it into the abyss below; and for Mallory it recalled an even more sinister incident, for in 1921, when he first discovered this route to the North Col, the whole surface *did* peel off between his party crossing it in the ascent and their descent an hour later.

Mallory's nerves responded as usual to the call on them, and he again insisted on taking the lead. We agreed that the safest way to negotiate the place was to climb nearly vertically up the steepest pitch and only traverse to the left at its top where the slope began to ease off towards the edge of the shelf above.[24]

The group reached the Camp IV site and dropped its loads. Mallory there and then insisted on opening the way from the ledge to the top of the col, and Odell at once volunteered to lead the way. Norton felt no inclination to go further:

I discovered an urgent need to drive some pickets for a fixed rope which should hang down the steepest part of our ladder of steps below — a ten-minute job. The task of the other two proved the affair of a long hour, and Mallory, who had borne the heaviest brunt of the previous work, looked nearly at the end of his tether by the time they rejoined me, for the site of Camp IV is separated from the Col by a maze of snow ridges and partially concealed crevasses — cruel hard work for a tired man.[25]

Norton had no intention of staying long at the North Col camp and at 3.45 p.m. set off back down. 'The less said about the descent the better. We took the 1922 route and, going very fast, had a series of slips and tumbles into crevasses, for which there could be no explanation but sheer carelessness.'[26]

Slips and tumbles! Unnoticed by the others, Mallory, scouting an alternative line, fell 10 feet into a crevasse, only saving himself from falling further by instinctively jamming his axe across its walls. Below was a very unpleasant black hole; 'above another and rounder hole where blue sky showed'. He yelled for help, frightened that if he started scrabbling to get out, he was more than likely to dislodge himself and fall deeper. The others were too far away to hear his shouts, so there was no option but for Mallory cautiously to extricate himself. When, exhausted, he finally wriggled through a hole cut in the side of the crevasse, he found himself on the wrong side of the chasm and had still somehow to get round the dangerous place without falling in again. He cut steps across a nasty slope of very hard ice to avoid the danger, but it was an exertion which, at the end of such an energetic day, almost finished him.

Irvine reports that, on the descent, Norton glissaded 'out of control', and Odell that Lhakpa Tsering had tied himself on to the rope by means of a reef knot that promptly slipped open upon the first fall. The porter 'was only saved from fatal consequences by a large patch of soft snow'.[27]

Any one of these accidents could have been fatal. After all their protestations, all their deliberations about the necessity of avoiding the 1922 line, the climbers still descended via this fatally easier route when they were thoroughly exhausted. Perhaps they had no choice. They may not have had energy enough left to retreat down the safer but more arduous route they had just created. All they could do was to trust to luck that the easy route would not avalanche. So thin is the line between safety and disaster that mountaineers daily tread. These climbers were often up against that line, and often crossed it.

Returning to the security of Camp III was no treat either. Norton describes the comforts of this little home:

> During all this phase Camp III was a truly horrid spot. The stones of the moraine on which it was pitched, stones which in 1922 radiated pleasantly the heat of the sun, were always covered with fresh snow; the little trickle of running water which their warmth would have produced was frozen stiff, and every drop of drinking water (I omit the usual reference to washing!) had to be melted over a Primus stove. Never a meal was eaten in the open, and I remember particularly the hatefulness of the evening meal, with the camp in the cold shadow and one's feet like stones. We made rather a point of collecting in a spare tent pitched for the purpose to eat our meals — a last flicker of the social amenities. We had a real live cook at Camp III this year. Three of our total staff of four cooks took it turn and turn about at each of Camps I, II and III; and if I shudder now at the recollection of some of those hateful meals, I am fain to admit that seldom has food been cooked under more difficult condition. Tea made with water which boils at a temperature in which you can bear the hand isn't very palatable even if it does not contain an admixture of paraffin oil and last night's 'mutton and veg'.[28]

'Alas, poor Kancha [one of the cooks] died of ptomaine poisoning in his own home a few days after our return to Darjeeling,' Norton records as an afterthought.

To warm up at night before turning into their tents, known as 'Balmoral' and 'Sandringham', they would each find a flat stone and for as much as ten minutes attempt a double mark-time on the spot.

The following morning Somervell, Irvine and Hazard guided a dozen laden porters up to the North Col. The plan was to leave Hazard in charge of the porters at Camp IV, and for Somervell and Irvine to return to Camp III to make ready for their later attempts. Odell and Bruce were to climb up, spend the night at the North Col, and then take the 12 porters up the North Ridge to establish Camp V at 25,500 feet.

The climbers and porters set off in intermittent sunshine with light, dry snow falling. Soon the air turned unduly warm, a portent of the impending monsoon. By 1 p.m. the snow turned wet, and began falling more heavily. Somervell and Irvine did not return until 6.35 p.m. They had hauled the porters' loads by rope up the steep chimney section of the climb, with Hazard tying the loads on below. It was a gruelling 2½-hour task, and in order to be able to get back to Camp III in the rapidly deteriorating weather, Somervell and Irvine left Hazard and the porters when they were still 150 feet short of Camp IV. 'Young Irvine was a perfect tower of strength, and his splendid physique never stood him in better stead,' Norton wrote upon hearing Somervell's report of the day's work.[29] The effort, however, had obviously taken its toll. In a moment of inattentiveness, Irvine too took a 'nasty slip' on the descent, but once more luck intervened, and the pair returned safely to Camp III.

The stage was now set for the expedition's second disastrous reversal. The next morning, 22 May, it was still snowing heavily, so that it was impossible for Geoffrey Bruce and Odell to join Hazard and his 'none-too-merry men' at Camp IV as planned. That night the temperature fell to −24°F which, according to Norton, was the coldest ever recorded in these parts. The morning dawned fine though bitterly cold, and Bruce and Odell set off with 17 porters. It began snowing again at 3 p.m. and they were forced to turn back just short of the ice chimney, having found the snow conditions too unsafe to continue. They could see Hazard's party retreating above them.

It was 5 p.m. when Hazard finally stumbled into Camp III with the alarming news that four of his men were stranded up at Camp IV. He had inexplicably left one man, the cook, behind in charge of the camp when he brought the others down. While he was leading across the upper traverse, three more had turned back. There was no European with them and little food in the camp. A bag of porters' rations had been lost down the cliff. Even more serious, two of the men were already suffering from frostbite. It was an extremely grave situation. The weather was worsening, and if they could not be brought down the following day, the expedition would almost certainly have another tragedy on its hands. Norton had been so determined that there should be no fatalities this year, and that the porters should be safeguarded at all times, yet once again events had galloped beyond his control.

Whatever the weather, an attempt would have to be made in the morning to reach those marooned. It was a task which was going to need three men, and they would have to be the three strongest — Norton, Mallory and Somervell. The effort required of them on a mission like this could well rule them out for any further action, though that was their last consideration in the urgency of the situation. In any case, it looked increasingly unlikely that the weather would ever improve enough for them to continue with an assault on the summit. Mallory and Somervell were already suffering badly with altitude cough, a form of bronchitis brought on by the cold air.

Neither Norton nor Mallory put the odds for getting all the men back safely at more than 2 to 1 on. After a very tricky operation Somervell, from a position on the traverse at the end of a 200-foot run-out of rope, began passing the porters down the taut line to the other two. In their anxiety to be off, two of the porters slipped and began sliding on their backs towards the ice cliffs. The build-up of ploughed snow under them was all that halted their progress. They were by then too terrified to move. There was only one thing for Somervell to do in this desperate predicament. He drove his ice-axe hard into the snow and hooked the rope over it. There was scarcely enough slack to reach down to the stricken men some distance below him. To gain a foot or two more, Somervell released the end from about his waist and slewed it round his right wrist. Gingerly he lowered himself, trusting his weight to the belay on his precariously-lodged ice-axe. With his free hand he was then able to haul the men up one at a time, gathering them 'to his bosom in a paternal manner worthy of Abraham'[30] before directing them back along the rope into the waiting arms of the others. Still they had the chimney to negotiate.

At last, in darkness, they reached the moraine above Camp III where they were greeted by Noel and Odell bringing welcome flasks of hot soup. Had the snow been any worse that day, Mallory told Ruth, things might have been very bad indeed. 'Poor old Norton was very hard hit altogether, hating the thought of such a bad muddle.'

When news of the rescue got home to London, it was rightly applauded as the most heroic feat ever seen on Everest. Longstaff congratulated the three men on an achievement of supreme skill, but thought it a 'terrible pity' it had been necessary. Writing a report for an Indian paper he was even more effusive in his praise: 'Talk about pulling the whiskers of Death — these folk crawled in through the chinks between his closed teeth! None of three expected to come out of it alive, [so] they could not take Geoffrey Bruce with them, for his local knowledge would be needed to shepherd the expedition home.'[31]

They were now only a week from the date that the monsoon broke in 1922. They could hope it would arrive later this year, but still it left desperately little time for a proper assault on the mountain. It was now a month since they had arrived in Base Camp and no progress at all had been made beyond the North Col, but as Mallory told Ruth, 'N[orton] had been quite right to bring us down for rest. It is no good sending men up the mountain unfit. The physique of the whole party has gone down sadly. The only chance now is to get fit and go for a simpler quicker plan. The only plumb fit man is Geoffrey Bruce.'[32]

A council-of-war was called, seven of the team coming together in Camp I, to examine all the possibilities now facing them. It was obviously courting danger to make use of armies of porters in such dangerous snow conditions; their two setbacks this year and the avalanche disaster of 1922 spelt that out clearly enough. Besides, when they started totting up how many porters were in a fit state for service as far as the North Col, only fifteen of the original fifty-five could be counted upon. This was serious. So far, all they had at Camp IV were four tents and sufficient sleeping bags for twelve porters and one climber. Food and fuel had still to be carried up, as had all the tents and stores for the higher camps, and whatever oxygen apparatus they decided they required.

The easiest saving on porter strength, in Norton's mind at least, would be to dispense with the oxygen. Ethically, he had never favoured its use, and remained unconvinced that any real benefit could be obtained from it. When he had been delegated to use it in 1922, he had quickly seized the opportunity to get away without it when Finch was off colour. Its chronic tendency to leak and break had done nothing to alter his views: 'In the end the simplest possible plan carried the day and was adopted *nem. con.* after I had made a careful analysis of the transport it entailed, as compared with that required by any other form of attempt. We decided to scrap oxygen altogether.'[33] Mallory alone was unhappy at this idea. He wrote bitterly to Pye,

All sound plans are now abandoned for two consecutive dashes without gas. Geoffrey Bruce and I the first party (provided I'm fit), and Norton and Somervell in the second — old gangers first, but in fact nothing but a consideration of what is likely to succeed has come in. If the monsoon lets us start from Camp

IV, it will almost certainly catch us on one of the *three* days from there. Bright prospects![34]

Why this concern by Mallory, and no one else — not even Irvine, who spent an enormous amount of time modifying and repairing the cantankerous equipment? Having convinced himself slowly and against his will, that using oxygen would indeed speed up the ascent and provide the energy he believed his age had caused him to lose, he found it hard to accept now that he would not be permitted to reap its benefit. Instead, he must force his weary body once more up the mountain against all resistance of will and played-out muscle power. There was another disappointing aspect occasioned by the change of plan, too, as he explained to his mother. It would mean that he and Irvine could no longer make their bid together, as he had hoped. Irvine voiced the same disappointment in his diary. 'Feel very fit tonight. I wish I was in the first party instead of a bloody reserve.'

As ever, Mallory took the mountain's rebuffs hard. He had written to Ruth in considerable despondency from Camp I, where through his tent door he could see nothing but 'a world of snow and vanishing hopes'. His cough had sapped his strength, and all that could force him on now was his spirit, but it was an indomitable spirit and he now set it in gear for one final intense burst of effort. 'The issue will shortly be decided,' he wrote in the expedition despatch. 'The third time we walk up East Rongbuk Glacier will be the last, for better or worse. We have counted our wounded and know, roughly, how much to strike off the strength of our little army as we plan the next act of battle.'[35]

He wrote to reassure his mother that he would take every care, and to Ruth, 'Darling, I wish you the best I can — that your anxiety will be at an end before you get this, with the best news, which will also be the quickest. It is fifty to one against us, but we'll have a whack yet and do ourselves proud. Great love to you.'[36]

Thus climbing without oxygen, Mallory and Bruce set out on 30 May for the attempt that Mallory believed would be 'the last, for better or for worse'. They reached the North Col camp the next day with nine porters. On 1 June they set out in a bitter north-west wind to establish Camp V. Leaving the relative shelter of Camp IV, the climbers were assailed by wind so strong it continually knocked them off their stride. At 25,000 feet four of the porters could carry no farther. They dumped their 20 lb loads and sat down exhausted.

Mallory, Bruce and the remaining four porters struggled on some

300 feet higher to a point where Mallory and three of the porters levelled out a platform and set up two tents. Bruce and the other porter – Sherpa Lobsang – each made two carries from the 25,000 ft dump up to Camp V, after which all but three of the porters returned to Camp IV. Those remaining jammed into one tent, and Mallory and Bruce spent a stormy night in the second. In the morning, none of the porters stirred. They were the pick of the expedition's 'tigers', but, despite Bruce's pleadings, they could not be coaxed upward. Bruce, too, was not feeling up to the mark after the previous day's exertions. They debated the position and saw little for it but to abandon the attempt. Mallory sent Norton a note with one of the returning porters.

Show's crashed – wind took the heart out of our porters yesterday and none will face going higher today . . . we are staying for the present to improve the camp, make the third emplacement and perhaps if you have better luck than us you will be able to establish VI tomorrow.[37]

This letter is curious for what it does not say. On the previous day, Mallory had spent considerable time building platforms for two tents. Now he proposed to level out a third – hardly an urgent task with the expedition frittering away its climbing opportunity. Should not Mallory and Bruce, at least, have continued without the porters and endeavoured to place Camp VI as planned? Such an act could have made a significant difference to the attempt of Norton and Somervell who were climbing up to Camp V at that very moment. It was not a suggestion anyone made, and indeed afterwards it was discovered that Bruce had strained his heart, and would probably have been unwise to go on though he was prepared to do so. Norton commented only on the deceptiveness of judging conditions higher on the mountain when they are 'quite perfect' lower down.

It is impossible to say when Mallory first began nurturing the idea of making an oxygen bid with Irvine after all, but through design or circumstance, he can be seen throughout this first attempt to have been conserving his energies. It may well be that even as he was making his way up to establish Camp V, Mallory was already regretting what he considered a forlorn oxygenless attempt, and one so unlike how he had envisaged the final climb. When they reached the camp-site, it could be considered out of character that Mallory, usually the first to seize the most difficult part of any climbing task, suddenly busied himself with setting up the Camp V tents, leaving Bruce to make the gruelling journey to retrieve the porters' loads 300 feet below — an hour's strenuous climb. Bruce and Sherpa Lobsang made the round trip twice.

Uncertain conditions would not have prevented the two continuing upwards the following day, even without porters. Norton and Somervell only had the usual difficulties in reaching Camp V on the same day, and in fact they did so in excellent time. Why was Mallory suddenly so ready to abort this summit assault if not that at some point he realized that he was simply not going to make it to the top? After the personal investment he had made in this mountain, failure was almost unthinkable. There was only one way to snatch victory from the jaws of defeat — Mallory could turn back now, before he was quite spent, rather than help others to attain what after all would only be another height record. He no longer believed there was a chance of any of them reaching the summit without oxygen. Oxygen offered the only hope of success and it was up to him now to prove it.

Mallory and Bruce left the little tents standing and retreated down the mountain, passing Norton and Somervell and their porters on the way. The cold wind prevented more than a brief exchange, and Mallory did not apprise Norton of his thoughts at that stage. Later, when they reached Camp IV, they met Odell and Hazard, who had just come up with fresh supplies and were very surprised to see them returning early. Mallory confided in Odell that any further attempt must be made with oxygen. It was his intention to go down to Camp III right away with Bruce, to see if sufficient porters could be mustered to bring up the oxygen apparatus. He conscripted Irvine to accompany him and organize which sets should be brought up.

With this bold decision, Mallory's energy returned threefold. After much vacillation, he now had a sense of purpose again. After being led by others to no avail, Mallory had finally seized control of his own destiny. He would climb as he originally intended — with oxygen and with young Irvine.

XV

The Great Couloir

Norton and Somervell set off from Camp IV at 6.30 a.m. on 2 June for their attempt on the mountain. As soon as they breasted the North Col they were met by the full blast of the west wind that had so taken the spirit out of Mallory and Bruce's porters at Camp V. A short while later, the first rays of the sun reached them and gave slight comfort. Norton has described the clothes he was wearing, which by today's standards sound pathetically inadequate. They comprised a thick woollen vest, flannel shirt, his Shackleton smock with flannel-lined gabardine knickers and soft elastic cashmere puttees, topped off with a fur-lined leather motorcycle helmet and a huge hand-knitted muffler. General Bruce had seen to it that the expedition was supplied with only the very finest puttees, because, as he said, 'Anyone who has worn a properly woven pair of puttees, from their original home — that is the mountains surrounding Kashmir — will never wish to wear any other, and for high climbing it is a fact that improper pressure round the calf and ankles gives extra work to the heart, and may be actually an assistant cause of frostbite of the feet.'[1]

After passing Mallory and Bruce coming down, Norton and Somervell went on to find the strips of cloth the pair of them had left to indicate where they should move off the ridge. They reached Camp V at 1 p.m., having climbed 2,500 feet in 6½ hours, or at a rate of 385 feet per hour. Norton describes the regimen:

The afternoon was spent as every afternoon must always be spent under these conditions. On arrival one crawls into the tent, so completely exhausted that for perhaps three-quarters of an hour one just lies in a sleeping bag and rests. Then duty begins to call, one member of the party with groans and pantings and frequent rests crawls out of his bag, out of the tent and a few yards to a neighbouring patch of snow, where he fills two big aluminium pots with snow, what time his companion with more panting and groans sits up in bed, lights the meta burner and opens some tins of and bags of food — say a stick of pemmican, some tea, sugar and condensed milk, a tin of sardines or bully beef and a box of biscuits.

Presently both are again ensconced in their sleeping bags side-by-side, with the meta cooker doing its indifferent best to produce half a pot of warm water from each piled pot of powdery snow. It doesn't sound a very formidable proceeding, and it might appear that I have rather overdrawn the panting and groans; but I have carried out this routine on three or four occasions, and I can honestly say that I know of nothing — not even the exertion of steep climbing at these heights — which is so utterly exhausting or which calls for more determination than this hateful duty of high-altitude cooking.

The process has to be repeated two or three times as, in addition to the preparation of the evening meal, a thermos flask or two must be filled with water for tomorrow's breakfast and the cooking pots must be washed up. Perhaps the most hateful part of the process is that some of the resultant mess must be eaten, and this itself is only achieved by will power: there is but little desire to eat — sometimes indeed a sense of nausea at the bare idea — though of drink one cannot have enough.[2]

The next morning Norton faced a problem similar to that which had confronted Mallory and Bruce. The porters were near comatose with fatigue and lack of incentive. Norton, who could speak their language, spent a long time exhorting them to further effort. 'If you put us up a camp at 27,000 feet and we reach the top, your names shall appear in letters of gold in the book that will be written to describe the achievement,' he promised. What bargain that might seem to illiterate porters is not clear, but carry they did, coming to within 200 feet of their goal. They put up a magnificent effort; the climbers were to fall far shorter of their goal than the porters did of theirs.

Having set out for Camp VI at 9 a.m., the two climbers and their three porters reached the point beyond which the porters could not continue at 1.30 p.m. They were now at 26,800 feet, and had therefore climbed at a rate of 290 feet per hour. The speed of the little group was held back somewhat by a porter, Semchumbi, with a badly-injured knee, otherwise they might have made a faster ascent. During this day's climb, Norton recognized and passed the highest point he, Somervell and Mallory had reached in 1922. 'I remember a momentary uplift at the thought that we were actually going to a higher camp than the highest point ever reached without oxygen. With a clear day ahead of us, and given favourable conditions, what might we not achieve!'[3]

After building the obligatory rock platform, for nowhere on the North Ridge is there a spot level enough to pitch a tent, the porters were sent back to Camp IV. Norton and Somervell passed an uneventful night, except that Norton's thermos flask – stored inside the sleeping bag to prevent it freezing – become uncorked and all the precious warm fluid leaked away. They were obliged to melt additional snow for their breakfast before they could set off at 6.40 a.m. – this time, as they hoped, for the summit.

It took an hour of slow toil to reach the 'yellow band' of Everest, a 1,000-foot high limestone bedding plane extending the full width of the North Face. It is a feature which changes the character of the slope dramatically for the better, as it is made up of a series of broad almost horizontal ledges, sufficiently broken to afford easy ascent. It marks a welcome relief from the loose sloping slabby rock which comprises the rest of the North Face – easy enough in clear weather, but exceedingly treacherous with even a light dusting of snow.

'The day was fine and nearly windless – a perfect day for our task – yet it was bitterly cold,' recalled Norton. Despite his woollen muffler, he began shivering so violently when he stopped moving that he suspected he was in for a malarial attack, like General Bruce. Alarmed, he took his own pulse and was surprised to find it only about 64, which was no more than twenty above his normal (very slow) resting pulse. Except when actually crossing patches of snow, Norton did not bother to wear his snow goggles. He found their rims obstructed his vision when looking down to place his feet on the loose rock. It was a mistake he would pay for dearly the next day, and indeed later this same day he began seeing double, which made finding footholds no less precarious a business.

Our pace was wretched. My ambition was to do twenty consecutive paces uphill without a pause to rest and pant, elbow on bent knee; yet I never remember achieving it — thirteen was nearer the mark . . . Every five or ten minutes we had to sit down for a minute or two, and we must have looked a sorry couple.[4]

At noon, they reached close to the point where the yellow band enters the Great Couloir. This is a huge vertical gully-like indentation that runs from the Rongbuk Glacier straight up to intersect the North-east Ridge at the final pyramid. They were now at an altitude of around 28,000 feet, the height at which the crux on any North Face climb of Mount Everest is met. The triangular final pyramid of Everest is guarded by a cliff band that encircles the mountain, and which meets the ridge at the First Step. The base of the cliff runs level across the North and South West Faces of the mountain, but as the North-east Ridge rises, the top of the cliff reaches higher. It rises abruptly at the Second Step to about 100-feet high — an almost impassable obstacle in the eyes of all early climbers. For this reason, anyone attempting what has come to be known as the 'Mallory route' is required to ascend the North-east Ridge no later than at the First Step. The seeming advantage of traversing across the North Face to the Great Couloir — the 'Norton Route', favoured by all early Everesters except Mallory — was that the Great Couloir splits into two gullies, each of which cuts through the cliff band and offers potential access to the final pyramid.

Mountaineers, especially rock-climbing specialists such as Mallory, always preferred to follow a ridge line wherever possible, offering as it did the prospect of many hand holds; they would only attempt a face climb if the ridge line was completely blocked. The Norton Route is such a face climb, trading the abrupt steepness of a cliff for a less steep, but generally holdless slope of uncertain, gravelly footing.

It was as they were approaching the Great Couloir that Somervell could not continue. The intensely cold dry air was having a disastrous effect on his throat. High-altitude throat afflicted all the climbers to one degree or other: Mallory had written how he would 'cough fit to tear one's guts'. None came so near to death over the condition, as Somervell. His trouble stemmed from the day they were obliged to rescue the marooned porters; he afterwards reckoned that he must then have suffered frostbite in the lining of his throat. Now great paroxysms of coughing forced him frequently to stop. Even more alarming, his throat appeared blocked and he was experiencing considerable difficulty drawing breath at all.

At midday Somervell announced he could go no further and urged Norton to press on alone and reach the top. Somervell found himself a sheltered rock in the sun and sat watching Norton's back move slowly across the face, taking several photographs of the receding figure.

Norton kept on the top edge of the yellow band, which led at a very slight uphill angle into and across the Great Couloir.

> To reach the latter I had to turn the ends of two pronounced buttresses which ran down the face of the mountain, one of which was a prolongation of a feature on the skyline ridge which we called the Second Step, and which looked so formidable an obstacle where it crossed the ridge that we had chosen the lower route rather than try and surmount it at its highest point.[5]

Here the going became a great deal more difficult. The slope was very steep and there seemed nothing firm beneath the light dusting of powdery snow underfoot. Though the terrain was very similar to that around the 'Eagle's Nest' chalet where he had spent his boyhood holidays, Norton could not feel at home. The whole face of the mountain was composed, he said, of slabs like the tiles on a roof, and all tilted at much the same angle as the pitch of a roof. Twice he was forced to retrace his steps and follow a different band of strata. The Couloir, when he reached it, was choked with deep powdery snow into which he sank sometimes to the knee, sometimes to the waist. The snow was too loose for making steps, or for offering any support if he slipped.

> Beyond the couloir the going got steadily worse; I found myself stepping from tile to tile, as it were, each tile sloping smoothly and steeply downwards; I began to feel that I was too much dependent on the mere friction of a boot nail on the slabs. It was not exactly difficult going, but it was a dangerous place for a single, unroped climber, as one slip would have sent me in all probability to the bottom of the mountain.[6]

Norton was tiring rapidly and the strain of such tentative climbing was beginning to tell. Moreover his double vision seemed to be getting worse. He supposed that above him was perhaps another 200 feet before he would emerge, so he believed, on to the north face of the final pyramid and the safety of the last stretch to the summit. But already time was running short. He realised that if he went on, he could not hope to get back in daylight. There was nothing for it: he would have to turn back.

Norton's decision to return was reached by using his uncommon good sense, and aroused in him none of the disappointment at failure that could be imagined. Altitude dulls all emotion, and it is only later that a sense of failure seeps in. He turned back, as he was to say later, 'on a favourable day when success appeared possible'. Somervell expressed the same sentiment:

> We are both rather done in, too, in general condition, but are satisfied that we had the weather and a good opportunity for the fight with our adversary. There is nothing to complain of. We established camps, the porters played up well, we obtained sleep even at the highest, nearly 27,000 feet, we had a gorgeous day for the climb, almost windless and brilliantly fine, yet were unable to get to the summit. So we have no excuse — we have been beaten in a fair fight; beaten by the height of the mountain, and by our own shortness of breath.[7]

Despite what Somervell says, their defeat was attributed to exhausting themselves in the early part of the expedition, rather than to any inability to function in the thin air. 'I still believe that there is nothing in the atmospheric conditions even between 28,000 and 29,000 feet to prevent a fresh and fit party from reaching the top of Mount Everest without oxygen,' remarked Norton.[8]

Norton had reached a height calculated at 28,128 feet. In his hour of solo climbing, when he thought he had a good deal left in him, he managed to gain less than 100 feet in height and traverse barely one quarter of a mile. Norton's usually steely nerve had begun to waver when exhaustion took him over. The mere process of turning around to face the other way seemed the most frightening move he had ever been called upon to make. Shortly afterwards he could not bring himself to cross a small snowy patch that was far easier than the section he had just covered. He called out to Somervell for help. Somervell came forward the 100 yards and, with surprise showing on his face but without comment, threw Norton the end of the rope to guide him across.

It was not long after this, and a measure of their coldness and fatigue, that Somervell lost grip of his ice-axe and saw it cartwheel away down the slabs. According to Norton, this was at about the spot where, an hour before, Somervell had taken his highest photographs. 'It is a proof of the deceptive picture of the true angle of the mountain conveyed by these photographs that it does not give the impression that a dropped axe would go any distance without coming to rest, yet his never looked like stopping, and disappeared from our view still going strong,' he remarked. This is an interesting observation in the light of the discovery in 1933 of an ice axe on similar slabby ground which must have belonged to Mallory or Irvine.

Norton and Somervell passed Camp VI, collapsing it with stones to prevent it from being blown to shreds, then headed back down towards the North Col. After passing Camp V, some hundred yards from the crest of the North Ridge, the going becomes much safer and the pair unroped. Norton again left Somervell behind by beginning a series of glissades, and soon put a considerable distance between them. But Somervell had not 'stopped to sketch or photograph the effect of the sunset glow', as he supposed. He was fighting for his life.

One of his fits of coughing had succeeded in dislodging the obstruction in his throat, but into such a position that he could breathe neither in nor out. Unable to voice any sound and, without the connecting rope, he had no way of catching Norton's attention. He sank into the snow, convinced death was seconds away, while Norton continued down in blissful ignorance of the drama being enacted behind him. Somervell: 'I made one or two attempts to breathe, but nothing happened. Finally, I pressed my chest with both hands, gave one last almighty push — and the obstruction came up. What a relief! Coughing up a little blood, I once more breathed really freely — more freely than I had done for some days.'9 The obstruction proved to be the entire mucous lining of his larynx.

Somervell's report says he was only a few yards behind Norton (probably to avoid any possible intimations of abandonment), but Norton, a great stickler for accuracy, admits there was a half-hour separation between them at the end. It is common in mountaineering, to the point of being standard practice, for the keep-together discipline of climbing to become unravelled when approaching the home stretch.

It was dark by the time Somervell caught up to Norton, and they switched on their electric torches. Approaching the North Col

213

Camp, Norton shouted to its inhabitants. A short but intricate maze of snow bridges and crevasses barred the last part of the descent, and it was a rule of this expedition that returning climbers, usually in the last stages of exhaustion, were to be met and guided down the last stretch.

> At last I made myself heard, and an answering shout informed us that our escort was coming and was bringing an oxygen apparatus and cylinder. But there was something we wanted far more than oxygen, for we were parched and famished with thirst. I remember shouting again and again, 'We don't want the damned oxygen; we want drink.' My own throat and voice were in none too good a case, and my feeble wail seemed swallowed up in the dim white expanse below glimmering in the starlight.[10]

It was Mallory and Odell who had come out to shepherd them home. Irvine remained in camp preparing them something to eat and drink. 'Somervell had a go at the oxygen, but seemed to get little benefit from it, and I tried it with the same result.' This was an interesting remark by Norton. All through this expedition, and as a standard procedure in the previous one, descending climbers — all excruciatingly dehydrated — were met with hot drink. Here is Mallory bringing them not tea, but oxygen! What could he be thinking about? It is surely indicative of his conversion to the notion that oxygen was a miracle elixir. Somervell made some pretence at feeling a bit better for breathing the oxygen for a few minutes, but later confessed in the Camp Log that it was merely politeness to those who had 'so gallantly provided it'.[11]

Mallory and Irvine had been using oxygen when they raced up in record time from Camp III to the North Col camp the previous day. Irvine wrote:

> We took exactly three hours going up, which included about half an hour at the dump selecting and testing oxygen cylinders. I breathed oxygen all the last half of the way and found that it slowed breathing down at least three times (using 1½ litres per minute). George and I both arrived at the Camp very surprisingly fresh.[12]

This was the first time Mallory had used oxygen for climbing, rather

than practising with it. Having slowly convinced himself of its
theoretic value, he must have been ecstatic to find this strong
confirmation of its utility. Yet, however convincing to Mallory and
Irvine, their display of climbing prowess had moved Odell to
grumble:

> On the evening of June 4th Mallory and Irvine with a few
> coolies came up from III, the two former using oxygen. They
> were able to cover the distance in the fast time of 2½ hours, and
> seemed well pleased with a performance which had no doubt
> been prompted by the wish to demonstrate the real efficacy of
> oxygen. But in my opinion the demonstration was hardly
> justified, and Irvine's throat at any rate, that had already given
> him considerable discomfort from the cold, dry air, that at these
> altitudes can reduce this delicate passage to the consistency of
> cardboard, was palpably aggravated by the effect of oxygen. [13]

Here again is the unassailable logic of the anti-oxygenists. When
the practical advantage of oxygen use is proved, as Mallory and
Irvine so ably did in their quick climb to Camp IV, the result is not
accepted as anything other than a *wish* to demonstrate the efficacy of
oxygen. When Irvine's throat is made sore by breathing the cold, dry
air, it is the fault of breathing oxygen. The fact that Somervell's far
more severe throat condition was most certainly not caused by
oxygen is omitted. Even more interesting is the fact that Norton and
Somervell both *did* try the oxygen apparatus, though, of course,
being on near level ground, and parched, they received no noticeable
advantage from it. Yet it will be this one ineffectual use that Norton
and Somervell will remember as reason for believing that oxygen
was unhelpful.

Resting up and preparing now for the last attempt Irvine had only
one problem. He was exceptionally fair-skinned and throughout the
expedition had suffered badly from sunburn; now it was becoming
nearly unbearable. 'My face was badly cau[gh]t by the sun and wind
on the Col, and my lips are cracked to bits, which makes eating very
unpleasant.' By the following morning, it was even worse: 'June 3rd.
A most unpleasant night when everything on earth seemed to rub
against my face, and each time it was touched bits of burnt and dry
skin came off, which made me nearly scream with pain.' [14]

While still at Camp III preparing for the oxygen attempt, Mallory
and Irvine heard what proved to be a false rumour from a descending

porter, that Norton and Somervell had returned to the North Col that evening. After breakfast the next morning, they learned the galvanizing truth: that Norton and Somervell had successfully placed Camp VI at 27,000 feet and were within striking distance of the summit. Mallory could wait no longer. After an early lunch, he summoned Irvine, rounded up a group of able porters, and set out at once for the North Col.

Just as in 1922 Mallory had become excited when Finch and Bruce started for the summit using oxygen, he had now again to face the fact that victory might slip from his grasp. Only in 1922 he had been able to rationalize, 'I shan't feel the slightest bit jealous of any success they may have. The whole venture of getting up with oxygen is so different from ours that the two hardly enter into competition', whereas now the boot was on the other foot. 'George believes he has seen their downward tracks some 700 ft. below the summit,' Irvine reported, an estimate that would have put them above the Second Step. Perhaps they were returning from the top!

As Mallory and Irvine made their rapid ascent up to the North Col, Hazard, in an unauthorized descent back to Camp III, had left Odell alone to receive descending climbers Norton and Somervell. This independent action infuriated Norton, as did some of Hazard's subsequent movements (most notably an unauthorized journey to the Tsangpo gorges on the way home). In Norton's eyes, Hazard was still to blame for the stranding of the porters.

That evening, lying in their Camp IV tent, Mallory told Norton of his latest plan, to make an oxygen attempt with young Irvine. Although agreeable to this third attempt, Norton was puzzled by Mallory's choice of Irvine as his climbing partner. It is certainly a choice that has intrigued several generations of climbing historians. David Robertson avoids the controversy by presenting a glimpse at both sides equally, and then hurrying on to other subjects. 'Were Irvine's sturdiness and mechanical genius enough to offset his inexperience?' is all he asks. David Pye makes no remark about the choice, but Walt Unsworth uses the question to suggest that Duncan Grant was perhaps correct when he said 'that no recognizable logic played a part in Mallory's decision'. Mallory chose Irvine partly on aesthetic grounds, but Unsworth does offer another possibility, safely posed as a question: 'Was he an ageing Galahad making a last desperate bid to find his Holy Grail and choosing as a companion a young man who embodied all he himself had once been?'[15]

It is a perceptive suggestion, one of many stabs made by Unsworth to provide an answer to this apparently puzzling choice. The reality is far more complex, however, than simply a question of aesthetics. Mallory's choice of Irvine may well reflect a fear of growing older, with the corollary premise that it is necessary to be youthful to obtain success. It also indicates his perception of oxygen as the elixir of youth, which in turn is intimately interwoven with his admiration of young Irvine's wizardry in this respect, too.

The alternative would have been for Mallory to choose to go with Odell, although this in itself may have been a factor in Mallory's decision. Mallory was a man ever impatient for action, a habitual early riser, whereas various colleagues of Odell's have noted affectionately what a long time it always took him to get warmed up. 'Odell is a notorious slow starter: after twelve hours going he is at his best,' wrote Tom Longstaff after Spitsbergen. Mallory may well have been irked by Odell's slow and methodical manner. Moreover, with Odell as partner, the two men would be near equals. If they felt differently about oxygen or about the choice of route, there could well be argument. With Irvine as companion, Mallory would clearly be the boss: it would be his decision which route to take, when to start and when to stop. In all probability, Irvine would even do all the cooking as well.

Yet the most likely answer is one that is not subject to controversial psychologizing. Mallory had long ago chosen Irvine as his oxygen climbing partner, and had said as much in a letter from the boat to his sister. It must have been tacitly understood by both from quite early on that they were a team. They were rarely separated, nearly always side-by-side in the expedition photographs. They were both disappointed when circumstances arranged for Mallory to make the first attempt with Bruce, and indeed, it could have been as much on behalf of Irvine as himself that Mallory resolved to make the final climb. They prepared for days for this particular assault.

The whole question of 'Why not use Odell?' is one that must have astonished Mallory. He had been 'using' Irvine during the entire expedition, and using him well. Irvine had proved to everyone that he was completely dependable, strong as an ox, and possessed astonishing endurance. Odell, on the other hand, had been the unknown quantity. He had been slow to acclimatize, and had not yet made his series of incredible climbs, and it was these climbs, made *after* the disappearance of Mallory and Irvine that firmly demonstrated what an astounding climber Odell had become.

No, if there is a puzzle about this, it is that there should be any puzzle at all. Norton's concern is academic, the natural stance of a leader with ultimate responsibility for all the climbers, worrying about the safety of the younger man. But the puzzle of Mallory's choice of Irvine later became a literary device. Norton was not nearly so concerned about Mallory's choice at the time, even if he might personally have substituted Odell for Irvine. 'It was not time to think of altering existing arrangements especially as Mallory was "leader of the climbing party" and organizing his own show, while I was a blind crock,' he told the Committee afterwards.[16]

At 11 p.m. (4 June), while Mallory and Norton were discussing the next day's assault, Norton suddenly experienced excruciating pain in his eyes. Because he had rarely worn sunglasses during his attempt, thinking they were required only when crossing snow, he was struck snowblind due to the intense ultraviolet radiation at that altitude, regardless of visible glare. He would be totally blind for the next 60 hours.

The following day, Somervell left for Camp III, while Norton lay suffering inside his darkened tent. Hazard was called up from Camp III by means of the blanket signal they were using. The time was spent quietly, as all prepared for Mallory and Irvine's attempt the following day. Irvine worked hard to get at least two sets of oxygen apparatus functioning properly. It was a brilliant day, with sun temperatures of 105°F, and air temperature below freezing.

XVI

The Last Climb

On the morning of 6 June, Mallory and Irvine strapped on their
oxygen systems, having breakfasted on 'a choice fry of sardines',
prepared for them by Odell and Hazard. They were anxious to be
off, and it was with some disappointment that Odell recorded, 'they
hardly did justice to the repast, or flattered the cooks!' Fetching his
camera from his tent, Odell snapped the two as they were about to
leave – Irvine standing stolidly by, hands in pockets, waiting while
Mallory fiddled to adjust a strap on his oxygen mask. Little did he
know then that his would be the last portrait there would ever be of
Mallory and Irvine.

The pair had restricted themselves to the very minimum of
baggage – lunch and their windproofs. Their loads consisted primarily of the oxygen equipment, about 25 lbs each, all told. Eight
porters carried similar weight loads, containing sleeping bags for all,
food, fuel and spare oxygen cylinders. The porters were not given
oxygen because that would have required a far larger supply than
the expedition had planned for. As it was, only 35 of the original
50 cylinders contained any gas at all on arrival at Base Camp. At the
rate of 30 hours of oxygen per man to reach the summit, they only
ever had sufficient oxygen to allow four attempts on the top.

The party moved off at 8.40 a.m. in a silence broken only by the
hissing and wheezing of the apparatus. Once kitted up, Mallory and
Irvine lived in private insulated worlds, denied normal camaraderie
because their face masks precluded all speech.

It was a beautiful day for the first stage of the assault. The two
climbers would have taken it steadily and slowly in order to let the

219

porters keep up with them, and to save themselves for their final climb. In such fine weather, the ascent to the first high camp was quickly made. Shortly after 5 p.m., four of the eight porters arrived back at Camp IV with a note from Mallory. 'There is no wind here, and things look hopeful.' What a change from his previous climb to Camp V![1]

The next day, 7 June, the two climbers with their four remaining porters were to ascend to Camp VI. At the same time, Odell would play a 'support' role, the exact nature of which is not immediately clear — nor is Odell's description of it:

> This method of support, a stage as it were behind, was rendered necessary by the limited accommodation at these high camps, consequent upon the inadequate number of porters available to carry up sufficient tentage, etc.[2]

The concept of 'support' was one taken very seriously by Norton. It was not a question of following after with additional supplies, although that sometimes came into it; it entailed the presence of one or more people to greet a returning party, so that in their exhausted state climbers did not have to bother with such mundane but life-saving chores as melting snow and brewing drinks. At the North Col, supporters had the additional role of steering tired climbers through the treacherous maze of crevasses that guarded the camp. What presumably persuaded Norton so strongly of the need for support parties was the realization of how close they had come to disaster in 1922, when, with Morshead seriously ill, they returned to Camp IV in pitch dark to find no food, no drink and no means of melting snow for water. Odell had always been particularly diligent in this respect, much of the time in tandem with Irvine, and Norton had effusive praise for the way this pair fulfilled 'for the first time in the history of Everest climbing, the official role of supporters':

> The most optimistic imaginations fell short of the reality, as produced by that 'well-known firm' [of Odell and Irvine]. For over a week those two have lived on the North Col and have cooked every meal — and only those who have done it can appreciate the recurring hatefulness of this operation. They have gone out day and night to escort and succour returning parties of porters and climbers over the intricate approaches to the camp, carrying lamps, drinks and even oxygen to restore

the exhausted. They have run the camp and tended the sick, and Odell, for one, has been down to Camp III and returned to Camp IV, escorting parties or fetching provisions on three consecutive days. Whether we reach the top or not, no members of the climbing party can pull more weight in the team than these two by their unostentatious, unselfish, gruelling work.[3]

Such a vital service, however, cannot be offered usefully from a camp or more away, yet it was hard for Odell to know where best to position himself to receive climbers returning after a summit attempt. If they were fit and well they were likely to leapfrog camps and need no 'support' at all until they reached the North Col. Anyone experiencing trouble above Camp VI, however, in urgent need of assistance, could hardly let Odell know where his presence was most required. He dared not wait for them in Camp VI after about mid-afternoon, since that camp — just one little tent — was not big enough to accommodate him as well as the returning climbers.

In the absence of a clear role, it is easy to imagine Odell, denied any summit attempt, simply climbing up as high as he could go. Acclimatization problems prevented him from being considered for any of the earlier summit bids. Now he was coming almost too late into his full and astonishing powers, with no place to go.

Toiling upwards toward Camp V, Odell found a spare oxygen set that had been set down on the ridge at some time previously. Irvine, he discovered, must have cannibalized the mouthpiece for a spare part on his way up the day before, but Odell attempted to use the set all the same. Instead of boosting his performance he commented, 'I was able to get along as well without its aid, and better without the bulky inconvenience of the whole apparatus.' A few days later, he would repair the mouthpiece of this set and again try to use it. Once more he reported that the effect was almost negligible. 'I wondered at the claims of others regarding its advantages,' he said. Odell, having now so well acclimatized, would have less use for extra oxygen, certainly, but it is strange that he felt so little benefit. It raises certain questions. In the first place, what was this abandoned set? Where did it come from? The only mention of an oxygen set taken above the North Col before Mallory and Irvine set off is the one that Mallory brought to revive Norton and Somervell after their summit attempt. They, too, derived no benefit from oxygen that night, so if indeed it was the same set on both occasions, was that particular set defective? That three men failed to receive any help from it suggests it could be because they were getting little or no oxygen out of it! Yet it is their experiences with this particular set (or sets) that permanently soured the attitudes of all of them against oxygen use for climbing.

Odell's remarkable ability, of seeming to climb better without oxygen than with it, became one of the keystones of the anti-oxygen argument. Surely his extraordinary performance proved that, for someone as well acclimatized as Odell, oxygen's added boost was at least offset by the weight of the heavy apparatus? Nor was this the first time he had tried to use oxygen: earlier in the expedition, when not yet comfortably attuned to altitude, he had experimented with it while climbing the steep slopes of the North Col with Geoffrey Bruce. His experience was similar then, too. He felt the device gave him so little advantage, and was so clumsy to carry, that he took it off and handed it to a porter! Perhaps Odell really was physiologically unusual in this respect. Or perhaps on that occasion, too, he had happened upon the rogue set! Modern physiologists find it inconceivable that properly-working apparatus would fail to give Odell a noticeable boost.

Soon the four porters who had accompanied Mallory and Irvine to Camp VI arrived back at Camp V. Their approach was heralded by a hail of stones bombarding the tents where Odell and his porter Nema were now in residence. Odell decided to send Nema down with the others that night and remain in the camp alone.

The porters had carried down from Camp VI two important messages — one for expedition cinematographer Captain John Noel, who was down at the North Col, and the other for Odell. The note Mallory had written to Captain Noel read:

Dear Noel,

We'll probably start early to-morrow (8th) in order to have clear weather. It won't be too early to start looking out for us either crossing the rock band under the pyramid or going up skyline at 8.0 p.m. [sic]

Yours ever,
G. Mallory[4]

The mention of the possibility of crossing the rock band suggests that up to the last minute Mallory had still not ruled out Norton's traverse if the ridge route proved not to be feasible. Captain Noel and the other team members were all convinced that it was the ridge Mallory intended to follow. This was borne out the next day by Odell's sighting.

It is surprising that both Robertson and Unsworth should leave out the phrase 'under the pyramid' when they quote this note in their books. As Captain Noel reproduces a photograph of the note in his book, *Through Tibet to Everest*, the other variation must have been obtained from a corrupt source.

If Mallory had calculated his climb rate from Camp IV to Camp VI, and his oxygen consumption, he would have realized that they had been climbing at some 800+ feet per hour. With only 1,300 feet left to climb to reach the skyline, he might well suppose, given no unforeseen difficulties, he could get up there in two hours, give or take half an hour.

Mallory was well known for his early starts, although how early one actually gets under way on the upper reaches of Everest is generally an unhappy surprise. Even so, the two climbers had everything in their favour. They were well-supplied, and there is even evidence that they might have used oxygen for sleeping — a lesson Mallory (but not Odell) learned from Finch — so as to assure a warm, restful night before the summit attempt. If they set off some time shortly before 6 a.m., it is not unreasonable to suppose Mallory reckoned to be moving up the ridge by 8 a.m. (not '8 *p.m.*', which is clearly a slip of the pen). To Odell Mallory had written:

Dear Odell,

We're awfully sorry to have left things in such a mess — our Unna Cooker rolled down the slope at the last moment. Be sure of getting back to IV tomorrow in time to evacuate before dark, as I hope to. In the tent I must have left a compass — for the Lord's sake rescue it: we are here without. To here on 90 atmospheres for the two days — so we'll probably go on two cylinders — but it's a bloody load for climbing. Perfect weather for the job!

Yours ever,
George Mallory[5]

This letter is pregnant with meaning, although it has not been subjected to nearly the same intensity of analysis as has the sighting of Mallory and Irvine on the Second Step. The anti-oxygenists thrilled to Mallory's 'bloody load'[6] comment, not realizing that this message in its entirety is a further confirmation of the efficacy of using oxygen.

There is a hidden meaning in this note because it is not generally appreciated that if two variables can be determined, the oxygen apparatus can act as a climber's speedometer. Given the oxygen flow rate, and the amount of gas used, it is possible to determine the climber's speed of ascent. A full tank of the 1924 apparatus could hold 535 litres of oxygen, stored at a pressure of 120 atmospheres (an atmosphere, abbreviated Atm., is 14.7 lbs/in.^{2}). If Mallory used 90 Atm., he used ¾ of his 120 atmospheres, or ¾ of his 535 litres, that is 400 litres in the two days' climb from Camp IV to Camp VI, according to his note to Odell.

Irvine had set the apparatus to deliver oxygen at a rate of 1.5 litres per minute when the two climbed from Camp III to Camp IV. So if Mallory continued to obtain oxygen at that rate, his 400 litres would last 267 minutes, or 4.4 hours (400/1.5 = 267). Climbing the 3,800 feet from Camp IV to Camp VI in 4.4 hours results in a climbing speed of 856 feet per hour (3800/4.4=856). Using oxygen at the highest rate the set was capable of — 2.2 litres per minute — results in an even faster climb speed.

If indeed he did experience such a high climbing speed between Camps IV and VI, Mallory might well expect, unaware as he was of rapid deterioration above 27,000 feet, that he and Irvine could tackle the summit with only two cylinders, rather than the full complement of three. True, it was still a 'bloody load' — but obviously not so bloody that they would rather climb without it.

With the loss of the stove and the left-behind compass, the message also reinforces, if indeed it is any longer in doubt, that Mallory certainly did scatter belongings behind him wherever he went. On his summit climb the next day he also forgot his torch and his lantern, which were found in the wreckage of the little camp by Jack Longland's porters in 1933. The other climbers watched late into the night for distress signals or signs of light from the upper face, but saw nothing. The sad fact is that if Mallory were still alive then, stranded by darkness on the mountainside, it is unlikely he had with him any means by which to signal his distress. His carelessness certainly led him to play his last poker game without a full hand of cards.

To find no stove must have been a particular pain to Odell.

Without it he would be unable to melt snow for drinks and was obliged to eat a cold supper and breakfast. He opened a few tins and did not go hungry. 'A meal of "Force" and a little jam varied with macaroni and tomatoes completed my supper.' Then he made himself comfortable in two sleeping bags and spent a relatively good night.

Odell was up at six the next day. So great is the effort required to get things done at these heights, it took him two hours to get ready to go — even without the lengthy chore of melting snow for his thermos. He packed provisions for Camp VI in case of a shortage there.

The weather had been clear and not unduly cold first thing, but as Odell made his way up towards the North-east Shoulder, great banks of mist began to form and sweep in from the west across the face of the mountain. He thought the mist might be chiefly confined to the lower half of the face because above him he detected a certain luminosity in the sky which would indicate comparatively clear conditions higher up. 'This appearance so impressed me that I had no qualms for Mallory and Irvine's progress upward from Camp VI and I hoped that by this time they would be well on their way up the final pyramid of the summit.'7

Odell continued upward, veering away from the ridge in order to explore untracked sections of the vast North Face. If he could not hope to be first to the summit, he had the consolation of being the first geologist to get to grips with the rocks on the upper part of the mountain. He was intent on carrying out a survey, and wandered backwards and forwards, eyes to the ground, practically lost to the world. The wind remained quite light and although there were occasional flurries of snow they were insufficient to distract Odell. Towards 1 p.m. he was feeling overjoyed at the discovery of what he believed to be the first fossils ever found on Everest. Coming to a rocky outcrop some 100-feet high, he decided to scramble up it for no other reason than that he was feeling very fit and particularly energetic. As he clambered on to the top, he was aware of a distinct lightening in the sky. Suddenly, the mists rolled back and revealed to Odell the brief glimpse of Mallory and Irvine that has so intrigued mountaineers for more than half a century:

There was a sudden clearing of the atmosphere, and the entire summit ridge and final peak of Everest were unveiled. My eyes became fixed on one tiny black spot silhouetted on a small

225

snow-crest beneath a rock-step in the ridge; the black spot moved. Another black spot became apparent and moved up the snow to join the other on the crest. The first then approached the great rock-step and shortly emerged at the top; the second did likewise. Then the whole fascinating vision vanished, enveloped in cloud once more.

There was but one explanation. It was Mallory and his companion moving, as I could see even at that great distance, with considerable alacrity, realizing doubtless that they had none too many hours of daylight to reach the summit from their present position and return to Camp VI by nightfall. The place on the ridge referred to is the prominent rock-step at a very short distance from the base of the final pyramid, and it is remarkable that they were so late in reaching this place. According to Mallory's schedule, they should have reached it several hours earlier if they had started from the high camp as anticipated.[8]

Odell continued on up to Camp VI, his mind swirling with the significance of the astonishing scene he had just witnessed. Mallory and Irvine were certainly much behind their own schedule. They still had enough time but only just to reach the summit and return in daylight. Certainly, too, from their position, they should have had no trouble getting on to the summit ridge. Once there, once so close, was there anything that could turn them back without success? He tried to envisage what could have brought them so late to this spot.

I had seen that there was a considerable quantity of new snow covering some of the upper rocks near the summit ridge, and this may well have caused delay in the ascent. Burdened as they undoubtedly would be with the oxygen apparatus, these snow-covered debris-sprinkled slabs may have given much trouble. The oxygen apparatus itself may have needed repair or readjustment either before or after they left Camp VI, and so have delayed them. Though rather unlikely, it is just conceivable that the zone of mist and clouds I had experienced below may have extended up to their level and so have somewhat impeded their progress.[9]

Odell arrived at Camp VI at about 2 p.m., just as it began to snow. The wind was bitter. Inside the tent he found a mess of food, oxygen cylinders and parts of the regulator, which suggests the two might have used oxygen for sleeping (something Mallory had suggested to Longstaff ought to be done at VI), as otherwise the bulky equipment could have been left outside along with the aluminium carrying frames. If Irvine had been working on the sets to repair a defect — which is the other possible explanation for their having been taken inside the tent — he would be quite likely to have left the system assembled in its frame. Then, once fixed, it would be immediately ready for use. But for sleeping, a frame is not necessary, and takes up precious room inside the cramped quarters.

After waiting an hour or so inside the tent, Odell began to wonder whether the snow squall was severe enough to cause the two climbers to cut short their attempt. This uncertainty indicates it was not as severe a storm as some have suggested (citing it as one of the reasons Mallory must surely have failed). Odell worried that the two climbers might experience difficulty in finding the tent, concealed as it was from the face (so he believed, although on this point Norton disagreed with him). He set out on to the North Face of the mountain, whistling and yodelling with the hope of attracting the descending climbers' attention. They were nowhere within hearing. After an hour, far longer than anyone would voluntarily spend in a real Everest storm, Odell returned to the shelter of Camp VI. As he reached it, the squall passed over and the entire mountain was bathed in sunlight. The fresh snow quickly evaporated, and Odell scanned the upper slopes of the mountain for sign or sight of his comrades, but he saw nothing.

In retrospect, Odell's 'support' mission would have been much more useful had he brought with him an extra tent, which would only have weighed some 10 lbs. Then he could have remained at Camp VI overnight in case the two climbers reached it *in extremis*. As it was, Mallory's instructions had been quite clear: Odell was to go down to Camp IV that evening and await the return of Mallory and Irvine there.

Odell closed up the little tent at 4.30 p.m. and began a rapid descent, stopping from time to time to scan the upper slopes. Due to the mix of rock and snow, he could pick out no trace of his companions. They would have been visible only if crossing one of the infrequent patches of snow or silhouetted against the skyline. By-passing Camp V at 6.15 p.m., 100 yards off the North Ridge, he began a series of glissades that brought him into Camp IV thirty minutes later. Odell used this remarkable descent to teach a lesson:

It was interesting to find, as I had earlier, that descending at high altitudes is little more fatiguing than at any other moderate altitudes, and of course in complete contrast to the extraordinarily exhausting reverse of it, and it seemed that a party that has not completely shot its bolt and run itself to a standstill, so to speak, should find itself unexpectedly able to make fast time downward and escape being benighted. And as I shall mention later, the unnecessity of oxygen for the properly acclimatized climber seems never more evident than in this capability of quick descent. [10]

Coming into Camp IV, Odell was ecstatic about the events of the past two days. He did not yet have cause to feel unduly anxious on Mallory's or Irvine's behalf. Consuming enormous quantities of liquids served up by Hazard, he ruminated on the tumult of emotions occasioned by his climb.

What a two days had it been — days replete with a gamut of impressions that neither the effects of high altitude, whatever this might be, nor the grim events of the two days that were to follow could efface from one's memory! A period of intensive experiences, alike romantic, aesthetic, and scientific in interest, these each in their various appeals enabling one to forget even the extremity of upward toil inherently involved, and ever at intervals carrying one's thoughts with expectancy to that resolute pair who might at any instant appear returning with news of final conquest. [11]

The question now in everyone's mind was how high had Mallory and Irvine managed to get? Had they indeed reached the summit? When would they return? Because they were behind schedule when seen on the Step, they might get no futher than Camp VI on this day's descent. A watch was kept at Camp IV far into the night, with hopes of spotting the returning climbers, or at least seeing a distress flare to mark their location. It was a clear night with sufficient moonlight to have permitted a night-time descent. The watchers saw nothing.

The next morning all the occupants at Camp IV carefully scrutinized the upper camps through binoculars for signs of life. Odell was beginning to fear the worst. By midday he could bear the suspense no longer and, requisitioning two of the remaining three porters to accompany him, set off once more for Camp V. Such was his

228

acclimatization, and so clear was the mountain of snow, that he reached it in 3¼ hours — a climbing speed of over 600 feet per hour. This quite remarkable pace provided further evidence against the need for oxygen.

In the tent was the spare oxygen set without the mouthpiece that he had carried up earlier, and he set about fixing it with a spare which he had brought with him. That night the oxygen lay beside him, but he did not think to follow Finch's valuable example and make use of it for sleeping. He spent an uncomfortable night. 'The cold was intense that night and aggravated by high wind, and one remained chilled and unable to sleep — even inside two sleeping bags and with all one's clothes on.'[12]

The bitter wind did not abate the next morning, and Odell found he was unable to stir the two porters into action. He had little choice but to let them return to Camp IV and leave him to continue the search alone. It is interesting to note that by this time it was no longer questioned that porters should be sent back down to the North Col unescorted, although it was one of those heinous acts for which Finch had been so heavily criticized on the last expedition.

It was on his second climb up to Camp VI that Odell determined to give the oxygen yet one more try, only to be disillusioned once more. 'Perhaps it allayed a trifle the tire in one's legs,' was the most he could say for it.

I switched the oxygen off and experienced none of those feelings of collapse and panting that one had been led to believe ought to result. I decided to proceed with the apparatus on my back, but without the objectionable rubber mouthpiece between my lips, and depend on direct breathing from the atmosphere. I seemed to get on quite as well, though I must admit the hard breathing at these altitudes would surprise even a long distance runner.[13]

Odell continued upward, taking shelter now and again behind rocks from the stiff breeze that had plagued him all through the night. Odell's thoughts were turning to the black side of things. He had not really expected to find Mallory and Irvine at Camp V (those at the North Col had been watching that tent too carefully) but now, on his way up, the full realization began to sink in that everything rested on him finding the pair at Camp VI. Yet there, too, no signs of life had been sighted, and it was two days since the climbers had made their summit attempt. Hopes looked very slim.

Reaching the solitary two-man tent that was Camp VI, Odell found his worst fears confirmed. Everything remained exactly as he had left it, except that one tent pole had collapsed. Dropping his oxygen equipment, he immediately set off along the path Mallory and Irvine would probably have taken.

This upper part of Everest must be indeed the remotest and least hospitable spot on earth, but at no time more emphatically and impressively so than when a darkened atmosphere hides its features and a gale races over its cruel face. And how and when more cruel could it ever seem than when balking one's every step to find one's friends? After struggling on for nearly a couple of hours looking in vain for some indication or clue, I realized that the chances of finding the missing ones were indeed small on such a vast expanse of crags and broken slabs, and that for any more expensive search towards the final pyramid a further party would have to be organized.[14]

Odell returned to the tent with heavy heart. He dragged out its two sleeping bags and hauled them up to a snow patch above the camp. Setting them out in the shape of a 'T', he signalled to the expedition members 4,000 feet below that he had found no trace of the missing climbers. Then, closing up the tent once more, and taking with him only the prismatic compass and the oxygen apparatus as proof of the modifications Irvine had made, Odell looked up once more at the mighty summit. 'It seemed to look down with cold indifference on me, mere puny man, and howl derision in wind-gusts at my petition to yield up its secret — this mystery of my friends.' Had they done right, he wondered, to violate the sacred refuge of Chomolungma, Goddess Mother of the World?

And yet, as I gazed again another mood appeared to creep over her haunting features. There seemed to be something alluring in that towering presence. I was almost fascinated. I realized that no mere mountaineer alone could but be fascinated, that he who approaches close must ever be led on, and oblivious of all obstacles seek to reach that most sacred and highest place of all. It seemed that my friends must have been thus enchanted also: for why else should they tarry?[15]

Resisting the siren call, Odell turned his back on the mountain, and began hurrying down in the biting cold. From time to time he would crouch in the lee of some rock shelter to escape the force of the incessant wind. As he approached the North Col, Hazard sent up the single remaining porter to assist Odell into camp. There was one final signal to make to those waiting anxiously below for news. Six blankets were dragged to the edge of the cliff and laid out in the form of a cross in the white snow. Now down in Camp III, they too knew to abandon all hope. The three then loaded up what equipment they could carry and descended the Col by means of the treacherous 'avalanche route'. In retreat, climbers relax their careful guard.

By 13 June, the team had come off the mountain and had returned to Base Camp. Norton considered briefly sending a party around to the base of the north Face, an arduous march up the trackless main Rongbuk Glacier, in the slim hope that the bodies of the two climbers might be found there, but it was an idea he wisely 'deprecated as a wild goose chase'. Hazard was later to pass that way on a survey mission and promised to keep a look out. Norton had no way of knowing whether the two climbers had fallen or not, and if so, off what side of the mountain. If they did fall, it seemed hardly likely that they would have reached the bottom of the mountain with its many terraces and outcroppings. Most of the remaining climbers were in one stage of exhaustion or another, suffering an assortment of strained hearts, stripped throats and frostbites; any form of search would be too dispiriting and taxing in the men's present condition. On medical grounds alone, Norton was right to rule it out. He wrote:

> We were a sad little party; from the first we accepted the loss of our comrades in that rational spirit which all of our generation had learnt in the Great War, and there was never a tendency to a morbid harping on the irrevocable. But the tragedy was very near; our friends; vacant tents and vacant places at table were a constant reminder to us of what the atmosphere of the camp would have been had things gone differently.[16]

XVII

Going Strong for the Top

'Work is the best specific against depression' was one of Norton's trusted maxims. It was fortunate that in the days following the disappearance of Mallory and Irvine 'there was work to do in plenty', more than enough to stop them brooding. By 13 June all survivors were back at base and all the upper camps stripped. An intense flurry of sorting and packing ensued as members quickly reassembled such equipment and stores as were worth taking back with them. They intended a short period of recuperation in the Rongshar Valley, under Gaurisankar, before starting the long caravan journey home. Hazard was to accompany the surveyor Hari Singh Thapa to the West Rongbuk and would rejoin them at Kampa. Captain Noel had unselfishly agreed to set off immediately for Darjeeling with the bulk of the porters and loads, travelling by way of Shekar Dzong and the Chumbi Valley. Animal transport and extra help was ordered for the 15th, when all three parties planned to get away. Before leaving, however, Somervell and Beetham set themselves the task of building a cairn in memory of the twelve Everest dead of all three expeditions.

Meanwhile Norton called a camp conference to discuss the implications of the loss of Mallory and Irvine and what they should tell the press and the people back home. He had hurried down to Camp III in order to despatch a brief cable as soon as he learned the import of the blanket-signal message from the North Col, but it had not been possible to include any details. The coded message left Base Camp by runner on 11 June and was transmitted from Phari Dzong eight days later. It read simply: OBTERRAS LONDON (England) MALLORY IRVINE NOVE REMAINDER ALCEDO, NORTON RONGBUK.[1]

232

Hinks found the cable waiting on his desk when he arrived for work at the Royal Geographical Society on 19 June, and soon had its cryptic message decoded. It told him that Mallory and Irvine were killed making a final attempt on the mountain and that the rest of the party had returned safely to Base Camp. To him now fell the unenviable task of advising the relatives, and the few pathetic details he had just learned were reworded and relayed once more by telegram to the two families. David Robertson suggests that Ruth Mallory might already have learned of George's death before the telegram arrived, for he says she 'received the news in Cambridge from a representative of the press'. Stunned, 'she went out for a long walk with old friends.'[2]

The news was released officially the following day (Saturday) in the newspapers, and the same day a cable went from the Society's offices to the expedition on behalf of the Everest Committee:

> Committee warmly congratulates whole party heroic achievements published today especially appreciate consummate leadership. All deeply moved by glorious death lost climbers near summit. Best wishes speedy restoration everyone health. Collie.[3]

Douglas Freshfield, for one, took great exception to the wording of this message, which he immediately attributed to Hinks, no matter whose name graced it. 'Warm congratulations' hardly sounded the appropriate way to address a leader who had just lost two men. 'Unfortunately,' he complained to Sidney Spencer, 'Hinks does not know what tact is.' He was concerned lest the impression be given that the Society and the Alpine Club were treating the expedition 'as a show without adequate recognition of its calamity', and remarked sourly, 'Between ourselves, Hinks with many qualities has no sense of taste and needs careful watching. I saw that during my presidency and since he has swollen in every direction.'[4] Hinks was certainly very moved by what he would keep calling the 'glorious news' and congratulated Norton on his own account for his 'nevertheless great successes' and the way he had handled affairs throughout the expedition:

> If anything could mitigate our sorrow in the loss of Mallory and Irvine it is the knowledge that they died somewhere higher than any man had ever been before, and it is possible for their

relatives to think of them as lying perhaps even at the summit.

What strikes us all in contrast to 1922 is the magnificent leadership and organisation of the whole thing by which everyone supported everyone else and there was none of the rather go as you please style of Camps III and IV in 1922. Whatever Hingston proved to you scientifically about the deterioration of the brain at high altitudes, you have routed him triumphantly by showing as fine a grip of circumstances as any man could have shown. Let me congratulate you especially upon your despatch of June 8th from Camp III, dictated when you were snow-blinded to a secretary with a strained heart. It was a superb performance.[5]

To Mrs Bruce, he wrote, 'The later news puts the tragedy upon an altogether higher level, and redeems it from being what might have been unredeemed disaster into a very fine and glorious achievement.'[6]

Response at large to the tragedy was unexpectedly warm. It suddenly became clear just how much interest the public had been taking in the Everest story, for it was by no means just mountaineers who were expressing real sorrow at the loss of the two men. A surprised Hinks wrote to Norton on 26 June, telling him, 'We have been overwhelmed with telegrams and messages of sympathy from the King, from many geographical societies and climbing clubs all over the world and from numbers of individuals in this country. The papers have vied with one another in paying their respect to the glorious memory of Mallory and Irvine.'[7]

Mallory's tutor from his Cambridge days, A.C. Benson, read of the accident in his Saturday newspaper. He failed to glory in the incident and saw only the sheer waste.

The dreadful news that George Mallory is killed on Everest. This entirely knocked me over. It is so utterly tragic. I think people have a right to risk their lives — but this is his *third* expedition, and he had a wife and two [three] children — and after all it is only a feat. He has been a very dear friend ever since he became my pupil here in 1905, and I have known him in all moods and stages. He has become much gentler and more tolerant of late.[8]

Norton's Base Camp conference revealed a consensus among

members that the deaths of Mallory and Irvine were caused by a simple mountaineering accident — a fatal slip. Odell alone clung to the belief that the two men perished from exhaustion and exposure after being overtaken by darkness on the way down from the summit. In considerable dejection, Norton related his own interpretation of what happened in a letter to Hinks two days after his brief cable. It was carefully worded so as to insinuate no blame on the part of either one of the lost climbers, or their equipment.

> I have little doubt in my own mind that the party was roped — one or other slipped and pulled the other down. I was near the ground where they were last seen myself, and it is a dangerous place — every single stone slopes outwards and with a powdering of new snow such as occurred while they were up there, it can become very nasty.
>
> Odell proved what we all guessed, viz., that men acclimatized as these were to 23,000 to 25,000 can dispense with oxygen as soon as they turn down hill. I don't think we need blame the apparatus.[9]

There were two anxious weeks from the receipt of Norton's cable before his fuller dispatches began arriving in London. His first report of the accident was published in *The Times* on 26 June, and from then he maintained a steady flow of letters and press communiqués throughout the following weeks. The sheer volume of his words is astonishing — official reports meticulously documenting every aspect of the expedition and all the conditions giving rise to them, graphic accounts for the press, besides letters of condolence to Mallory's and Irvine's relatives. No wonder in some exasperation he complained to Hinks on 23 June, 'I have had a bellyful of writing'. It was as if he was writing his way through his grief and disappointment. The expedition had started off with such high expectations, but, so he still believed, not unrealistically ambitious hopes. The turn of events was due more to ill fortune, as he saw it, than to any flaw in basic planning.

All the same, such faith did not lift the burden of responsibility from Norton's shoulders. He reviewed the entire expedition to assure himself there was nothing else he could have done which might have changed matters. He had prided himself throughout on the democratic fairness of his show, discussing everything with Somervell, Mallory and Bruce. He had taken a genuine caring interest in all his European and native personnel, and in return, as he told Hinks, 'No leader of any Expedition can have been more loyally and splendidly supported than I have. Team work has been the keynote throughout. There hasn't been a hint of jealousy and the way in which everyone has worked to the bone to try and achieve success under circumstances which made the 1922 Expedition seem a picnic by comparison baffles my power of description.' All he wanted now was to ensure that no individual and no single decision should be deemed at fault.

He well knew those areas that were open to criticism. Mallory's judgment in making a third ascent was one; for Irvine, with his unproven climbing ability, to go into unknown territory was another; then there was the old bugbear, oxygen. People would want to know if failure of the oxygen equipment could have contributed to the disaster. Norton was determined that no accusations would reflect badly on Mallory or Irvine. That was all he could see to salvage from this sorry situation.

Hinks, who never missed an opportunity to denigrate the use of oxygen, could see its potential as a useful scapegoat now, and was puzzled by Norton's seeming reluctance to admit such a possibility. 'Your belief that the loss was due to an ordinary mountaineering accident has, as you doubtless intended, switched off people from discussing whether it was due in any way to difficulties in the oxygen apparatus.' He was prodding Norton for a response, but as none was forthcoming, he put the question more suggestively in his next letter: 'You have been careful to divert speculation from the oxygen apparatus . . . I suppose that the question of the apparatus and its difficulties will have to be the subject of a Committee inquiry when you all come home?'[10]

He had a point. It was not a question that could reasonably be avoided in view of the damning report on the condition of the apparatus Norton had encouraged Odell to send from Shekar Dzong. What Hinks did not foresee as well as Norton could was where such an inquiry might lead. Without any evidence as to how they died, nothing more than an academic case could be put against oxygen, but there was every possibility that in the crossfire of accusation and counter-accusation, mud would stick to expedition members and their representatives.

In response to Odell's report, Siebe Gorman wrote predictably, disclaiming all responsibility. Whether or not the shortness of preparation time was sufficient reason for the workmanship to have been quite so shoddy, the suppliers had a strong case when claiming that no members of the expedition team had liaised with them properly beforehand. Had the Chief Oxygen Officer visited the factory, seen the apparatus tested, and had its internal construction and working explained to him, they contended, 'he would have been able readily to deal with any of the matters in question in a practical way, and put them right, and the points raised in the report need never have arisen.'[11] In Siebe Gorman's opinion, much of the leakage could have been prevented if anyone had understood how to use the new-style control valves which had been fitted.

Throughout the design and construction, Siebe Gorman had dealt almost exclusively with P.J.H. Unna of the Alpine Club, a very able engineer, who did not travel with the expedition. Oxygen Officer Odell was working in Persia prior to departure and had received no first-hand briefing. Irvine's interest in the apparatus seems not to have been taken very seriously. No doubt his innate modesty prevented him thrusting himself further forward at the time.

What really put Siebe Gorman in an unassailable position, however, was the fact that Irvine had so exhaustively modified the equipment once in Tibet. It exonerated the manufacturers of any responsibility for it. To make use of low pressure tubing in Irvine's reconstructed sets for high pressure functions, they alleged, was so far to exceed its design specification as to invite leakage. These would have been very difficult points to argue, and the Committee wisely decided against further action.

With the expedition packed and ready to leave, Norton confided in a letter to Spencer: 'I feel the loss of Mallory and Irvine very much. Mallory and I shared a tent off and on for days and weeks; he was more than my right hand for all matters pertaining to the mountain and simply backed me up through thick and thin. Young Irvine was a real winner. I wish one could know whether they succeeded or not before the end.'[12]

Somervell, too, was trying to come to terms with the loss. On the 11th he wrote, 'No news. It is ominous . . . They may never come back. They may be dead. My friend and fellow-climber, Mallory, one in spirit with me – dead?' By the 12th, forced to accept the inevitable, he was trying to rationalize. 'It is terrible. But there are few better deaths than to die in high endeavour, and Everest is the finest cenotaph in the world to a couple of the best of men.' Three days later he wrote:

Especially do I feel the loss of Mallory, who was a particular friend of mine, and one of the few people on this show with whom one could really talk freely of more serious things — he had a good knowledge and appreciation of literature, and although highbrow in some things, was always ready to laugh at his own highbrowisms. Moreover, he was a first-rate mountaineer, and the nicest and most patient of companions if one couldn't go quite as fast as his furious pace uphill. His loss as a friend is made up by the privilege of having known him, and whenever I read the *Spirit of Man*, I shall be reminded of times, both in 1922 and 1924, when he and I read selections aloud to each other in our little tent at No. III Camp. His spirit is indeed the Spirit of a Man . . .[13]

Norton included 'Mr. Odell's Story' in his bulletin of 14 June in *The Times*, but confided in a letter to Spencer, 'I'm very sorry Odell put in that bit about their dying of exposure in his communiqué, he is the only member of the party who holds that view; all the rest of us are agreed that it is any odds on a "fall off" '.[14]

It was not just that Norton 'could hardly picture Mallory ever succumbing to exhaustion'. What so thoroughly convinced him that the two could not possibly have been trapped out overnight was the absence of any sign of light on the upper slopes that night. A watch had been kept for the first three hours of darkness of that evening and the next, and not a flicker had been seen. It was inconceivable to Norton that Mallory could have failed to carry a torch. Having run into trouble before by being benighted without a light (in 1922), he would never again 'have started unprovided in this respect'. Moreover, he asserted, the climbers had flares with which to signal distress. There were flares inside the Camp VI tent when Odell visited it, which suggests they were left behind on the fateful day to lighten the 'bloody load'. In 1933 Longland's party found a torch, still in working order, among the pathetic debris of the camp. As Bruce had so wryly observed, Mallory could leave even his boots behind.

If Norton's belief in a fall as the most likely cause of an accident was based on the dubious logic that Mallory could not again have forgotten his torch, what of Odell? Why was he so convinced that the two had been overtaken by darkness, taken shelter in some rock recess and fallen asleep, never to wake? Such a solution would at least guarantee his friends a painless death, leave them unmutilated, and – even more important – would place no onus on Irvine's inexperience. One has only to consider Odell's position to realize the subconscious pressures that could have affected his personal response to the loss of Mallory and Irvine.

In the first place, Irvine was Odell's discovery. Before Odell proffered the Spitsbergen invitation, and later Everest, it had never occurred to Irvine to take up mountaineering. His instinctive loves had been motorbikes and rowing. It would be natural for Odell to feel a strong sense of moral responsibility for what happened to Irvine. It would not be easy for him to avoid a measure of self-reproach at the abrupt curtailment of so much unrealised life and talent. He knew it would fall to him when he returned home to face Irvine's family and friends, and explain to them what had happened. He had lost his own brother in the War; he well knew the pain of losing someone dear.

So much was inescapable, but the manner of death would affect, to some extent, the degree of responsibility Odell might feel impelled to bear. If Mallory and Irvine fell, as most believed, inevitably the assumption would be that it was the inexperienced Irvine who slipped. That calls into question Irvine's suitability for a summit attempt. If Irvine was not ready for Everest, then to a degree that would be (as Bruce would say) Odell's 'blob'. If death had come through some malfunction of the oxygen apparatus, again, Odell (as Oxygen Officer) would bear some measure of blame.

Even so, such considerations take no account of how, at the time of the final climb, Odell might have felt about being excluded from the action. Though he claims none, would it be surprising if he had nursed even a small sense of injustice or frustration at being left behind, especially as he was so exceptionally fit? Odell has said that he would happily have sacrificed his geological survey for a crack at the summit. Would it have been a different story if he had accompanied Mallory on that final climb – or would he have died in place of Irvine? Can we be sure, either, that he had not suppressed a long disgruntlement throughout the expedition at the way Mallory had monopolized Irvine, who was after all his friend and protégé? Indeed, did it ever flicker across Odell's mind to make a solo bid if Mallory and Irvine returned without success?

After closing up Camp VI for the last time, Odell admits to 'something alluring in that towering presence', which enchants all who approach and leads them on 'oblivious of all obstacles'. Was he recognizing wistfully that his one opportunity had passed, that tragedy had placed once more an unbridgeable barrier between him and the ultimate? It had been so temptingly lifted for a short interval two days before when, finding himself high enough to make his own crack at the summit, he could so easily have just kept on climbing. More than anyone else in the expedition, he had reached an astonishing peak of physical agility and mental equanimity. He had been so selfless and dependable in his support of others, he had trudged up and down with supplies from the North Col, had brewed and cooked, without once being considered a serious contender for the summit. If, after all, he had yielded to personal ambition, who could have blamed him? Yet he did not. Staunch and supportive to the end, Odell had thought only of his obligations to the two men above him, and to the rest of the team below.

It was with some reluctance that the climbers finally took leave of 'this old Base Camp of conflicting memories, so bleak and inhospitable after the sunny plains of Tibet, so homelike and cosy after the far bleaker glacier camps.'[15] It marked a final severing with the life that had included Mallory and Irvine, and an acceptance of a new life without. Behind them they left an imposing conical monument, 15-feet high, bearing five carved stone panels with the names of their dead. It had been very hard work, building and carving it in two days, but it would stand, Somervell hoped, 'for many years — to greet the next expedition and tell of the dangers of the mountain.'[16]

Most of the porters went back with Captain Noel to be paid off in Darjeeling, only a few travelling with the team to the Rongshar Valley as personal servants. These were selected from those men who had performed best at high altitude. Norton has recalled how Odell was allotted 'the ruffianly but stout-hearted Narbu Yishé':

Now if you know no Oriental language and have to talk to a man who has no English, there is more than one way of doing it. Beetham adopted the ordinary methods of John Bull on the Continent: he talked good simple English rather loudly and slowly and produced surprisingly successful results. Odell adopted a more sonorous style, and addressed the Sherpa porter in rolling periods worthy of Doctor Johnson. I was much intrigued one day at overhearing a conversation between Odell and his new valet in the tent next to mine. The latter, to my surprise, did know one word of English, which was 'yes,' but I'm not sure that this really helped matters. It went something like this:

Odell. 'Ah, good morning, Narbu Yishé. I understand you are undertaking the duties of my personal servant.'
N.Y. 'Yes, Sahib.'
Odell. 'Well, I have been excellently served in the past by Pu and Nambya and I am very sorry to part with them, but I am convinced that if you display the same spirit that they have done we shall get on together to our mutual satisfaction.'
N.Y. 'Yes, Sahib.'
Odell. 'Let us examine my luggage and I will show you how my various belongings are disposed.'
N.Y. 'Yes, Sahib.'

After this auspicious beginning there must have been a hitch in the proceedings, and in a few minutes Narbu Yishé appeared at my tent with his best military salute. 'Please ask the Sahib,' said he, 'to give me his keys and leave the rest to me; I quite understand the duties of a bearer, and he will find that his kit will be looked after and all his work perfectly done.'[17]

As the climbers moved down into a lusher, vegetated land, their spirits began to lift, although when they reached the Rongshar gorge itself, with its high confining walls which seemed to go on for ever, they found it unexpectedly oppressive. Norton and Somervell drew solace from sketching. They spent three days away from the rest of the party up in the hills above the little rocky village of Trobdje, hoping for a glimpse of the beautiful elusive peak of Gaurisankar, which Wollaston had photographed from a distance during the reconnaissance expedition. Through shifting mists, they were rewarded with what Norton described to Spencer as the finest mountain view either of them had ever seen, 'Perfect in outline, with a most amazing ice ridge facing you. 15,000-feet of sheer mountainside — just fancy it! When the top appeared through the mist it was an utterly incredible height. We sketched like the devil.'[18] Somervell was equally impressed. It towered so high above, he said, 'that when I saw it I felt my balance was wrong and fell over backwards!'[19] It was a dream mountain. They came down spiritually replenished, with five sketches apiece, and immediately despatched Beetham and his camera up for an official photograph for the expedition record. He was too late. The mountain was once more obscured.

Norton's despatch from Rongshar was quite skittish, in sharp contrast to recent communications from Rongbuk. He told of topless girls working in the fields, of Gargantuan repasts of fowls and potatoes and succulent bamboo shoots. It was the letter of a man welcomed back into the world of mortals after long privation, and relieved, for the moment at least, of almost unbearable tension. Its tone did not suit the sombre mood of those back home. Freshfield was prepared to allow that the fault probably lay 'with the man who edited the dispatches', but (as he complained to Spencer) 'unfortunately the jocosity of Norton's last letters from under Guarisankar and the concluding remark of his intentions about having a jolly in the Alps have made an impression that I am sure was never intended.' It displayed, he felt, careless insensitivity towards the family and friends of Mallory and Irvine, and, like Hinks's telegram, ran the risk of 'making a popular show of the disaster'.[20]

General Bruce was still in India at the time of the loss of Mallory and Irvine. After recuperating from his illness at the home of F.M. Bailey, the Political Officer of Sikkim, he had decided to postpone going home until he could travel back with the rest of the party. He kept in touch with expedition affairs as best he could by spending time in Captain Noel's Darjeeling photo laboratory. News of the accident, however, he learned from the newspapers. 'I would give anything to be up now and take the job off their hands and let them rest,' he told Spencer. 'It is a terrible but very wonderful story . . . in fact the whole story should rank with any effort, Arctic and Antarctic etc or in the mountains: and to my mind amply justifies itself and is a complete answer to the "What's-the-use"-s which are bound to spring up . . . I still, though without information, believe that the accident was probably due to a terrific gust of wind catching tired men in a difficult place.'[21] When he read Odell's account, however, he was quite prepared to change his view. He wrote to Hinks:

> I think that he gives a very reasonable opinion that the top was reached and that Mallory and Irvine were overtaken on their way back, probably by dark; possibly they were much longer getting up, their oxygen being exhausted, and were unable to get back in consequence and after this is the possibility of their being obliged to rest owing to night coming on . . . Anyhow it's dreadful — heartbreaking but wonderful.[22]

Longstaff, too, had no difficulty in believing that Mallory and Irvine had made it.

It was my good luck to know both of them: such splendid fellows. Mallory wrote in the last letter I got from him: 'We are going to sail to the top this time and God with us — or stamp to the top with our teeth in the wind.' I would not quote an idle boast, but this wasn't — they got there all right . . . You cannot expect of that pair to weigh the chances of return — I should be weighing them still — it sounds a fair day: probably they were above those clouds that hid them for Odell; how they must have appreciated that view of half the world; it was worthwhile to them; now they'll never grow old and I am very sure they would not change places with any of us.[23]

Freshfield had always doubted the expediency of sending a party of two. It was a practice, as he told Spencer, that had grown out of sharp and short rock climbs and was 'wholly unsuitable, if not suicidal in the case of great ascents'.[24] His point was that a party of three were in a better position, if necessary, to render assistance to a disabled member, and events, he now claimed, had proved him right. From the evidence of Odell's sighting, he presumed that Mallory and Irvine had climbed just over 1,200 feet in about six hours. At that rate the final 800 feet would have taken them another four hours at least. He was sure they could not have had more than three hours of oxygen left. In such circumstances, he failed to see how they could possibly have made it to the summit. Winthrop Young disagreed. He had implicit faith that they had, and was incensed to note that Norton, in his latest press statement, no longer seemed to be giving them the benefit of the doubt.

After nearly 20 years' knowledge of Mallory as a mountaineer, I can say . . . that difficult as it would have been for any mountaineer to turn back with the only difficulty past — to Mallory it would have been an impossibility. I could go into this at length but it is not necessary. The fact that Norton has to depend on this alone in opposing Odell's opinion rather confirms than shakes my own opinion that the accident occurred on the descent (as most do) and that if that is so, the peak was first climbed, because Mallory was Mallory.

Of course there must always be an inclination in such an open question for those who hope to return to the attack to care to think the summit still unclimbed. It is an emotion which above all things these fine fellows should avoid giving to the public unless there is more evidence to contradict the probable interpretation of the facts as we all know them now equally.[25]

The long weeks it took for the expedition to make its way home was a sort of no man's time. The members were making their personal adjustments to the events of Everest, accommodating their loss, coming to their own conclusions about what might have happened. They knew that when they reached home several weeks later they would be required to relive everything as the endless accounting began. In England, too, for those waiting for answers, it was a period of vacuum. Though letters flew back and forth, the time lag made the dialogue strangely stilted. In the several weeks it took for responses to return, events moved inexorably on. It was like corresponding with the past. Already, as can be seen, opinions were shaping and hardening, based as often as not on conviction rather than hard fact. Even for those who had been most intimately concerned in the drama, perceptions of it were subtly changing.

This slow metamorphosis would continue for several months until the 'official version' emerged, and that then could be expected to remain virtually unchallenged — until some new ingredient had to be incorporated into the story, such as the finding of an ice axe in 1933. It is interesting to chart this slow transformation, from the first letters and bulletins written at the time, through the more considered reports and addresses given to the parent bodies on the expedition's return, to the version recorded a year later in the expedition book. This latter could be deemed to be the 'official version', the party line — although it may not have coincided exactly with any one person's individual experience.

The most obvious example of change of opinion about Mallory and Irvine's climb can be found in comparing the despatches sent from Base Camp to *The Times* in London to the version which appeared in *The Fight for Everest* in the middle of the following year. The single most crucial variation concerns Odell's epochal vision of Mallory and Irvine struggling up an obstacle and emerging on top. What exactly did Odell see?

It is easy to understand why it was so important to establish precisely *where* Odell caught sight of the two men. If they were surmounting the Second Step, most agree they would then have a good chance of reaching the summit. At first this possibility delighted Alpine Club members. Then a sea change of opinion occurred, and it became universally accepted that Odell must have been

244

mistaken in believing it to be the Second Step. How could anyone climb a step of 80 feet or so in five minutes at that altitude? It must have been the First. Odell's sighting of the two climbers became the most heavily 'interpreted' part of the entire Mallory and Irvine episode. Within a few years the revisionist version modified every point he originally made. It was even suggested he had not seen anything: perhaps he was confused by rocks or choughs; maybe even, he was suffering from altitude-induced hallucinations and saw nothing at all.

In so much confusion, it was no wonder that Odell, too, began to doubt what he did see. It would be worth at this stage comparing Odell's original description published in the despatches (see Chapter XVI), and the account that appeared in the expedition book *The Fight for Everest*:

At about 26,000 feet I climbed a little crag which could possibly have been circumvented, but which I decided to tackle direct, more perhaps as a test of my condition than for any other reason. There was scarcely 100 feet of it, and as I reached the top there was a sudden clearing of the atmosphere above me and I saw the whole summit ridge and final peak of Everest unveiled. I noticed far away on a snow slope leading up to what seemed to me to be the last step but one from the base of the final pyramid, a tiny object moving and approaching the rock step. A second object followed, and then the first climbed to the top of the step. As I stood intently watching this dramatic appearance, the scene became enveloped in cloud once more and I could not actually be certain that I saw the second figure join the first. It was of course none other than Mallory and Irvine, and I was surprised above all to see them so late as this, namely 12.50, at a point which, if the 'Second Rock Step' they should have reached according to Mallory's schedule by 8 a.m. at the latest, and if the 'First Rock Step' proportionately earlier . . . Owing to the small portion of the summit ridge uncovered I could not be precisely certain at which of these two 'steps' they were, as in profile and from below they are very similar, but at the time I took it for the upper 'Second Step'. However, I am a little doubtful now whether the latter would not be hidden by the face. I could see that they were moving expeditiously as if endeavouring to make up for lost time.[26]

Several apparently minor alterations occur between the two versions, besides the really important change of place. There is also a curious inconsistency in the second version, when, having said that he saw 'the whole summit ridge and final peak of Everest unveiled', Odell later remarks — 'Owing to the small portion of the summit ridge uncovered, I could not be precisely certain at which of the two steps they were.'

The first minor change was altering the words 'a black spot' to 'a tiny object', and this probably reflected an attempt by Odell to counter suggestions that he might have mistaken two rocks, or cloud shadows, for the two climbers. Then, 'Mallory and his companion' became, far more naturally 'Mallory and Irvine'. The only remark to be made here is that it was an extraordinary omission for Odell not to have named Irvine in the first version, since of the two men, it could be supposed that Irvine was his closer friend.

The third change is not an easy one to decipher: 'The first [black spot] then approached the great rock-step and shortly emerged at the top; the second did likewise' becomes '. . . a tiny object moving and approaching the rock step. A second object followed, and the first climbed to the top of the step. I could not actually be certain that I saw the second figure join the first.' To have 'emerged' at the top suggests the figure rose above the skyline, and 'the second did likewise'. A perfect description of surmounting a step. It is hard to see why this aspect of the story should change. If, as it was thought, the step was impossible to climb quickly, Odell might question whether he could have seen either man reach its top. He did not, only the second. However strong the logic of the anti-Second Step lobby, it was not strong enough to erase totally his impression of what he saw.

By next changing 'snow crest' to 'snow slope', Odell was merely clarifying ambiguous wording in his first version. He was indicating that the snow slope itself lay *below* the crest of the ridge. This gives a much clearer picture: if the figures were not after all on the 'crest', or skyline, all the time, it explains how they could disappear — or blend with the rock background — before 'emerging' again, silhouetted against the sky at the top of the step.

The fifth change is the critical one. Originally, Odell unequivocally asserted that where he saw the two climbers was the Second Step. That was his instinctive interpretation at the time the stimuli were pouring into his brain. However, unable to re-create the image accurately afterwards, except in imagination, by the time he wrote the revised version, Odell could no longer 'be precisely certain at which of these two steps they were'. His second description, therefore, is not of what he saw, but what he subsequently *came to believe he saw*.

Finally there is the discrepancy about whether it was the whole, or only part, of the summit ridge that was revealed to Odell through the rent in the clouds. Clearly by the time he came to rewrite his contribution for the *Fight* book, he was no longer trusting his memory on any point of detail. If he could not pin-point where he saw the two climbers, presumably he could not have seen the whole ridge.

But why go to such great lengths to analyse these original clues when it is possible simply to ask Odell exactly what he did see? We have done this, of course, as have other historians, and have also consulted other 'Everesters' for their impressions. The passage of more than half a century naturally dims the freshness of vision, and it is now too late for any new first-hand interpretation. That is why it is necessary for us, like Biblical scholars, to examine carefully the two written versions. Each change of an original expression deserves comment, if only to ask why any change is being made at all. Odell can hardly be blamed if he has made his own choice and declines to be drawn into further controversy. It is for others to weigh the balance of probability.

The expedition book was published in the summer of 1925, and the manuscripts for it would have been required several months earlier. Odell's 'conversion', therefore, must have been completed by the beginning of that year. At the Joint Meeting of the Alpine Club and the Royal Geographical Society held in the Albert Hall on 17 October, the Second Step was still being taken for the location of the sighting, as an article in *The Times* the next day, entitled 'Endurance and Sacrifice', clearly indicates:

In 1922 all previous records were beaten when Mallory, Norton and Somervell without oxygen, and Finch and Geoffrey Bruce with oxygen climbed to close on 27,000 feet and 27,250 feet, respectively. This year those records had in their turn been beaten by Norton and Somervell when they climbed to 28,130 feet without oxygen and by Mallory and Irvine when they reached *28,230 feet* for certain, and probably a greater altitude, with oxygen. (Cheers.)[27]

247

'*28,230 feet*' (italics added) is Norton's assessment of the height of the top of the Second Step, based on theodolite measurement. Even so, at this meeting, the first signs of the transfiguration of Odell's story were already appearing. The words 'the last step but one' had crept into his dissertation though he did not spell out the significance of this. Norton, on the other hand, was still allowing it to be the Second Step in a talk he gave in December, reproduced in the *Alpine Journal* as late as May 1925:

> The approach to the final pyramid appears to be the only other place [apart from the North Col slopes] entailing any danger, except perhaps when new snow is lying. Here there are two possible routes; the first, which Mallory always favoured, and which he followed in his last climb, is by the crest of the N.E. Arête.
>
> There was always the doubt that a feature in this route, which we called the Second Step, might cause considerable difficulty; it presents a vertical face to the S. and E., but seemed surmountable, though evidently steep, to the N. Mallory and Irvine were last seen on the top of the step, and so must have climbed it; but this is not quite sufficient to guarantee this route, as they may well have fallen from it on the descent.[28]

At some time early in 1925, therefore, the last sighting came to be 'officially' demoted from the Second to the First Step. Odell was already isolated from the rest of the team by suggesting that the climbers were benighted rather than that they fell. By changing his mind over which step he saw them on, he was responding to strong peer-group pressure – but conceding so much and no more. He took great exception to the suggestion that he might have been misled into believing other objects to be the climbers, and through-out his life has staunchly refused to amend his original conviction that Mallory and Irvine could have made it to the summit – even though to believe this, while at the same time accepting that they had only reached the First Step by 1 p.m., required Odell to make what amounts to a leap in faith:

> The question remains, 'Has Mount Everest been climbed?' It must be left unanswered, for there is no direct evidence. But bearing in mind all the circumstances that I have set out above, and considering their position when last seen, I think myself

there is a strong probability that Mallory and Irvine succeeded.[29]

Is Odell's noble constancy a delusion — a stubborn refusal to bow to conventional wisdom? Could it perhaps be an unconscious effort to maintain the wholeness of his great vision despite the way it was being whittled away by intellectual bickering? It had, after all, been a magical episode for him, and one which happened when he was already in a state of high elation. The buoyant mood brought on by believing them to be 'going strong for the top' with no further obstacles in their path, sustained him throughout the rest of the day as he returned to his tent on the North Col. His vision was far too powerful an experience to deny. It was his last link with Irvine, and it somehow fused him with the fate of the two men. Just how much this meant to him is revealed in the obituary notice he wrote for his young friend in the *Alpine Journal:*

> My final glimpse of one, whose personality was of that charm-
> ing character that endeared him to all and whose natural gifts
> seemed to indicate such possibilities of both mind and body,
> was that he was 'going strong', sharing with that other fine
> character who accompanied him such a vision of sublimity that
> it has been the lot of few mortals to behold; nay, few while
> beholding have become merged into such a scene of
> transcendence.[30]

Regardless of any personal significance, however, the main reason Odell would cling so tenaciously to the key elements of his vision, even in the face of apparent logic, is because he cannot do anything else: that is how it was. To have it otherwise, he would need to invent. The inconsistencies in his account only began to creep in when he felt compelled to change the location of his sighting. If later discoveries are measured against his original description, they tally surprisingly well.

Members of the British expedition that went to Everest in 1933 found an ice axe on the slabs leading up towards the First Step. They also inspected the Second Step from close quarters and found it perhaps 100 feet high, steeper and more difficult than earlier descriptions had suggested. All but Longland came back convinced that the Second Step was an impossible proposition. Hugh Ruttledge, leader of the expedition, made a point of questioning Odell closely about his sighting. His climbers were having difficulty reconciling Odell's evidence with their own findings and were inclined to dismiss the whole episode, openly expressing doubt that Odell had seen anything at all.

Odell, on the other hand, having studied the photographs they brought back, thought that it might well have been on the Second Step after all where he had last seen Mallory and Irvine. In response to Ruttledge's interrogation, he pointed out, with some irritation, that it was incorrect to suggest that he had ever declared Mallory and Irvine to be moving fast on *rock*. What he had said was that they were moving up a *snow slope* and *approaching* a rock step; nor had he said 'quite fast', but 'expeditiously'. What he wanted to convey by that was the notion that there was nothing halting about their movements. 'In the few minutes of visibility, I felt certain of seeing one of the figures, lost for a short time against the rock face above the snow slope, appear in profile on the top of the rock feature.'[31]

So far as the ice axe was concerned, he agreed it would always be a matter for speculation, but too much could be made of it. It could have been discarded on ascent (unlikely, certainly), or left or lost on descent. Nothing Ruttledge's team said made him doubt his version of events – but, equally, nothing Odell said had any effect on the views of the 1933 men. It is interesting that Longland described watching the Second Step coat up with snow in a way that suggested there were faults on its north face, 'which might conceivably be linked together into a route from the ridge'. Longland still believed the ridge route might just be possible, though he now says that both he and Mallory were wrong. It was a formidable obstacle, unclimbable by the standards of the time. The other 1933 climbers all favoured Norton's traverse. None of them believed it remotely possible that Mallory and Irvine might have made it.

It is hard to be so dogmatic today. The ridge route has been successfully climbed by the Chinese, the Japanese and the Catalans, following those fault lines Longland observed on the upper part of the Second Step. In 1985 five members of the Catalan Expedition reached the summit following Mallory's route under the extra burden of monsoon snow. They climbed without oxygen, and found the section between the two steps, and the Second Step itself, extremely dangerous. It took them fourteen hours to reach the summit from their Camp VI near the North-east Shoulder, and they were forced to bivouac at the foot of the Second Step on their way back. None the less they were left with the impression that it was perfectly feasible for Mallory and Irvine, climbing the ridge when relatively clear of snow, to have reached the summit, though they would have had insufficient time in hand to get back down to their last camp. It is interesting that *none* of the expeditions which have so far reached the summit by this ridge have made it back to their Camp VI the same day. They have all had either to bivouac or place an additional camp.

Long after 1924, Odell was contacted by a man from the Shetland Islands, a retired artist called Williamson, whom he knew only slightly, with news of the ultimate fate of Mallory and Irvine. It appeared that Williamson had a psychic friend who had just died and had been 'in touch' with Sandy Irvine. For what it was worth, he wished to pass on Irvine's message from 'the other side', which told of his last climb with Mallory. They had reached the summit of Everest, the story went, though very late, and were utterly exhausted when they tried to pick their way back down again in the gathering darkness. They were unroped. On the way, Mallory slipped to his death, leaving Irvine to continue alone. He had gone only a short distance before he was so overwhelmed with fatigue that he sank down to rest on a rock not far below the ridge, setting down his ice axe on the slabs beside him. Huddled there in the bitter cold, the image of Mallory floated before him. 'Come on, old chap,' Mallory said. 'It's time for us to be getting along.'

This was not the first extra-sensory manifestation to 'reveal' the fate of Mallory and Irvine – a number of similar stories circulated just after their deaths – but for Odell, Williamson's version was one which offered a plausible sequence of events as well as an explanation of how the ice axe came to be lying free on the angled rocks. It had always been a puzzle why the axe, if it was lost in an accident or dropped from above, had not bounded down the slopes as did Somervell's on similar ground some days before. It did not strike Odell as particularly odd that Irvine should seek to get a message to him in this way, and Somervell, when he heard the story, agreed there might be something in it. Having lived a long time in India, where he had made a study of oriental religions, Somervell kept an open mind on para-normal matters. For Odell, however, the wish to believe, backed up by Somervell's encouragement, may have been overwhelming: it is Mallory, not his inexperienced young protégé, who falls to his death. All doubt about oxygen malfunction is swept away, so leaving neither Odell nor Irvine culpable on that score. Having attained the summit, Irvine's readiness for Everest could no longer be in question. He is even spared the lonely agony of freezing to death by a visitation from 'the other side' as Mallory returns, like an angel of mercy, to ease the passage for him into the next life.

Odell's request to join the expedition in 1936, in order to complete his geological survey, was flatly refused by Ruttledge. Bitterly disappointed he went instead to Garhwal Himalaya, where with H.W. Tilman, another 1936 reject, he had the satisfaction of making the first ascent of Nanda Devi. Until 1950 it remained the highest mountain ever climbed.

XVIII

Friends and Relations

What is so difficult to know about 'heroes' is where and when they start to be so. Are they visibly different from other people when they are alive, recognizable even then, or is it the dying that makes them? Do heroes make themselves, or are they the products of others? At very least, do they collude in their own myth? Do they strike attitudes, make statements that, even if a little absurd at the time, destine them for immortality? To judge by other 'heroes' of the early twentieth century — Robert Falcon Scott, Rupert Brooke, T.E. Lawrence — we clearly do not require them to be perfect. Perhaps failure, or the futility of their gesture, is a desirable ingredient. Maybe we even require our heroes to be flawed in some way, so that having raised them as paragons, we can make them once more humanly accessible.

What then affects the intensity with which heroes are perceived? Would Mallory and Irvine have come to symbolize the same striving spirit of enterprise if Odell had not caught his tantalizing vision of them forging bravely upwards? If his last glimpse had been of them coming down, or if he had seen one man only, or if he had come up that day and seen nothing at all, would the Mallory and Irvine myth be so potent? Was the moment Odell lost them in the swirling mists also the moment when they stepped into legend? Was the image then gilded by well-chosen words of friends who came to honour them? By embracing them as heroes, did a wondering public rob them of their personalities?

'Picturesque and vivid lives are of more service to their kind than lives of conventional eminence.' So began Geoffrey Winthrop

253

Young's obituary notice for George Mallory, in the *Nation* on 5 July 1924. He concluded:

> In [Mallory's] last despatch we can read his mind: the limits of experience were past, reason might counsel retreat, but if the age-long fight of humanity with its unknown environment were to be carried this one step further, chivalry, with its fickle ally, chance, must take up the challenge. In that final magnificent venture of himself and his gallant younger companion against the unknown, we are thrilled by the knightly purpose, by the evident joyousness of the attempt, as much as by the audacity and endurance. It is the burning spirit of chivalrous, youthful adventure, flaming at the close, higher than the highest summit of the known world.
>
> However the end of that great contest came, to those two alone with unimaginable height, space, and silence, that flame, we know, burned radiantly to the last. George Mallory — 'Sir Galahad' always to his early friends — gave back to the hills their life of inspiration, content. The greatest mountain upon earth is the monument to his clean and selfless use of his rare manhood. While there are hearts to quicken still at tales of heroism, merciless Everest — terrible to us — will remain for them a mountain of beautiful remembrance.[1]

Do carefully-chosen words like those of Winthrop Young, which seek to preserve and celebrate the essence of their friend, perhaps bar us, who did not know him, from the real man? Words are codes — they strike a response when the experience is shared: vital, vivid, radiant, flame-like. Those to whom Mallory was these things, will seize Winthrop Young's words saying 'Yes, yes, that's it! That is exactly what he was like!' But, for us, without such personal experience, separated by a gulf of generations, words alone are insufficient to conjour a living, beating presence. Chivalrous, knightly . . . again, produce an air of unreality. Sir Galahad? The maiden knight, the purest and noblest of the Arthurian company: to how many of our own acquaintance could we attach such a high-minded epithet? Yet the knightly comparison is the one most often associated with Mallory. Bruce called him 'the Bayard of the Mountains — *"sans peur et sans reproche"* '. For us to hope to come to an image or an atmosphere of the man, we need to superimpose description upon description, in the hope that from such a composite, a consistent outline will emerge. We must give precedence where we find it to the unconscious description, written in life, before the legend took root.

The appearance should be the easiest to re-create. There are photographs, yet as Ruth Mallory wrote to her husband in France, 'I've got your beautiful face looking at me now, but it won't move, it stays always the same. Photographs are not much real good I'm afraid, not when you know a person very, very well.' Not much good, either, when you know them not at all. There are a few paintings and there are descriptive portraits by friends.

We know Mallory's height (just under six foot), his weight (11 stone 5 lbs), his build (that of an 'ideal athlete, unspoilt by over development in any part'). We know he looked ridiculously young for his age, certainly until he was well into his thirties, and that he was fine-featured and moved with an easy grace. R.L.G. Irving, who knew him throughout his life, from his schooldays at Winchester, gave what in some ways is a curious description:

He had a strikingly beautiful face. Its shape, its delicately cut features, especially the rather large, heavily lashed, thoughtful eyes, were extraordinarily suggestive of a Botticelli Madonna, even when he had ceased to be a boy — though any suspicion of effeminacy was completely banished by obvious proofs of physical energy and strength.[2]

To make such a point of denying effeminacy indicates that it is an inference that could otherwise be drawn, and this is reinforced when Irving goes on to say, 'Neither at school nor at the Varsity was his simple chivalrous nature even temporarily affected by the adulation that knaves and fools are ready to bestow on youths like him.' Irving is referring to the hero-worship that was lavished on Mallory, by such as Lytton Strachey, who on first setting eyes on Mallory in Cambridge in 1909 wrote in a transport of rapture to Clive and Vanessa Bell,

Mon Dieu! — George Mallory! When that's been written, what more need be said? My hand trembles, my heart palpitates, my whole being swoons away at the words — oh heavens! heavens! I found of course that he'd been absurdly maligned — he's six foot high, with the body of an athlete by Praxiteles, and a face — oh incredible — the mystery of Botticelli, the refinement and delicacy of a Chinese print, the youth and piquancy of an unimaginable English boy. I rave, but when you see him, as you must, you will admit all — all![3]

To dismiss Strachey's adoration, is to overlook the fact that by whatever means Mallory came to know Strachey, he developed a close and affectionate friendship with him and certainly did not himself regard Strachey as either fool or knave. Rather, he told Ruth, just before they were married, when he was expecting Lytton to come and stay the night at Charterhouse,

He is very, very queer — not to me, of course, because I know him as a friend, but to the world. He must be very irritating to many people. My profound respect for his intellect, and for a sort of passion with which he holds the doctrine of freedom, besides much love for him as a man of intense feelings and fine imagination, make me put up with much in him that I could hardly tolerate in another. I haven't seen him for I don't know how long — much more than a year, more like two — which for a *great* friend is rather a long time.[4]

Certainly, it falls to the lot of exceptionally good-looking young men to be the target of considerable attention from male and female alike, although in the sheltered university world of those Edwardian days, feminine company would have been in short supply. Mallory would soon have come to the realization that he was physically attractive, whatever reaction that knowledge kindled in him. Yet we have it from his tutor, the diarist Arthur Benson, that when he first went up to Magdalene College in the autumn of 1905, Mallory still wore an air of unknowing and luminous innocence:

I had noticed in King's in the morning a fine-looking boy, evidently a freshman, just in front of me — lo and behold the same came to call on me; and turns out to be MALLORY from Winchester, one of our new Exhibitioners at Magd[alene]. He sate some time; and a simpler, more ingenuous, more un-affected, more genuinely interested boy, I never saw. He is to be under me, and I rejoice at the thought. He seemed full of admiration for all good things, and yet with no touch of priggishness.[5]

256

From Benson's diaries it is possible to glean much about Mallory and his friendships at Cambridge, and also about the prevailing atmosphere during the time he was there. Benson was a bachelor don, who took a paternal and individual interest in his charges, and it must be said, derived emotional comfort from his frequently-tangled but essentially chaste associations with attractive undergraduates. Though perennially self-absorbed, he could be a warm and sympathetic friend and earned considerable popular success from the publication of several uplifting books that appealed — as he himself said — to 'the unctuous and sentimental middle classes'. For twenty-eight years until his death in 1925, a year after Mallory's, he kept a diary which chronicled not just the events of his days, but his inmost dreams and desires. It betrayed little of the same avuncular fluency of his books; privately he was a wry and often waspish observer. Realising that pain and offence might be caused by some of its more intimate revelations, Benson decreed an embargo on publication to extend for fifty years after his death.

The diaries were not, therefore, available in their entirety to Mallory's earlier biographers, although Benson did pass a sketch he had written of Mallory to David Pye, and this was later drawn upon again by David Robertson. At the time Benson doubted if Pye's book would reach fruition. 'Nothing will be done, or worse than nothing. It is amazing how amateurs will let a thing fall through. A real beautiful little sketch could be made of G.M. I would do it only Mrs. M. doesn't like me, or won't ask me,' adding spitefully, 'I really rather hate Mrs. M. She is so uncivilised.'[6]

The lifting of Benson's embargo has now revealed more of interest, and it is perhaps worth a digression here to say a little about Arthur Benson himself, not only to obtain a clearer perspective on his observations, but also because he was such an important influence in Mallory's development.

At the time Mallory went up to Cambridge, Benson was forty-four. He had been at Magdalene himself for only one year. Before that he was a housemaster at Eton, where he was deeply respected for his kindly and liberalizing influence, preferring to run his house on trust rather than severity of punishment. Benson challenged such educational traditions as the domination of the classics and the worship of sport, placing instead a high value on the civilizing qualities of tolerance and friendship. His ideal was that 'friendship that cuts across the generations and achieves the union of youth and age'. He moved to Cambridge largely because he wished to further

257

such bonds of friendship in a way which he considered impossible with young boys, especially when placed in a position of authority over them.

Generation gaps meant little to Mallory. Throughout his life he enjoyed the friendship of older men — like Benson, like R.L.G. Irving and Winthrop Young, like Farrar and Reade, like Arthur Clutton Brock and indeed, like Ruth's father, Thackeray Turner — men with whom he would confide his developing ideas and from whom he would frequently imbibe attitudes and general philosophy. In many of the decisions or directions he took, the discernible influence of such mentors can be seen. Benson influenced Mallory academically, as one would expect, encouraging particularly his talent for essay-writing, but perhaps even more in the way he prized and cultivated friendship. When Mallory, in his turn, later railed against traditional teaching methods at Charterhouse and eventually left with the expressed desire to teach more mature students, he was, like Benson, on a quest for better understanding between youth and age, the Greek ideal.

Benson came from a privileged background but was all his life conscious of the difficulties of being the son of a famous man. His father, a distinguished theologian, rose from headmaster of Wellington College through ecclesiastical ranks to become Archbishop of Canterbury under Queen Victoria. He was a stern, overbearing man who handled emotional affairs with an odd, stilted, matter-of-factness, which Benson came later to realize was due more to a chronic inability to communicate affection than want of it. He early decided his cousin Minnie Sidgewick would make him a suitable wife, apprising the young lady of the fact when she was only eleven years old. Accordingly, as soon as Minnie reached her eighteenth birthday, they were married. It proved a tense and unhappy union, but none the less six gifted children were produced. The eldest, Martin, his father's favourite, died as a schoolboy, leaving Arthur, as second son, to shoulder with his own grief the extra burden of responsibility for all his father's hopes. Devoted as they were to each other, none of the Benson children was able outside the family to make satisfactory relationships with the opposite sex. Even Benson's mother, after his father's death, shared the rest of her life — and the family bed — with the daughter of the previous Archbishop. Both sisters formed Sapphic liaisons. One brother, Hugh, became a Roman Catholic monseigneur whose name was linked with the infamous 'Baron Corvo'; and the other, Frank, was the society

258

satirist E.F. Benson, who, had he lived today, could only have been described as camp.

Arthur survived on a succession of warm friendships with favoured young men among his students, friendships which he recognized to be based on a transmuted sexual attraction, but which he kept perfectly restrained. 'These romantic attachments may do great good both to the inspirer and the inspired,' he wrote, 'but they should be conducted with some seemliness and decorum.' Passion without taint, was his watchword. What he always most enjoyed was the 'courtship' period of each new 'romance', with its mutual absorption, and the sharing of risqué confidences. He shied from physical contact and deplored sentimentality or mawkish displays of affection. It was a life, as he recognized, lived on the Edge. Even so, it made overwhelming demands on his emotions. Twice he suffered disabling fits of depression, and was always prone to the torment of petty jealousies.

Arthur Benson's friendship with Mallory was one of the more enduring of his romantic attachments, though there were later fluctuations of affection and times when Mallory profoundly irritated him. The initial attraction, as it usually was for Benson, was the unconscious beauty of a young male. Mallory was at first unresponsive to Benson's overtures, though at all times polite and cordial. Benson was intrigued. Mallory's spirit was evidently as full of pure beauty as his face. 'A *very* straight-forward, pure-minded, wholesome, manly youth,' he wrote, but was he also, Benson wondered, a little stupid? The idea was dismissed as Mallory gradually unbent in his company and Benson saw great promise and intelligence in the history essays the boy produced. Increasingly Benson's diary records what a charming creature Mallory was, with a 'combination of energy, modesty and virtue that I have seldom seen equalled'. All the more puzzling, therefore, that disturbing reports should reach him from other sources that his 'good Mallory' was growing unpopular among fellow students for his habit of laying down the law on everything.

Benson had a house out on the Cambridgeshire fens at Haddenham, and for a few days in the summer of 1906, and again before Christmas, he invited Mallory to stay with him. He was hoping to penetrate the last of Mallory's reserve; he could not put his finger on what troubled him about his young friend. At times it almost seemed as if he was devoid of emotion, hard and unsympathetic, though Benson knew him to be generous and kind: 'It is

259

simply that I do not feel in *contact* with him — yet he likes me, I believe, and I certainly like him.' The two men bicycled out across the fields on a damp, grey day in mid-December. The first night Benson recorded in his diary:

> Mallory is a delightful creature . . . one of the most ingenuous and purest-minded creatures I know. He is very beautiful, too, to look at, and finely proportioned, so that it is a pleasure to me to see him move, or do anything . . . He comes with the least little touch of shyness.[6]

By the third evening Mallory had relaxed sufficiently to discuss religion, confiding the difficulties he was experiencing in accepting the existence of miracles, even though he was expecting to follow his father into the church. Later, Benson was able to steer the conversation around to romance and Mallory related his own early experiences. 'Most interesting,' commented Benson ' — and I thought him rather a kind of *Ion* in this respect.' After seeing Mallory off on the fourth day, Benson had no further cause to regret any diffidence on the part of his 'dear companion'. All barriers had broken down: 'This boy has grown much into my heart,' he confided to his diary, 'he is romantic, but not at all sentimental, like H[ugh] W[alpole], and I feel that his liking for me is a kind of filial confidence. Never mind what it is, it is sweet and encouraging.' They were photographed together at the door as Mallory left, but Benson found the results 'grotesque'. 'He appears impish', he said, 'I like an old bear.'

There was no need to force the friendship and apart from supervising Mallory's studies, Benson saw little of Mallory over the next few months. It was not until early summer (1907) that they again achieved closeness. Benson received an invitation to take tea with Mallory, which he accepted with a degree of reluctance. Prolonged company of the young had of late the effect of reminding him he was growing middle-aged, even though in himself Benson felt haunted by a sense of youth and rashness. More than anything, he dreaded appearing boring and was already beginning to avoid encounters where he felt this likely. It was something which would trouble him for the rest of his life.

When he arrived at Mallory's rooms, he found his young friend ill and miserable, and immediately concern for Mallory eliminated his own worries. 'He confided to me a love-affair with a girl of 16, the daughter of a doctor.' It was hardly a matter for wonder, Benson felt, that any girl should fall in love with Mallory, but he felt obliged to offer conventional counsel. When young, he said, it is so easy to mistake fancy for passion. 'It is no good telling people in such moods that they are silly,' his diary records. 'Indeed I told him that I frankly envied him. It touched and pleased me greatly that he wanted to tell me about this. He is a fine creature.' Benson often admitted to himself a deep longing for a son, and this incident suggests that his relationship with Mallory was still one of such affection as might be shared between father and son.

Mallory's illness proved to be jaundice, which kept him in bed for some days. When Benson visited him on 1 May he found the room full of flowers and a young boy from the florist's was delivering yet another bouquet, some lilies of the valley from a gentleman who gave no name. With them came a mysterious note in printed capital letters, 'FROM A FAIR UNKNOWN'. A touch of sentiment, Benson reflected, seemed admissible among men when a friend is ill. This expression of sentiment was a permanent preoccupation of Benson's. It should be there, he felt, 'like a warm summer air, not expressed, but quietly permeating everything'.

The weeks of convalescence following Mallory's illness curtailed his rowing training. He and Benson took frequent walks and cycle rides, when he would confide the latest news of his doomed 'engagement' to the doctor's daughter. 'His father will be vexed with me for not warning him, but one can't give people away!' These walks and the fine spring weather caused Benson's sagging spirits to soar miraculously. 'It is nice to be wanted!' he exclaimed. 'Mallory is a boy I'm really fond of and like to be with, even think about when he is not near.' On 25 May, they went together on a long country walk and Benson could no longer conceal from himself his real feelings for Mallory:

Why should I pretend that I do not love this young friend, and take deep pleasure in his company. I did my best to amuse him and interest him but I did not sentimentalize for an instant — except just at the end to say that I enjoyed the day. I do not think sentiment would please him, and moreover, I don't want to be sentimental myself. It is a different sort of feeling from that. It is a pleasure in the sight of him, the sound of his voice and his company. Pleasure in a direct, original and thoughtful mind, unlike my own — pleasure in a very virginal kind of innocence — and that he likes and trusts me. But he would dislike anything

261

emotional, and so should I; and yet one seems to want *something*. There is some haunting wish to establish a *permanent* feeling, a tie which is impossible. And I suppose that, in reality, far off, disguised, refined, transmuted, it is really the instinct of passion: but how unrecognisable!

It had been a sweet day of summer, a day of almost impossible and golden sweetness, not in the least clouded by the fact that Mallory was due to sit for his Tripos on the morrow. He told Benson, 'I think I am happiest on the eve of the fray — it is a stimulus which suits me.' It was an uncanny insight into Mallory's later search for adventure, but it was not an instinct Benson felt he could share:

Well, so we rode together, and walked together, and had tea together, and said many absurd things that came into our heads and smiled at each other like two good comrades. The church at Guilden Morden had the gate tied with a wreath of shepherd's purse — a good omen.

For the rest of that summer, Mallory remained for Benson a figure much in the foreground of his mind, and, Benson believed, he in turn featured much in the foreground of Mallory's:

but how strange that this being so, we cannot draw together more! Only drift along side by side, in a kind of vague longing, for what? Anyhow, my heart goes out greatly to him. I desire to see and hear and understand him. But I cannot communicate this to him, because of some stupid shame-facedness, or say frankly how much it means to me. And so it is that the years slip by, and one gets no hold, no permanent hold, in any heart. To matter to someone, why does one desire that?

Increasingly, Benson was beginning to sink under the depression that was to grip him for the next two years and keep him away from Cambridge for many months, but as yet Mallory still had the power of charming away his blackest moods. They spent a few days together at the start of the long vacation. 'I do not think I could have a companion more to my taste,' Benson reflected. 'I only grudge the flight of the pleasant hours of his company.' They walked, rowed, talked, motored in Arthur's new chauffeur-driven car, and in the evenings played music, read and wrote poetry. 'One does not often get the society of an ingenuous and congenial young man who is also sincerely affectionate; perhaps it is rather a dangerous luxury — still it has beguiled my depression in these gloomy days as nothing else could have done. He has walked with me as the angel walked with Tobit.'

The shadow fell again when it came time for Mallory to leave:

> I hated him going and he was sorry to go. I wonder what these affections mean, whether there *is* something real and permanent behind them — or if we merely meet as fellow pilgrims, love each other, are sorry for each other, and then fall back into the stream. I fell into considerable depression.

Benson's melancholia was compounded by family problems and on several occasions brought him close to suicide. In desperation he tried a variety of cures, including hypnotism. On a brief but disastrous return to the university in March 1908 he could not help but observe how close a friendship had grown up between Mallory and Stephen Gaselee, who was shortly to succeed Percy Lubbock as the new Pepys Librarian at Magdalene. Peevishly Benson remarked, 'Very good for both. G. is a fine old crusted Tory, with a strong dash of the world about him. M. a rather sentimental radical, and they may learn to see if not respect other points of view.' It is easy to judge the degree of Benson's hurt by his application of the despised word 'sentimental' to Mallory. Throughout Benson's illness, however, Mallory maintained friendly contact, and visited him twice during the summer of 1908. Benson afterwards remarked how touched he was at the concern Mallory showed, particularly upon his return to Cambridge, still far from well; Mallory was the only undergraduate to visit him regularly and try to jolly him out of his gloom.

In July 1908 Mallory was invited to stay at Benson's family home Tremans, near Horsted Keynes in Sussex. Apart from disgracing himself by giggling hysterically throughout a sermon at Benson's church, the two enjoyed easy companionship and talked much of politics and religion. They did have one argument, however, on the bases of morality, that got very heated — Benson maintaining that the word 'moral' did not stand for any absolute reality, 'Polygamy and wars of annihilation were considered righteous once, but immoral now'; and Mallory arguing equally trenchantly that morality was not variable. They were able to agree on common ground at the end. Another afternoon some months later they were having

263

what Benson described as 'an odd conversation about the expression of sentiment', when Benson suddenly became aware that a strong undertow of emotion threatened the calm:

> I had the feeling . . . rather an uncomfortable, semi-physical feeling — that in my companion's spirit there was a great and deep perturbation of emotion. I felt scorched, as by a fire. Now my own emotions do not scorch — they merely shine and ripple like the waters of a lake; and when I come near this sort of *fire*, it makes me, I think, uncomfortable. His point was that we should *never* express such things. Mine, that if one can *trust* a person absolutely, not to give one away, there is no objection to an easy and natural frankness. I do think we English people are absurdly reticent.

Benson had noted the tendency at Cambridge for people to have great emotional affections for each other, but to be ashamed of speaking of them — or indeed of admitting to them — even though they were held to be right and holy and altogether admirable. That seemed to him an absurd nonsense. 'Either the whole thing is wrong, sentimental and effeminate,' he declared, 'or else people should not be ashamed to speak of it — among the right people of course. It is the wrong kind of reticence.'

Clearly, in his conversation with Mallory, Benson managed to achieve a level of oblique frankness that suited him, even if it was less than the easy openness he was advocating. Discussing the amount of romantic friendship in the air they dipped into what Benson called that 'darker moral region, the shadow that lies behind such friendships', and it was usually at mention of this darker force that Benson, in his turn, became reticent, despite his brave protestations. Why was Mallory so agitated? It could not have been the first time he was forced to acknowledge that such a 'shadow' existed behind even this friendship with Benson? Mallory's puritanical streak may well have demanded such matters be kept fiercely submerged and Benson's obvious delight in discussing them disturbed this resolve. Or did Mallory's distress go deeper than that?

It had taken Mallory a long time to make friends when he first came up to Cambridge, and many of his acquaintances then were older men. Benson's diary contains frequent references to an awkward manner Mallory adopted with his equals, a derisive, dogmatic truculence — also recorded by David Pye — and it is easy to understand how such a strident attitude could put off people at first meeting. During 1907, however, Mallory had been admitted into Charles Sayle's menagerie and discovered there others who shared his liking for vigorous, adversarial debate, and with whom he found music, poetry and much else in common. Many of those who met regularly in Sayle's little house in Trumpington Street were to number among his inner circle of friends, and it was with Sayle's encouragement that the Marlowe Dramatic Club came into being. Rupert Brooke, whose radiant beauty was the talk of all Cambridge, Geoffrey Keynes, James Strachey, Cosmo Gordon and Justin Brooke were all regular visitors. Great value was placed on friendship and there was a strong feeling of brotherhood among students and younger dons alike. John Lehmann, describing this period in his book, *Rupert Brooke, His Life and His Legend*, maintains that:

it would be no exaggeration to say that they [the younger dons] were all inspired, to a greater or lesser degree, by a dream of re-creating the atmosphere and ideals of the Athens of Socrates in their University. They were basically agnostics if not atheists, pagans who had assimilated Christian ethics rather than Christian morals or metaphysics. With such ideals, there was a strong homosexual element in their attitudes.[7]

For Mallory — as a Christian with wavering intent to become a priest, and one already experiencing difficulty reconciling the necessary acceptance of dogma with a natural instinct for enquiry — this emergent spirit of free thought must have presented a conscientious dilemma. How could he cleave to the traditional virtues required of a churchman when confronted with the heady allure of mental and sensual exploration? As Benson liked to say, 'Isn't it really rather dangerous to let boys read Plato, if one is desirous that they should accept conventional moralities?'

Politically, Mallory was an instinctive socialist and readily embraced Fabianism as soon as it reached Cambridge. A belief in God and a desire to work for the betterment of the human condition, that too was instinctive. He knew he wanted to do some form of work that offered service to the community. Benson had long been concerned that Mallory's idealism might founder on disappointment. 'Like all generous reformers,' he said, 'he counts too much upon mankind being both disinterested and reasonable.' Moreover,

Benson doubted whether Mallory had the emotional stamina for reading theology. Now, as Mallory felt his convictions shifting and resettling, there arose the added problem of what he should do about it. It would grieve his father to know that his religious views had subtly altered, and he supposed, strictly speaking, it would not be necessary to tell him, but he saw keeping quiet as a confirmation of insincerity. Should he, therefore, make a frank confession and knowingly inflict pain on his father in the service of honesty?

Faced with a conflict of emotions, Mallory's sensitivity was such that he frequently became taut and excitable — as he did in the year leading up to his marriage, and also when his efforts to get into the War were being frustrated. Captain Noel remarked upon it on Everest. The entry in Benson's diary indicates that Mallory was enveloped in similar emotional turmoil that September afternoon when he was forced to accept, perhaps for the first time, the true nature and implications of the situation and society in which he now found himself. He could no longer, like Peter Pan, remain insulated by his ingenuousness. When it came to the freer society of his contemporaries, the New Pagans, he would need to adopt a conscious moral stance or abandon himself to hedonism and throw morality to the winds. It is doubtful if he fully resolved the dilemma until he made the decision to become a schoolmaster rather than enter the church — if indeed he ever fully did.

Mallory was now meeting men who were less discreet about displaying their feelings than Benson. Charles Sayle, for one, was quite unable to conceal his worship of the Young Apollos. 'I do not know if these undergraduates love me, but I know they love me to love them!' he wrote, and would refer to them in his diary as his 'swans': 'A very happy evening. So many swans in the room at once, and all happy. Time only broke us up.' He hung their picture in a 'shrine' in his drawing room, would fawn and fuss, and even in formal company babble about his current flames. To Benson, the man was a foolish sentimentalist and his behaviour, if harmless, was effeminate and horrifyingly embarrassing. But he was a product of the prevalent mood and not, it would seem, particularly exceptional. Sayle developed an infatuation for Rupert Brooke, giving him presents and inviting him to tête-à-tête suppers. With Mallory he shared a love of mountains, and their friendship endured long after Mallory had left Cambridge. It was of course Sayle who introduced Mallory to Geoffrey Winthrop Young.

When Benson recovered sufficiently from his nervous collapse to resume his duties at Magdalene, it seemed to him that Cambridge had never been so highly-charged with romantic talk and open, intensely emotional friendships. He was amazed at the 'public fondling and caressing' seen after a Feast at King's College, 'friends and lovers sitting with arms enlaced, cheeks even touching'. He supposed such Saturnalia did no harm, and could even be considered beautiful in a way, but he could not resist the uncomfortable feeling that, like reading Plato, it was really rather dangerous.

Mallory was now in his fourth and final year at Cambridge. He managed in the previous year to improve the grade of his History Tripos from third to second class, and Benson had made it possible for him to stay on at Magdalene in the hope that further advantage might be gained. He was writing an essay on James Boswell for the Members' Prize Essay. It was a year in which Mallory continued to widen his circle of friends. Through Geoffrey Keynes and James Strachey he came to know their more famous brothers, Maynard Keynes and Lytton Strachey, and the Stracheys' cousin, Duncan Grant. Lytton Strachey came to stay in Cambridge for two weeks at the end of April. There is a story that Mallory rescued him from being ducked in the Trinity fountain by a mob of boisterous undergraduates. Whatever the truth of their meeting, at his first sight of Mallory, Lytton was completely bowled over. He had been told before his visit, by both James and Duncan, that Mallory ranked easily first among all the handsome young undergraduates; even so, Lytton was quite unprepared for so perfect a vision. He felt he could 'curl up within its shadow, and sleep', and wrote his ecstatic 'Mon Dieu! – George Mallory!' letter to Clive and Vanessa Bell (21 May 1909).

'Mallory, had he known of this effusion, would certainly have felt abashed,'[8] declared David Robertson in 1969 – but would he, though, given the climate of the time? Lytton is unlikely to have made any secret of his infatuation. Mallory may well have been initially disconcerted, as Michael Holroyd suggests in his biography of Lytton Strachey, by Lytton's 'mixture of irreverence, indecency and outrageous coyness', but Holroyd also tells how the first thing that struck Lytton, on his arrival in Cambridge – as it also struck Benson – was how 'the colleges seemed thick with amorous crises and stupendous rumours'. It did not take Lytton long to discern that Mallory nurtured an unrequited affection for James, Lytton's brother. Lytton's letter to the Bells continued:

The amazing thing, though, was that besides his beauty, other things were visible, more enchanting still. His passion for James was known, but it so happened that during my visit he declared it — and was rejected . . . Poor George! I met him for the first time immediately after this occurrence, and saw in my first glance to the very bottom of his astounding soul. I was écrasé. What followed was remarkable — though infinitely pure. Yes!! Virginia alone will sympathize with me now — I'm a convert to the divinity of virginity, and spend hours every day lost in a trance of adoration, innocence, and bliss. It was a complete revelation, as you may conceive. By God! The sheer beauty of it all is what transports me . . . To have sat with him in the firelight through the evening, to have wandered with him in the Kings Garden among violets and cherry blossom, to have — no, no! for desire was lost in wonder, and there was profanation even in a kiss . . .[9]

Lytton concluded: 'For the rest, he's going to be a schoolmaster, and his intelligence is not remarkable. What's the need?' Such intellectual snobbery was a feature of the 'Bloomsberries', who were always ready to dismiss lightly lesser talents. Michael Holroyd considers that Lytton — and Duncan Grant, too — were scornful of Mallory's intelligence because he seemed so unaware that their admiration for him was physical. Yet it is hard to believe that Mallory would not recognize even coded overtures. A strong element of moral puritanism existed in him and if he presented an attitude of virginal innocence, it is far more probable that he had set his own limits, either from considerations of morality or from personal inclination. Lytton Strachey has referred to a 'fond of prudery', and Cottie Sanders has described an argument which took place at Pen-y-Pass on Easter Sunday 1912 between Mallory and an Irishman who declared that the only reason for having principles at all was to break them:

It was not difficult for him [the unnamed Irishman] to make George's insistence on the importance of thinking right and doing right look pedestrian and priggish, and he was very unsparing. And the sense of the meeting was on the whole against George — at the start, anyhow. George stood up to it superbly, really: no irony, no dialectical skill, would budge him from his position — that it might and must be necessary to alter the letter of principles to suit fresh facts as they entered into a person's experience, but that the spirit informing them would remain the same. There *was* a right, and if you wanted to you could find it, and it was supremely important. The discussion grew very heated. George was really outmatched; but the thing that gradually emerged most, for me, was the practical demonstration he was giving of living up to the principle of keeping one's temper in an argument — in spite of shrewd blows given and received. And his extraordinary insistence on purity of motive. [10]

It was this championship of purity, and the 'right' of things, that of course earned Mallory his 'Sir Galahad' label. Later in life he was to develop it into a humanistic philosophy. By replacing God with Good, Mallory simply side-stepped his religious difficulties, although he staunchly maintained he was a Christian long after he had dismissed the divinity of Christ.

Between themselves, and within their own intimate circle, Lytton Strachey and Duncan Grant knew no reserve, and relished outrageous revelation and gossip. Events were quite naturally dramatized for effect and there is little to indicate where fact departs into fantasy. Both fantasized over George Mallory, and egged each other on. Lytton wrote to Duncan in October 1910, after a visit to Mallory, to say he was sure Mallory would sit for a painting — 'If the nude's an impossibility (there are very many clergymen about!) couldn't you do a small full length sitting, in romantic watercolours?' They might even fall in love, he suggested,

I don't think, in the long run, you'd enjoy it, but such calculations affect no-one. Fortunately, so far as I'm concerned, I needn't make them, because I'm not in love with him, and never will be — though how I've avoided it I hardly know — perhaps his mind is really a little too far gone. But would that matter with you? I think you're a shade less particular . . . But, oh heavens! his body! — the supreme beauty of the face has I'm afraid gone — that wonderful bloom — but it's still intensely attractive, with the eyes, and the colour, and the charming expression, and the strange divine ears, so large and lascivious — oh! [11]

Many years later, recalling Mallory with affection, Grant remarked to Lytton that at one time he would have been willing to give Mallory a hundred pounds a year, to have him as his mistress. Grant was known for his constant lack of money, and when asked where he would have found the hundred, laughed and said he would have borrowed it from Maynard (Keynes).

Lytton believed Mallory's feelings to be 'as exquisite as his face', though he did detect a certain 'indifference' (along with the 'fond of prudery'). David Pye, whose affection for Mallory was beyond question, also recognized 'something virginal and cold' about him; Benson at first had found him 'unsympathetic, hard and self-absorbed'; Dr Raymond Greene, who knew him later in the Climbers' Club, found him so cold and distant it was as if he was covered in a thin coating of glass.

No doubt a certain reserve, a shyness, a retention of privacy, had made it hard for Mallory to initiate friendships in his first years at Cambridge — but, once made, what he certainly achieved with his friendships was durability. Whatever their basis (and so often, it is true, it was a response to his astonishingly good looks), Mallory superimposed upon each a genuine delight in, and concern for, the other party, that cemented the bond of intimacy between them. He was never a temporary plaything, dropped by his admirers when the novelty wore off; nor did he readily let established friendships lapse. When Benson was apathetic with the 'black dog on his back', Mallory coaxed him into good humour; when Lytton Strachey was seeking sanctuary in Cambridge between bouts of those mysterious and debilitating ailments that so constantly afflicted him, Mallory arranged for him to take over his own rooms in Pythagoras House, and went to stay with Benson. When Mallory moved to Charterhouse at Godalming, he still kept in touch with his Cambridge friends, visiting them whenever possible and welcoming them to stay with him. Lytton, James, Geoffrey and Maynard Keynes all came down, and Mallory's friendship with Duncan Grant flourished at this time.

XIX

Green Chartreuse

To Mallory, Grant must have seemed an exotic figure — charming, flamboyant, uninhibited, and on the brink of international recognition. Though there was only a year's difference in age between them, the two young men were light years apart in worldliness. From childhood Grant had led a gregarious and vagabond existence. He was sent home from India as a boy to grow up in the eccentric household of his Strachey cousins, surrounded always by music, literature and art. It was his aunt, Lytton's mother, who encouraged him to make a career out of art, rather than to go into the army as his own parents had planned. He studied at Westminster School of Art and the Slade before moving to Paris to work under Jacques Blanche, and his early paintings were strongly influenced by those of Cézanne. He travelled widely throughout Europe, Turkey and North Africa, and had introduced himself to Matisse and Picasso long before their work was seen in London at the First Post-Impressionist Exhibition of 1910. He had had a number of love affairs — with men and women — and was now living with Adrian. Stephen (brother of Vanessa Bell and Virginia Woolf) in Brunswick Square.

Mallory was an admirer of Post-Impressionism. Through Grant, he glimpsed a world of glamour which he could not have failed to find seductive, and he seized every opportunity of widening his interests. He affected a more Bohemian style of dress. Benson did not altogether approve of the change. 'Mallory arrived in the evening,' he noted, 'very handsome but with too much hair and not enough collar. He would be so much more attractive if he only were

271

not so determined to dress unconventionally. Long hair cannot be comfortable.'[1]

Grant, for his part, took trouble to understand Mallory's world. In March 1913, he accompanied him to the Easter climbing meet in North Wales, and also stayed at his family home in Birkenhead. When Mallory with some of his students launched a new school literary magazine called *Green Chartreuse*, Duncan Grant painted a large poster to advertise it, depicting a brilliant green monk with uplifted glass. This quaffing friar, Pye tells us, was 'flaunted on the cricket pavilion', where it caused quite a sensation. It is unclear from Pye's account whether it was the poster or the magazine itself which so offended the 'decorous upholders of public school proprieties', but it was, Pye said, 'Mallory's counterblast to traditional school philistinism', a symbol of his derision of 'cherished shibboleths'.[2]

On those weekends when Mallory visited Grant in London, he would often pose for him. A series of paintings produced in Duncan's Brunswick Square Studio in 1913 speak of the erotic attraction the naked sitter held for the artist. A number of drawings and photographs also survive, and these may well have provided studies for later decorative panels of dancers and musicians that Duncan executed for the Omega Workshops.

Green Chartreuse was not Mallory's only brush with the school establishment. The friendly relations he cultivated with the older boys in particular were frowned upon, but were, he felt, necessary for establishing an incentive to learning. Pye gives no indication that he thought these relationships reflected anything other than Mallory's eccentric teaching methods, but was quick to point out their dubious merit: 'I do not think Mallory felt, in the end, that his methods had been justified by results,' he wrote, 'and I remember him saying in later years that if he were to begin again with the same outlook and enthusiasm, but armed with his own experience, he would not attempt the same methods. The process was too exhausting and the results too nebulous.'[3]

Perhaps this was the point. Mallory was trying to apply methods before he had clearly worked out the principles. Benson had noted, 'he overflows with youthful enthusiasm and ideas, but he is a slipshod performer and none the better for being so artistically wedded to his own imperfect thoughts. He has enough spirit and feeling for two poets: but the power of expression seems denied him.' The next time he saw him, however, he was prepared to concede that it was wonderful how much schoolmastering had

'widened, mellowed and tranquillised' Mallory, though he suspected he was not tactful. 'He is full of the idea of being frank with
everyone, but this seems to end at times in a rather unpleasant
chopping at toes with a cutlass.' He was too ready to 'interpose in a
talk with a dash of acid. I think he is a little proud of candour and
fearless talk.' This to Benson's mind had the result of being both rude
and disconcerting. He wondered sadly if perhaps it was just the
inevitable drifting away. 'I think I rather bore him.'[4]

Mallory's informality prevented him from keeping good order in
the classroom, and he placed little value in doing so. It worried Pye
that Mallory's discursive style of teaching, laced with anecdote and
intrusions of philosophical propaganda, was disliked by the boys as
well as being unproductive. But there were those, like Robert Graves
and Raymond Rodakowski, who benefited enormously from the
personal interest Mallory took in them, particularly those he had
introduced to climbing.

Early in 1913, Mallory had written, 'My life even now is one of the
most pleasant I know. When the sun comes out again in this green
paradise, I shall effervesce into a spirit.'[5] That summer instead of
going to the Alps, he and Geoffrey Winthrop Young camped and
climbed in Cornwall, then sailed with Conor O'Brien along the
coast of Ireland. Writing to Geoffrey Young in September, Mallory
described provocatively climbs and bathes he had enjoyed with one
of his young recruits, but the same letter disclosed a growing
restiveness with the pattern into which his life had fallen. In what
seems an endeavour to resolve his complicated emotions into their
essential elements, he continued, enigmatically, 'Perhaps I've
already caught the habit of vomiting complacent enthusiasm, which
may well be the reaction of boys upon one of my temperament.'[6]

It was not long after this that Mallory met Ruth Turner, and found
in her someone with whom he could rediscover his innocence,
whom he could instruct and mould. He tried to explain to Benson
what this meant to him.

The most wonderful thing about it is the knowing of someone
else in a quite different way — I know what is noble in another
human being much more deeply than ever before; the beauty of
a soul known this way and the fineness and delicacy of it is
overwhelming: and it really does make one good — already.
But then, though it adds so much it changes nothing, only
intensifies all that one thought best before. I'm more wholly

devoted to my work here than ever I was; and Ruth shares my
ideals, wants to know my friends among the boys, is prepared
in fact to acquire the same devotion. I can't believe it can make
life anything but more strenuous in the pursuit of virtue.[7]

And to Geoffrey Young, 'Ruth is too wonderful and splendid, good
enough for two. She has the sublime capacity for disregarding
unessentials always and is quite imperturbable about everything that
doesn't really matter. Life really is going to be good with her.' At
Mallory's insistence, Young hurried down to Charterhouse to meet
her and found, with pleased surprise, that his friend was not
exaggerating. 'I have never met anyone who brought such an
atmosphere of reality, such a certainty of true nature,' he wrote
enthusiastically on 5 May. 'It is *big*, just *big* that nature . . . I know
just a bit what you must be feeling. I could *shout*.'[8]

Not only did Ruth share Mallory's ideals, her unflurried calm and
common-sense lent them a better chance of success. She appreciated
his restlessness and accepted his need for the mountains. They
enjoyed walking holidays together, and he took her rock-climbing in
the Lake District and in Wales; she also raised no objection to his
taking the occasional climbing holiday without her. He was delighted that she took so readily to all his friends and was welcomed
into the hill company.

It was in 1917, at the time their second child was born, that
Mallory received the alarming news that Geoffrey Young had been
severely wounded in the Battle of Monte San Gabriele. He was in
a serious condition and surgeons had been forced to amputate his
left leg above the knee. Mallory wrote at once to Lady Young,
Geoffrey's mother.

I can't tell you how much worse I feel it that he should lose a
limb than anyone else I know. It's the spoiling of some flaw-
less, perfect thing . . . So graceful; his light movements were
always reminding me of the inner alertness.

I can hardly get to thinking of what the loss will mean to his
life, the rush of memories is too strong. We had promised each
other days on the mountains together if we should meet again —
and I can't separate my own loss in it from his; our friendship
has been woven very much out of that texture and you must
know as well as I how much all that part of living was to him.[9]

He wrote, too, to Geoffrey, and was surprised and delighted from the reply to learn that he was eagerly looking forward to getting into the hills again, 'I couldn't, at forty-two, have *bettered* my old hill-going,' Geoffrey had written. 'Now I shall have the immense stimulus of a new start, with every little inch of progress a joy instead of a commonplace. I count on my great-hearts, like you, to share in the fun of that game with me.'[10] Mallory reassured him eagerly, 'I see we shan't have exhausted life's store of delights for an arm or leg less . . . there shall be a rope's length between us again.'[11]

They were indeed to climb together again, but it was, as Geoffrey Young said, Mountains with a Difference. The first problems Winthrop Young needed to overcome with an artificial limb were those of awkwardness, balance and sheer fatigue. To save unnecessary effort, Mallory would drive him up the Miners' Track from the Pen-y-Pass to the very foot of Lliwedd, invariably backing his little blue car into the lake when turning it around for the journey back.

The old, careless sensual delight could never quite be recaptured. Neither would know again the same buoyancy as on the long summer's day when they had ranged over Amphitheatre Buttress and its outliers, drawing energy from the gritty, sunsoaked rock while the 'laughing hours chased each other unnoticed'. Or when they had discovered a secret cleft in the rocks not far from Land's End, with a floor of firm silver sand, and had raced down its gentle slope to fling themselves into green Atlantic breakers. On days like these, Young has written, 'and in movement, Mallory was wholly in harmony within himself and with the world, and nothing could give him pause.'

The fluency of Mallory's movement is a theme Geoffrey Winthrop Young returned to many times. 'He swung up rock with a long thigh, a lifted knee, and a ripple of irresistible movement,' he wrote in *Snowdon Biography*. 'A perfect physique and a pursuing mind came together as it were in a singleness of power as he rushed into motion.'[12] In *The Nation* obituary he declared that Mallory could make no movement that was not in itself beautiful.

As a sportsman, Mallory also displayed a highly charged competitive instinct. Letters he wrote home from Winchester expressed his pride and delight at becoming the only boy in the school to master the giant swing in gymnastics, or of being a member of the Shooting VIII which won the Ashburton Shield at Bisley. In France towards the end of the War he organized a Sports Day on the beaches to buck up his men.

The fifth [event was] improbably cock-fighting on horseback. The Major mounted Wilson and Pemberton, Nibs, and after a most stirring contest the first two were defeated . . . In the second round I mounted a corporal and took on Pemberton and Nibs. We had a good fight which was evidently very amusing. It was said that I was out for blood, but I'm not conscious of having done more than present a resolute face to an opponent who knew all the tricks of the game . . . In the end we crashed down together, but he was bottom so I was victor.[13]

A similar competitive urge would have been noticed in young Sandy Irvine when Mallory got to know him on the way to Everest in 1924. In Irvine, too, this instinct had manifested itself during schooldays. He had written home to his mother in 1919 after taking part in the final for the Elsenham Cup at Henley against Bedford School, 'They are all (with the exception of their captain) the most dirty looking loathly crew I have ever known and so we were ditirmined that it would be too disgraceful to let them win.'[14] And they did not. Mallory commented to Ruth that Irvine was the only one of the new expedition members to possess a winning spirit. He was stoical too, though not perhaps as impervious to discomfort as Mallory. So reputedly tough were conditions at Shrewsbury School when Irvine was there, that a story circulated of one unfortunate boy cleft in two when the icicle fell from the standpipe under which they were obliged to wash.

Irvine was thoughtful and considerate, which counted highly in Mallory's book as civilized characteristics. Mallory had high hopes of winning him over to a love of poetry, and though he betrayed a certain shyness when Mallory first produced *The Spirit of Man* and began reading from it, he seemed, Mallory noted, 'to be favourably impressed by the Epitaph to Gray's Elegy'.

Irvine was in love with adventure. To him, Mallory, fifteen years older, may have seemed something of an old campaigner, but there was no gainsaying his adventurous record, or his romantic dash. Mallory's sensitive, almost effete air, belied an overall hardiness which first became apparent to Irvine when blizzards thwarted their initial attempts to move up the mountain during early May. When morale among the native personnel was low and sinking, and Irvine was suffering badly from his first exposure to altitude, that 'energetic beggar' Mallory was striding up and down the glacier, chivvying porters and trying to get loads shifted.

On 7 May, after a night when the temperature dipped to −21°F (53 degrees of frost), Mallory decided to begin escorting the sick and exhausted porters down from Camp III to Camp II, and again worked tirelessly when all Irvine could do was potter around for most of the day feeling sick and listless. The two were now sufficiently good friends for Mallory to begin featuring as 'George' in Irvine's diary. Irvine noted solicitously, 'George looks rather worn out tonight − he has had a heavy day of it.'[15]

Of all the expedition members, Mallory would have appeared to Irvine as the most youthful spirit, ready for anything, and he was delighted that Mallory should consider him his partner and want to climb with him. Putting aside the drawback of Irvine's inexperience, there were other reasons why Mallory should have wanted to climb with him − his 'real guts' for one but it is a persistently intriguing question, and one asked by every generation of mountain historians: why, *why* for that very last climb, Irvine and not Odell?

Could it have been, as Walt Unsworth suggested in his book *Everest*, that Mallory had formed a *romantic* attachment for the handsome young undergraduate? Unsworth consulted Duncan Grant shortly before the artist's death. 'Was Mallory bisexual?' Grant's reply was swift and emphatic. 'No, certainly he was not.' In his view, the reason Mallory favoured Irvine was purely aesthetic. Given that Odell and Irvine were both good with oxygen, it would have been characteristic of Mallory, he said, with his own superb proportions, to choose of two equal objects the more beautiful.[16]

This might seem perverse reasoning in the context of Everest, but it can be seen that if Irvine were indeed the more attractive, it would have the effect of making the whole enterprise more perfect. If the attempt were rewarded with success, glory would shine brighter shared with Irvine. This train of thought has a tendency to circle around on itself, however: if beauty is the attraction, is it a romantic attraction after all? Despite Duncan Grant's loyal denial − and he had been known to give far more equivocal replies to other enquirers than he did to Unsworth − could there have been an element of physical attraction? There is nothing to suggest, if that were the case, that it was more than an unacknowledged sense of kinship on Mallory's part, or that it was even recognized by his young companion. Their friendship does, however, fulfil the Greek ideal Mallory earlier professed: the bonding of youth with age, enthusiasm with wisdom, strength with experience, to produce the most unassailable union of all.

277

The two men shared an ideal and a strength of purpose to pursue it. Was it a reasonable quest? There is a point at which the pursuance of an ambition can so override normal limitations as to tip into obsession; when a fixity of purpose drives a person beyond the point at which legitimate caution should have turned him back – if, that is, one is to assume that survival is as important as success. After all, these questions would never be asked had they reached the summit and returned to tell the tale, as they are not asked of Reinhold Messner after his astonishing solo ascent of Everest in 1981. Yet Messner would surely recognize that degree of obsession which is vital to the accomplishment of any human endeavour that seems to most ordinary mortals to be beyond the bounds of possibility. As Geoffrey Winthrop Young had said, 'if the age-long fight of humanity with its unknown environment were to be carried this one step further, chivalry, with its fickle ally, chance, must take up the challenge.'

Somervell went further: 'I verily believe his death, as that of his well-loved and splendid companion, is a clarion call to our materialistic age, which so terribly needs the true unselfish spirit typified by George Mallory alike in his life and in its ending.'[17]

It was a symbolic death, certainly. No climbers before Mallory and Irvine were so honoured. The King, The Prince of Wales, The Duke of York, The Duke of Connaught and Prince Arthur of Connaught were all represented at the Memorial Service held for the two climbers in St Paul's Cathedral on 17 October. Arthur Benson was impressed by the pomp, but remained curiously unmoved. 'It all seemed so unlike George to be so celebrated, unlike his unaffected modesty.'[18]

For the families, it was difficult to adjust emotionally to the publicity of such a heroic death. Mallory's mother paid a visit to Benson, who wrote in his diary:

A friendly, homely woman but strangely exaltée over his death – the frame of mind I find it most difficult to sympathise with. She spoke of the benefits which might come to the whole world by his example and sacrifice, and with wild transcendental ideas of how influence like his might spread in the other world. I could make no answer because the *speculations* may be beautiful in one's own mind, the spirit scaling the clouds in search of castles, but uttered in very plain English in a matter of fact voice over a plate of roast chicken, they seem to have no meaning.[19]

Benson found it hard to divine grief in such an attitude. Rather, Mrs Mallory seemed to him to be 'stirring the situation with both hands like a stewpot over a fire'. Ruth, he had heard, was being wonderfully brave and calm. 'Everyone is — more shame to them!'

Ruth Mallory, still numb with shock, felt she must write to those who knew and loved George best of all. To Geoffrey Winthrop Young, 'It is not difficult for me to believe that George's spirit was ready for another life and his way of going to it was very beautiful . . . I do not think this pain matters at all.' She wrote to him again, a short while later, 'I know George did not mean to be killed . . . Oh Geoffrey, if only it hadn't happened! It so easily might not have.'

All his adult life, George Mallory saw an ideal world where truth could not be compromised, and where the value of any action depended solely on the integrity of the thought from which it sprang. To liken him, as Geoffrey Winthrop Young so often did, to Sir Galahad has a haunting aptness. By virtue of his purity, Galahad was the only one of Arthur's knights destined to find the Holy Grail. Legend has him vanishing from the mortal world when, after long quest, the mystical vessel comes at last within his grasp.

. . . Then you see, I also think it very possible that although this life was undoubtedly very good for George, there is something better he was ready for. So, if I love him entirely, I must try to be content that he should have it.

Of course, you share George with me, the pain and the joy. I never owned him. I never even wanted to. We all had our own part of him. My part was tenderer and nearer than anyone else's, but it was only my part. Geoffrey, shall I keep my love fresh and pure and strong as it is now till I die?[20]

XX

In Perspective

by Audrey Salkeld, 1995

The idea that Mallory and Irvine might have reached the summit before they died was never relinquished by their most loyal supporters. Geoffrey Young, Mary Ann O'Malley, Tom Longstaff, R.L.G. Irving, David Pye always maintained the two had been successful, as of course did Noel Odell throughout his ninety-six years. Captain Noel claimed psychic proof of the fact; and yet, within a short while of their disappearance, the consensus of mountaineering opinion had swung firmly against such an optimistic view. It had to be so. Scepticism was not merely the logical response where conclusive proof was lacking; but those taking on the Everest challenge needed a belief in the virginity of the summit if their quest was to have any validity.

For nine years after 1924 no other expedition was permitted to approach Mount Everest. At the time, this was said to reflect the displeasure of the Dalai Lama's government over Hazard's wide-ranging survey work after his compatriots had left for home, but it is easy to see now that Hazard was being used rather as a scapegoat in this. Certainly, he exceeded the bounds of the team's passport and the Tibetan authorities had always been uneasy about these expeditions roaming their countryside. Resistant to all outside influences, they feared the impact such godless cavalcades might have on a naive populace. The concept of climbing mountains for anything but spiritual merit or military gain was beyond imagining to the Tibetan mind; how else could you explain the deplorable loss of lives in 1922 and 1924 than that the mountain furies resented such intrusion? Yet, without doubt, the overwhelming objection after

the 1924 'show' was to the 'enticing away' of Tibetan monks to per-
form 'devil dances' as a publicity stunt for Captain Noel's Everest
film. And, back in England, this was not something the expedition
organisers wanted widely known.

Sir Francis Younghusband, Chairman of the Mount Everest
Committee, was Chairman also of Noel's Explorer Films Ltd. If he
did not personally sanction the monks' visit, it is inconceivable he
was unaware in advance that these holy men were being brought
over. He personally conducted the head monk around the country,
using his influence to arrange meetings for him with eminent
churchmen and politicians. On the face of it, Sir Francis was foster-
ing intercultural understanding. He certainly could not afford the
implication to be made that his dancing lamas were in any way
responsible for Britain's newly-soured relations with Tibet.
(Younghusband's reputation in that quarter was already dented,
after all, following the controversial Mission to Lhasa two decades
before.) No, Hazard's wayward journey provided a far readier and
perfectly convincing excuse for the ban.

There is suspicion that F.M. Bailey, a former double-agent who
was Political Officer in Sikkim at that time (and a man moreover
who in his youth had nurtured designs of his own on Everest) was
instrumental in hardening the Tibetan attitude. Be that as it may,
no further requests for expeditions were entertained by Lhasa until
after Bailey's tour of office was ended. Then, during the 1930s, four
official British attempts were directed at the mountain, as well as an
ill-judged illicit solo bid by the eccentric Maurice Wilson. Yet,
despite the inclusion of more and younger alpinists in the team, no
one during those years exceeded the altitude known to have been
achieved by Norton and Somervell in 1924. Norton's North Face
traverse was favoured over the ridge line Mallory always cham-
pioned, and the only clue to emerge to the fate of Mallory and his
companion was the 1933 discovery of an ice axe. Lying free on bare
slabs, it prompted more questions than it answered. Markings on its
shaft matched others etched on a swagger stick belonging to Irvine,
so that although known in Everest folklore as 'Mallory's axe', in all
probability it belonged to the younger man.

World War II and the political climate thereafter put an end to
British activity in the Himalaya throughout the next decade, by
which time the Chinese had marched into Tibet and sealed the
mountain's northern approaches to all Westeners for the next thirty
years. Edmund Hillary and Sherpa Tenzing made their indisputable

ascent of Everest from the southern Nepalese side in 1953, and seven years later, Chinese mountaineers surprised the world by announcing that they, too, had been to the top of the world, completing, they said, Mallory's route along the upper North-east Ridge.

From the outset, the news was treated with suspicion outside China. How could men new to the sport of mountaineering have succeeded on a route which had defeated traditional climbing heroes – a route, moreover, which was assumed by most to be unfeasible? There were no summit photographs and only the vaguest of details to back up the Chinese claim. On the other hand, plenty of reasons could be found for suspecting the creative hand of propaganda at work, especially since announcement of the feat coincided with serious expansionist threats all along China's Himalayan frontier and a violent Sino-Nepalese squabble over territorial ownership of the world's highest mountain. Official accounts of the climb were so heavily overlain with ideological tub-thumping that their authenticity could not easily be stomached.

Wounded by the almost universal scepticism, China wasted no time in planning a further ascent which none could dispute. After a series of training climbs, Everest would be climbed again, so it was hoped, in 1967. As it turned out, the Cultural Revolution delayed this demonstration until 1975, when eight men and a woman planted a conspicuous red survey tripod on the mountain's summit for the world to find. And it was during this expedition that the late Wang Hung-bao stumbled across his dessicated 'English dead', lying on a terrace somewhere between 8,100 and 8,200 metres (c. 26,750 ft). As near as can be ascertained, this was directly below the spot where the ice axe had been discovered forty-two years earlier.

These, then, were the clues in 1986 when we (the authors of this book), undertook our expedition to Everest in the hope of learning more of the fate of Mallory and young Irvine. Three clues only: the ice axe – tangible enough; but the two sightings – of Mallory and Irvine by Odell, climbing a rock step with alacrity, and the body described by Wang Hung-bao – have to be treated as more nebulous, since neither could be corroborated by other witnesses. Even the statement extracted from Mr Zhang in Beijing on our way home only gave weight to Wang's description of a find, not to the find itself. All the same, that said, the circumstances of its communication are very interesting. First Song, our liaison officer, and then his expedition colleague, climbing leader Mr Liang, firmly denied Wang's story when pressed by Tom; in other words they maintained the official Chinese position. But instead of that being the end of the matter, they then each went to extraordinary lengths to pass him on to someone else, thereby making sure he did not relinquish faith in the existence of the body on the terrace. It is difficult to interpret this otherwise than that they knew the true answer to Tom's questions and were shepherding him towards confirmation of that truth, without themselves having to utter it.

What, if anything, did our expedition prove? Was there more evidence to go on? Images were clearer in our minds, certainly – the topography, the difficulties facing those pioneer climbers, the way a mountain can totally absorb one's being. Opinions we held or subsequently formed could be reinforced with rather more than wishful thinking. Even so, at the end of it we were still short on what could be called hard evidence. Perhaps that is the way it will be, no sudden revelations, just soft evidence piling up silently over the years like snow, until its accumulation cannot be ignored.

With increased traffic on the mountain's northern slopes, it had seemed inevitable that sooner or later another climber would confront the 'English dead'. Yet the years went by. Everest yielded up other victims – Hannelore Schmatz on the South-east Ridge, Peter Boardman and, more recently, Joe Tasker high among the Pinnacles, the inevitable Maurice Wilson (churning regularly from his glacier tomb below the North Col), but still the only one of real significance to the Mallory and Irvine story remains the Chinese climber who in 1975 had fallen from near the First Step. In other words, Wu Tsung-yueh, who lost his footing near the ice-axe site and fetched up on the same high terrace where the slumbering British is believed to lie. Japanese climbers confirmed seeing him there in 1980.

In the ten years since the Catalan ascent of 1985 (described on page 250), the summit has been reached several more times by Mallory's North-east Ridge. Indeed, over fifteen days in the spring of 1995 an astonishing sixty-seven ascents were made this way, including that by George Mallory's eponymous grandson. By the end of June that year 125 men and five women were known to have completed the climb now called 'Mallory route', either in its entirety or with variations. Truly, it is surprising that none of these ascents has thrown fresh light on the fate of Mallory and Irvine beyond producing conflicting opinions over whether or not the two pioneers could have surmounted the Second Step back in 1924.

Jon Tinker published an important 'photo-guide' to the upper North Ridge in *High* magazine in March 1994. Tinker's climb avoided the treacherously steep slopes which skirt the First Step by adopting an oblique, lower traverse from his team's top camp and striking the ridge further to the west, at the Second Step. It meant picking a cunning line through the awkward mixed ground which had defeated pre-war expeditions. One of Tinker's photographs looks back down the route from about 28,710 feet. You see clearly over the Second Step to the sloping terraces above and below the Yellow Band, and all the way down to Advanced Base.

Describing Tinker's approach to the ridge as a 'new' variation does carry the qualification that we cannot be entirely sure how Mallory and Irvine arrived on the Second Step to be spotted there by Odell (if indeed that is where they were, and he did). The enigmatic ice axe need not indicate that they ascended by the line on which it was found; it is more likely to mark the site of a mishap coming down, when they could have taken an entirely different course, either mistakenly or by design.

One German enthusiast of the Mallory and Irvine story, Jochen Hemmleb, who has been collecting data about the north side of Everest from around the world, reminds us[1] of an old rope and pole discovered by Chinese climbers in 1960, a find not revealed at the time but first documented some twenty years later when expedition leader Shih Chan-chun visited the United States. The pole was wooden and unpainted, about an inch in diameter. They had found it sticking out of the snow, he said, with about three feet of it exposed, and lying on a rock nearby was the end of a piece of old hemp rope. The rest of the rope was still buried under the snow; it was not attached to the pole. The find had been made at about 8,500m, or 200m below the Second Step, down on the slabs of the North face, not down the ridge.[2]

No serious speculation attended this belated news, beyond a mild curiosity about the origin and purpose of the pole. It was assumed the relics must have belonged to climbers of the 1930s who vainly attempted to gain the Second Step from below. But, they could have been older, Hemmleb suggests. There is just a chance that Mallory, finding the ridge line trickier than he thought, opted on that fateful morning to gain the Second Step by way of a lower traverse – in the same way as Tinker had done. It will be remembered that in his last note to Noel (see page 222) Mallory was still holding both options of route open. And the Second Step itself? In Tinker's opinion, there were 'several places where Mallory and Irvine could have got up', though he added 'to downclimb would have been very difficult.'

Much was made at the time and since of the supposed lateness of Mallory and Irvine when spotted by Odell, yet there has been so much variation in time taken by others to negotiate this tricky summit section that the pioneers' missing hours evaporate away. Dawson Stelfox, making the first Irish ascent in the spring of 1993, and using oxygen (as we assume Mallory and Irvine to have done[3]), kept to the ridge line between the two steps and found that almost nine hours were required from his high camp just to surmount the Second Step, from which it took another three to reach the summit. Tinker's variation later that same year was six hours shorter overall, and in 1995, young George Mallory climbed First and Second steps to complete the ascent from Camp 6 at around 27,000 feet to the summit in just four and a half hours. He too sucked artificial oxygen and, it is true, was following a route already prepared by other climbers, a route moreover abnormally clear of snow. Even so, we can take this as being inordinately fast going. Nowdays some seven hours is normally assumed as the time needed to get from high camp to the top of the Second Step. If Mallory and Irvine got away at 6 a.m., as was their intention, they were making reasonable time when Odell saw them at 12.50. If they were delayed by faults in the apparatus, which is possible – or even climbing without oxygen[4] – they were doing very well indeed. There were no 'missing hours', just a fatal misjudgement of the distance involved.

Tinker's down-the-mountain photograph prompted another observation from Hemmleb. The spot marked by Tinker as his 'Camp 3' (Tinker numbers camps only from the North Col upwards) approximates the site of the Chinese 'Camp VB' in 1975, occupying a rocky rib on the critical 8,200m (26,900 feet) snow terrace. All at once it is clear how easily Wang Hong-bao could have wandered west along the terrace to discover his 'English Dead' within the twenty minutes he claimed. Tinker could have done the same. Unwittingly, Tinker's 'Out There Trekking' expedition had come as close as anyone since Wang to rediscovering Irvine (or Mallory).

*

Have we learned anything more in recent years about Mallory himself and those early expeditions?

As more letters and diaries emerge from family chests and attics, and more studies of the main or peripheral characters in the story come to be written, new perspectives are gained. But these are less often of a surprising nature than satisfactory confirmation of what was already suspected.

Wakefield's letters home in 1922, for instance, throw up no revelations to prompt a historical rewrite, but they do paint some very vivid pictures of life on the road on the way to Everest. Wakefield came out to Tibet straight from Labrador, where he worked at Dr Grenfell's medical mission. Arriving at Tinki Dzong, he held his first sick parade, alone, since Longstaff was laid low with the 'tummy wobbles'. A long line of patients gathered, but given Karma Paul to interpret and lend a hand, and sheltered from the usual stiff breeze among all the expedition boxes, things went well enough to start. Then Paul was dragged away by the General to help interview the local Dzongpen, at which moment the capricious wind blew up more strongly:

> Without Paul's aid things began flying everywhere. To cut a bit of lint and spread with ointment became a rare feat of skill. Meanwhile every sort of dust and filth was blowing into the dressings – whatever would asceptic surgeons working in their cosy surgeries have said! Whew! A mighty gust swept lint, dressings, cotton wool; whirling wildly over the veldt. Most of my patients promptly scattered . . . To see a roll of lint flying a wild race with dust and papers across the veldt with half a dozen coolies chasing it was a sight for the gods.

A few days later, Wakefield wrote from Shekar Dzong: 'I have just had a gorgeous 'all over' bath in my canvas camp bath, followed by a gorgeous grease-up of hands and face, which were getting pretty sore, and now I am feeling a new man!' Elsewhere, he explains that the grease was a special concoction of his own, made from glycerine, seline and tincture of benzoine compound, which he found served better than the popular lanolins.

Rather, surprisingly, a Tibetan point of view also came to light, and although we have so far been unable to track down its author, there is no reason to believe that it is not genuine.[5] One of the issues of *Kailash,* a scholarly Nepalese Journal of Himalayan studies, carried a translation of the Rongbuk lama's chronicles for 1922. In it, the holy man describes being visited by Karma Paul, who advises him to grant an audience to at least the leader of that year's expedition. 'If one meets one heretic, there is no point in keeping all the others back,' the lama replied wearily, but by his own admission he 'was feeling very sick.' Nonetheless, the following day he greeted the General, along with three other sahibs and their interpreter and, receiving from them a photo of the Dalai Lama and a length of gold brocade with a ceremonial scarf, had tea and rice-with-curds served to his visitors.

His account deplores the unnecessary loss of life that year and concludes with the story of how twenty young local people crept up to one of the food caches after the expedition had gone home, only to be sent screaming for their lives when seven bears emerged from a cleft among the rocks – a sure sign of the displeasure of the mountain's guardian spirits.

Many treasures relating to 1924 have also turned up. Still, our knowledge of Sandy Irvine, remains scant, although among Odell's papers when he died was one very enthusiastic letter from Irvine (addressed to 'Schol' and spattered with exclamation marks), saying how 'awfully' he was looking forward to starting the Everest show, having come back 'whole' from his skiing holiday in Murren.

I never thought I would – I took the Nose Dive straight my second day and Lone Tree my third, and stood, which shook some of the expert skiers to the core – I got the nickname of the Human Avalanche; so you can guess how I crashed about!! God it's a good place – I'm dying to go there again. Aren't the mountains wonderful, just asking to be climbed!

Among Hingston's mementoes, a letter from Longstaff outlining the *do*'s and *don't*s of natural history collecting is guaranteed to give a shudder to modern conservationists, since there appear to be very few *don't*s at all:

You must especially remember that at and after Khamba Jong all taking of life, even of insects, must be done by stealth. But you must collect every grasshopper you see . . . Bruce will probably have to make you promise not to shoot at all. But if you can, get the common wren (very scarce), which may be new . . .

Molluscs, Longstaff tells his friend, have never been found. So he should issue a pill box to everyone from Phari onwards and tell them to pick up snail shells. Toads and frogs are also wanted, including tadpoles. To these injunctions a few medical tips are added,

'At first squitter give 1 lead and opium pill . . . if squitters bad I give wine glass full of castor oil and one third grain opium.' Further teaspoonsful of castor oil, taken every two or three hours till the diarrhoea stops, will effect a cure within 24 hours, Longstaff promises confidently.

From various sources, a handful of previously unpublished letters by George Mallory have emerged, including the last he wrote to his mother, which she was to receive after the news of his death. Penned in the 'vanishing hopes' period before the summit attempts, it strikes a note of almost Peter Pan bravado, 'It will be a great adventure, if we get started before the monsoon hits us – with just a bare outside change of success and a good many chances of a very bad time indeed.'

Hazard's relatives shared with us the poignant pages from his notebook that set out the elaborate code of blanket signals by which Odell was to send down news of his search of the upper slopes, and Hazard to relay them further, on down to Norton at the foot of the mountain.

The brief entry in Odell's diary for 8 June must surely be his first stab at recording the momentous sighting of Mallory and Irvine. However, an evenness of handwriting does raise [a] faint suspicion that the diary could have been recopied later, or several days' entries written up at a single sitting, and when this might have been we cannot know. That said, the lack of any reference to first step, last step, or last-but-one steps on the ridge would seem to indicate that it precedes all other versions, including the dispatch Odell penned for *The Times* as soon as he got back to base:

> *Sun 8 June 1924 Whit Sunday.* Up 6. Off 8. Went up and over N ridge on to N face frequent mists. At 12.50 saw M & I on ridge nearing base of final pyramide. Had a little rock climbing at 26,000, at 2 on reaching tent at 27,000 waited [*illegible, but must be:* '1'] hr then went out & whistled & shouted to give M & I direction. Blizzard cleared so decided to go back, reached IV c.6.45, no signs, lights, on mt.

It has always appeared surprising that Odell, with his scientific training, should have had any problem at all differentiating between the two prominent and quite dissimilar rocky features on the ridge, whether or not they were glimpsed through breaks in the clouds. If he were confused at the time of his tantalising sighting, you would have expected him to satisfy himself which feature it was when he climbed to the high camp again after his friends failed to reappear. By not mentioning steps at all, you wonder now if that could possibly be because he saw the climbers neither on the First, nor the Second Step. Could they have been on the diminutive Third Step, or merely scrambling up along the ridge? Odell's diary entry suggests that wherever it was he saw them, the wavering between steps only occurred under heavy questioning afterwards. As if, on coming back to base, he was suddenly bombarded from all sides by his comrades, 'Yes, yes, you saw them on the ridge. Below the pyramid. But where exactly? What were they climbing? Point out the spot? It must have been one of the steps, wasn't it? Was it the lower one or the upper one? Come on, which one? You must remember.' By that time the vision was several days' old, and a thousand emotions had washed over him. Mallory and Irvine were already slipping into the past: Odell could not be sure.

Mallory's family preserved the letter of sympathy Ruth received from Norton after the tragedy, in which can be noticed the struggle most of his friends had in reconciling Mallory's almost obsessive need to stand on Everest's summit with a refusal to contemplate that he might have taken any unnecessary chances towards that end. 'I really believe,' Norton had written, 'the struggle between him and the mountain had become a personal matter':

> He simply would not accept defeat and yet (from a thousand talks on the matter) I know how his determination was temp-ered with discretion; he fully realized his responsibility as leader of the climbing party. He and I saw eye to eye over the question of the absolute necessity of avoiding a single casualty, even to conquer the mountain . . .

Norton always felt he had usurped the place Mallory would other-wise have filled had the latter not joined the expedition at the last minute. To Ruth, he confessed he was very conscious of his own inferior qualifications for the role of climbing leader and was grateful to George for backing him through thick and thin, working with him, ever ready with sound advice. 'His determination to win were my prop and stay,' he declared, and 'his innermost soul . . . pure gold.' Norton would not go so far as to suggest, he told her, that George never uttered a rude word to anyone. 'He was too much of a man. He cursed Somervell and me soundly for loitering or lagging when there was serious business in hand on at least two occasions. But it was worth it for the warm-hearted apology which always followed so quickly.'

A similarly heartfelt letter went to the Irvines:

I can hardly bear to think of him now as I last saw him (I was snowblind the following morning and never really saw him again) on the N. Col – looking after us on our return from our climb – cooking for us, waiting on us, washing up the dishes, undoing our boots, paddling about in the snow, panting for breath (like the rest of us) and this at the end of a week of such work, all performed with the most perfect good nature and cheerfulness . . .

He went on to describe Irvine's various displays of strength during the expedition – how several times, for faltering porters, he shouldered 'heavier loads than any European has ever carried here before', and how he and Somervell had hauled porters' loads up 150 feet of ice cliff on their way to the North Col.

Norton died in 1954, Somervell in 1975 and Odell in 1987. Captain Noel was in his hundredth year when he passed away in 1989. It was assumed then that the last link with the pioneer expeditions of the 1920s was broken. Yet in the spring of 1993 an Australian friend of mine, Mike Dillon, told me of someone he knew in Melbourne who, as a boy, had accompanied the 1924 Everest expedition. The story was not common knowledge, he said, and needed to be drawn from this modest but tough Empire hand who, refusing to accept retirement, was now at the age of eight-two running a flourishing vegetable oil farm and factory. The man's name was Micky Weatherall and his father, a friend of General Bruce, had been local trade agent in Darjeeling for the early Everest expeditions. In 1924, when one of the General's Gurkhas broke an ankle during training, young Micky, with his knowledge of local languages, was given the opportunity of replacing him at very short notice to lend a hand with the transport and with Captain Noel's photographic effort.

What an extraordinary story. Could it possibly be true? With no one left to ask, it was easy to be sceptical. The older Weatherall, of the Indian Civil Service, was certainly Bruce's trade agent, and reading between the lines, it looked as if Noel's photographic laboratory was situated in a wild part of the Weatherall garden. But where was evidence that the lad, only fifteen at the time, had actually gone to the mountain, stayed with the group for all or some of the time and climbed – as he claimed – as high as the North Col?

Dillon, a filmmaker, recorded an interview with the old man on his farm and sent a videocopy to me in England. There were some inconsistencies in Micky's story when compared to the known sequence of events, as indeed I found when we interviewed Odell and Noel for David Breashears' television film about the Mallory and Irvine mystery. Sixty or seventy years was a long time to retain precise detail. Micky grew up to follow a distinguished career in engineering and foreign aid work, earning an OBE for services to Nepal, building roads and bridges.

Supposing it were true that he went to Everest – and why would he invent the story with so much in his life to boast about? – should we be surprised to find no record in the official accounts or the expedition book? Bruce (always his own boss when it came to insinuating preferred personnel on to the trips he organised) would not have banged the drum about taking along a juvenile supernumerary, especially since he was already in trouble with the Mount Everest Committee over his friendship with Weatherall senior. Micky's father, Vivian Weatherall, had been receiving regular payments from Everest funds for the storage of returned expedition gear between 1922 and 1924, and Bruce had the strictest instructions to sell off everything this time round to avoid any more unnecessary expense. Do we, after all, know the names of all the Gurkhas, or the transport assistants, or even the European members of Noel's photographic retinue? There were literally hundreds of helpers attached to the expedition to and from base camp, and doubtless for much of the time between. Still, that does not explain why there are no obvious references to a European boy in *private* papers – all those letters home and diaries we have been shown from time to time. Nor why a likely Micky cannot be identified in any of the photographs?

The story must remain a mystery – as unprovable as what actually happened to Mallory and Irvine. But were we to accept the basis of it, what could Micky – now dead – have been telling us that we did not already know? He had one colourful story of a wall painting in the Rongbuk monastery which portrayed a man on horseback, wearing a solar topee, riding towards a high white mountain – the Englishman cometh, obviously. Behind him, seven natives are impaled on a single spear. After the loss of Mallory and Irvine, when the shocked survivors pulled back past Rongbuk again, they were surprised to see that the fresco had been altered. The lance, longer now, had additional figures skewered upon it. I was aware that, on the way in, several among the team (Irvine included) had photographed a painting in the monastery of Everest taking her vengeance, and the story has been told in more or less similar fashion elsewhere, so, graphic as it is, this anecdote is not new.

Irvine was reluctant to make that last climbing attempt, Micky asserted. Now, that *is* a deviation from the standard line, which maintains the stouthearted young man 'was every bit, if not more, obsessed to go "all out" as was Mallory'.[6] It is upsetting to picture him dragging his feet at the last, agreeing to make the climb only to gratify Mallory's desire for that ultimate 'fifty to one against' whack ... to do themselves proud. Given that image, a chilling prescience overtakes Geoffrey Young's uncomfortable caution of 1910, when he told Mallory 'your weakness, if any, is that you . . . do not hold back from allowing yourself to sweep weaker brethren, carried away by their belief in you, to take risks or exertions that they were not fit for.' Disturbing, yes, but does it square with the final entries in Irvine's diary? Forgetting for a moment, the impulsive 'God, I'd like to have a whack at it myself' (on *4th June*, when it looked for a moment as if Norton and Somervell might have stolen the march), there *is* a discernable hint of resignation in the entries for those last days, alongside stoical references to the hideous discomfort of his chronic sunburn: 'George decided that I should go down . . . and prepare apparatus for an oxygen attempt' (*2nd June*. George's idea, then, not his. He is doing what he is told.) 'My face was badly caut (sic) by the sun and wind on the Col, and my lips are cracked to bits' (*same day*. A misery that makes the prospect of wearing an oxygen mask almost too painful to contemplate.) After a bad night, when even the touch of his sleeping sack is agony, Irvine welcomes 'Restful morning in camp'. Two days later on the North Col, the conditions are 'very trying for everyone with freezing air temperature and a temperature of 120 in the sun, and terribly strong reflection off the snow. My face is perfect agony' (*5th June*). Nonetheless he has 'prepared two oxygen apparatus for our start tomorrow morning.' And those are the last words he is ever to write.

It should be said that these are typical end-of-expedition sentiments when, after weeks of effort, enthusiasm has suffered serious corrosion. Who would need to feel ashamed at that stage if forced into honourable defeat? Everyone but Mallory appeared quite prepared to accept it. But another of Mallory's weaknesses, if any, lay in failing to recognise when he had given enough. In 1922, after the team had made its two valiant assaults, he was plagued by the notion that it seemed 'too early to turn back, and too easy – we should not be satisfied afterwards.'[7] So the third bid was launched – and seven porters died. Despite his very real remorse over that tragedy, here again was his personal sense of duty prodding him to give one more ounce of effort with the monsoon all but upon them. This fixity of purpose he always found fatally hard to switch off.

According to Micky, Norton and Mallory had a heated exchange over the selection of Irvine for this last climb. We knew the decision had been questioned, but not with any loss of equanimity. Mallory told Norton of his proposed 'last whack' in their tent at the North Col camp on the evening of 4 June, and raised voices might well be heard by others on the Col at this time. Yet surely these could not have included Weatherall? The taped interview hinted that he had visited the col, at a time unspecified; it seems unlikely he could have been there at this critical juncture and remain unmentioned in any dispatch or diary.[8]

Inevitably the Micky-story is little more than a diversion from the main drama, bringing us no nearer to a conclusion as to what happened up among the drifting clouds on 8 June 1924. There is greater readiness these days to accept the Second Step as the site of Odell's beguiling vision, and with it the increased possibility that Mallory and Irvine achieved their goal before dying. Doubtless one day, the 8200-metre terrace will again disclose its secret, although in 1995 George Mallory II found nothing when he 'strolled about' up there without oxygen before his own summit day, 'to see what I could see.' His camp was further east than Tinker's had been, and he remarked only how infinitely difficult it would be to pick out anything in that broken waste of rock and snow.

George Leigh Mallory had always intended to bury a photograph of his wife Ruth upon the summit. In the fifty minutes young George spent upon the highest pinnacle on earth, he commemorated the successful completion of 'family business' by planting a laminated photograph of both his Mallory grandparents, George and Ruth, in the summit snows. He would always remember it as a 'profoundly emotional' moment. Down in base camp a few days earlier, George's own father – George Leigh Mallory's son John – on his first pilgrimage to the Rongbuk Valley, had dedicated a memorial stone to the lost pioneers. The spring of 1995 was very much Mallory Season on Everest. It is interesting, in this age when so many heroes are chopped from their pedestals, to note how much affection and good will still clings to the haunting memory of those two 'Brothers till death' who found their wind-swept grave on this preposterous mountain.

When Howard Somervell saw their deaths as a clarion call to a materialistic age, he could never have imagined how much more materialistic we were to become seven decades along the line, nor foreseen that the clarion call might even yet be feebly heard. Even so, the families of Mallory and Irvine paid dearly for our inspiration.

A.S., August 1995

*

How I wish I had you with me! . . . Supposing that you, instead of Hazard, had been sharing my cabin and I could have peeped over in the morning from my perch and seen you lying below, and we would have gone up into the bows together in our silk dressing gowns to breath the fresh morning air, and sat together here where now I am alone – dear girl we give up and miss a terrible lot by trying to do what is right.

(George Mallory, wistfully, to his wife Ruth, from RMS California, Everest-bound for the last time, 3 March 1924.

Epilogue

Mallory in a sense left his own epitaph in the famous phrase, 'Because it's there!'

The enigmatic response he is said to have given at one of his American lectures when pressed to know '*why* climb Mount Everest?' has passed into legend. For years people have tried to fathom exactly what he meant by the remark, 'Because it's there!' Was it a profound metaphysical observation, as some believe and as many have since employed it, or was it a dismissive brush-off? Ambiguity is a feature of much that Mallory wrote. Brevity, on the other hand, was not.

Why climb Everest? It was a question Mallory posed rhetorically in his lectures, and his response was usually some variation of that given to the Harvard undergraduates: for the stone from the top for the geologists, the knowledge of the limits of human endurance for the doctors but, above all, for the spirit of adventure to keep alive the soul of man. It being so similar in essence to the declaration made by Sir Francis Younghusband in 1920 when he first announced the Everest programme, it could almost be said to be the 'manifesto' of Everesters.

'Because it's there!' What were the circumstances of its utterance? Where, indeed, was it uttered? Not, it seems, at any of those lectures where Mallory took satisfaction in having sent the audience away 'fizzing'. The quotation appeared in the *New York Times* of Sunday 18 March 1923, long after Mallory lectured in that city. (He was not in New York at the time either, although he was shortly to pass through it again between engagements.) It was in the first paragraph of a half-page feature entitled 'CLIMBING MOUNT EVEREST IS WORK FOR SUPERMEN':

> Why did you want to climb Mount Everest? This question was asked of George Leigh Mallory, who was with both exped- itions toward the summit of the world's highest mountain, in 1921 and 1922, and who is now in New York. He plans to go again in 1924, and he gave as the reason for persisting in these repeated attempts to reach the top, 'Because it's there.'

Prompted by the reporter's question, 'But hadn't the expedition valuable scientific results?' the article's second paragraph goes on to give Mallory's standard remarks about geology and adventure:

> . . . The geologists want a stone from the top. That will decide whether it is the top or the bottom of a fold. But these things are by-products. Do you think Shackleton went to the South Pole to make scientific observations? He used the observations he did make to help finance the next trip. Sometimes science is the excuse for exploration.

On the face of it, this response sounds much more typical of Mallory, although the sentences are still far more clipped than is his usual style. Taken together, the two paragraphs rather dismiss the idea that 'Because it's there' might have some mystical significance. There is even strong temptation to suspect that the journalist (or his sub-editor), conscious of the newspaper requirement for short para- graphs and punchy openings, in some way massaged Mallory's rather verbose explanation to fit the format. Or, in interview, he may have 'led' Mallory to produce the statements he wanted. 'Sometimes science is the *excuse* for exploration' has a similar ring to it; this, too, could be regarded as good, provocative 'copy'.

The *New York Times* reporter continues:

> This is pure romance, call it what else you will, and every man recognizes its touch. It leads into jungles and over deep waters and up through the high thin reaches of the air. Its glamorous trail goes through the doors of moving-picture houses and up one flight to the chop suey restaurant. It beckons to all that is strange. It is inherent in the 'dares' of childhood. It makes the timid boy dive from the pierhead, and it sent the British Royal

Geographical Society's and the Alpine Club's expedition nearer the sky than any man had climbed before without taking unto himself wings.

It is pure romance all right, but it is the romance of a reporter infatuated with his subject: 'Mr. Mallory says that personally he can use with equanimity at the sky end of a few thousand feet of cliff or ice wall, any footing that would serve him at lower levels.' As proffered, that does not sound very much like George Mallory either. After weaving the story of the 1922 expedition in a series of colourful vignettes — 'The insane wind threatened every minute to sweep them and their tiny tent off the slope, and the cold gripped them with fatal creeping numbness' — the unnamed reporter wound up with a crescendo of bravado:

For this quiet young man's casual comment raises the ghost of such a tremendous adventure as the fireside mind can scarce conceive; of crawling along knife edges in the teeth of a bitter wind; of chopping footholds up the face of a wall of ice; of moving on where each step may reasonably be expected to be the last, and yet taking that step, and the next, and the next after that; of pushing up and up in spite of laboring heart and bursting lungs, until death is certain just ahead, and then turning back just as steadily, to wait for the next opportunity.

There is an intelligence at work here, well able to fashion a catchy phrase. Might it not have been he who portrayed Mallory uttering as heroic an epigram as his pungent passages required?

Even so, the phrase might have remained unremembered, but for the deaths of Mallory and Irvine the following year. Searching through the newspaper's clippings in preparation for writing an appreciation of Mallory, a reporter happened once more upon the catchy words, 'Because it's there', and ran them again. The *Philadelphia Public Ledger*, on the other hand, which also published a major article on Mallory and picked up on the same question, 'Why climb Everest?', having no such pithy phrase in its cuttings' files, reproduced the Mallory answer it did have:

If one should ask me what 'use' there was in climbing, or attempting to climb the world's highest peak, I would be compelled to answer 'none.' There is no scientific end to be

297

served; simply the gratification of the impulse of achievement, the indomitable desire to see what lies beyond that ever beats within the heart of man. With both poles conquered, the mighty peak of the Himalayas remains as the greatest conquest available to the explorer.

If the phrase was Mallory's, it being such a patently good one, it is curious he did not think to mention it to Ruth in one of his letters. No mention of it appears either in the loving, uncritical memoir by his long-time friend David Pye, published only three years after Mallory's death. If the words are someone else's, some curiosity over their authorship is forgivable. Here, there *is* a clue among Mallory's letters to Ruth. On 1 February he wrote,

> Mr. Carson came in, a curious, shrivelled, respectable, disillusioned, observant journalistic person, who was once attached to Northcliffe and wrote a life of him and is now a newsmonger in part for Keedick — a very long talk, rather interesting, with him.

Could this be our anonymous reporter? From the beginning of February to 18 March is a long time between interview and article, certainly, but if the reporter were working for the publicity-conscious Keedick, the time to run an article on Mallory would be just before his arrival in New York City, or re-arrival in this case, in hopes of catching a last elusive lecture booking.

Having once allowed the possibility that the words 'Because it's there' may not accurately represent any single utterance of Mallory's, it is interesting to find that others who knew him well, also had doubts. Howard Somervell wrote in his Valedictory Address to the Alpine Club in 1964, 'My old friend George Mallory's much quoted remark about climbing Everest "because it is there" has always given me a shiver down the spine. It doesn't smell of George Mallory one bit.' But whether it was Mallory, or Carson, or a journalist unknown, who put together the words that have become so firmly associated with Mallory — that to many people they have become the most memorable thing about him, like the cakes to Alfred — does not really matter. If he did not say them himself, the phrase is nevertheless a perfect summation of the man and his passionate quest to conquer Everest. 'Because it's there' will remain for ever Mallory's epitaph.

Acknowledgments

Many friends have helped with encouragement and advice during the extended period of research for this book. We are particularly indebted to those 'Everesters' and their families who have helped with reminiscence, interpretation and by allowing us access to manuscript material and photographs; also to our own families who have had to put up with our divided attention for so long.

No study of George Mallory would be possible without leaning heavily on earlier biographical studies by David Pye and David Robertson, and no history of the early attempts on Mount Everest without recourse to the official expedition books and the journals of the Alpine Club and the Royal Geographical Society, who jointly sponsored this early exploration. To these and to the Mount Everest Foundation we offer our grateful thanks.

Mrs Kelly, Archivist at the Royal Geographical Society, has steered us through the many boxes that make up the Everest Archive, and V.S. Risoe has been similarly helpful at the Alpine Club, as have Dr Richard Luckett and Mrs Coleman at the Pepys Library, Magdalene College, Cambridge, and Denise Thomas at the Philadelphia Free Public Library. At Merton College, Oxford, Dr Roger Highfield made available Irvine's Spitsbergen and Everest Diaries; Charles Sayle's diary was seen in the Cambridge University Library; George Ingle Finch's Everest Diary in the National Library of Scotland; and correspondence of Lytton Strachey and Duncan Grant, together with the various papers that make up the *Blakeney Collection*, at the British Library in London.

To the families of Mallory and Irvine we would like to extend our gratitude for their help and understanding: Mollie and Sally Dalglish, Barbara Newton Dunn, Alec Irvine, George Mallory II, John Mallory, Clare Millikan, Elizabeth Osborne and David Robertson. Our special thanks, too, go to Captain Noel and his daughter Sandra for so often welcoming visits of enquiry, and to Professor Noel Odell, Peter Odell and Sir Jack Longland for patiently answering our many questions concerning the climbers, climbing and equipment of early decades of this century. For T.G. Longstaffs writings we are grateful to Mrs Charmian Longstaff.

For letters, advice and other assistance we thank: Peter Bicknell, T.S. Blakeney, David Breashears, Herbert Carr, David Cox, Mike Dillon, Xavier Eguskitza, Andy Harvard, Michael Holroyd, Bob Lawford, Peter Lloyd, Francis Nevel, S. Marsh Tenney, Mrs Joyce Norton, Dr and Mrs R. Scott Russell, Richard Shone, Frank Solari, Jon Tinker, Antoni Sors of the Catalan Everest Expedition, Hiroyuki Suzuki, Dr Charles Warren, Kaye Weatherall, Nicholas Wollaston, and Mrs Eleanor Winthrop Young.

Finally, without Tony Colwell, our tireless editor at Jonathan Cape, whose ideas we have gratefully incorporated and whose constant support has sustained us throughout, our efforts would be poorer by far.

AUDREY SALKELD   TOM HOLZEL
Clevedon   California
Avon, England   USA

Notes on Sources

Abbreviations used

AC	Alpine Club
AJ	*Alpine Journal*
BL	British Library
Bruce	Bruce C.G. Bruce et al., *The Assault on Mount Everest 1922*, London, Edward Arnold, 1923
EA, RGS	Everest Archive, Royal Geographical Society
GJ	*Geographical Journal*
GLM	George Leigh Mallory
Magd.	Magdalene College, Cambridge
MEC	Mount Everest Committee
NLS	National Library of Scotland
Norton	E.F. Norton et al., *The Fight for Everest: 1924*, London, Edward Arnold, 1925
Pye	David Pye, *George Mallory, a Memoir*, London, Oxford University Press/Humphrey Milford, 1927
Robertson	David Robertson, *George Mallory*, London, Faber & Faber, 1969

Introduction

1 The British pre-war Camp I is no longer used. Our first camp above Base Camp was the old British Camp II at 19,000 feet. Advance Base Camp (ABC) was the old Camp III, and the camp on the North Col we called

Camp IV. This nomenclature is maintained in order to correlate to the Mallory and Irvine literature.

2 The appearance of the summit so close to the Second Step is a deadly illusion. Three hours is an optimistic estimate; it can take about five hours to get there and four hours back to the Second Step. Many modern climbers have been benighted underestimating this distance.

3 The Chinese Camp V was in the usual place, but a temporary dump camp, which I am calling 'Camp VB', was laid in at 26,600 ft (8100m). Camp VI is the regular post-World War 2 location of 27,500 ft (8375m). The Chinese also put in a small bivouac – Camp VII – just northeast of the First Step.

I The Call of Everest

1 Telephone conversation, Hargreaves/Salkeld, June 1995.
2 T. H. Somervell cable EA, RGS (Box 34).
3 Letter in British Library – BL 63119.

II The Young Recruits

1 R.L.G. Irving, *The Romance of Mountaineering*, London, Dent, 1935, p.148.
2 'In Memoriam — George Herbert Leigh Mallory', *AJ* No. 229, Vol. XXXVI, November 1924, p. 383.
3 GLM to Sir Francis Younghusband, letter, 31 March 1921, EA, RGS (Box 3).
4 R.L.G. Irving, 'Five Years with Recruits', *AJ*, No. 183, Vol. XXIV, February 1909, pp. 367–8.
5 Ibid., p.453.
6 T.S. Blakeney in *AJ*, No. 317, Vol.LXXIII, November 1968, p.265.
7 GLM to G. Winthrop Young, letter, 16 February 1909 (quoted in Robertson, p.47).
8 Geoffrey Winthrop Young, Geoffrey Sutton and Wilfrid Noyce, *Snowdon Biography*, London, Dent, 1957, p.40.
9 GLM to G. Winthrop Young, letter, 2 May 1909 (AC Archives).
10 Mallory gained *prox. accessit* for the Members' Prize of 1909 with his essay on James Boswell. He later expanded the material into a book, *Boswell the Biographer*, published by Smith, Elder, London, 1912.
11 Geoffrey Winthrop Young, *On High Hills, Memories of the Alps*, London, Methuen, 1927, p.179.
12 GLM to G. Winthrop Young, letter, 30 December, 1909 (AC Archives).
13 GLM to G. Winthrop Young, letter, 6 July, 1910 (AC Archives).
14 Lytton Strachey to James Strachey, 1910 (quoted in Michael Holroyd, *Lytton Strachey: A Biography*, London, Penguin, 1971, p.431).

15 Robert Graves, *Goodbye to All That*, London, Jonathan Cape, 1929, p.91.
16 Ibid., p.91.
17 Geoffrey Keynes, *The Gates of Memory*, Oxford, Clarendon Press, 1981, p.96.
18 Graves and Keynes both claim to have been in North Wales with Mallory in the spring of 1914, but he spent Easter of that year in Italy — one week in Venice with the Turner family and another walking in the Apennines with George Trevelyan and Stephen Tallents. D. Robertson has noted that although Mallory's name appears in the book of Pen-y-Pass photographs among those present at Easter 1914, it is signed in G. Winthrop Young's hand, not his own.
19 Graves, op. cit., p.96.
20 Alan Goodfellow (quoted in Robertson, p.87).

III   *The Third Pole*

1 'A Journey to Tashirak in Southern Tibet, and the Eastern Approaches to Mount Everest', *GJ* No. 5, Vol.III, May 1919, p.299.
2 Major Cecil Rawling, 'The exploration and ascent of Mount Everest', paper, c.1914 (RGS Archives).
3 Sir Francis Younghusband in the *Observer*, 2 June 1920.
4 MEC Minute Book.
5 EA, RGS (Box 12).
6 J.P. Farrar to H.F. Montagnier, letter, 20 March 1919 (AC Archives).
7 J.P. Farrar to H.F. Montagnier, letter, 15 May 1919 (AC Archives). Marcel Kurz was a leading Swiss mountaineer who knew and climbed with the Finch brothers in Zürich.
8 George Mallory, 'The Mountaineer as Artist', *Climbers' Club Journal*, March 1914.
9 George Mallory, 'Mont Blanc from the Col du Géant by the Eastern Buttress of Mont Maudit', *AJ* No. 218, Vol. XXXII, September 1918.
10 GLM to G. Winthrop Young, letter, 5 December 1917 (AC Archives).

IV   *The Two Georges*

1 Cottie Sanders (Lady O'Malley), reported in Robertson, p.70.
2 Robertson, p.224.
3 GLM to G. Winthrop Young, letter, 25 August 1920 (AC Archives).
4 Aldo Bonacossa, 'Reminiscences', *AJ* No.311, Vol. LXX, November 1965, p.218.
5 John C. Case, *AJ*, No.322, Vol.78, 1973, p.284.
6 GLM to Ruth Mallory, letter, 27 August 1916 (Magd.).
7 J.P. Farrar to GLM, letter, 22 January 1921 (quoted in Robertson, p.148).
8 Sir Francis Younghusband, *The Epic of Mount Everest*, London, Edward Arnold, 1926, p.28.

9 Geoffrey Winthrop Young, *Mountains with a Difference*, London, Eyre & Spottiswoode, 1951, p.131.
10 GLM to Geoffrey Winthrop Young, letter, 21 February 1921 (quoted in Pye, p.106).
11 GLM to his sister Avie Longridge, letter (quoted in Pye, p.106).
12 GLM to Robert Graves, letter, 15 April 1921 (quoted in Robertson, p.150).

V Bald-headed into Battle

1 A.R. Hinks to Col. C.H.D. Ryder, Surveyor General of India, letter, 20 June 1921, EA, RGS (Box 4).
2 EA, RGS (Box 3).
3 GLM to A.R. Hinks, letter, 11 March 1921 EA, RGS (Box 3).
4 J.P. Farrar to H.F. Montagnier, letter, 20 March 1919 (AC Archives).
5 GLM to G. Winthrop Young, letter, 21 February 1921 EA, RGS (Box 3).
6 GLM to G. Winthrop Young, letter, 9 March 1921 EA, RGS (Box 3).
7 GLM to A.R. Hinks, letter, 27 March 1921 EA, RGS (Box 3).
8 GLM to Sir Francis Younghusband, letter, 31 March 1921 EA, RGS (Box 3).
9 GLM to G. Winthrop Young, letter, 3 April 1921 EA, RGS (Box 3).
10 *AJ*, No.222, Vol.XXXIII, March 1921, p.466.
11 MEC Minute Book, 1 April, 1921.

VI The Opening Round

1 GLM to Ruth Mallory, letter, 17 (?) May 1921 (Magd.).
2 GLM to Ruth Mallory, letter, 21 May 1921 (Magd.).
3 GLM to David Pye, letter, 9 June 1921 (quoted in Pye, pp. 109–10).
4 GLM to Ruth Mallory, letter, (?) (Magd.).
5 GLM to G. Winthrop Young, letter, 9 June 1921 EA, RGS (Box 3).
6 GLM to Ruth Mallory, letter, 17 May 1921 (Magd.).
7 GLM to G. Winthrop Young, letter, 9 June 1921 EA, RGS (Box 3).
8 Ibid.
9 GLM to Ruth Mallory, letter, 15–22 June 1921 (Magd.).
10 Ibid.
11 Mary Wollaston (ed.), *Letters and Diaries of A.F.R. Wollaston*, Cambridge, Cambridge University Press, 1933, p. 225.
12 GLM to Ruth Mallory, letter, 28 June 1921 (Magd.).
13 GLM in C.K. Howard-Bury et al., *Mount Everest, The Reconnaissance 1921*, London, Edward Arnold, 1922, p. 214.
14 GLM to Ruth Mallory, letter, 9 August 1921 (Magd.).
15 GLM to Ruth Mallory, letter, 22 August 1921 (Magd.).
16 Ibid.
17 GLM to Ruth Mallory, letter, 1 September 1921 (Magd.).

18 GLM to Rupert Thompson, letter, 12 July 1921 (quoted in Pye, pp.123–4).
19 A.R. Hinks to C.K. Howard-Bury, letter, 6 September 1921, EA, RGS (Box 12).
20 GLM to Ruth Mallory, letter, 1 September 1921 (Magd.).
21 C.K. Howard-Bury to A.R. Hinks, 3 September 1921, EA, RGS (Box 12).
22 GLM to H.V. Reade, letter, 15 September 1921, EA, RGS (Box 3).
23 GLM to Ruth Mallory, letter, 15 September 1921 (Magd.).
24 G. Winthrop Young to GLM, letter, 20 July 1921 (quoted in Robertson, p.172).
25 GLM to G. Winthrop Young, letter, 9 September 1921, EA, RGS (Box 3).
26 GLM to Ruth Mallory, letter, 15 September 1921 (Magd.).
27 GLM to Sir Francis Younghusband, report, 13 October 1921 EA, RGS (Box 3).
28 Ibid.
29 GLM in Howard-Bury et al., op.cit., p.26.
30 'The Everest Expedition, 1921: Diary of G.H. Bullock', AJ, Nos. 304, 305, Vol.LXVII, 1962, p.305.
31 GLM in Howard-Bury et al., op.cit., 269.
32 GLM to Sir Francis Younghusband, report, 13 October 1921 EA, RGS (Box 3).
33 GLM to G. Winthrop Young, letter, 11 November 1921 EA, RGS (Box 3).
34 GLM to Ruth Mallory, letter, 29 September 1921 (Magd.).
35 GLM to David Pye, letter, 11 November 1921 (quoted in Robertson, p.177).
36 GLM to G. Winthrop Young, letter, 11 November 1921, EA, RGS (Box 3).

VII   The Damnable Heresy

1 GLM to David Pye, letter, 11 November 1921 (quoted in Robertson, p.177).
2 GLM in C.K. Howard-Bury et al., Mount Everest, The Reconnaissance 1921, London, Edward Arnold, 1922, pp.243–4.
3 P.J.H. Unna, 'The Oxygen Equipment of the 1922 Everest Expedition', AJ, No.224, Vol.XXXIV, May 1922, pp.235–6.
4 J.P. Farrar to Sir Francis Younghusband, letter, EA, RGS (Box 3).
5 GLM to David Pye, letter, 12 March 1922 (Clare Mallory collection).

VIII   Preparing the Attack

1 GLM to his sister, Avie Longridge, letter, 10 November 1921 (quoted in Robertson, p.177).

2 A.R. Hinks to GLM, letter, 15 November 1921, EA, RGS (Box 3).

3 C.G. Bruce quoted in *Western Mail*, 11 June 1923.

4 A.R. Hinks to C.K. Howard-Bury, letter, 14 July 1921, EA, RGS (Box 12).

5 General C.G. Bruce to Sir Francis Younghusband, letter, 1 November 1921, EA, RGS (Box 18).

6 C.K. Howard-Bury to A.C. Hinks, November 1921, EA, RGS (Box 12).

7 Jack Longland, 'Between the Wars, 1919–39', *AJ*, No.295, Vol.62, November 1957, p.88.

8 J.P. Farrar to A.R. Hinks, letter, 21 April 1922, EA, RGS (Box 12).

9 A.R. Hinks, writing anonymously in *GJ*, No.V, Vol. IX, May 1922, pp.379–80.

10 A.R. Hinks to J.P. Farrar, letter, 27 April 1922, EA, RGS (Box 12).

11 J.P. Farrar to A.R. Hinks, letter, 28 April 1922, EA, RGS (Box 12).

12 G.I. Finch, *The Making of a Mountaineer,* London, Arrowsmith, 1924, p.294.

13 Manuscript diary of G.I. Finch NLS, Acc. 8338.

14 GLM to Ruth Mallory, letter, 7 March 1922 (Magd.).

15 GLM to Ruth Mallory, letter (undated) (Magd.).

16 GLM to Ruth Mallory, letter, 7 April 1922 (Magd.).

17 E.L. Strutt to Sir Francis Younghusband, letter, 24 November 1921 (BL, 63121).

18 John Morris, *Hired to Kill*, London, Hart-Davis/Cresset, 1960, p.145.

19 Manuscript diary of G.I. Finch NLS, ACC 8338.

20 GLM to Ruth Mallory, letter, 27 March 1922 (Magd.).

21 GLM to Ruth Mallory, letter, 26 April 1922 (Magd.).

22 GLM to Ruth Mallory, letter, 18 April 1922 (Magd.).

23 Ibid.

24 Ibid.

25 General C.G. Bruce to A.R. Hinks, letter, 7 May 1922, EA, RGS (Box 18).

26 Manuscript diary of G.I. Finch (4 May 1922) NLS, ACC 8338. Finch was wise to treat the Leonard Hill apparatus cautiously. Later after conducting tests, he was forced to condemn it as too hazardous for use.

27 G.I. Finch, *The Making of a Mountaineer,* p.295.

28 Manuscript diary of G.I. Finch (22 May 1922) NLS, ACC 8338.

29 The highest point recorded by the first attempt was 26,985 feet, measured by theodolite in 1922. Camp VI in 1924 was some 100 vertical feet higher, but was, Norton believed, still under 27,000 feet. Realistically, therefore, the high point of the first 1922 party must have been c.26,000 feet.

30 Major H.T. Morshead, quoted in *Western Morning News*, 6 August 1923.

IX A Bitter Defeat

1 GLM, in Bruce, p.173.
2 Ibid., p.174.
3 Ibid., p.181.
4 Ibid., p.205.
5 Ibid., pp.213–14.
6 Ibid., p.219.
7 Ibid., pp.206–7.
8 G.I. Finch, in Bruce, p.255.
9 G.I. Finch, quoted in *Muswell Hill Record*, 26 October 1923. (The oxygen experts could not agree among themselves. Finch favoured the opinions of Professor Dreyer; the 'certain fashionable gentleman' would therefore be one of the 'opposing camp', most probably Professor Haldane.)
10 G.I. Finch, *Climbing Mount Everest*, London, George Philip, 1930, p.54.
11 G.I. Finch, in Bruce, pp.255–6.
12 G.I. Finch, *The Making of a Mountaineer*, pp.325–6.
13 Ibid., p.327.
14 Ibid., p.331.
15 General C.G. Bruce, in Bruce, p.116.
16 GLM to Ruth Mallory, letter, 1 June 1922 (Magd.).
17 GLM to David Pye, letter, 1 June 1922 (quoted in Pye, p.131).
18 T.H. Somervell, *After Everest*, London, Hodder & Stoughton, 1936, p.64.
19 GLM to Ruth Mallory, letter, 9 June 1922 (Magd.).
20 GLM to G. Winthrop Young, letter, 11 June 1922 EA, RGS (Box 3).
21 General C.G. Bruce to E.L. Strutt, letter, 13 June 1922 (BL, 63121).

X Casting Asparagus

1 Manuscript diary of T.G. Longstaff (AC Archives).
2 T.G. Longstaff, 'Some Aspects of the Everest Problem', *AJ* No.226, Vol.XXXV, May 1923, p.64.
3 GLM to Ruth Mallory, letter, 1 June 1922 (Magd.).
4 John Morris, *Hired to Kill,* London, Hart-Davis/Cresset, 1960, p.147.
5 Manuscript diary of T.G. Longstaff (AC Archives).
6 E.L. Strutt to A.R. Hinks, cable, 22 June 1922, EA, RGS (Box 18).
7 T.G. Longstaff to A.F.R. Wollaston, letter, 19 August 1922 (Nicholas Wollaston).
8 Ibid.
9 A.R. Hinks to Norman Collie, letter, 19 July 1922, EA, RGS (Box 11).
10 A.R. Hinks to Norman Collie, letter, 21 July 1922, EA, RGS (Box 11).
11 Norman Collie to A.R. Hinks, letter, 25 July 1922, EA, RGS (Box 11).
12 E.L. Strutt to GLM, letter, 2 August 1922 (quoted in Robertson, p.203).
13 G. Winthrop Young to GLM, letter, 18 August 1922 (quoted in Robertson, p.204).

14 Sir Francis Younghusband to GLM, letter, 23 August 1922 (quoted in Robertson, p.205).
15 General C.G. Bruce to A.R. Hinks, letter, 1 June 1922, EA, RGS (Bo¯ 18).
16 General C.G. Bruce to A.R. Hinks, letter, 4 July 1922, EA, RGS (Box 18). His shyness to sing the praises of G. Bruce and Morris is because they act as Bruce's secretaries and would therefore see the report.
17 General C.G. Bruce to A.R. Hinks, letter, 1 June 1922, EA, RGS (Box 18).
18 A.R. Hinks to Mrs Bruce, letter, 10 April, 1922, EA, RGS (Box 18).
19 G.I. Finch, quoted in *Muswell Hill Record*, 26 October 1923.
20 A.R. Hinks to J.E.C. Eaton of the Alpine Club, letter, 11 July 1922, EA, RGS (Box 12).
21 D.W. Freshfield, 'The Conquest of Mount Everest', *AJ* No.228, Vol. XXXVI, May 1924, p.8.
22 G.I. Finch, 'The Second Attempt on Mount Everest', *AJ*, No.225, Vol. XXXIV, November 1922, p.440.
23 J.P. Farrar, 'The Everest Expeditions. Conclusions', *AJ*, No.225, Vol. XXXIV, November 1922, p.455.

XI   Epistolary Warfare

1 G. Christy to A.R. Hinks, letter, 17 July 1922, EA, RGS (Box 10).
2 G.I. Finch to GLM, letter, 5 October 1922, EA, RGS (Box 3).
3 A.R. Hinks to G.I. Finch, letter, 15 December 1921, EA, RGS (Box 3).
4 G.I. Finch to A.R. Hinks, letter, 21 December 1921, EA, RGS (Box 3).
5 GLM to A.R. Hinks, letter, 14 September 1922, EA, RGS (Box 3).
6 J.P. Farrar to A.R. Hinks, letter, 12 October 1922, EA, RGS (Box 12).
7 GLM to A.R. Hinks, letter, 31 October 1922, EA, RGS (Box 3).
8 A.R. Hinks to GLM, letter, 31 October 1922, EA, RGS (Box 3).
9 GLM to A.R. Hinks, letter, 2 November 1922, EA, RGS (Box 3).
10 Lee Keedick to MEC, letter, 9 September 1922, EA, RGS (Box 10).
11 G. Christy to A.R. Hinks, letter, 13 October 1922, EA, RGS (Box 10).
12 General C.G. Bruce to S. Spencer, letter, 1 March 1923 (BL, 63119).
13 S. Spencer to T.G. Longstaff, letter, February 1923 (BL, 63120).
14 General C.G. Bruce to S. Spencer, letter, 30 June 1923 (BL, 63119).
15 J.P. Farrar to S. Spencer, letter, 5 July 1923 (BL, 63120).
16 J.P. Farrar to S. Spencer, letter, 10 July 1923 (BL, 63120).

XII   George and Ruth

1 GLM to Ruth Mallory, letter, 9 February, 1923 (Magd.).
2 GLM to Ruth Mallory, letter, 26 January 1923 (Magd.).
3 GLM to Ruth Mallory, letter, 19 January 1923 (Magd.).
4 GLM to Ruth Mallory, letter, 2 February 1923 (Magd.).

5 GLM to Ruth Mallory, letter, 9 February 1923 (Magd.).
6 Pye, pp.136–7.
7 *Harvard Crimson*, 28 February 1923.
8 *New York Times*, 21 January 1923.
9 GLM, 'The Second Mount Everest Expedition', *AJ*, No. 225, Vol. XXXIV, November 1922, p.436.
10 GLM to Ruth Mallory, letter, 5 March 1923 (Magd.).
11 Ibid.
12 GLM to G. Winthrop Young, letter, 30 March 1914 (AC Archives).
13 GLM to his mother, letter, 1 May 1914 (quoted in Robertson, p.94).
14 GLM to Ruth Mallory, letter, 15–16 May 1914 (Magd.).
15 Ruth Mallory to GLM, letter, 29 May 1914 (Magd.).
16 Rosamund Wills to Lady O'Malley, letter, May 1914 (quoted in Pye, p. 71).
17 GLM to Ruth Mallory, letter, 16 May 1914 (Magd.).
18 G. Winthrop Young to GLM, letter, June 1914 (quoted in Robertson, pp.98–9).
19 GLM to Ruth Mallory, letter, 31 October 1918 (Magd.).
20 Ruth Mallory to GLM, letter, 3 August 1916 (Magd.).
21 GLM to Ruth Mallory, letter, 27 July 1916 (Magd.).
22 GLM to Ruth Mallory, letter, 24 November 1916 (Magd.).
23 GLM to Ruth Mallory, letters, 9 February and April 1917, (Magd.).
24 GLM to Ruth Mallory, letter, 14 October 1918, (Magd.).
25 GLM to A.R. Hinks, letter, 18 May 1923, EA, RGS (Box 3).
26 GLM to Ruth Mallory, letter, 18 October, 1923 (Magd.).
27 A.R. Hinks to GLM, letter, 24 October, 1923, EA, RGS (Box 29).
28 GLM to G. Winthrop Young, letter, 8 November 1923 (AC Archives).
29 GLM to his father, letter, 25 October 1923 (quoted in Robertson, p.221).
30 In conversation with Eleanor Winthrop Young, June 1985.
31 Geoffrey Keynes, *The Gates of Memory*, Oxford, Clarendon Press, 1981 (paperback edition), p.98.
32 A.C. Benson, Diary, 192 (Magd.).
33 GLM to Ruth Mallory, letter, 8 March 1924 (Magd.).
34 Ruth Mallory to GLM, letter, March 1924 (Magd.).

XIII   *Out of the Blue*

1 N.E. Odell, 'Explorations in the Mountains of Eastern Spitsbergen', *AJ*, No. 227, Vol.XXXV, November 1924, p.237.
2 N.E. Odell, 'In Memoriam. Andrew Comyn Irvine', *AJ*, No.229, Vol. XXXVI, November 1924, p.386.
3 George Abraham to Charles Meade, letter, 10 October 1923, EA, RGS (Box 28).
4 Charles Meade to A.R. Hinks, 21 October 1923, EA, RGS (Box 28).
5 GLM to G. Winthrop Young, letter, 18 October 1923 (AC Archives).

6 Sir Arnold Lunn, 'In Memoriam. Andrew Comyn Irvine', *British Ski Year Book* 1924, p.369, and quoted in Carr (ed.), *The Irvine Diaries*, pp.41–2.

7 Andrew Irvine to Arnold Lunn, letter (quoted in Sir Arnold Lunn, *A Century of Mountaineering, 1857–1957*, London, George Allen & Unwin, 1957, p.201).

8 Andrew Irvine to Geoffrey Milling (quoted in Carr, op.cit., 69).

9 GLM to his mother, letter, 16 May 1924 (quoted in Robertson, p.242).

10 General C.G. Bruce to S. Spencer, letter, 5 February 1924 (BL, 63119).

11 General C.G. Bruce to A.R. Hinks, letter, 4 April 1922, EA, RGS (Box 18).

12 General C.G. Bruce to 'Mr President and Mr Secretary', Progress Report, 3 April 1924, EA, RGS (Box 33).

13 General C.G. Bruce to 'Mr President and Mr Secretary', Progress Report, 25 March 1924, EA, RGS (Box 33).

14 General C.G. Bruce to Sir Francis Younghusband, letter, 7 May 1922, EA, RGS (Box 18).

15 Ibid.

16 General C.G. Bruce, quoted in *Weekly Scotsman*, 3 November 1923.

17 General C.G. Bruce, in Norton, p.23.

18 General C.G. Bruce, quoted in *The Times*, 28 January 1924.

19 Dr C. Wilson to General C.G. Bruce, letter, 6 November 1921, EA, RGS (Box 18).

20 Dr C. Wilson, 'On Limitation of Effort in Heart Disease', *British Medical Journal*, 9 June 1923.

21 Dr C. Wilson to Dr F.E. Larkins, letter, 9 November 1923, EA, RGS (Box 29).

22 Dr F.E. Larkins to Dr C. Wilson, letter, 10 November 1923, EA, RGS (Box 29).

23 General Bruce to 'Mr President and Mr Secretary', Progress Report, 3 April 1924, EA, RGS (Box 33).

24 T.H. Somervell, *After Everest*, London, Hodder & Stoughton, 1936, p.110.

25 GLM to Ruth Mallory, letter, 7 April 1924 (Magd.).

26 Major Hingston to MEC, letter, 14 April 1924 (BL, 63119).

27 A.R. Hinks to Mrs Bruce, letter, EA, RGS (Box 22).

28 GLM to Sir Francis Younghusband, letter, 19 April 1924 (BL, 63119).

XIV Vanishing Hopes

1 GLM to Sir Francis Younghusband, letter, 19 April 1924 (BL, 63119).

2 GLM to Ruth Mallory, letter, 14 April 1924 (Magd.).

3 A.R. Hinks to E.F. Norton, letter, 15 May 1924, EA, RGS (Box 26).

4 E.F. Norton, in Norton, pp.35–6.

5 GLM to Ruth Mallory, letter, 17 April 1924 (Magd.).

6 GLM to Ruth Mallory, letter, 24 April 1924 (Magd.).

7 Ibid.
8 GLM to his sister Mary, letter, 17 March 1924 (quoted in Robertson, p. 226).
9 GLM to T.G. Longstaff, letter, 18 March 1924 (AC Archives).
10 GLM to Ruth Mallory, letter, 24 April 1924 (Magd.).
11 GLM to T.G. Longstaff, letter, 18 March 1924 (AC Archives).
12 GLM to Ruth Mallory, letter, 24 April 1924 (Magd.).
13 Andrew Irvine, diary, 29 April 1924 (Merton College).
14 Geoffrey Bruce, in Norton, 62.
15 Andrew Irvine, diary, 11 May 1924 (Merton College).
16 Captain J.B.L. Noel, *Through Tibet to Everest*, London, Edward Arnold, 1927, p.233.
17 GLM to Ruth Mallory, letter, 16 May 1924 (Magd.).
18 GLM to Ruth Mallory, letter, 30 April 1924 (Magd.).
19 Howard Somervell, *After Everest*, London, Hodder & Stoughton, 1936, p. 104.
20 Ibid.
21 *Harvard Crimson*, 28 February 1923.
22 Andrew Irvine, diary, 17 May 1924 (Merton College).
23 GLM, in C.K. Howard-Bury et al., *Mount Everest, The Reconnaissance 1921*, London, Edward Arnold, 1922, p.269.
24 E.F. Norton, in Norton, p.79.
25–9 Ibid., pp.80–4.
30 GLM in 'The Mount Everest Dispatches', reprinted in *AJ*, No.229, Vol.XXXVI, November 1924, p.207.
31 T.G. Longstaff, report, 27 July 1924, EA, RGS (Box 28).
32 GLM to Ruth Mallory, letter, 27 May 1924 (Magd.).
33 E.F. Norton, in Norton, p.94.
34 GLM to David Pye, letter 28 May 1924 (quoted in Pye, 180).
35 GLM in 'The Mount Everest Dispatches', reprinted in *AJ*, No.229, Vol.XXXVI, November 1924, p.203.
36 GLM to Ruth Mallory, letter, 28 May 1924 (quoted in Robertson, p.246).
37 GLM to E.F. Norton, note, from Camp V (Norton family collection).

XV   The Great Couloir

1 General C.G. Bruce, in Norton, p.14.
2 E.F. Norton, in Ibid., p.106.
3–6 Ibid., pp.109–12.
7 T.H. Somervell, in 'The Mount Everest Dispatches', reproduced in *AJ*, No.229, Vol.XXXVI, November 1924, p.215.
8 E.F. Norton, in Norton, p.113.
9 T.H. Somervell, *After Everest*, London, Hodder & Stoughton, 1936, p.132.
10 E.F. Norton, in Norton, p.115.

11 Somervell, in 'Log of Camp IV', 3 June 1924 (BL, 63121).
12 A.C. Irvine, diary, 4 June 1924 (Merton College).
13 N.E. Odell, in Norton, pp. 122–3.
14 A.C. Irvine, diary, 2 and 3 June 1924 (Merton College).
15 Walt Unsworth, *Everest*, London, Allen Lane, 1981, p. 124.
16 E.F. Norton to MEC, letter 13 June 1924, EA, RGS (Box 33).

XVI   The Last Climb

1 N.E. Odell, in Norton, 125.
2 Ibid., p. 126.
3 E.F. Norton, in 'The Mount Everest Dispatches', reproduced in *AJ*, No. 229, Vol. XXXVI, November 1924, p. 211.
4 GLM to Captain J.B.L. Noel, note [7 June 1924] (photographically reproduced in J. Noel, *Through Tibet to Everest*, London, Edward Arnold, 1927, facing p. 214).
5 GLM to N.E. Odell, note [7 June 1924] (photographically reproduced in *AJ*, No. 230, Vol. XXXVII, May 1925, frontispiece).
6 The word 'bloody' has been overwritten to appear as 'beastly' — when and by whom is not clear. (Presumably it was sanitized for publication in *AJ*!)
7 N.E. Odell, in Norton, p. 129.
8 N.E. Odell, in 'The Mount Everest Dispatches', reproduced in *AJ*, No. 229, Vol. XXXVI, November 1924, p. 223.
9 N.E. Odell, in Norton, p. 131.
10–15 Ibid., pp. 133–9.
16 E.F. Norton, in Norton, p. 145.

XVII   Going Strong for the Top

1 E.F. Norton's cable, EA, RGS (Box 37).
2 Robertson, p. 250.
3 MEC cable, EA, RGS (Box 22).
4 D.W. Freshfield to S. Spencer, letters 22 and 27 August 1924 (BL, 63120).
5 A.R. Hinks to E.F. Norton, letter, 26 June 1924, EA, RGS (Box 26).
6 A.R. Hinks to Mrs Bruce, letter, EA, RGS (Box 22).
7 A.R. Hinks to E.F. Norton, letter, 26 June 1924, EA, RGS (Box 26).
8 A.C. Benson, Diary 175 (Magd.).
9 E.F. Norton to A.R. Hinks, letter, 13 June 1924, EA, RGS (Box 33).
10 A.R. Hinks to E.F. Norton, letter, 10 July 1924, EA, RGS (Box 26).
11 Siebe, Gorman & Co Ltd. to P.J.H. Unna (AC), letter, 14 June 1924, EA, RGS (Box 30).
12 E.F. Norton to S. Spencer, letter, 28 June 1924 (BL, 63119).

13 T.H. Somervell, *After Everest*, London, Hodder & Stoughton, 1936, p.136.
14 E.F. Norton to S. Spencer, letter, 28 June 1924 (BL, 63119).
15 E.F. Norton, in 'The Mount Everest Dispatches', reproduced in *AJ*, No.229, Vol.XXXVI, November 1924, p.221.
16 Somervell, op.cit., 1936, p.137.
17 E.F. Norton, in Norton, p.153.
18 E.F. Norton to S. Spencer, letter, 28 June 1924 (BL, 63119).
19 Somervell, op.cit., 1936, p.142.
20 D.W. Freshfield to S. Spencer, letters, 22 and 27 August 1924 (BL, 63120).
21 General C.G. Bruce to S. Spencer, letter, 29 June 1924 (BL, 63119).
22 General C.G. Bruce to A.R. Hinks, letter [end July], EA, RGS (Box 22).
23 T.G. Longstaff, report, 27 July 1924, EA, RGS (Box 28). (Longstaff first wrote 'such absolute fizzers', but amended it to 'such splendid fellows'.)
24 D.W. Freshfield to S. Spencer, letter, 29 August 1924 (BL, 63120).
25 G. Winthrop Young to D.W. Freshfield, letter, August 1924, EA, RGS (Box 26).
26 N.E. Odell, in Norton, p.130.
27 *The Times*, 18 October 1924.
28 E.F. Norton, 'The Problem of Mount Everest', *AJ*, No.230, Vol.XXXVI, May 1925, p.11.
29 N.E. Odell, in Norton, p.143.
30 N.E. Odell, 'In Memoriam. Andrew Comyn Irvine', *AJ*, No.229, Vol.XXXVI, November 1924, p.388.
31 Manuscript notes (by T.S. Blakeney?) (BL, 63120).

XVIII Friends and Relations

1 G. Winthrop Young, 'Obituary Notice: George Mallory', *The Nation*, 5 July 1924.
2 R.L.G. Irving, 'In Memoriam. George Herbert Leigh Mallory', *AJ*, No. 229, Vol.XXXVI, November 1924, p.382.
3 Lytton Strachey to Clive and Vanessa Bell, letter, 21 May 1909 (quoted in M. Holroyd, Penguin p.417).
4 GLM to Ruth Mallory, 23 May 1914 (Magd.).
5 A.C. Benson, Diary, 74 (Magd.).
6 Ibid., 87 (Magd.). *All other Benson quotations in this chapter are from his diary* (Magd.).
7 John Lehmann, *Rupert Brooke, His Life and His Legend,* 1980 (Quartet paperback edition, 1981, p.26).
8 Robertson, p.50.
9 Lytton Strachey to Clive and Vanessa Bell, 21 May 1909 (quoted in M. Holroyd, *Lytton Strachey, A Biography,* Penguin, p.417).
10 Quoted in Robertson, p.71.
11 Lytton Strachey to Duncan Grant, 19 October 1910 (BL, LSDG 114).

XIX Green Chartreuse

1 A.C. Benson, Diary, 113 (Magd.).
2 Pye, p.66.
3 Ibid., p.67.
4 A.C. Benson, Diary, 127 (Magd.).
5 Pye, p.70.
6 GLM to G. Winthrop Young, letter, 26 September 1913 (AC Archives).
7 GLM to A.C. Benson, letter (quoted in Pye, pp.71–2).
8 G. Winthrop Young to GLM, letter, 5 May 1914 (quoted in Robertson, p.95).
9 GLM to Lady Young, letter, 16 September 1917 (copy in AC Archives).
10 G. Winthrop Young to GLM, letter, 26 September 1917 (quoted in Robertson, p.120).
11 GLM to G. Winthrop Young, letter, 5 December 1917 (AC Archives).
12 G. Winthrop Young, Geoffrey Sutton and Wilfrid Noyce, *Snowdon Biography*, 1957, pp.36–7.
13 GLM to Ruth Mallory, letter, 28 September, 1918 (Magd.).
14 A.C. Irvine to his mother, letter, 1919 (Irvine family collection).
15 A.C. Irvine diary, 7 May 1924 (Merton College).
16 Duncan Grant to Walt Unsworth, letter, 1977, quoted in Unsworth, *Everest*, London, Allen Lane, 1981, p.111.
17 T.H. Somervell, 'In Memoriam. George Leigh Mallory', *Journal of the Fell & Rock Climbing Club*, 1924, p.385.
18 A.C. Benson, Diary, 175 (Magd.).
19 Ibid.
20 Ruth Mallory to G. Winthrop Young, three undated letters, EA, RGS (Box 3).

XX In Perspective

1 Jochen Hemmleb: *The Second Step: Unravelling the Mystery* (20p 'Personal account'.) Unpublished, 1993.
2 There is some confusion about which step the Chinese meant here; they may have been counting from the summit downwards, thus reversing First and Second.
3 Modern oxygen sets are capable of delivering a faster flow than those of the pioneers. However, climbers do not always employ maximum rate: Stelfox talks of 2 litres a minute to the top of the Second Step and then switching to 4; George Mallory II also started at 2 litres, switching to 2·5 above the same step. Mallory and Irvine would have set their apparatus to deliver the maximum rate of 2·2 litres a minute.
4 Odell told Salkeld (in 197?) that there was such a jumble of oxygen frames and bits and pieces in and around Mallory's and Irvine's high camp, he could not say with any certainty that they had taken oxygen with them on their last climb. The distance from which he caught his last glimpse of the

pair was too far away to make out whether or not they were carrying the apparatus. However, these parts may have belonged to the extra set brought up by the porters, which could have been cannibalised for spare parts.

5 Alexander W. Macdonald: *The Lama and the General*, in *Kailash vol 1, no 3*, Kathmandu 1973.

6 Mallory's report to the Mount Everest Committee on 'the Coolie Accident', RA, RGS.

7 Sherpas and photographic assistants largely went about their business unremarked: but even in his role as 'a helper', we must ask ourselves if the young Weatherall could possibly have been identified with the 'native' personnel and rendered thereby almost invisible? It seems unlikely, and equally so, that he could have been on the North Col at this time.

Select Bibliography

ANON, *Another Ascent of the World's Highest Peak* — *Qomolangma*, Peking, Foreign Languages Press, 1975.

ANON, *High Mountain Peaks in China* — *Newly Opened to Foreigners*, Peking, The People's Sports Publishing House of China, 1981.

BRUCE, C.G., et al., *The Assault on Mount Everest 1922*, London, Edward Arnold, 1923.

CARR, HERBERT (ed.), *The Irvine Diaries: Andrew Irvine and the Enigma of Everest 1924*, Reading, Gastons-West Col Publications, 1979.

DITTERT, R., et al., *Forerunners to Everest, the Story of the Two Swiss Expeditions of 1952*, London, George Allen & Unwin, 1954.

FINCH, GEORGE INGLE, *The Making of a Mountaineer*, London, Arrowsmith, 1924 (to be reissued by Arrowsmith in 1988).

——*Climbing Mount Everest*, London, George Philip, 1930.

GRAVES, ROBERT, *Goodbye to All That*, London, Jonathan Cape, 1929.

HOLROYD, MICHAEL, *Lytton Strachey: A Biography*, London, Penguin, 1971.

HOWARD-BURY, C.K., et al., *Mount Everest, The Reconnaissance 1921*, London, Edward Arnold, 1922.

HUNT, JOHN, *The Ascent of Everest*, London, Hodder & Stoughton, 1953.

KEYNES, GEOFFREY, *The Gates of Memory*, Oxford, Clarendon Press, 1981.

LEHMANN, JOHN, *Rupert Brooke, His Life and His Legend*, London, 1980 (Quartet paperback edition 1981).

LUNN, SIR ARNOLD, *A Century of Mountaineering 1857–1957*, London, George Allen & Unwin, 1957.

MESSNER, REINHOLD, *Everest, Expedition to the Ultimate*, London, Kaye & Ward, 1979.

——*Der gläserne Horizont, Durch Tibet zum Everest*, Munich, BLV, 1982.

MORRIS, JOHN, *Hired to Kill*, London, Rupert Hart-Davis/Cresset, 1960.

MURRAY, W.M., *The Story of Everest*, London, Dent, 1953.

NEWSOME, DAVID, *On the Edge of Paradise, A.C. Benson: The Diarist*, London, John Murray, 1980.

317

NOEL, J.B.L., *Through Tibet to Everest*, London, Edward Arnold, 1927.

NORTON, E.F., et al., *The Fight for Everest: 1924*, London, Edward Arnold, 1925.

PYE, DAVID, *George Leigh Mallory, a Memoir*, London, Oxford University Press/Humphrey Milford, 1927.

ROBERTSON, DAVID, *George Mallory*, London, Faber & Faber, 1969.

RUTTLEDGE, HUGH, *Everest 1933*, London, Hodder & Stoughton, 1934.

SAYRE, WOODROW WILSON, *Four Against Everest*, Englewood Cliffs, New Jersey, Prentice-Hall, 1964.

SOMERVELL, T.H., *After Everest*, London, Hodder & Stoughton, 1936.

UNSWORTH, WALT, *Everest*, London, Allen Lane, 1981.

WOLLASTON, M. (ed.), *Letters and Diaries of A.F.R. Wollaston*, Cambridge, Cambridge University Press, 1933.

YOUNG, GEOFFREY WINTHROP, *On High Hills: Memories of the Alps*, London, Methuen, 1927.

——*Mountains with a Difference*, London, Eyre & Spottiswoode, 1951.

——SUTTON, GEOFFREY and NOYCE, WILFRID, *Snowdon Biography*, London, Dent, 1957.

YOUNGHUSBAND, SIR FRANCIS, *The Epic of Mount Everest*, London, Edward Arnold, 1926.

Index